Robin Barker is a nurse midwife with ten years experience as a lactation consultant. She currently works as a paediatric nurse practitioner and has over twenty-five years hands on experience with families and babies.

Robin has a great interest in the trickier aspects of babycare such as crying, sleep, and normal habits in babies. She also finds the intricacies of breastfeeding an absorbing and challenging part of her work.

Robin has baby and toddler information published regularly in magazines and on the Internet.

She has two delightful children, now young adults, and found the adolescent years a breeze compared to the toddler years.

Other books by Robin Barker

*Baby and Toddler Meals*
*The Baby Love Guide to Crying*
*The Baby Love Guide to Feeding*
*The Baby Love Guide to Sleeping*
*The Baby Love Guide to the First Three Months*
*The Mighty Toddler*

# BABY LOVE

## ROBIN BARKER

M. EVANS AND COMPANY, INC.
NEW YORK

NOTE TO READERS

*All care has been taken to provide accurate, safe information, but it is impossible to cover every situation, so please consult a competent health professional whenever you are in doubt about your baby's health or behavior. A book can never be a substitute for an individual professional consultation. The author and the publishers cannot accept legal responsibility for any problems arising out of the contents of this book.*

*M. Evans and Company, Inc.*
*216 East 49th Street*
*New York, NY 10017*

First published 1994 in Pan by Pan Macmillan Australia Pty Limited
St Martins Tower, 31 Market St, Sydney

Illustrations by Susie Baxter-Smith

ISBN 0-87131985-3

Printed in the United States of America

9   8   7   6   5   4   3   2   1

*For Babe and Adam and Kate.*

# He, she, and so on

*In this book the mother is she, the father is he, and the baby is she . . . (for no particular reason).*

# Contents

# Introduction

*Baby Love* is the result of the many years I have spent talking to women about their babies. For over twenty-five years my job was to help them by providing the technical knowledge they needed to do the job as well, to help them sort out the vast range of ideas about babycare that drives modern parents mad.

In the process I learned an extraordinary amount from the women I helped, as well as, of course, from their babies. And it's all in this book.

*Baby Love* is not meant to be read from cover to cover like a novel (heaven forbid!). It is structured in the manner in which I worked, so it is easy to find the information you need at the time you need it by using the index or going to the age-related information. As it is intended to be a professional mother's working manual, some information is repeated when relevant. References to the related subject matter are listed at the end of each chapter to help you find more information on the topic when you need to.

General baby books tend to fall short of comprehensive breastfeeding information. I feel strongly that this information is becoming so highly specialized that there is a growing need to balance this. We need more breastfeeding information that relates to the whole baby experience. Separating breastfeeding from the rest of women's lives can make it seem like an unachievable activity in modern life in the suburbs.

*Baby Love* has complete breastfeeding information that covers the whole of the first year. The information is set in the context of the baby's age and development, bearing in mind the extensive range of baby behavior and the varying lifestyles of women and their families today.

The biggest concerns of parents in the first year after feeding are sleeping, settling, and baby crying. *Baby Love* looks at all these topics in a detailed, structured way, providing answers when there are answers and options when there aren't. Often just knowing that even the "experts" don't know and that a particular worry falls into the normal range of baby behavior is a relief.

I have come to see that group childcare for the under twos is a growing dilemma for families in the United States. I think there is ample evidence to suggest that group day care does not provide the optimum quality of life for most babies and toddlers. It is unfair to those parents who have a choice to keep giving bland reassurances about the childcare options that are available; they need to be fully informed in order to make the best decision about paid work and non-parental care that is available to them.

I recognize that options for many families are limited as they try to work out how they are going to meet the needs of their children, the economic needs of the family, and their own personal needs and it is certainly not my intention to make parents feel guilty. However, it is only by raising everyone's awareness that things on the childcare front are far from rosy that governments and employers might seriously start to consider options other than group day care for employed parents with babies and toddlers.

Finally, after years of talking to mothers, I know that women approach motherhood seriously and professionally and count on the health professionals they seek advice from to provide them with accurate, practical, safe information suited to their baby and their lifestyle. *Baby Love* is written for you with this in mind as the start of your baby's life unfolds.

part **one**

# BIRTH TO
# 3 MONTHS

# chapter **one**

# Preparing
# for
# Parenthood

*Life is what's happening to you when
you're busy making other plans.*

John Lennon

Parenting information is everywhere. Many books and articles are
written on the subject, parenting magazines are flourishing along
with parenting classes, yet the most common phrase heard from
the lips of new parents, especially new mothers, is still *Why didn't
anyone tell me it would be like this?*

Preparing for birth is different from preparing for motherhood,
which is usually different from preparing for fatherhood. It is very
difficult to understand this in the excitement of pregnancy and
birth, and I am convinced there is no way to totally prepare anyone for the incredible event of the birth of their baby and what
follows. An element of mystery remains thatis impossible to antici-
pate or provide for. No two babies are alike; no two mothers or
fathers are alike. This is why no one can tell you what it will really
be like *for you.*

The trend to use the word *parent* instead *mother* is a hopeful way of suggesting that the work and lifestyle changes related to having a baby are now equally shared between men and women. While in some families this is so, the reality is that most of the babycare and the household administration is still done by women.

*Baby Love* is addressed mainly to women because when children are babies the mother and father role is not interchangeable for the vast majority of families. I hope fathers will forgive me for often not referring to them specifically throughout the book. The information is there for them too; it is set in a context that regards their participation as much needed, even essential.

The hidden surprises about life with a baby are usually centered around unexpected difficulties with babycare and feeding, unrealistic expectations of the time and attention babies need, and the overwhelming conflict of emotions that are often very hard to deal with and quite unexpected.

Before meeting your baby it is impossible to know how profound the feeling of love is and how intense the anxious feelings about your baby's survival and well-being can be.

Babies bring indescribable joy. They are funny; they make you laugh. Having a baby makes you feel like you've joined the human race. A baby opens up avenues of communication with other people—you become a member of an exclusive club. Caring for your baby and watching her grow gives you a great sense of achievement and is one of the most creative things you can do. Babies help you appreciate small things (like a good night's sleep). Babies change your priorities in life, develop your tolerance, and have the capacity to bring two people closer by sharing an exceptional experience. Caring for a baby is fulfilling, rewarding, and exciting. A baby brings unconditional love that motivates you in ways you never thought possible. Babies give us all a reason for living and hope for the future.

4

I often ask parents to tell me the positives and negatives of life with a baby. Most parents find it much easier to talk about the negatives rather than the positives, even though most find the whole experience overwhelmingly positive. This book, in order to be of assistance, is full of information about the negatives—crying babies, sore nipples, sleep problems, relationship difficulties, stress, fatigue, anger, depression, crying mothers, and so on and so on. *Eeeeek!* What are babies all about? How come everyone wants one? Does *anyone* have a nice time with their baby?

The answer is yes, but the positive aspects are harder for many parents to express, identify, and enjoy when they are trying to adjust to a completely new lifestyle that may place more physical and emotional demands on them than they ever felt possible. And a book like this has to cover the wide range of things parents may experience—including the possible difficulties—so that they can get help or reassurance if they need it.

Certainly it's easy to get bogged down by the sleepless nights, the messy moments, and the chaos and disorganization that babies bring, but if life with babies meant only this, the human race would have died out. Becoming a parent means learning how to savor and share the joys as well as the stresses and strains.

And the best thing anyone can do for another human is to be a true blue, loving parent. The benefits flow on for generations. You deserve congratulations for taking the opportunity to grow and to help someone else grow as well.

Part of preparing for life with a baby is about realizing and accepting the element of surprise and unknown, but you can do plenty of practical things beforehand that will help you manage when things don't go according to plan. Here are some suggestions:

# Attend childbirth education classes

Most of these classes are primarily concerned with the birth, however, there are also many other advantages in attending. Attending puts you in touch with other people who are sharing the same experience. The classes are excellent resource centers that help you find out what help is available in your local community after your baby is born. You will also be taught relaxation skills that prove invaluable long after the actual birth.

Childbirth Education Classes are offered by hospitals, certified childbirth educators, and a range of accredited organizations. Hospitals are the least expensive but can be crowded. Ask your obstetrician or midwife about other classes or call the International Childbirth Education Association at 952-854-8660 or email them at info@icea.org.

# Parenting Classes

Parenting classes concentrate on the practical aspects of babycare such as bathing, dressing, diaper changing, massage equipment to buy, breastfeeding, crying, common worries, and queories about the early weeks. Ask your local hospital or your midwife, pediatrician or obstetrician. Alternatively, go to Advanced Search at www.google.com. Enter "parenting classes" and scroll through to find what's available in your area.

Alternatively, if classes and groups aren't your scene, you can select something from the huge range of videos, magazines, and books that deal with caring with new babies.

# Can you borrow a baby?

Your baby will be blissfully unaware of your inexperience as a parent, but if you have a few babycare skills it can make the first few weeks more enjoyable for you. Many of us have never held a baby until we hold our own, so if you have a friend or relative with a young baby who is prepared to let you bathe, change, and handle your baby, give it a try. Being able to change a diaper, dress and undress a crying baby with confidence will help you feel less nervous. Never feel inadequate or silly because you need to learn basic babycare skills. Babycare skills don't come naturally to most people—men or women—and usually have to be learned.

# Plan to live with fatigue

Extreme tiredness—both physical and emotional—is the most common problem in the first few months. It's worth taking the time to discuss with your partner what you both imagine will happen after the birth.

Speculate out loud (even if it feels strange).

• What will it be like when the baby cries in the middle of the night?

• What do we do when she cries incessantly and we can't sleep?

• Who will stay up with the baby?

• As the father, will you change diapers, do the shopping, cook sometimes?

• As the mother, will you tell your partner when you want him to do something? This is new to him too and he is not sure what is expected of him.

- As the father, how much time are you able to spend with the baby?

- As the mother, what will you do when you are exhausted, the baby won't stop crying, the dishes are in the sink, there's nothing for dinner, and there's no clean clothes to wear? Who can you turn to for help?

Talking about these things with your partner may seem trivial and unnecessary, negative even, but imagining the reality together and discussing all possibilities means you will both learn to manage the changes much better.

Here are a few practical things you can do in advance.

- Get as much rest as you can before your baby arrives. If possible, do not continue your paid work until the first contractions—give yourself a few weeks of self-indulgence.

- Stay healthy by eating properly and exercising—this sounds boring and predictable but makes a great positive difference to your energy and stress levels.

- If you are an active superwoman, afternoon naps probably aren't your style, but prepare yourself mentally for daytime sleeping after the birth, as a stint of night duty is almost always unavoidable. Changing your sleep patterns for a short time is easier than changing your baby's **as there is no safe way of making young babies sleep through the night.**

- Learn about breastfeeding. Breastfeeding is covered in detail in the baby-feeding sections of this book. Breastfeeding is not always easy to begin with, and the more you and your partner know and understand, the easier it is.

- Give yourself as much room to move as possible. If your life is run on a tight string, everything takes on a nightmarish quality the minute the smallest thing goes wrong. Babies are unpredictable; they need time and peace to adjust to their new world, and some need more time and peace than others.

- Try to avoid moving and doing major renovations when your baby is very young. Visitors who arrive at the same time as the baby and stay for months create a great deal of stress. Women often agree to things like this in order to show they are managing well, but it is most unfair for others to assume arrangements like this are all right. Make sure relatives understand when and if they are needed.

- Any major lifestyle change is harder for you when you have a new baby; for example, your partner changing jobs, starting a new business (especially if you're the one doing the books as well as caring for the baby and doing the housework!), and overseas trips. These things are often unavoidable, but if you talk about them *before* the birth, alternative plans or compromises can sometimes be made.

- Mad shopping expeditions after your baby is born are exhausting. Plan your clothing, bedding, and equipment carefully and have it ready and waiting.

- Often women are told to forget the housework, yet even in households that share the load the expectation remains that the mother will keep everything on the home front running smoothly as well as taking care of the baby, even when she is utterly sleep deprived. Furthermore, many women find that living in a shambles increases their stress rather than the reverse, and if they don't attend to the household chores, no one else will. Ideally, some sort of system should be worked out in advance. Don't be shy about asking for help. Is your partner pre-pared to share the housework more evenly? Can your mother or partner's mother help? Is there a possibility of paying someone to do some cleaning for the first few months?

- Going back to your other job raises many important issues that are discussed in detail on page 406, so before you make any firm decisions, please read this section carefully. It is vital to give seri-ous thought to the pluses and minuses for babies and toddlers in care under the age of two that so you are not locked into a deci-sion you may regret.

- If returning to paid work is unavoidable in the first year, allow plenty of time to plan for your baby's care. If possible, limit the hours your baby has in group day care (daycare centers and home daycare) by choosing part-time work or sharing the care with your partner or a close relative. For a detailed summary of childcare that includes fees go to www.babycenter.com. Another resource that can help you find accredited childcare in your area is the National Association for Education of Young Children. Phone:800-424-2460 or 202-232-8777 or go to www.naeyc.org

## Knowing how to relax

You are likely to become very irritated at the number of times well-meaning people (usually health professionals) tell you to just relax when you are in situations not at all conducive to relaxing. Know-ing how to relax is an art, especially when the going gets tough. It's useful to learn about and practice a few relaxation techniques when you are in a calm frame of mind so that you can draw on them when things get tense.

Here is a very simple way to help you relax in a tense moment.

- Whenever you feel stressed or uptight, take a few minutes to regain control.

- Stop whatever you are doing, making sure your baby is safe.

- Clench your fists and close your eyes, taking in a deep breath.

- Breathe in slowly through your nose . . . and breathe out *very slowly* through your mouth.

- As you breathe in, tighten your fists while keeping your eyes closed. As you breathe out, open your fists.

- Shake your arms gently. If you are standing, give your legs a shake at the same time.

- Drop your shoulders and take a few more deep breaths, relaxing your neck, shoulders, chest, and abdomen.

- Tell yourself that you will remain calm—that it is all okay.

# *For fathers*

Being a father is obviously very different from being a mother. Working out precisely why is a little more difficult.

The mother has already started a relationship with the baby during pregnancy, and her new work in caring for the baby is quite straightforward. A father, on the other hand, outside of his career, can do as little or as much as he chooses, and his role in relation to the baby is not straightforward at all. The father has to build a relationship with his baby and keep one going with his partner. Lots of men find this is a strange experience for which there are no clear and precise guidelines. Unless a man has some previous hands-on experience with a baby, he is unlikely to know what to do with one of his own.

# *A great opportunity*

Many men now have a more hands-on presence in their children's lives either from choice or necessity or a little bit of both. The benefits of this both for the children and the community are incalculable. But, understandably, men feel there is no recognition of the fact that the provider role is still mostly theirs. They have to single-handedly take care of the mortgage and can feel locked into an inflexible work role from which there is no escape. The currently high unemployment rate is also contributing to extra stresses and strains for men who are the providers.

Very often, after the euphoria of the birth fades, the mother disappears into the mother world and the father disappears into the father world with a general lack of understanding from both about each other's worlds. This seems to happen to most couples despite the best-laid intentions beforehand to share the load, so the housework and babycare ends up belonging to the woman while the man dedicates himself to paid work. Women often feel disappointed, tired, and alone while men are often concerned about money, feel they have no leisure time, and that life is no longer any fun.

Is this unavoidable? Yes, to some extent, depending on how much the couple wants to avoid it. Often, fathers don't know what to do or how to change the way things are, and many mothers don't know how to separate from their babies and include their partners in their new lives. Research shows that these are probably the main reasons most relationships go through a difficult period during the first six months after a baby arrives.

When you're a new father, chances are you need some information and ideas to help you become a family man instead of the distant, non-participating breadwinner. Granted, there will be times when the latter role is more attractive and indeed a handy escape from the daily humdrum of domestic life, but the men who become hands-on fathers discover a profound dimension to their lives, difficult to describe but never to be missed. Many men over fifty express disappointment about not having helped more and not having spent more time with their children throughout their lives, especially when the children were babies. Older men who become fathers the second time around frequently become participating fathers the way they never were the first time.

Don't let the opportunity pass you by!

## Some inside information

- Unfortunately it is still a commonly held idea among men who have only experienced paid work that babycaring and housework is not really work, and the person earning a salary has a right to clean shirts, nourishing meals, and a good night's sleep no matter what. Men and women who have experienced working at home caring for children and working outside the home generally agree that wage earning is easier, so remember you are both working. Tolerance and flexibility are needed.

- Help your partner have a peaceful, pressure-free home after the birth, free of unwanted visitors and relatives.

- Try not to have unrealistic ideas about your baby. She will amaze and delight you, but she will also cry, throw up, poo everywhere, and disrupt your life. Your partner will not instinctively know what to do a lot of the time, so don't expect this and make her feel she should know. On the other hand, she might know. Either way, if you can gain some understanding of normal baby behavior and give some practical help rather than advice, you will be doing a lot to support her.

- Your partner is the baby's mother, not yours, so resist the temptation to call her Mommy.

- Accept change. Burying your head in the sand and pretending life will go on as before means the changes will be for the worse, not the better. A lot of the changes are temporary, but some are permanent, and to keep on waiting for things to get back to normal creates friction and makes the time with your baby much less satisfying. What is normal in your life with a baby is not at all what it used to be.

- Some of the temporary changes are things like less or no social life and maybe less or no sex for a while. Babies are very good at creating chaos in the evenings, so being prepared to come home and take over until this stage has passed will mean an enormous amount to your partner.

- It's very good for your baby to have lots of physical contact with you as well as her mother. Dressing and undressing her, changing her diaper, bathing, cuddling, and playing with her is a great way to get to know her and for her to get to know you. Don't worry if she cries in the early weeks whenever you do anything with her—this stage is only temporary and passes quickly. Lying with her on your bare chest and stroking her back will help calm her, and you will both enjoy the skin-to-skin contact. Carrying her in a sling at home, or when you are out and about, and bathing and showering together are other ways of enjoying each other.

- Sleep deprivation is always an issue. I find parents, and fathers in particular, think there is some way very young babies can have their sleeping and crying patterns changed so that adults are able to sleep the way they did before the baby arrived. This is not possible, and since no one, father or mother, can exist indefinitely on little or no sleep, cooperation and planning will make living with broken sleep easier until the baby is older.

  For example, if your baby is waking a lot at night, your partner will be under a lot more stress if you constantly complain about your lack of sleep. She then feels she is dealing with two babies, not one (or three if you have twins). Talk things over. It may work better if you sleep in another room on some nights so that you can remain lucid at work the next day. On the weekends you can help by bringing your baby to your partner for breastfeeding, or feeding her yourself if she's bottle fed, and then taking the responsibility to settle her after the feeding (which might mean walking the floor if she's not ready to sleep).

  When your partner is up a lot at night, she will have to rest when the baby sleeps during the day, which means you may come home to no dinner at times. If you are prepared for this and for sharing the household tasks more evenly, especially the shopping and the cooking, your family life will be much more harmonious.

- The first few months after giving birth is a very teary, emotional time for many women. While that great scapegoat, hormone imbalance, possibly contributes to a minor degree, many other reasons exist for these erratic feelings, and these mainly center around the shock of motherhood. The shock of motherhood affects every woman's self and lifestyle and is a mixture of a sense of gain, a sense of loss, intense joy, intense fatigue, intense worry of the sort never felt before (which fades but never quite goes), boredom, wonder, delight, and lingering fears that the former body she once occupied has gone, never to return. You don't have to find solutions—listen, comfort, and give her practical help.

- The shock of fatherhood means you will feel some of these things too as well as other feelings particularly related to fatherhood—like a mixture of jealousy toward and overwhelming feelings of love for your baby. A sense of losing an exclusive relationship with your partner as well as enormous respect for her for enduring the mystery and pain of childbirth, plus confusion about reestablishing a sexual liaison with a woman who is now a mother, are all strange new feelings you might have to work through. It helps to acknowledge them and talk about them together.

- Give your partner some time to herself whenever you can. Take your baby for some long walks—don't come back in ten minutes. Offer to care for your baby while she has some time out with friends or goes to the hairdresser. If you can come to reliable arrangements about time out without constantly having to be reminded, she will have something to look forward to and plan for each week, even if it's only a couple of hours. Don't worry—healthy breastfed babies who won't take bottles can last two to three hours without a breastfeed.

- Last but not least, support your partner's care of your baby. Many options are possible when caring for babies, which gets a bit confusing at times. A cooperative approach works best, so help and encourage her decisions.

    Breastfeeding, for example, works much better when those around the mother have a basic knowledge of how it works and show confidence in the mother and baby's ability to breastfeed.

# *Finally*

Having a baby is one of the most wonderful events in life. The next twelve months are the beginning of an extraordinary adventure, and you will find it is a moving, loving, fearful, exciting, boring, and muddling time. You probably don't think you know much or you might think you know everything—either way you're likely to be surprised by the extent of your ignorance or knowledge.

In the past, the extended family supplied a lot of help and information, and, in many families, still does. By today's standards, the advice of years gone by was often rigid, but it supplied consistency and structure unlike today, where the plethora of baby and childcare information provides an endless supply of conflicting advice.

The sweeping lifestyle changes over the past thirty years have not only given new parents more independence and freedom but more uncertainty and soul searching about what they should and shouldn't do.

Being a parent is not always easy and is certainly not simple, but when sifting through the maze of information it's important to remember that babies' and children's basic needs have never changed. **They need lots of love, the right food, a safe place to grow, lots of cuddles, the chance to learn the skills they need to take their place in the world, and constant interest in their progress through life from the same one or two adults in a peaceful home.**

It's possible to give your baby all this in your own way according to your own particular beliefs, culture, and lifestyle. Safe options are always available—the trick is working out the best plan for you and your baby and not getting too bogged down by preconceived ideas or completely impractical theories that sound great "pre" baby but fall apart in the realities of life after birth.

**FOR MORE INFORMATION**

Chapter 6: Breastfeeding Your Baby for the First Two Weeks, page 78

Chapter 16: For Parents (*childcare/returning to paid work page 406*)

# chapter two

# More Than One Baby

*They've shared the womb, they've been born together.*
*They're on their journey together.*

Helen Townsend, *Baby Crazy*

Twins now occur in about one in forty births. Twins are more likely when there is a strong family history of twins or in recent times because more women are taking fertility drugs and turning to in vitro fertilization (IVF).

Twins may be identical (monozygotic) or fraternal (dizygotic). Identical twins occur when one egg and one sperm join then split into two halves. Each half has and identical genetic make-up and both halves are usually joined to a single placenta by two cords. Identical twins are the same sex and look very similar.

Fraternal twins are more common. They come from two different eggs being released instead of one. Each egg is fertilized by a different sperm, so there are two placentas and two cords. Fraternal twins are just as different to look at as any two children of different ages with the same parents.

It's more common for women over thirty-five to release two separate eggs at the same time when they ovulate, so fraternal twins are more common when the mother is older. As there is now a higher incidence of women over thirty-five having babies, twin births are increasing.

It's rare for twins to arrive unannounced these days—most are diagnosed well ahead of time. A twin pregnancy is like a single pregnancy but with both the delights and discomforts somewhat magnified. Women having twins need plenty of rest—and this is often difficult when there's another toddler in the house. A premature birth is more likely as are minor complications, which means one or both babies might need special care for some time after birth.

Knowing twins are on the way evokes a joy, difficult to describe, that is, and most parents with twins are irritated and annoyed by the generally negative comments commonly expressed by people who only have one at a time. It is certainly a surprise, but the initial feelings of shock are quickly replaced by feelings of excitement and delight with the anticipation of the arrival of two little people.

Like having one baby, there are negative aspects about having twins. These are perhaps most noticeable during the first year, but parents of twins find the rewards and sense of achievement for twice the work give twice the pleasure. Here are some thoughts from parents of twins:

- *It's a great ego trip to have two beautiful, healthy babies.*

- *Two babies keep each other entertained, especially when they're in the bath together. I love watching the two of them—it makes me melt inside.*

- *There's an enormous feeling of accomplishment and pride watching them grow. The pleasure of seeing two of them smile and talk and having two of them hug you is indescribable.*

- *Twins attract an enormous amount of attention, which can be a nuisance, but also makes you feel very special and part of an exclusive club.*

- *My girls are a joy that is impossible to describe—starts at my toes and works its way right up to my heart.*

If you are having twins it's a good idea to get in touch with friends who have twins and the National Organization of Mothers of Twins Clubs as they will be your best source of advice and support. Unless health professionals have had twins themselves they are unlikely to have much to offer in the practicalities of day to day management.

Everyone chooses slightly different equipment and everyone ends up managing in their own way, so it's important to be flexible and not to have too many set ideas. The early months will be a time of trial and error until you work out what suits you and your babies.

You may feed simultaneously or you may feed separately. A baby carriage is likely to be a waste of money. Options for strollers include either the tandem or side-by-side models. Tandem strollers generally maneuver more easily and fold up more compactly but the lightweight side-by-side strollers seem to be the most popular choice. Some of your equipment and clothes can be borrowed, hired or bought secondhand.

Obviously any sort of useful help should be snapped up if offered voluntarily, or arranged and paid for if you are financially able to do this.

Lots of women breastfeed twins. It can be a struggle for the first six to eight weeks as can breastfeeding one baby, but mothers who persevere find it extremely rewarding and feel great satisfaction knowing their babies are getting the best baby food. If you are planning to breastfeed, and especially if you haven't breastfed before, learn all you can with your partner about breastfeeding so that you will get plenty of encouragement. If possible, visit someone who is breastfeeding twins and can show you how she does it. Talking to another woman who is breastfeeding twins also gives you a chance to learn about the practicalities.

Of course, it's unrealistic not to be prepared for extra work and some conflicting emotions along the way. As well as the joy expressed, parents have also talked to me about some of the difficulties:

- *The first year is hectic. It's easy to get completely bogged down by the chores and miss the good bits—the playing, the laughter, the cuddles, and the amazing way they learn about the world.*

- *It's isolating because it's very often hard to motivate yourself to go anywhere; it's such a hassle and so difficult doing simple things—like catching a bus, getting up and down stairs, and so on. I know how disabled people feel.*

- *It's exhausting having two babies crying and wanting attention at the same time. It's essential to learn to tune out and deal with them one at a time.*

- *Two babies means two of everything and costs more.*

- *The safety factor is much more of a concern, especially when the babies become more mobile. Keeping them safe is constant hard work, which is exhausting at times. Long bouts of sickness are very difficult.*

## Triplets

Triplets happen a lot less than twins, and caring for triplets is an exaggerated version of caring for twins. Every mother is a working mother, but a mother with twins or triplets works even harder. I am constantly in awe at the way women with twins or more not only adjust and carry on with their lives but find many rewards in looking after and loving twins. Most of the information in this book is as relevant to twins as singles, and any helpful tips relating to twins will be mentioned as we go.

## FURTHER READING

*The Art of Parenting Twins: The Unique Joys and Challenges of Raising Twins and Other Multiples*, Patricia Maxwell Malmstrom, Janet Poland, Ballantine Book, USA, 1999.

chapter **t h r e e**

# Premature and Small Babies

*The baby's limbs are like threads. They do not bend at angles as older babies' do, but lie curved like pieces of apple peel.*

Kate Llewellyn, *Dear You*

A small baby is one who weighs less than 5 pounds (2.5 kg) at birth. Babies may be born small because their parents are small, because they are born before the expected forty weeks' gestation, or because they are born smaller and frailer than would be expected for the number of weeks they were in the womb.

A full-term small, healthy baby born to small parents does not need any special care.

Babies born before thirty-seven weeks' gestation are called premature babies and usually need help with some important body functions such as breathing, eating, digesting, and maintaining body temperature and sugar levels. The earlier a premature baby arrives, the more help she is likely to need.

The survival rate for premature babies is three times higher than what it was in the early seventies. Because of improved technology and skilled staff care the chance of a positive outcome for even very premature babies has doubled in the last decade. Babies born up to eight weeks early who are well at birth have the same survival rate and health for term babies. Those who are more premature (born after twenty-seven weeks) have survival chances almost as good as term babies, only five percent of these babies have major handicaps. The risks of survival and permanent disability increase for those born at 23–25 weeks and/or weigh less than 25 pounds (750 grams). Even so, of the 40 percent of these babies who survive, more than half do well.

Premature babies needing specialized care have a much better chance when they are cared for in the biggest and best hospitals and are transferred to these hospitals when necessary by a ambulance with highly trained teams giving intensive treatment along the way.

If you know in advance there is a possibility of a premature birth, do an intensive care nursery tour if one is available at the hospital where you expect to give birth. Doing this can help prepare parents—but make sure you have plenty of tissues and a sympathetic health professional with you.

Small-for-dates babies may be full-term or premature babies who have not grown as much as they should have during the pregnancy, usually because the placenta did not function efficiently during the last few weeks before birth. A small-for-dates baby needs extra attention as well—the amount depends on the number of weeks she is at birth and how much she weighs. Some babies can stay with their mothers their breathing, body temperature, heart rate, and blood sugar levels are regularly checked by nurses. Others may need to be in an incubator for a short time.

Healthy, full-term small-for-dates babies usually have a good appetite, suck well, and put on weight appropriately in the first three months.

# What causes prematurity and/or small-for-dates babies?

- About half are unexplained. Some women just seem to give birth a little earlier. This may happen with all their pregnancies, so knowing an early birth might happen can help the mother and her family prepare for the event.

- Medical problems such as kidney trouble, high blood pressure, high blood pressure of pregnancy, or bleeding during the pregnancy can contribute to an early birth and/or a small baby.

- The chances of an early birth and/or smaller babies are increased when twins or triplets are expected.

# Who are more likely to have premature babies?

- Teenagers having a baby for the first time.

- Older women (over thirty-seven) having their first baby.

- Smokers—ten percent of all premature births can be attributed to smoking and it is recognized that smoking during pregnancy also contributes to babies being born small for dates.

- Drug and alcohol abuse increases the risk of a premature birth.

When babies are very small, premature, or sick, they need special care in a neonatal intensive care unit.

The care is aimed at keeping the baby alive and well while her body matures. Immaturity of heart and lungs, nervous and digestive systems, as well as problems with breathing and temperature control and the possibility of infection, requires skilled one-to-one nursing combined with highly sophisticated technology.

The atmosphere of a special care nursery can be daunting, but hospital staff try hard now to care for families as well as babies. You will be encouraged to spend as much time as possible with your baby, but if you find everything completely overwhelming, take it slowly until you feel more comfortable about being in the nursery.

Ask lots of questions—write them down as you think of them no matter how silly or frightening they seem. Every parent wants to ask things like, *Will she live?* or *Will she be normal?* and *How long before we can take her home?*

# Feeding

If your baby is too premature to suck and digest food, she will be fed either by a fine tube directly into the stomach or by a tiny direct drip into the vein. The staff will show you how to express and store your milk which can be used for your baby straight away or once she is able to tolerate milk, feeds depending on her condition.

You can participate in the care of your baby by changing her and tube feeding with instructions from the staff as soon as you feel up to it. Many mothers say the out-of-control feeling is one of the hardest things to deal with, and caring for their babies while they are in the intensive care nursery helps them feel more in control.

# Feelings

As well as dealing with the practical issues, you might find yourself overwhelmed by some unexpected emotions.

Feelings of numbness, of being out of control and in a dream-like state, are very common. Sadness, anxiety, and guilt are also very powerful emotions that parents feel when their baby has a problem after birth, and those feelings may make you angry with each other, the staff at the hospital, and even, perhaps, the baby. All these hurt feelings are part of the accepting and healing process which will happen in time. Some parents benefit from sessions with a skilled counselor.

You might find people, even close friends, don't congratulate you or send the usual gifts and flowers, which can be distressing. Jealous feelings toward other mothers with their full-term babies and pregnant women obviously due soon are often felt by mothers of premature babies. Leaving your baby behind when you go home is sad and very hard to come to terms with, but nowadays every effort is made to get babies home as soon as possible.

# Going home

There isn't likely to be a predetermined age or weight at which your baby is allowed to go home. Various factors are considered, such as her general condition and how well she is feeding and putting on weight. Some babies are discharged quite early when there is a follow-up team from the hospital who can visit the family at home. Babies may be discharged even though they still need oxygen for lung problems.

Follow-up support varies throughout the country. Capital cities always seem to have more resources and more help available for parents who have sick and/or premature babies. Some hospitals continue to give specialized care from staff who come to your home for a time. This is a great help. Apart from this, you can seek assistance from your pediatrician, your family doctor, and your nurse practitioner. And in the immediate weeks following your baby's departure you can continue to call the medical staff, who can answer your questions about her care.

Nervous feelings about taking your tiny baby out are normal for a while. When you do take the plunge, you will find everyone stops you to comment on how small she is. One mother told me it made her feel as if she never fed her baby.

Premature babies who are born healthy follow the same range of crying, eating, and sleeping patterns as full-term babies.

Very-low-birth-weight and sick premature babies may be erratic and tense and can be a great challenge to care for until they become more settled and predictable. Very-low-birth-weight babies may also need extra care throughout the first year for wheezing conditions and gastroenteritis. Surgical repair of an inguinal hernia is also common.

Premature or sick babies benefit from a specific way of positioning and handling and by avoiding the use of bouncers, walkers and doorway jumping seats. Good help with this can be obtained from physiotherapists and occupational therapists.

A premature baby has to spend the first weeks or months of life making up for lost time in the womb, so naturally she'll reach developmental milestones later. By the time premature babies reach their fourth birthday, four out of five have caught up with their peers and many catch up long before this, some in the first twelve to fifteen months.

While it's wise to bear in mind your baby's prematurity when assessing development, it's also a good idea to start to treat your baby normally as soon as you can and encourage those around you to as well. All the information in this book is as applicable for babies who have been premature or sick as it is for any other baby. In areas where I think mothers of premature babies need a little reassurance or extra information, I have included it.

## FOR MORE INFORMATION

Chapter 8: Breastfeeding Your Baby After the First Two Weeks (*expressing and storing breastmilk, page 125*)

## FURTHER READING

*Preemies: The Essential Guide for Parents of Premature Babies,* Dana Klechsler Linden, Emma Trenti Paroli, Mia Klechsler Doron M.D. Pocket Books, USA, 2000.

*Caring for your Premature Baby: A Complete Resource for Parents,* Alan H. Klein, Jill Alison Canon Harperregjence; USA, 1998.

chapter **four**

# Doing it
# Alone–
# Sole Parents

*This baby is society's future and resources need to be given
to assure this future is sound.*

Norma Tracey, *Mothers and Fathers Speak on the Drama of Pregnancy,*

*Birth and the First Year of Life*

I'm sure one of the irritating things about being a sole parent is the constant assumption in pregnancy and baby information that there are always two doing it. Pictures of mothers and babies in magazines and tend to always depict smiling, happy, well-groomed mothers who invariably have smiling, well-groomed, caring men sitting beside them. The reality is that nearly a quarter of America's parents live on their own with their children and many more parents are on their own a great deal of the time because of absent partners.

I am guilty myself of not mentioning sole parents specifically throughout this book, mainly because of the difficulties in constantly referring to the total range of parenthood experiences. I talk to sole parents of newborns often in my work who range in age from as young as fourteen to as old as forty-eight. They are usually women, but occasionally I meet one who is a man. All of their stories and reasons for being on their own are different. Some women choose to be pregnant alone so that they don't miss the experience, but for most not having a partner is not their choice; rather, it is the result of an unplanned pregnancy or relationship problems.

The lovely things that babies bring are there for everyone whether they have a partner or not, but not having anyone to share the physical and emotional demands of babycare with makes the job harder. While our society has moved away from the moral judgments and harsh treatment of single mothers of twenty years ago, economic and emotional support for them is still lacking. They are still often seen as irresponsible women getting a meal ticket at the expense of the community, which adds to the difficulties that women caring for babies on their own are already facing.

Being a sole parent takes determination and guts. All the information in this book is here for you too. I certainly had you in mind while I was writing it.

## A few tips just for you

- Make staying healthy and sane a top priority as there is unlikely to be an easily available person around to give you a break. Try to eat well and regularly, do some simple exercise (walking is great) and catch up on sleep when you can instead of doing chores. Take up all offers of practical help. When someone offers give them specific ways in which they can be of assistance.

- As you emerge from the first year, start to make plans for an optimistic future. Working for a qualification part-time helps you feel better about yourself, meet new people and start a new career path. It's a good way to move back into the wide world again.

# chapter **five**

# Choosing Baby Products

*Away in a manger no crib for a bed*

Martin Luther

Part of the excitement of preparing for your baby is deciding what clothes and equipment to buy, and this chapter is to help you buy the things you need before your baby arrives. The range of products is endless, and it's often hard to sort out useful and essential items from those that are merely decorative or simply duds. Buying for babies is flavored with emotion. It's easy to get completely carried away gazing at a quaint cradle or a tiny, elaborate nightgown and end up spending more than you can afford on something that is of no use at all, so it's worth taking your time and doing some research.

Here are some resources to help if you are in doubt when you purchase baby products.

• **U.S. Consumer Product Safety Commission (CPSC)**

CPSC is an independent federal regulatory agency created to protect the public against unreasonable risk of injuries and deaths associated with consumer products. The CPSC covers a wide range of baby and child consumer products. Telephone: (301) 504-0990. Toll-free consumer hotline: 1-800-638-2772, 1-800-638-8270 (TTY) Web site: http://www.cpsc.gov

- **U.S. Consumer Gateway (Consumer.gov)**

Consumer.gov is a resource for consumer information from the federal government and has a category for children with information ranging from childcare to immunization to product recalls. *Telephone Federal Information Center:* 1-800-688-9889 *Web site:* http://www.consumer.gov/children.htm

- **National Highway Traffic Administration (NHTSA)**

NHTSA, under the U.S. Department of Transportation was established to carry out safety and consumer programs in all areas relating to traffic and motor vehicle safety. NHTSA has a wide range of valuable information about baby/child motor vehicle passengers that includes a list of child safety seat recalls. *Telephone nationwide toll-free number:* 888-DASH-2DOT (888-327-4236). TTY number is 800-424-9153. *Web Site:* http://www.nhtsa.dot.gov

- **National SAFE KIDS Campaign**

SAFE KIDS is dedicated to the prevention of unintentional childhood injury and has 300 state and local SAFE KIDS coalitions in all 50 states. SAFE KIDS provides information on all aspects of baby and child safety including a product recall list. *Telephone:* (202) 662-0600 *Web site:* http://www.safekids.org

- **Juvenile Products Manufacturers Association, Inc (JPMA)**

JPMA is a national trade organisation of over 400 companies that manufacture and/or import infant products such as cribs, car seats, strollers, bedding and a wide range of accessories and decorative items. JPMA developed an extensive Certification Program to help parents select baby/child products that are built with safety in mind. Parents can look for the seal on product packaging. *Telephone:* 856-638-0420 *Web site:* http://pwww.jpma.org

- **Consumer Reports**

Consumer Reports Magazine and Consumer Reports Online is an independent, nonprofit testing and information organization that tests products, informs the public and protects consumers. The organization has a comprehensive Babies and Kids category that includes detailed ratings and reports for hundreds of products. Address: 101 Truman Avenue, Yonkers, NY 10703. Telephone number and email address is only given to subscribers. *Web site:* http://www.consumerreports.org

# Clothes

It's a good idea to wait until late in your pregnancy before buying clothes for your baby. As relatives and friends tend to like to give clothes as presents you may find you only need a set of basic clothing items.

A useful list follows. Variations can be made to allow for hot or cold climates.

- 3–4 undershirts for extra warmth, with side snaps

- 3 bodysuits with crotch snaps

- 3–4 nightgowns

- 3–4 stretchies with feet (sometimes called footed rompers)

- 4 sweaters

- 3–4 receiving blankets

- 1 sleeping bag for winter babies

- Hats, socks and leggings (depending on the climate and season).

- Bibs

## Tips on clothing

- As babies grow out of clothes very quickly suggest that friends and relatives buy bigger sizes (6–12 months) so you don't end up with a lot of unused tiny clothes

- The simpler the clothes the better. Cotton is best next to your baby's skin, but there are many artificial fabrics or combinations of natural and artificial fabrics that are soft and easy to wash and dry so it's not essential to go solely for cotton.

- Stretchies with feet are incredibly practical, summer or winter, which is why you see so many babies wearing them, but it's nice to have one or two other outfits for special times or a morale boost when you need it.

- Winter babies need hats when out and about. Pull-on hats are the best as ribbons under chins are a nuisance, sometimes irritating and can also be dangerous. Babies need lightweight hats once they are exposed to the sun, even on cloudy days. Hats should provide shade for the face, ears and neck.

- Leggings are obviously for cold weather. Socks are useful most of the year round. Mittens are not needed unless your baby is out of doors and it's very cold. Babies prefer having their hands free.

Learning what their fingers are for and finding out what they can do with them is an important part of babies' development.

- Avoid frills and ribbons on bibs and clothing (especially around the neck) and open weave fabric that baby fingers can get caught in. Loose threads in socks, mittens and clothing can wind around fingers and toes, sometimes causing serious injury.

- Bibs are often more decorative than useful. Bibs need to be large and absorbent as most babies throw-up to some extent and some do it all the time. Just about all babies dribble a lot for at least a year. A dozen soft square gauze weave diapers to use as mopper-uppers is a very useful purchase.

# Diapers

Years ago diapers were a major consideration. No liners, no diaper-soaking solutions, no diaper service, no decent diaper covers and no disposables.

Modern ways have managed to eliminate most of the hard work and inconvenience associated with baby bowels and bladders. There are several choices:

## Reusable diapers (you will need 2–4 dozen)

Heavy weight cotton cloth is the most effective. Cotton flannel diapers are useful when babies are young but are not absorbent enough once they are over three months. Soft gauze weave diapers are not very effective as diapers but are excellent as bibs and general purpose wipes. Most reusable diapers come prefolded. There is also a range of all-in-one diapers that are ultra-absorbent and machine washable.

## Cleaning cloth diapers

• Soak diapers for 24 hours in one cup of borax per gallon of water. Use pails with tight-fitting lids and store them out of the reach of toddlers and young children.

• Wash in washing machine or washtub. Rinse well.

• If diapers become hard use a water conditioner in the rinse cycle. Avoid fabric softeners as these leave a deposit on the diapers which is irritating to some babies' skins.

## Diaper Covers (you will need 3–4)

Diaper covers are made of waterproof material and go over cloth diapers. They are essential to prevent leaking and dampness. Diaper covers do not cause diaper rash as long as the diaper is changed regularly.

## Diaper Liners (optional)

Diaper liners can be disposable or made of cloth. Diaper liners make washing easier because they collect the poo, which can then be neatly disposed of into the toilet. They are also useful when using disposable diapers as the poo can be collected and placed into the toilet instead of thrown into the trash can. Liners can also help prevent friction of the skin from wetness. If you are using reusable diapers it's probably worth buying one box of disposable liners to start with and see if they are needed.

Non-disposable liners are made from soft fabric that allows the moisture to pass through and so helps keep the skin dry. They are not needed by most babies but can be a boon for babies with extra-sensitive skin who are prone to diaper rash.

## Diaper Service

A diaper service brings you a couple of plastic bags full of clean diapers as well as a bin with a liner bag for the used diapers. You decide how many you need—up to seventy or eighty a week is standard for one newborn baby. On an agreed day each week (or twice a week if needed) the used diapers are taken away, clean diapers left. A diaper service is an ideal gift and is an alternative to disposable diapers. If you intend to use a diaper service, sign up in the eight month of your pregnancy then let the company know as soon as you give birth. If you are only going to use the diaper service temporarily you need to consider what you are going to do when you have finished using it.

## Disposable diapers

Disposable diapers are convenient, easy to use and come in many brands. In general, the more expensive the brand, the more effective the diaper. Different sizes and shapes are available according to age and sex. It's best to only buy a limited number of size 1 diapers because some newborns are already too big for the smallest size. You may decide to use them all the time or only on holidays or in emergencies.

# *A word about the great diaper debate*

From a point of view of your baby's personal comfort, it is unlikely to matter which she wears—cloth, diaper service diapers, or disposables. Individually some babies' bottoms do better with disposables, some with cloth. A small number of babies are allergic to disposable diapers. When this happens the skin in the diaper area turns bright red and the redness follows the exact shape of the diaper.

When estimating cost, convenience and baby comfort have to

be considered. Cloth diapers aren't great if you don't have a washing machine. Disposables are a worry if you happen to have a baby who is allergic to them. The most economical option, especially when they come as a gift, is thirty good-quality diapers which last several children. The most expensive is either exclusive use of top-brand disposables or a diaper service. Both these options are an ongoing expense that has to be budgeted for and met every week.

In some respects the advances in disposable diapers in the past ten years are like a dream come true, especially in certain situations—multiple births, lots of babies close together, overseas trips, holidays, long bouts of sickness, and so on. The downside is that like many environmental issues relating to housework, the whole issue ends up back in the female basket. While the marketing people of the disposable diaper industry come up with more and more efficient diapers and brighter and better ways to sell them, the environment movement is turning the diaper debate into an either/or issue, which is not stopping their use but simply making women feel guilty when they do use them. It is not an issue just for women—it is an issue for all parents and the whole community. Environmental costs such as overlaundering versus landfill and waste disposal are involved in both disposables and cloth diapers, neither of which have been analyzed in their entirety.

Disposables are a solid-waste disposal problem. Energy could perhaps be directed more toward ecologically accepted methods of production and disposal of disposable diapers rather than trying to eliminate their use and the concept.

In the meantime, if you are using disposables remember:

- Don't try to flush them down the toilet.

- Put the poo in the toilet where it belongs. This might mean using diaper liners to make poo disposal easier. Oddly enough, once disposable diapers are used, normal rules of hygiene seem to be forgotten and poo gets dumped in the most inappropriate places to the discomfort of those left behind with a diaper in their wastepaper basket. Take the same care at home for the sake of the crew who empty your garbage.

# Sleeping equipment

- Six or more bassinet and/or crib sheets: You can't have too many of these. They can easily be made up from larger sheets. A pillowcase works well over some small mattresses while your baby is in a bassinet.

- A mattress protector for bassinet and/or crib: These are available from any stores that sell baby goods. A mattress protector is made of suitable material with a waterproof backing. Alternatively a piece of blanket is an option during the first three months.

- Two blankets and a quilt (plain, no fringes).

- Something to sleep in: Most parents prefer to have their baby in a small bed (bassinet) in the first three months, but there is no reason not to put your baby into a crib from the start if you are happy to do this. Parents with triplets, for example, put their babies into cribs from birth so that they don't have to buy two lots of beds.

   If you are looking for a small bed for the first three months, don't overspend. Look for something that's not too narrow or too heavy. If it's on a stand, make sure it's stable. It's important to have the bassinet at the right height for you so that you don't have to lean over your baby—there may be times when you have to pat her to sleep and it's essential that you can do this comfortably.

   Cute, colonial wooden cradles are quite impractical, but if you do buy one, check the security of the pin. If the pin comes out, it may force the cradle on an angle which can cause suffocation.

- **MATTRESSES:** Mattresses are sometimes sold with an indirect message that they are safer and protect against crib death. This message is implied, not stated outright, but parents do buy these products believing they give protection against sudden infant death syndrome. A conclusive link between SIDS and any nursery product has not been established, so do not be misled by manufacturers' claims when buying your baby mattress.

  Babies are easier to settle and do seem to sleep better on a firm mattress.

- **CRIBS:** Federal regulations and a voluntary industry standard apply to crib design and safety but also look for a sticker that shows that the crib meets the minimum requirements of the American Society for Testing and Materials voluntary standard and that its manufacturer participates in the Juvenile Products Manufacturers Association.

Other things to look for:

1. Check construction and workmanship. Ask for the store to assemble the crib, either there or at your home so you can inspect the assembled crib on the spot. The slats should not be loose. There should be no sharp bits sticking in or out of the crib. If you assemble it yourself at home, follow the instructions carefully and assemble it in the bedroom so there is no difficulty getting it through the doorway once it is up.

2. The crib should have high sides so your older baby can't fall out. The recommended measurement from the base of the mattress to the top of the crib side is 2 feet (600mm).

3. The lock-release mechanism should be child resistant and work smoothly and efficiently.

4. The space between the bars should be between 2 and 3¼ inches (50–85mms).

5. Decorative transfers, counting beads or cut-outs in the head-board or footboard are all potential hazards.

6. There should be nothing in the cot that older babies and toddlers can use as a step to climb out (for example, mattress supports must be low enough in their lowest position so a toddler can't easily climb out when the sides or ends are in their highest position).

7. If wheels are fitted, two should be removed.

- **CRIB MATTRESSES:** Once again, a firm mattress is preferable, so look for innerspring or dense latex. Make sure the mattress cover is completely sealed, so your baby can't get her head stuck between the cover and the mattress. Nothing should be tied or attached to the mattress with tapes or elastic. A good-quality secondhand mattress is fine—give it a couple of days in the sun before you use it. The mattress should fit snugly, no gaps between the crib and the edge of the mattress.

  There's no need to use pillows until your baby moves into a bed—usually some time between eighteen months and three years.

- **CRIB BUMPERS:** A crib bumper is a fabric or foam liner about 12 inches (30cms) high, that surrounds the inside of the crib above the mattress. It is held in place by ties or elastic. Crib bumpers are designed to prevent babies banging their heads against the crib or getting their legs caught between the bars.

Crib bumpers are not recommended in many countries as their use has been found to pose significant safety risks of strangulation and suffocation. Some experts in the area of Sudden Infant Death Syndrome have also registered concern about the decrease in air-flow when bumpers are used. To date no evidence exists to show babies have ever come to harm because they bang their heads on the crib sides or get their legs caught between the bars so consider giving crib bumpers a miss.

# Staying mobile

## In the car

It is mandatory in all fifty states for babies to be safely restrained in an approved infant car seat that is correctly installed. Here is some information to help you choose a car seat but if you have any doubts about any aspect of purchasing or installation please call or go to the website of the National Highway Traffic Administration (see page 35) or your local police department.

Many different brands are available. Child car seats (also called child restraints) must meet federal standards so all brands should provide good protection for your baby.

You have a choice of two models:

- Single-purpose (non-convertible) infant car seats are used for babies up to 20 pounds. These car seats are in a *rear-facing* position and anchored to the body of the car independent of the seat belts. Once the baby weighs more than 20 pounds. (which can happen anytime from 9 to 12 months of age) a toddler car seat will need to be purchased which is a *forward facing* car seat and can be used for babies from 20 pounds to

40 pounds (up to 4 years).

- Dual-purpose (convertible) car seats are designed to face the rear of the car for babies/toddlers up to 20 pounds and the front of the car from 20 pounds to 40 pounds.

## RECOMMENDATIONS

- Select the car seat that most suits the size and type of your car (convertible car seats sometime do not fit very well into small cars). Put similar-looking models side by side to compare features. If possible bring the seat to your car to see whether it fits. If the store won't allow that make sure you can return it if it doesn't work.

- Never buy a secondhand car seat. The seat may have been in a crash or recalled or it may have been manufactured before 1981 when strict federal standards went into effect.

- New car seats cost between $80 and $300.

- Check for recalls with the National Highway Traffic Administration.

- Remember all this will have to be organized before you leave hospital. If you've bought a convertible seat and your baby is born prematurely, check with your hospital about hiring a preemie car seat until your baby is big enough to fit into the convertible.

- Many baby seat accessories are available to buy. Most are unnecessary and can compromise the safety features of the infant car seat. Nothing should be placed between the liner of the car seat and your baby. Accessories such as head supports, receiving blankets and padded mattresses are not necessary for your baby's comfort and may interfere with the safe working of the car seat.

  Sunshades over the car seat can reduce airflow, trap heat and increase body temperatures. It's much safer to attach sunscreens to the car windows than to drape something over the baby (for more on car safety please see page 264).

## Dashing About

As well as buying a baby car seat you need to make some decisions about what you will use for baby transport when you are on foot or on public transport.

**SLINGS, CARRIERS AND BACKPACKS:** Slings and carriers, worn on your front are an extremely useful way of keeping your baby next to you and your hands free. They are excellent for trips to the supermarket, on public transport and for times when carrying her next to you is the only way to calm her during an unsettled period. They are not so practical for long walks or in any situation where you have to carry your baby for long stretches of time. If you use a sling or a carrier you are unlikely to use it much after six months when your baby becomes heavy.

**SLINGS:** A sling is a simple device that slips over one shoulder across the chest. Your baby lies inside the sling across your body so her head is on your chest. Some women find slings a great breastfeeding aid when breastfeeding in public. Slings are more for newborns and up to the first three months although some parents use them for the whole of the first year. Most babies, however, find slings too restrictive after the early months and prefer to be upright, watching what's going on. And many parents find slings uncomfortable as the baby gets bigger, because the weight tends to be distributed unevenly.

**CARRIERS**: A carrier is more complicated and it can be tricky getting one on and off until you get the hang of it (it won't take long) but they are designed to distribute the baby's weight more evenly.

Needless to say there are many varieties to choose from. Some hold your baby inward until she is around four to six months, at which time she can be turned outward to face the world. Others convert to a backpack when the baby is between six and nine months.

**Tips for carriers**

- Look for one that's easy to adjust (especially if different people are using it) and easy to get on and off on your own.

- A wide bottom and padded shoulder straps are more comfortable for both baby and parent.

- Make sure your baby's head is still supported securely when both your hands are free.

- Try to find a carrier that is strongly made without being bulky and hot.

- **BACKPACKS:** Backpacks are designed for babies from about six to nine months who have good head support and are sitting (or close to sitting) on their own. A baby/toddler backpack is similar to a hiking/camping backpack. If you are going to use it a lot, it is worth getting a more expensive model with a frame that stands on it's own acting as a seat with the toddler in it, a waist belt and weather protection. Backpacks are more for the hardy. They can be useful for older babies and toddlers who refuse to sit in strollers.

- **FINALLY:** Slings, carriers and backpacks are not for everyone and may not be a good idea for those with back problems.

## Carriages and Strollers

Selecting a carriage or stroller can be confusing, as there is now a wide variety to choose from. Take your time and do some research so you can work out what is best for your lifestyle and your budget. You will need some sort of transport system from early babyhood to age three (sometimes four).

A sample of what's available:

- **CARRIAGES:** (heavy sometimes weigh more than 30 lbs) Carriages are becoming a thing of the past especially for people who live up flights of stairs, in small dwellings, in crowded cities or anywhere where there is rough terrain to negotiate. Carriages are very comfortable for young babies and protect them well from the elements. They also have a springy, rolling motion that can calm fussy babies, and they usually have a removable carry bed that can be used as a bassinet. Sometime between six and nine months you will find you will need to change to a stroller, which means making an extra purchase.

- **TRAVEL SYSTEMS:** A travel system allows you to snap an infant car seat into a frame (lightweight) or a stroller (larger, heavier) which means your baby can be transferred from car to stroller with minimal disturbance. If you use a frame you will need to buy a stroller when your baby grows out of the car seat. The stroller system saves you having to buy another piece of equipment.

- **CARRIAGE/STROLLERS:** These models convert from a carriage (so young babies can lie flat) to a stroller (once they are old enough to sit up or be propped up). Some models have a removable carry bed that can be used as a bassinet. They are expensive and relatively heavy (compared to the lightweight strollers) but do grow with your baby.

- **MIDWEIGHT STROLLERS:** (weighs 17–35 lbs) These can be heavy and bulky but are sturdy and stable with deep comfortable interiors and provide good protection from the weather.

**49**

**A comment on both of the above:** Parents report that some of these models are too bulky and cumbersome for city living and difficult to negotiate on uneven sidewalks.

- **UMBRELLA STROLLERS:** (12 lbs) Are so called because they have curved umbrella-like handles. They are easy to maneuver in tight spots and easy to store (great for travelling on planes, trains, buses). Step-up models include a canopy, an adjustable seat and padding. Durability is often poor, you may need several for one child, and the wheels (like the wheels on supermarket trolleys) may not perform well on bumpy terrain (or sometimes even on smooth terrain).

- **LIGHTWEIGHT STROLLERS:** (12 lbs) Like an umbrella strollers these models have curved handles but there the similarity ends. These models are the most sophisticated (and often the most expensive) on the market. They feature smooth folding mechanisms, thick padding, a reclining seat, weather protection extras and built-in shock absorbers in the wheel assemblies.

  **NB:** Care has to be taken with umbrella strollers and lightweight strollers when hanging bags on the handles as heavy items can make the stroller tip backward onto the ground.

- **JOGGING STROLLERS:** Jogging strollers have three large bicycle wheels mounted to a lightweight frame. They are perfect for rough terrain and for taking your child on runs or hikes. But the big wheels take up a lot of space in the trunk of the car and they can be difficult to maneuver around small spaces and up and down stairs.

**Things to consider**

Each system and particular model has positives and negatives. Strollers have become smaller, lighter and easier to push around in the last ten years but the perfect design to suit every purpose remains to be invented. You may have to make a compromise.

**Essential**

- **SEAT BELTS:** Many strollers have inadequate restraints (for example, too loose, no shoulder straps, non-adjustable). Ideally the stroller should have a shoulder harness and a waist and crotch strap (especially for jogging strollers) however most models only have waist and crotch straps. The buckle should be easy for you to operate but impossible for your baby/toddler to unfasten.

- **BRAKES:** Test them in the store. The wheels should lock when you engage the brake.

- **LEG HOLES:** Carriage/strollers that can fully recline must have leg holes that close so an infant can't slip through one of them.

- **STURDINESS AND FLAWS:** Shake the stroller and check that all the mechanics work smoothly and efficiently remembering you will often be opening and folding your stroller while holding your baby. Look for flaws such as malfunctioning wheels, frames that are likely to bend out of shape, faulty locking mechanisms, loose seat belts, flimsy buckles.

**Important**

- **MANEUVERABILITY:** Can you push it and turn it with one hand? The best wheels are the swivel type that move in all directions and can be locked when you are going over rough surfaces.

- **STORAGE AREAS:** How big is the storage bin under the stroller? Check how strong it is by pressing on it—it shouldn't drag on the ground when loaded. Storage nets fastened onto the handles are suitable only for lightweight articles.

- **WARRANTIES AND RETURN POLICES:** Purchase your stroller from a store, catalog or web site that offerS 100% satisfaction guarantee.

### A final check list

- Ask friends with toddlers what they recommend.

- What is your price range? The range is $20 (umbrella strollers) to $450 (top of the range lightweight strollers). Bear in mind that high price and good quality doesn't always match up. *Consumer Reports* tests have shown that some economical strollers can perform as well as highly priced models.

- Do you have back problems? Think about the weight of the stroller and how much you might have to lift it.

- Will you be using public transport a lot, walking a lot, jogging?

- Will you be frequently lifting the stroller in and out of the trunk of the car?

- Do you have many stairs to climb up and down daily?

- Do you want the stroller to last several children?

- Are you looking for a single item to last from birth to three years, or are you prepared to buy new equipment as needed?

- What sort of terrain are you going to be pushing your stroller over?

- What is provided for shopping? What happens to your shopping items when you want to collapse the stroller to get onto the bus?

- Is it the right height for you and your partner? Can you push it without damaging your shins? Do you need adjustable handles?

- What extras do you need for weather protection?

# Baby cosmetics and baby baths

## Toiletries

There is an unlimited array of toiletries and tubs available for babies. Most are unnecessary. Here's a short list of essentials:

- Cotton balls and tissues

- A mild, simple soap

- A moisturizer—choose a hypoallergenic, paraben-free, lanolin-free and fragrance-free brand, such as Moisturel lotion.

- Alcohol-free, fragrance-free disposable baby wash clothes to clean the diaper area when you are out and about. At home, water and tissues are fine.

- A small jar of petroleum jelly

- Two soft bath towels and two washcloths

- Small blunt-ended scissors for cutting your baby's fingernails

The use of special baby bath lotions instead of soap is common practice. As well as commercial lotions designed specifically for your baby's bath time, oils such as jojoba or almond oil can be used. All of these products are acceptable but not essential. Simple soap, water and moisturiser are sufficient for babies unless they have a dry skin condition such as eczema, in which case soap is not advised.

Buy toiletries in small quantities until you know for sure what products suit your baby. Wait until you need specific items before

**53**

buying out the store.

## Tubs

An extraordinary selection of baby tubs is available—from cradling bath seats to sling baths to beanbag tubs to huge tubs that will last a year! Amazing when you consider that many babies around the world are wrapped up tight for the first six months and never go near a bath.

Some thoughts on the matter of tubs:

- A large plastic wash bowl is fine

- Bathing in a sink is an option. Infant bath seats are available to support your baby in the sink. Make sure she can't bump against the spouts or get burnt on hot faucets.

- Other bathing devices designed for young babies, such as sling baths, bath pads and beanbag tubs, will have to be replaced as the baby grows.

- Double check duel purpose baths to make sure they work the way they are meant to.

- Large roomy plastic moulded tubs are popular. Make sure the one you buy gives you easy access to your baby. One of the problems with the bigger tubs is emptying them when they are full, without causing an injury to yourself or making a terrible mess everywhere. Some models sit across the regular tub, which solves the drainage problem, but check that it fits your tub.

# Child safety products

In keeping your baby safe nothing can replace constant vigilance, planning, and making sure your basic equipment is not hazardous. At each age and stage of your baby's life, however, you'll find there are items worth buying to help make her life safer and your life easier. Child safety products are available in stores across the country as well as from babycare websites.

During the first three months, babies are fairly immobile, but there are a few basic items worth buying:

- A low-power night light in your room, your baby's room and the hall.

- An efficient flashlight.

- A childproof lock or handle to the baby's room.

- A childproof lock on the laundry door.

- A child-resistant cabinet for medicines.

- An outlet cover.

- An emergency telephone number listing.

- A non-slip mat in the shower.

- An automatic doorstop.

- A chair for you: A suitable chair for you to breastfeed your baby is essential. In general, low, soft lounge chairs or rocking chairs are not great to learn to breastfeed in. You need a reasonably wide, firm chair with good back support that is about 14–16 inches from the floor.

# Optional extras

## Change tables
Change tables are specially constructed tables to put babies on

while you change them, dress them, and so on. It's much easier for you and kinder to your back to be able to attend to your baby without bending over all the time. A variety of change tables are available, some with storage space and many with restraining straps. As babies can fall off things, safety is an important consideration when a change table or any high surface is being used.

The change table should be stable and strong, especially if there are small children in your family who are likely to try climbing it. It should not be on wheels. Some mothers couldn't manage without change tables; others feel they are a waste of money. If the change table can double as a place to store diapers, diaper-changing equipment, clothes, and so on, it's a lot more useful.

Do you have room for one? Maybe a changing pad on a table or chest of drawers would suit you better.

## A portable baby chair (often called a baby bouncer)

Most parents find that portable baby chairs are very useful. Portable chairs provide a place for your baby to sit in and look around at the world, and can be carried from room to room (or place to place) with ease. Many portable chairs are designed to bounce or rock and come with sun-shades, rockers, and activity centers. All of these things are attractive to parents but the main thing to look for when you buy a portable baby chair is a stable chair that gives your baby good support and does not move when your baby moves. Firm, stable chairs encourage better posture. This is especially important for premature babies or babies with developmental problems.

## Specialist baby bags called change bags, diaper bags

Important if you're the sort who likes to be highly organized; alternatively, any large bag will do. Make sure it is cleanable and fits over the handles of your stroller or buggy (remember heavy bags tip strollers over).

# Breast pumps

I find this is the most common piece of equipment that is never used or rarely used, so don't rush off and buy one early on. For more on breast pumps, see pages 129–130.

# Pacifiers

A pacifier is not an essential item, and before you start using one, it's worth looking at the advantages and pitfalls.

## ADVANTAGES

- Relieves baby and parent distress in the early months.

- Allows the baby to fulfill her need for non-nutritive sucking without being constantly on the breast.

- Pacifiers can be useful in helping establish some sort of routine with feeds so that mothers have a more predictable day.

- Pacifiers are very useful for calming sick babies, premature babies, or babies under lights who are jaundiced.

## DISADVANTAGES

- Can interfere with initiating and establishing breastfeeding.

- May increase the incidence of thrush. At times, causes contact dermatitis around baby's mouth under the plastic shield that surrounds the nipple.

- Pacifiers contribute to sleep problems in older babies.

- Pacifiers are an extra hassle to worry about—life is easier without them.

- Hazards such as tooth decay and safety risks are associated with improper use.

- Occasionally the use of pacifiers contributes to excessive dribbling in the toddler years as the saliva pools under the tongue and falls out instead of being swallowed. The prolonged use of the pacifier interferes with optimum muscular development around the mouth and encourages tongue thrusting.

If you decide to use one, which type should you buy?

Choices center around material and shape.

Shapes are either the bell shape or the more recently developed orthodontic shape, which manufacturers claim resemble, women's nipples and is in some way advantageous to babies. This is based on very flimsy evidence. Orthodontic pacifiers are not pliable and responsive like women's nipples, so it is misleading of companies to make these claims.

Bell-shaped pacifiers come in a variety of sizes ranging from small to large. There are no advantages to any particular size apart from your baby's personal preference. If she prefers a small size, there's no need to change the size as she grows.

The material is either latex or silicone.Latex is softer, cheaper, and more flexible. Silicone is the other option. Silicone pacifiers are more expensive, harder, less flexible, and more durable. Because they are less flexible, they are more prone to tearing and being bitten through, so choking is a possible risk you should be aware of.

## Washing baby clothes

Baby clothes can be washed with the rest of the family clothes. They do not need to be washed separately unless there is a medical reason for doing so.

# To buy or borrow—basic equipment for the first three months

## Clothes
3–4 undershirts

3 body shirts with crotch snaps

3–4 nightgowns

3–4 stretchies with feet (footed rompers)

4 sweaters

3–4 receiving blankets

1 sleeping bag for winter babies

Hats, socks, leggings (depending on the climate and season)

## Bibs
3 receiving blankets

1 packet of soft square gauze weave diapers (for mopping up, wrapping summer babies in)

## Diapers
Reusable diapers (squares, pre-folded or all-in-ones)

Diaper covers, safety pins

Pails with lids

Disposables

Disposable liners

Sleeping

Bassinet and stand (optional) and firm mattress

Crib and mattress

6 or more bassinet and/or crib sheets

Waterproof covering for mattress

1–2 blankets

## Staying Mobile

Sling, carrier (optional, most parents find these useful if not essential)

Stroller

Baby bag (optional, any big bag will do)

## Car Safety

An approved baby car seat

Baby bathing and toiletries

Basic toiletries

Blunt-ended scissors

Change table or pad (optional)

## Miscellaneous

Appropriate child safety products

A comfortable chair for you

Portable baby chair/rocker (baby bouncer)

## For More Information

Chapter 12: Safety, page 253 *(for safe use of equipment, including car safety and safe use of pacifiers)*

Chapter 16: For Parents *(SIDS, page 413)*

Chapter 11: Daily Care *(for use of baby cosmetics, page 250)*

Chapter 17: Equipment *(portable cribs, page 263)*

Chapter 15: The Crying Baby, page 331

Chapter 28: Sleeping and Waking, Six Months, and Beyond, page 539 chapter **six**

# Breastfeeding Your Baby for the First Two Weeks

*As usual, pedagogy has brought us to the point where new mothers view breastfeeding as a skill, a schedule, a kindly kingdom of motherly feelings. It will surprise her to find that breastfeeding is above all a relationship, and that it occupies the mind in a way you don't even realize until you step outside that tired dreamy bubble.*

Marni Jackson, *The Mother Zone: Love, Sex and Laundry in the Modern Family*

Breastmilk is the best baby food there is. Breastfeeding and the benefits of human milk have been promoted much more vigorously in the last twenty years as research reveals more and more about the special qualities it has, how they benefit babies and impact on adult health. Some of the information is difficult to come to terms with but does not mean it should be withheld or watered down.

People who support, protect, and promote breastfeeding do not do so to make women who struggle with breastfeeding and wean feel guilty—some of them bottle fed their own babies. Their information and efforts to change our society's approach to how babies are fed is aimed at the product (human milk and formula), not the person.

If an interest had not been taken in breastfeeding by passionate individuals and groups, breastfeeding may well have disappeared from our culture. If the art and act of breastfeeding is lost, it is reasonable to assume there will be far-reaching negative effects on the human race in the same way irresponsible use of the environment is a potential threat to us all.

Think about the implications of our babies being completely reliant on manufacturers to provide indefinitely safe artificial milk in the absence of competition from a superior product. Producing a suitable substitute for the few babies who need it is very different from completely replacing an optimum system that has been in place for thousands of years. One of the spinoffs of the renewed interest in breastfeeding research has been a great improvement in the manufacture of formula, which has made bottle feeding much safer, so the protection of breastfeeding is also about the protection of baby feeding.

Unfortunately, in the rush to promote breastfeeding, the ease and enjoyment of it is at times unrealistically portrayed and the practicalities of life as we live it overlooked. A woman's decision to keep breastfeeding is always influenced by support systems, and we have not reached a stage yet where appropriate support, resources, education, and community awareness are in place in the U.S. to have most babies breastfed for six months. I am made very much aware of this by the women I see in my work, so breastfeeding in this book is presented from a practical, realistic perspective. We also need to recognize that very few women choose not to breastfeed. When breastfeeding is abandoned, it is usually not a matter of choice; rather it is because the circumstances surrounding the breastfeeding make it impossible to continue. The few women who do *choose* to formula feed usually do so because circumstances make it impossible to continue or because a previous breastfeeding experience was painful and stressful and/or their babies did not thrive.

To help overcome the difficulties that can occur in the first six to eight weeks, it helps enormously to know what the advantages of breastfeeding and breastmilk are for you and your baby. Doing what you can to prepare yourself and your partner and having access to accurate information to solve the solvable problems when and if they occur makes a great deal of difference during the early weeks. Not all breastfeeding problems are solvable, but the ones that aren't can often be overcome with good support, the right advice, and a little time.

Feeding your baby cannot be seen as separate to other aspects of her life or yours. Bear in mind that many of the difficulties with babycare have nothing to do with feeding but simply with the way babies are, which most of us find a challenge, and sometimes a trial, especially when we are doing it for the first time.

# Why breastfeed?

## It's best for your baby

Breastmilk is perfectly balanced and contains everything your baby needs to grow and develop the way she is meant to. It's easy to digest, contains antibodies to protect her from illness and foster optimum brain growth. Breastfeeding is good for your baby's jaw development and speech, and breastmilk enhances her eyesight.

Exclusive breastfeeding for about six months delays the onset and reduces the severity of conditions such as asthma, eczema, and food intolerance. Breastfed babies rarely get constipated when they only have breastmilk and no other food or milk. Their poo is always soft. Current research also suggests that breastfeeding may reduce the incidence of heart disease in later life and that breastfed children may have a lower risk of developing juvenile diabetes and celiac disease.

## It's best for you

The hormones your body secretes when you breastfeed keep you calm. Many women find the hormones also help with weight loss by making their bodies work more efficiently.

Breastfeeding helps your uterus return to normal size after birth and speeds up the blood loss, so the bleeding after the birth is over quicker.

Breastfeeding delays the return of menstruation. Exclusive breastfeeding without use of pacifiers, bottles, or any other food is effective, natural contraception.

Once you and your baby are breastfeeding well, it is easy, convenient, and, of course, milk is freely given and freely obtained, so it is easy on the family budget.

A possibility that breastfeeding may reduce the incidence of pre-menopausal cancer of the breast, cervix, and ovaries is indicated in some research. The research also suggests that women who breastfeed are less likely to suffer from osteoporosis and heart disease in later life. Research in these areas is difficult and there are no guarantees, but are an added bonus that you should be aware of.

Breastfeeding is potentially sensual and pleasurable for mother and baby alike. Skin on skin, close body contact—it is a richly emotional and physical time, a delicate balance of nature, and a wonderful way for you and your baby to get to know each other.

Women's experiences of breastfeeding are as diverse and individual as everything else to do with babies. The issues surrounding baby feeding are emotional, psychological, social, and political. The concepts are complex and a challenge for all of us to deal with whether we are parents, health workers, baby food industry workers, or bureaucrats who set policies on infant nutrition.

The following are letters written to me about breastfeeding. I am including them because I think they reflect the thoughts and experiences of women generally, and it may be comforting to read them if you are going through a few dilemmas yourself.

## A POSITIVE ATTITUDE

*I guess I've been very lucky in that I grew up with very positive attitudes on breastfeeding. I am one of nine children and my mother breastfed all of us for about nine months each. When I had my first child, I had no doubts about my ability to breastfeed. To me, choosing to breastfeed in preference to formula feeding is like choosing to feed the family fresh food as opposed to canned and frozen food. Many women are not given a real choice about baby feeding due to a lack of knowledge on the subject.*

## WHY AM I DOING THIS?

*I am currently breastfeeding my two-month-old son. If I were to give my expecting friends any advice regarding this topic, it would be to breastfeed. My rationale for this is as follows:*

*When you have a baby such as mine that wants to be fed every two and a half hours, could you be bothered, screaming child in hand, heating the bottle only to find that the baby has fallen asleep on you after five minutes and the bottle has gone to waste?*

*You are portable. I can't imagine what a pest it would be to go out if you are bottle feeding. Have you got enough bottles? Are they sterilized? How can you keep them cool? When you breastfeed, wherever you go your milk goes in a nice simple package. It is*

**65**

*cheap. I have not had to buy formula, but I can imagine that it becomes very expensive.*

*Breastfeeding also helps you lose weight, or so I am told. Personally I think you lose weight due to all the walking up and down the hall pacifying the little gem.*

*Bonding? Well I am sure bottle-fed babies bond just fine too, but I am the one feeding him. For the moment I am his lifeline. It is one hell of a responsibility and perhaps one of the only times in your life when you are truly useful.*

*Breastfeed just for the experience of it. I mean, we go back to our animal forebears when we bear the child, and breastfeeding is another one of those experiences you do simply because you can. I am a bit vague on this point, but in the same way people go parachuting for the sensation, breastfeeding, while not as dangerous, is still done for the experience and sensation.*

*Off the top of my head these are the issues I find to be most important. However, let's not kid ourselves—why don't any of the books ever describe the associated hassles with breastfeeding?*

*I think that we should all accept that there are people who want to bottle feed for their own very good reasons. I think there are far more potentially harmful things in store for our children; whether it be an electrical fault, some misplaced medicine, or an accident when they get their driver's licence.*

*I mean, if I could have more than two hours of consecutive sleep, I would be the happiest person in town right at the moment.*

## WAY OF LIFE

*My belief is that unless a comfortable breastfeeding relationship is established within the first two to four weeks, many mothers quickly opt for the bottle. It seems many problems arise in those first few days of a baby's life. This is particularly distressing as every hospital, birth center, La Leche League Counsellor appears to have different and often conflicting ideas. Without the support of loved ones at this time, it's not surprising the number of women who turn to formula feeding to help them cope.*

*Probably the greatest thing I have learned about breastfeeding is that it is a way of life. Much of our parenting skills are a direct spinoff of the "breast is best" attitude. I am grateful to be parenting in this manner as my son is a delight.*

## ENCOURAGED TO BREASTFEED

*The lack of breastfeeding is a sad affair, but it slowly seems to be coming back. I was encouraged to breastfeed my son, which I did happily for a year. He was ten weeks premature and I expressed my milk for eight weeks until he was strong enough to feed from the breast. It was quite an ordeal at first, expressing milk by hand and electric pump, but all worthwhile. My son took to the breast as if it was what he was waiting for. It was a great experience for both of us.*

## A NON-BREASTFEEDING EXPERIENCE

*I am writing to let you know of my experience of not breastfeeding. I am aware that there are pressures on women who decide to either breastfeed or not to breastfeed. These are discussed in many publications and books for pregnant women and new mothers.*

*There is almost complete silence on the subject of those women, like me, who fail to produce milk at all. Does this indicate almost complete ignorance about this problem? My experience indicates that it does.*

*My husband and I were in Canada for the birth of our son. Despite help from a doctor, La Leche League, a lactation consultant, and tests from an endocrinologist (which showed my hormone levels were normal), there was no reason any of them could come up with for my lack of milk.*

*This time was very upsetting for my husband and me, and we are still upset and disappointed that breastfeeding information for prospective parents does not make it clear that some mothers (if only a small number) are unable to breastfeed. After telling friends of my problem, they related stories of people they know with similar problems. Thus I know I am not alone in having this problem.*

## DIDN'T CONNECT WITH BREASTFEEDING

*While I was pregnant with my first child, I had every intention of breastfeeding. I read all the appropriate information. Unfortunately there isn't enough literature stating that not all mothers and babies can connect with breastfeeding. This is agonizing for a new mother as she is constantly told to persist. Meanwhile her child is losing weight and crying continually with hunger.*

*Sadly, I will never have the first seven weeks of my son's life back to enjoy; instead it was misery for this time due to so much emphasis being put on breastfeeding. I don't think I'll breastfeed again because the experience was far from fulfilling for me or my baby.*

## LET'S PREPARE WOMEN FOR THE DIFFICULT ASPECTS OF BREASTFEEDING

*To some first-time mothers, the pain and stress involved in breastfeeding comes as a total shock. The literature aimed at them only talks about the pleasurable, positive aspects. Breastfeeding promoters need to realize that talking about the difficult aspects of breastfeeding will help mothers overcome the initial and subsequent hurdles to experience the positive and pleasurable aspects. If health professionals cannot be realistic about the difficulties of breastfeeding, then how can emotional and sleep-deprived mothers remain positive about the advantages breastfeeding offers themselves and their babies?*

## THE PERFECT PRODUCT

*My baby is now fifteen weeks old and I am breastfeeding her. Both she and I are thriving. In the beginning I found breastfeeding painful and stressful for both my husband and myself. I thought I wanted to give it up. My nurse practitioner gave me lots of sensible advice and loads of encouragement to continue. When I complained about breastfeeding, she pointed out two important facts:*

- *Breast milk is the perfect food for babies.*

- *If I hang in there, it will get easier.*

*She was right on both points.*

## THE DREADED FORMULA

*I enjoyed the twelve months I breastfed my first baby. With my second baby, I had feeding difficulties from day one. He was placed in special care because he was a low weight. Once my milk came in and we thought he was feeding okay, we went home to what was to become hell on earth. The next six to eight weeks consisted of a screaming baby who was not gaining weight. Eventually my family doctor (who was very supportive of breastfeeding) was concerned that my son needed to gain weight, so I ventured to the store and bought the dreaded formula, which I then fed to my son. He not only drank it happily but then slept for five hours, the longest he had ever done. It suddenly dawned on me that through my stubborn desire to breastfeed and the feeling that mothers who bottle feed weren't really "good" mothers, I had probably done my son a disservice who, in hindsight, had probably been hungry most of his life.*

*He went on to thrive on artificial milk and I think I have recovered from my guilt and have tempered my feelings about breastfeeding. If I had another child, I would still do my utmost to breastfeed, as it is ideal, but I no longer look down on mothers who bottle feed.*

## BREASTFEEDING WORTH THE STRUGGLE

*I am breastfeeding my six-month-old son and would not have it any other way—now. However, feeding was a nightmare for the first eleven weeks of his life and a desolate time for me. I so wanted to breastfeed and I'd read about the techniques to use, but "your nipples may feel a little tender at first" was the understatement of the year. I wanted to throw a hand grenade at those whose books had given me the expectation that breastfeeding would be warm, comfortable, and pleasurable. It is now, but it wasn't then.*

*After struggling through sore nipples and recurrent mastitis, almost weaning then having to reestablish my milk supply, I finally did it by the time my baby was twelve weeks old. A supportive husband helped me stay sane.*

*Establishing breastfeeding can be a lengthy, demoralizing process. It's no wonder some of us, used to snapping our fingers to deal with difficulties, reach for formula to solve the problems. I can still recall being amazed that I, a tough high school teacher who'd been able to maintain discipline in all sorts of school situations, should be so beaten by a tiny baby who simply needed to be fed.*

*I don't think we should back away from saying breast is best. It is a scientific fact that formula only approximates breastmilk, but we need more realistic education about what can go wrong. We need it given in detail so that we can be prepared.*

## BREASTFEEDING IS SENSUAL AND PLEASURABLE

*My son was born by cesarean section. Breastfeeding him was and is a natural experience that is convenient and economical. The staff at the hospital were very encouraging and actively promoted breastfeeding through lactation consultants giving presentations and providing all the support needed.*

*I'd like to address some aspects about baby feeding. Firstly, mothers who bottle feed feel at odds with breastfeeding mothers.*

*When I learned that some of my friends weaned at two to five weeks, I asked how they found it in an attempt to learn of their experience. Their responses were consistent—"it's great," "more convenient." I did become aware of some minor conflict between the two methods from the mothers' viewpoint. I feel that breastfeeding moms feel compelled to defend their position.*

*Secondly, breastfeeding is sensual and pleasurable.*

*I found it interesting and comforting that you wrote of breastfeeding being frequently sensual and pleasurable. I certainly found it to be both. It's something one feels inhibited to express, but it does feel quite nice. This aspect, I believe, is not made known by health workers.*

# What's in breastmilk?

I think we sometimes lose sight of what it is the baby is getting and why it's worth persevering through the hard times to make sure your baby doesn't miss out, so let's look briefly at what it is.

Breastmilk is a living substance. Despite the wealth of information now available, lots of things about breastmilk remain elusive and unanswered, so we are still a long way from manufacturing a substance that is equivalent.

One of the reasons precise breastmilk analysis is so difficult is because human milk changes constantly. Breastmilk components vary from woman to woman, from breast to breast, during the course of a feed and over time. Human milk adapts to babies' ages and needs and to climatic conditions. Its taste varies, so breastfed babies are exposed to a variety of interesting tastes from feed to feed. Women are usually aware of the difference in the way their milk looks when it changes from the first milk, colostrum, to the later milk known as mature milk. Colostrum is rich-looking and yellow while mature milk is a fine fluid often with a bluish hue. Milk from different women can look quite different, and all variations are fine. Human milk doesn't look like formula, which is thick and white. They are different substances, so this is to be expected.

Everything your baby needs is in her own special milk made by you. There are over one hundred known ingredients. Let's look at the main ones and some of the amazing features of human milk.

## Water

There's lots of water in breastmilk. Water quenches your baby's thirst and during the early weeks helps make up for the water she loses from evaporation from her lungs and skin. This evaporation is normal and is one of the reasons new babies lose body heat quickly, so breastfeeding contributes to maintaining your baby's body temperature after birth. Even in very hot climates, babies get all the water they need from breastmilk, clean and uncontaminated—your baby doesn't need extra water in a bottle.

## Fat

Fat makes up the next biggest part of breastmilk after water. The fat in breastmilk is very well absorbed because of a special enzyme present in the milk that makes the fat instantly ready to digest without having to be broken down in your baby's liver. Fat satisfies her hunger and is the main way she gets her calories and puts on weight. The special fats in breastmilk are quite different from fats in any other food or milk, and so far unable to be replicated. These fats give your baby energy and provide essential nutrients in the

72

correct amounts and proportions that are needed for growth and development of her central nervous system.

Breastmilk also has plenty of cholesterol, needed by babies for optimum brain development at this time of their lives.

## Protein

Protein is important for growth and development of every part of the body, down to the tiniest cell. Humans grow slowly compared to other mammals, so the protein in their milk exactly suits the growth rate of human babies.

The two types of protein are casein and whey. The casein, or milk curd, is soft and small and easy to digest. The whey, which is the clear fluid left when milk clots, is also easy for your baby to digest. The whey protein contains a lot of the antibodies that protect your baby from disease.

## Carbohydrates

The main carbohydrate is lactose. Lactose makes it easier for babies to absorb calcium—which compensates beautifully for the relatively small amounts of calcium in breastmilk. Lactose also supplies energy to your baby's brain and contains a special carbohydrate known as bifidus factor, which helps stop harmful germs from growing in your baby's gut.

## Some other special things about breastmilk

Breastmilk contains living cells like those found in blood. They have complex functions but are important in protecting your baby from illness and delaying the onset of possible allergies.

Many hormones are found in breastmilk. Hormones are substances the body produces that have a specific effect on a particular part of the body. One of the hormones found in breastmilk is a growth hormone. The exact role of many of the hormones found in human milk is still to be discovered. It is reasonable to assume they all play some part in the growth and development of babies. Breastmilk also contains vitamins, minerals, iron (which is very well absorbed), and trace elements.

Breastmilk is an intriguing, living substance—the real benefits of which are only just beginning to be understood. Breastfeeding is an extension of birth and part of nature's grand plan to help babies adjust to life outside the womb.

# Getting ready for breastfeeding before the birth of your baby

Getting ready to breastfeed doesn't mean doing things to your nipples and breasts. Past ideas of toughening your nipples or pulling them out have now been found to be unnecessary and even harmful. Preparation is about learning how breastfeeding works, getting an idea of the best things to do to make it work the way it should, and doing a little bit of flexible planning.

Learning to feel comfortable handling your breasts by gentle massage (using a technique similar to that advised for self breast examination) is also helpful. If you are curious to see what your milk looks like or tastes like, express a little, gently, and see.

Here are some planning suggestions:

• Read the early breastfeeding parts of this book before your baby is born.

• Breastfeeding is usually part of childbirth education classes, so make sure you go the night it's on. Alternatively, many maternity hospitals conduct breastfeeding classes.

- La Leche League International (LLLI) is a nonprofit, voluntary organization that provides breastfeeding information, education and support. LLLI has 3000 groups and 8000 leaders across the country. LLLI leaders and counsellors are women with personal experience of breastfeeding as well as special training in helping other mothers; making use of this wonderful resource is strongly recommended.

  If you feel very unsure about breastfeeding, making an appointment to see a lactation consultant before the birth will give you confidence before you start, and will help with any difficulties that may arise once your breastfeeding is underway. Lactation consultants are health professionals with special training in breastfeeding. They may be on staff at obstetric hospitals, in paediatricians' offices or they may work in private practice.

- Plan to rest more than you usually do during the first six weeks until your body adjusts to your new life and breastfeeding. The matter of housework rears its head again and can't be ignored— talk to your partner about possible strategies.

- Having someone around who believes in breastfeeding whom you can rely on for consistent advice and encouragement is a great boon. A nurse practitioner, a La Leche League counsellor, a lactation consultant, a midwife, a friend who has breastfed, or a relative might fit the bill.

- Think about ways of avoiding the three S's which are smoking, stress, and supplements. Women who *smoke* often find they don't have quite enough milk to keep their baby happy, especially after the first two or three months. Constant *stress* makes you feel unhappy and ill, which means your body doesn't work as well as it is able to, so try to change stressful areas in your life before the birth. Learning relaxation techniques also helps. *Supplements*, which are fluids given in bottles to babies, may mean the end of breastfeeding if they are given in the first six weeks, so avoid them. Water and juice are not necessary.

# A word about flat or inverted nipples

Flat nipples are nipples that do not stand out when they are stimulated by touch or cold. Flat nipples usually start to stick out once the baby is feeding well and drawing the nipple out, but feeding can be tricky in the early weeks.

Inverted nipples turn into the breast, so there is a dip instead of a nipple standing out. It is more difficult to breastfeed if your nipples don't stand out as it makes it harder for your baby to get a good mouthful of the breast tissue around your nipple. Inverted nipples provide a real challenge, but women can succeed with patience, perseverance, help from a skilled adviser and a baby who sucks well. Having said that, it must be acknowledged that inverted nipples often present a considerable hurdle that prevents some women from breastfeeding. In these cases, breastmilk can be expressed and given in a bottle.

Having flat or inverted nipples might discourage you from breastfeeding. If you are concerned, check it out with someone reliable like a midwife, a La Leche League counsellor, or a lactation consultant.

Special exercises and wearing breast shells (devices made of rigid plastic that are placed over the nipple and held in place by a firm bra) during pregnancy have been shown to be of little benefit; however, the use of a nipple shield after the milk comes in, for the first six to eight weeks after birth, can be a worthwhile strategy if the baby has trouble taking the breast because of flat or inverted nipples. For more on nipple shields, see page 100.

# How breastfeeding works

Breastfeeding involves not only your breast but your areola, nipple, and several hormones that are released by the brain. The areola is the area of colored skin that surrounds your nipple. The size and color of the areola varies a great deal between women and has nothing to do with the way breastfeeding works. Dark hair on or around the areola is common and doesn't interfere with breastfeeding in any way.

## Milk production

Milk production is inhibited during pregnancy by the hormone progesterone, which is produced by the placenta. Once the placenta is expelled after birth, the progesterone levels in your body fall. During the next thirty hours as the progesterone decreases, milk production increases, and while this is happening your baby takes in small amounts of colostrum. Colostrum is rich in good things that protect her digestive tract, respiratory tract, and urinary tract against infection, as well as helping her gut and bowel to function efficiently. After this time, milk production rapidly increases to meet your baby's needs.

Recent research suggests that breasts can produce more milk than required by the baby and that within a few days of birth each breast begins to regulate its rate of milk production according to the amount of milk the baby removes at each breastfeed. Feeding well and often in the first days and early weeks means your breasts get a clear message to keep making milk. As your baby and your body become more skillful at breastfeeding, the milk supply and release becomes very efficient, which is why sucking time decreases as your baby grows, not increases as you may imagine.

## Releasing the milk

After the milk is made, the breast has to release it. As your baby sucks, the nerves around your nipple send a message to your brain to release another hormone called oxytocin. Oxytocin contracts the muscles around the milk-producing sacs in the breast, squeezing the milk down toward the nipple. Oxytocin is the same hormone that contracts the muscles of the uterus, drawing it tight—a feeling ranging from pleasant to painful. Painful contractions of the uterus while breastfeeding are not permanent and only last for a short time after birth. The contraction of the milk sacs by oxytocin is called the let-down, a feeling that may range from not being able to feel anything, to tingles, to pins and needles, to a needle-sharp sensation that is painful for some women for a while. Some women who breastfeed well never feel a let-down. Let-downs occur in between feeds, from one breast while you are feeding from another, at times when you are thinking about your baby or if you hear her cry. Feeling sexy can also start a let-down or alternatively a let-down can make you feel sexy—the latter doesn't happen to everyone, so if it works for you—enjoy it!

# Getting started—the first two weeks

Breastfeeding is natural but not something all mothers and babies know how to do. There's no doubt that a lot of babies and breasts go well together right from the start, and the whole experience is a smooth operation that just happens. For others, it's a skill to be learned like riding a bike or learning to swim. The learning is made more complicated because there's two learning together, a bit like learning to have good sex.

There are two important things to remember when you start breastfeeding:

- Frequent good sucking removes the milk, which tells the breast to make more milk and stops the milk from banking up. Banked-up milk causes painful breasts, sore nipples, much less milk, and a hungry baby.

- When your baby takes the breast the right way, everything works well. Good sucking and comfortable feeding depends on you both being in the right position.

## Let's look at getting the position right

Getting both your posture and your baby's position right each time you feed is sometimes not easy in the beginning, although the basics are fairly simple. Like any practical procedure, learning how to breastfeed from written instructions is difficult—imagine learning to drive a car from a book! It's of great benefit to get help from an experienced person who can guide you and your baby for the first several feeds. This is likely to be a nurse or a lactation consultant. The following basic guidelines are suitable for most mothers and babies. However, as all breasts and babies are different, a number of women find they need specific help tailored to their requirements. Many hospitals and communities have lactation consultants available who are skilled at working out what changes individual mothers and babies need to make to help their breastfeeding become more effective and comfortable. If you find you are having difficulties after you leave hospital, ask your practitioner or pediatrician how to contact an experienced lactation consultant. She/he can closely watch you feed and help you by making recommendations adapted to you and your baby.

While the ideal time for the first breastfeeding is within a few hours after birth, there are times when this can't happen, so don't panic if something delays the first feeding. Breastfeeding can work at any time after birth, even weeks later.

Here are the main things to think about and do when you breastfeed your baby:

- When your baby is awake and ready to nurse, make sure you are both comfortable before you start. In the beginning you need to think things through step by step. Empty your bladder, wash your hands, and have a glass of water close by (breastfeeding makes you thirsty). Have a footstool or telephone book handy in case you need something to put your feet on. Don't worry about changing your baby at this stage if changing her is going to result in a distressed, screaming baby (unless there is poo everywhere).

- Finding a comfortable position for yourself is easier if you are not holding your baby at the same time. Ask someone to hold her if she is crying or leave her somewhere safe within easy reach until you are ready.

- While you are getting used to handling your baby and getting the position right, sitting in a straight-backed chair (like a dining room chair) that gives you good back support is best.

- Lying on your side may be a better way to feed after a cesarean or if your bottom is sore, but as it is difficult to see what your baby is doing, ask for help.

- Most women find it easier to use a pillow to support their babies while they are learning to breastfeed. Your lap needs to be almost flat, your trunk facing forward and your back straight (not tilted back or leaning forward). Sit, so that your legs are down with your feet flat on either the floor, a footstool, or a telephone book.

- Feeding babies unwrapped has many advantages. It lessens the likelihood of the baby becoming too warm and sleepy to nurse well, there is more direct skin contact, and the baby's hands on the breast help stimulate the milk supply. You may find, however, that you prefer to wrap until you are more used to handling your baby and your breast (it won't take long). Make sure if you do wrap that your baby's hands are wrapped either down or up and *not* across the front of her chest, as this forms a barrier between her and your breast.

- Hold your baby so that she faces you, her chest against your chest. Support her behind the shoulders with her body flexed around your body so that her nose (not her mouth) is level with your nipple. You may find it helpful to tuck both her legs into your armpit area, holding them firmly in place with the top of your arm (like a set of bagpipes—forgive the comparison).

- There are various ways to support your breast, and you may try several before you find one that suits you both. For starters, try placing your palm and fingers flat on your rib cage, bring your fingers forward along the side of your breast, and cup the breast between the fingers and thumb.

- She needs to take a good mouthful of breast, so wait until her mouth is wide open before you bring her to the breast. When your baby's cheek is touched, a reflex called the rooting reflex makes her turn her head in the direction of the touch and open her mouth to suck. You can help her open her mouth by gently brushing your nipple against cheek and lips or by running your nipple lightly over her nose and lips.

- When her mouth is wide open, move your baby quickly up to your breast. Her chin should reach the breast first and tuck well into the breast with the bottom lip curled back. Support your baby's head and shoulders that so the nose and forehead can extend slightly, allowing for good air circulation while your baby feeds. When the position is correct, you do not have to press the breast with your finger so that she can breathe. If her nose and forehead are pushed into the breast, it becomes more difficult for her to suck and breathe, and she may go to sleep after only a short suck.

- A lot of the areola will be in her mouth, but you will still see some of it above the nipple—the bigger the areola, the more you will see.

- When she starts to suck, take a deep breath, make your shoulders go floppy, and feed away. Once your baby gets going, she will suck deeply and strongly at a regular pace. You will see her jaw moving and her ears moving slightly.

- You may experience a drawing sensation at first; some women find this painful for about thirty seconds. If any discomfort or pain persists after this or if your baby sucks quickly and lightly all the time and is sucking her cheeks in, take your baby from the breast. To do this, place your finger in the corner of her mouth to break the suction, then gently remove her. Try again. Sometimes it takes several tries before it feels right.

- Every time you nurse, think carefully about how you are doing it. This may seem tedious, especially in the middle of the night, but it is the best way to prevent sore nipples. After the first six to eight weeks, you will find you and your baby are such an efficient team you won't have to think about what you are doing, where you are sitting or even have to use a pillow.

## A good mouthful of breast

A good mouthful of breast means your baby takes in part of the breast tissue around the nipple as well as the nipple and draws the

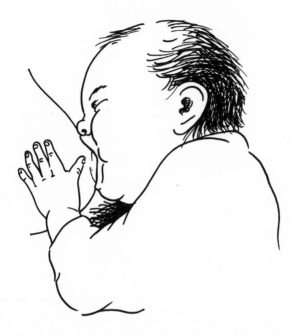

nipple right back past her hard palate. This protects the nipple and is a major factor in preventing painful feedings.

Think about the difference between sucking the skin on your forearm and sucking your finger. To suck the skin on your forearm, you need to open your mouth wide to get a good mouthful of skin, and it is a similar action to what your baby does at the breast. Sucking your finger, however, does not require an open mouth or a big mouthful. When babies suck like this to feed, nipples quickly become sore, the breast is not well drained, and no one has a nice time.

## A summary of the most important points

- Sit with a straight back and flat lap with good support for your back.

- Hold your baby so that she faces you, her nose in line with your nipple.

- Bring your baby up to your breast. Let her take a good mouthful. Don't lean forward and give her your nipple.

- Her chin should be tucked well into the breast, her nose and forehead slightly extended.

- Take a deep breath and make your shoulder go floppy.

- If it hurts after thirty seconds, gently take her off. Avoid pulling. Try again.

## What about twins?

Women's marvelous bodies respond to the stimulation of two babies sucking and can produce enough milk for more than one baby.

The basics are the same. The decision has to be made whether the babies will be fed separately or together. In the early weeks, it is probably better to feed one at a time until you become more confident and the babies are feeding well. After a while, it may be easier at times to feed them together. You will need help to master this as well as privacy and peace and quiet.

Trying different positions, feeding one at a time and two at a time while you are in hospital with the support of the staff, is a good idea. I find that everyone who breastfeeds twins does it slightly differently, so don't get bogged down by rules.

Eventually it is a good idea to swap breasts regularly, as some twins become so attached to one breast that they will not use the other one, which may cause great inconvenience later.

Sitting in a chair

Sitting on the floor

Lying down

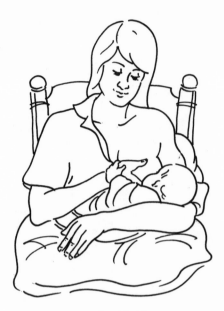

Front hold

Underarm (twin) hold

Here is one way to feed twins

# Weighing babies

Some health workers, both in the past and present, have been obsessed by the issue of a baby's weight. This is seen as disadvantageous to breastfeeding by many mothers and people involved in supporting breastfeeding. Constant weighing of breastfed babies with an unsympathetic health professional who makes incorrect assumptions from the baby's weight can indeed be most unhelpful and work against successful breastfeeding. Test weighing (weighing a baby before and after a feed to see how much she gets) is a pointless, stressful exercise that should never be inflicted on a mother—so if it's ever suggested to you, change your health provider.

When a baby is breastfeeding well, has six to eight pale, wet diapers a day and a good soft poo frequently throughout the day, or one every day or two, and there are no problems, weighing is unnecessary apart from the nice buzz it gives a mother to see a tangible sign of the great job she's doing. It can also be a very positive, reassuring thing for women who are breastfeeding for the first time.

If problems arise, there are times when weighing the baby to assess weight gain (as opposed to static weight or weight loss) is necessary to give the mother appropriate guidance, particularly when the problem is a crying, unsettled baby. Certainly, many problems can be sorted out without weighing, so whenever I suggest weighing in this book it is because I think the baby's weight is very useful information on which to base advice in that particular instance.

# How long and how often to feed?

There are no set rules about the length of time babies need to suck to get the milk they need. Some babies get all they need quickly; others take longer. In the past, problems were caused because the general guidelines suggested short rather than long feedings; now we are seeing problems with the current standard advice that suggests leaving the baby to decide when to come off the breast. There is also a lot of unnecessary advice about foremilk and hindmilk.

Many women are being needlessly worried by the whole concept of foremilk and hindmilk, so let's get that out of the way now so you can forget about it.

The composition of breastmilk changes as milk is removed from the breast at a feeding. Usually the milk at the beginning of a breastfeed (the foremilk) has a fine blue appearance that changes to a whiter appearance (the hindmilk) as the breast becomes emptier at the end of a feeding. The change in appearance of the breastmilk occurs because the fat content of the milk increases as the breast is emptied. However, these changes vary greatly as the baby rarely removes all the available milk at any particular feeding.

The important point is that the changes in breastmilk even out over each twenty-four-hour period and you do not have to be concerned about it. It is not possible to change your baby's energy intake by altering your pattern of feeding—your baby cannot consume consistently either low-fat foremilk or higher-fat hindmilk.

The role of foremilk/hindmilk imbalance in what is called colic is minimal, if it exists at all. I have seen no clear evidence in my work that it is a reason or answer for crying, unsettled breastfed babies. The main thing for you to be aware of is that you don't have to worry about foremilk and hindmilk: just think of your milk as breastmilk.

It would be nice if breastfeeding just happened and there was no need to offer advice to mothers, but if you're doing it for the first time you may be looking for something to hang your hat on in the early weeks. Some women breastfeed in whichever way suits them and never have a problem, so if you're doing just that, for goodness sake don't change a thing. **Others find the current standard advice is fine; again, if you and your baby are happy, carry on.**

However, if you are looking for a little more structured breastfeeding advice to help you through the first six to eight weeks, here are my guidelines.

- The longest babies need to get enough milk and comfort is twenty minutes or so of good sucking on one or both breasts. Lots of babies finish in under twenty minutes, which is fine. **If you are happy to leave your baby sucking longer than twenty minutes, keep going.** If you would sooner finish the feed, gently take her off and offer the second breast. It's quite all right for you to end the feeding after about twenty minutes rather than wait for her to come off the breast by herself.

- Always offer the second breast—there are no advantages to one-breast feeding apart from times when there may be temporary difficulties with an oversupply (see page 147). Before you offer the second breast, wake your baby up so that she is alert and ready to nurse. Change her diaper if you have to or tickle her feet. If she is not interested in the second breast, she is getting all the milk she needs at this time from one breast. This is rarely a permanent arrangement and may vary from feeding to feeding and over time. As babies grow, they usually take both breasts at most feeds.

- When your baby only takes one breast, you may need to hand express the other breast for comfort. If the breast is comfortable, don't worry about expressing.

- The number of times you feed your baby in the first week or two varies from six to eight every twenty-four hours. After your milk is flowing, six to seven feedings suit most mothers and babies. Less than six feedings over twenty-four hours usually lessens the milk supply over time; more than six is fine as long as you are both happy. Some of the feedings will be two hours apart, some three to four, and your baby may have one long sleep of five or six hours. Stay flexible about feeding times. If you are looking for some sort of pattern, it is better to think in terms of the number of feedings every twenty-four hours rather than three-hourly and four-hourly feedings. Expecting a set four-hourly feeding routine is unrealistic for most babies.

## How can you tell if the baby is hungry?

Working out whether babies are hungry or not is confusing as babies cry, suck their fists, and make mouthing signs when they are overtired, overstimulated, or generally distressed, as well as when they are hungry. Feeding breastfed babies to comfort them for any of the above—rather than because they are due for a feeding—is not harmful to the baby in any way, but being worn out from too many feeds and an unsettled baby is a common problem for many women in the first three months. If this is happening to you, here are two simple things to check:

- Your baby's position at the breast and sucking technique. If you have an advisor to call on, so much the better.

- That your baby is getting enough milk. The best way to do this is a quick weigh with a sympathetic adviser who uses the weight as a guide to help you and your baby—not worry the life out of you.

Most of the time, endless feeding and an unsettled baby fall into the broad range of normal baby behavior and are not breastfeeding problems, so there is rarely a quick, easy answer once hunger and poor positioning are ruled out. If your baby is bright-eyed and alert, sucks well, is gaining some weight, and is wetting and pooing but is never off the breast and you are feeling very tense, see if you can limit some of her feedings. Limit the time at each breast to about twenty minutes and wait two to two and a half hours before feeding again. Try other ways of settling her. This advice is for your sanity, not because endless feedings will harm her—you cannot overfeed a breastfed baby. You may also find it helpful to refer to other sections of the book that deal with low milk supply, crying and sleeping and the crying baby (see the index).

Very few women breastfeed in exactly the same way. What works for another mother and baby may not work for you, so stick to your own style and ignore unwanted, uncalled-for advice. On the other hand, you can always change what you're doing if someone suggests something that suits you and your baby better.

# Common difficulties in the first week

## Your baby won't suck

**FULL-TERM HEALTHY BABIES:** Recommendations for getting breastfeeding off to a good start include offering the baby the breast as soon as possible after the birth. And while many babies do take the breast well soon after birth, others are simply not interested. It can be very stressful for the mother when those around her keep trying to encourage a reluctant baby to take her breast. When the birth is a normal one and the baby is full-term and healthy, it is best to stay relaxed about the early breastfeeds. Some babies do not start sucking well for two or three days. Remember that newborn babies have quite a lot of food in reserve.

**SLEEPY BABIES:** Babies may be sleepy if they are jaundiced, a few weeks premature, or if they are recovering from a long or difficult labor. Sometimes it can take two to five days before they start to suck well. Try to stay relaxed and patient. Sleepy babies start to feed very well when they "wake up" two to four days after birth. Unwrap your baby when you put her to the breast as skin-to-skin contact helps stimulate her senses.

**BABIES WHO FIGHT THE BREAST:** Some babies thrash about, move their head from side-to-side, and scream. Like a lot of things babies do, it's often difficult to know exactly why they do it because they can't tell us. If this is happening to you, it can turn into a cycle where your baby becomes more and more tense and you become more and more distressed, dreading the thought of putting your baby to the breast. Happily, this sort of situation is usually short-lived. The cycle can be broken by having a third person, not as emotionally involved with the baby, to help. If there is no professional help available, a calm neighbor or friend could fill the bill.

**HERE ARE SOME TIPS FOR YOUR HELPER:**

- Separate mother and baby. Calm the baby and see if you can help her go to sleep.

- Nurture the mother. A cup of tea, a bath, or a shoulder massage all help.

- When the mother and baby are calm and comfortable, try another feed. The mother should express a little milk before starting the feed to encourage the baby to suck. This softens the areola, making it easier for the baby to take the breast.

- Skin-to-skin contact can be very helpful, or if the mother is comfortable with the idea, feeding the baby in the bath helps.

- Expressed milk or boiled water may be given by bottle if necessary. This is usually not required as these babies do tend to start feeding well before any extra fluid is needed.

## Engorged breasts

What a terrible term this is and what visions it conjures up—rising breasts! What are engorged breasts? Engorgement refers to painful, swollen breasts usually caused either by the milk not flowing well or because the breasts are temporarily producing far more milk than the baby needs at each feed. It can happen in the early days or later.

- In the first two to four days, your breasts may feel full and heavy because of the increased blood supply to your breasts as they get ready to make milk. Discomfort is variable and passes quickly as long as your baby feeds frequently and she is positioned so that she can suck well to drain the breast.

- Later engorgement—painful, swollen breasts persisting after the first few days—means too much milk is stored because too much is being made and not enough is being removed. The areola is stretched and distended, which makes it difficult for your baby to get a good mouthful.

## WHAT CAN YOU DO?

- Nurse often, up to eight times in twenty-four hours.

- Waking babies to feed often doesn't work, so put your baby to the breast whenever she is awake and ready to suck.

- Ask for help if it's available to make sure your baby is in the best position to suck well.

- Avoid giving any fluids from bottles.

- Gently hand-express a small amount of milk before the feeding to soften the areola to make it easier for your baby to take the breast.

- Stand with your back to the shower so that the hot water spraying down doesn't increase the discomfort. To relieve the pain and full feeling, express a little milk in between feedings under the shower. Placing cold packs on your breasts also helps them feel better. To make a cold pack, soak a clean washcloth in cold water. Wring out hard and place in a plastic bag in the freezer.

- If it all becomes unbearable, the cycle can be broken by completely draining both breasts with an electric pump after a feeding. This brings relief and makes it easier for your baby to take the breast at the next feeding. It should be done once only, preferably at the end of the day and with some help from a your health care provider.

- Talk to your doctor about taking acetaminophen (Tylenol, Panadol) for pain, if you need it.

## Baby won't burp

Burping babies is more tradition than necessity. For some reason it is indeed very satisfying to hear a baby burp (I enjoy it too), but medical problems don't happen because babies don't burp and in many cultures it is an unknown practice. An unnecessary emphasis is placed on "getting the gas out" in our culture, which is unfortunate as it worries the life out of new mothers. Whether a baby burps is not related to unsettled behavior, vomiting, or interesting colored poo. It's fine to put your baby to bed without hearing a burp first. Babies won't always oblige with a burp no matter how experienced the burper, so don't think everyone in the world knows how to burp a baby better than you. No secret tricks exist! Try for a few minutes, then forget about it.

## Sore nipples

Sore nipples remain one of the most troublesome aspects of early breastfeeding for many women. Past theories on sore nipples concentrated on the necessity of having to toughen up the nipples and making sure babies didn't suck for too long. Current research shows that neither of these things are relevant in avoiding and treating nipple problems; rather, the way the baby takes the breast is the crucial factor.

This is why there is now so much emphasis on getting the mother's and baby's position right for a feeding. If positioning is right for all the early feedings, nipple problems can be avoided a lot of the time. However, despite current knowledge and the best efforts with correct positioning, sore nipples are still with us. This may be because the damage can be done during only one feeding in the early days when the mother is tired or uncomfortable and the baby doesn't quite take the breast in the best way. Once nipples become sore, comfortable feeding is difficult, so the problem gets worse.

Sometimes nipples get sore even when the feeding position seems to be right. This may be because the nipple and areola are being used constantly in a new way, which causes discomfort until the relevant parts of our body adjust to being used.

Nipple discomfort, pain, and damage can be experienced in a number of ways.

- Many women find their nipples are sensitive when hormonal changes take place—for example, pre-menstrually, during early pregnancy, and the first few days after having a baby. If you have sensitive nipples, you may find breastfeeding uncomfortable or painful at the beginning of a feeding. The discomfort should only last up to thirty seconds. Sensitive nipples become less sensitive as the weeks go by, but a small number of women have sensitive nipples for up to three months while they are breastfeeding.

- Sore, grazed, or blistered nipples are all signs of a damaged nipple. The nipple looks red and raw and sometimes there may be a blister is filled with blood or clear fluid. See if you can get help as soon as possible to position your baby.

- Cracked nipples: A split appears that may be on the nipple or areola or both. A common place is where the nipple joins the areola.

## WHAT CAN YOU DO?

- Get help to get the position right. If you are in hospital, ask for help from the staff.

- You can visit your nurse practitioner, talk to a nurse, or in some areas there are nurses/lactation consultants who help with breastfeeding problems at home.

- When you remember to think carefully at every feeding about your posture and position as well as your baby's. Don't leave your baby sucking if it continues to hurt after the first thirty seconds. Gently remove her and try again. Sometimes in the early weeks you might find you have to do this three or four times before it feels right.

- Fresh air and a little reflected sunlight helps.

- Gently hand express for about thirty seconds before feeding to soften the areola, draw out the nipple, and start the milk flowing.

- Much as it would be nice to apply a magic cream or cure, there is no consistent evidence that any of the commonly used creams, sprays, and ointments make any difference. Other "cures" such as grated carrot, geranium leaves, and so on all appear at regular intervals, often hailed as the long-awaited answer to sore nipples. I have never seen any evidence that these things fix the problem either. Nevertheless, some women do find comfort in using some of these preparations. They can make the nipple feel better, which in turn stops breastfeeding from being abandoned even if they don't actually hasten the healing process. Gently massaging some expressed milk onto the nipple at the end of a feed appears to be as useful as anything else and has the added advantage of being free, safe, and non-allergenic.

  If you do use something other than breastmilk on your nipples, be careful. Some preparations make things worse. Avoid nipple sprays in aerosol packs. They have ingredients that interfere with natural lubrication and the normal protective barrier of the nipple that prevents infection. They also contain a local anesthetic that prevents you from having any idea if the level of discomfort the baby's position is not right.

Cortisone, antifungal, or antibiotic creams should not be used unless a specific skin problem is diagnosed. Most sore nipples are related to the way the baby takes the breast, not to skin conditions.

For most women with sore nipples, getting the position right, fresh air, a little indirect sunlight, plus massaging expressed milk into the nipple are all that's needed. Most nipples improve rapidly in the first few weeks.

For those who find feeding painful beyond the first few weeks, there are other things to try. Unfortunately all of these suggestions involve doing things that might upset the supply and demand system of breastfeeding and so cause more problems. These strategies include such things as using a nipple shield, limiting feedings, or temporarily stopping breastfeeding from one or both breasts. Trying any of these tactics is best done with help from an experienced person who will help you get your baby back on the breast as quickly as possible. Such help, however, is not always available, so please go ahead and try them yourself if the thought of another breastfeed fills you with despair.

**LIMITING FEEDINGS AND SUCKING TIME:** It's often difficult to separate hunger from other aspects of baby behavior when you're breastfeeding for the first time. Lots of normal, healthy, well-fed babies cry a lot, wake frequently, or have endless fussy, unsettled times when they don't sleep. It's easy to see this behavior as a breastfeeding problem and fall into a pattern of endless, frequent feedings that seem to run into each other all day and all night.

Very long sessions at the breast in the early weeks can contribute to sore nipples. When babies are left on the breast for a long time and mothers are tired, the position can go wrong during the feeding and nipples get hurt. Twenty minutes or so is all babies need to get what they require and drain the breast. If there are no nipple problems and you are happy, it's fine to nurse as long and as often as you like, but if your nipples are sore or damaged, try limiting your feedings to twenty minutes or less (depending on your baby) and to about six every twenty-four hours until your nipples are feeling better.

**TEMPORARILY STOPPING BREASTFEEDING ON ONE BREAST:** Sometimes only one nipple is sore. This may be the right one if you are right-handed or the left one if you are left-handed because you are not as skilled at positioning your baby with whichever arm and hand you don't use as much.

Stopping feeding from the breast, with the sore nipple and only feeding from the other breast for twenty-four hours works well for some mothers. Express the unused breast (by hand for comfort) if your baby is content on one breast, or express enough for supplements (by hand, or electric pump if hand expressing is too tedious) from a bottle or cup if she needs extra. If you can't express enough for supplements and your baby is not content with one breast, use formula when necessary.

After twenty-four hours, put your baby back to the breast with the sore nipple, paying a lot of attention to your posture and her position. You may like to try the gradual approach, where you put her back to the breast by introducing one feed daily until you are fully breastfeeding again.

**TEMPORARILY STOPPING BREASTFEEDING ON BOTH BREASTS:** If both nipples are very sore, you might consider stopping breastfeeding for a period of time until they feel better. You will need to express every three to four hours during the day to keep your supply going. Hand expressing is often advised in this situation.

If you can hand express easily, go ahead, but many women find it easier to use a hand pump or an electric pump. The expressed milk and/or formula is given to your baby from a bottle or cup. Complications can arise from doing this that you need to be aware of:

- Your milk supply may decrease.

- Expressing and feeding from a bottle or cup is tiring and time-consuming.

- Some babies are reluctant to go back to the breast after having bottles.

- Some babies will not drink from a bottle and miss the sucking if they drink from a cup, which makes them unsettled.

**NIPPLE PROTECTORS (NIPPLE SHIELDS)** A nipple protector is a soft-silicone shield that fits over the nipple and areola. Using a nipple protector helps some women to breastfeed more comfortably until the nipple pain or discomfort gets better. It sounds great but there are disadvantages to using nipple protectors, which is why they are often not mentioned in general breastfeeding information. I am including them because despite their limitations, a number of mothers do find nipple protectors very useful and, for them, prolongs their breastfeeding.

If you decide to use one be aware of the following:

- A nipple protector forms a barrier between your breast and your baby's mouth, so as your breast doesn't get a clear message to make milk, using a nipple protector can gradually reduce your supply.

- When you become accustomed to using a nipple protector it is often hard to stop using it when you need to. That is, if your

**100**

supply starts to decrease.

- Babies beyond the newborn stage often object to nipple protectors, so starting to use one after about three weeks of age is not highly successful.

- Some women find nursing just as uncomfortable with a protector as without.

And here are some tips for their use:

- Only ever use a thin soft silicone shield. Avent makes suitable nipple protectors.

- Remember to continue to follow the guidelines for your posture and your baby's position when you nurse her.

- Dry your nipples and areola gently. Lubricate the shield with a little breastmilk so it will stay in place. Once it's in place, hand pump a little milk into the nipple part of the shield before bringing your baby to your breast.

- Allow your baby to suck longer than she normally does to compensate for less stimulation to your breast.

- Plan to use the nipple protector as a short-term strategy only— try some feeds without it.

- If possible, stay in touch with an advisor who can help you try some feedings without the protector and make sure your milk is flowing.

On the positive side, nipples always get better, most in the first two to six weeks. Think of all the wonderful benefits of breastmilk and try to see sore nipples as a short-term problem in relation to the whole time you will be breastfeeding. Support from family and friends and help and encouragement from health workers do make an incredible difference.

Nipple problems are not inevitable, but they are common. Everybody's pain threshold varies, so some women decide to wean. This is quite understandable when life is a constant round of painful feedings that never seem to improve and neither you nor your baby are happy.

## Tongue tie and breastfeeding

Tongue tie refers to a condition where the baby's tongue is attached to the floor of the mouth rather than floating free. Mild tongue tie is very common in newborn babies and does not cause breastfeeding problems. Serious tongue tie is rare and more likely to be found in babies where such a condition runs in the family. A tiny number of babies have a degree of tongue tie that interferes with successful breastfeeding, resulting in damaged nipples and low milk supply (the baby is unable to adequately extend the tongue under the nipple). The incidence of this happening is unknown and surgical release of the tongue for breastfeeding problems in selected situations is occasionally performed. Case studies where this has been performed report successful outcomes, but it remains a controversial procedure and should only be considered after a full assessment of the baby and the breastfeeding problems.

## Needle-sharp pain

A few women experience a piercing, stabbing breast pain that may happen while the baby is sucking or in between feedings. Apart from these spasmodic pains, the breast feels fine. Needle-sharp pain is different from mastitis or a blocked duct where discomfort or pain is felt all the time. Needle-sharp pain is possibly due to the release of oxytocin (which tightens the muscles around the milk sacs in the breast). As it is spasmodic and gradually fades, it is something women learn to live with and it disappears some time in the first three months. It's possible for a woman to experience it with one baby and not another. Needle-sharp pain is often confused with the possibility of a yeast infection of the nipple, but there should be some other signs a yeast infection exists before treating the mother and baby for this condition.

## Delays in getting breastfeeding started

Sometimes it is not possible for babies to go straight to the breast; for example, premature babies or babies who have problems at birth and need to be in an intensive care unit for a while. Many women and babies breastfeed well after difficult beginnings. Your milk flow can be stimulated and kept going by massage and expressing until your baby is able to take all her feedings from the breast. Here's a guide:

- It's a good idea to start expressing as soon as possible after birth, but don't panic if there are delays. If you are very tired, distressed, or in any discomfort, wait until you feel you can handle learning how to express. When you are ready, a midwife can show you how to hand express. Hand expressing is best to begin with. After the milk is flowing, a hand pump or electric pump can be used. Keep asking for help after you are shown what to do if your technique doesn't seem to be working. See How to Express and Store Breastmilk, page 125.

- Regardless of the amount of milk you express, don't give up. In the beginning you might only express a few drops of colostrum—don't throw it away; even tiny amounts are good for your baby to have. Once the mature milk is flowing, try not to compare how much you express with how much someone else expresses. Remember, babies stimulate and remove the milk much more efficiently than expressing does; once your baby is sucking regularly, your supply will build up.

**103**

- The transition from tube feeding or bottle feeding to breastfeeding is a challenge. Many premature or sick babies take the breast well and suck strongly; others take quite a long time to learn what to do. When this happens, expert help from the midwives and lactation consultants who work in hospitals is needed for a while.

## FOR MORE INFORMATION

Chapter 16: For Parents *(contraception and breastfeeding, page 402, health professionals you might come in contact with, page 386)*

Chapter 13: Growth and Development *(rooting reflex, page 296, weighing babies, page 293)*

Chapter 14: Sleeping and Waking in the First Six Months *(settling techniques, page 315)*

Chapter 15: The Crying Baby *(wind, page 342)*

Chapter 10: Early Worries and Questions *(blue around baby's mouth, page 195)*

Chapter 8: Breastfeeding Your Baby After the First Two Weeks *(Candida albicans [thrush], page 155)*

## FURTHER READING

*The Politics of Breastfeeding*, Gabrielle Palmer, Pandora Press, 1994. (A fascinating look at the growth of artificial feeding. Read it with an open mind—it can give you a whole new perspective on infant feeding.)

*Breastfeeding Matters*: Maureen Minchin, Alma Publications, 1998. (As with the above book, much of the information gives a fresh perspective to many of the dilemmas surrounding infant feeding.)

Both available on Amazon.

chapter **seven**

# Bottle Feeding Your Baby for the First Two Weeks

*Bottle or breast, there are some wonderful aspects of feeding a baby and terrible ones. Feeding is a very basic function, an integral part of mothering, and as such, immensely satisfying. But it can also be frustrating, and, at times, unbelievably disgusting.*

Helen Townsend, *Baby Crazy*

Breastfeeding and formula feeding are very emotional issues for lots of reasons. There may be feelings of disappointment when breastfeeding doesn't work out and a sense of loss or even anger that something promoted as easy and pleasant turned out to be problematic and stressful.

Women usually wean because breastfeeding problems arise that either seem impossible to solve *or are* impossible to solve any other way. Whatever the reason, it's just as important for women who are bottle feeding to have accurate, detailed information about formula feeding as it is for women who are breastfeeding.

Bottle feeding babies is so much a part of modern living that it is very much taken for granted. It's important to remember that safe bottle feeding depends on a healthy water supply, enough money to meet the costs, refrigeration, clean surroundings, and satisfactory arrangements for cleaning and storing equipment. Parents without literacy skills or parents who do not speak English need extra help to make sure their bottle feeding is done safely.

If you are unsure of whether you want to breastfeed or not, remember weaning and formula feeding is always an option at any time. Breastfeeding isn't, and once you start to wean, it can be difficult to go back to breastfeeding.

When babies are not breastfed or have a combination of breast-milk and formula, it is very important to make sure that the substitute milk they are receiving meets as much of the baby's nutritional needs as possible. It is also important to make sure it is mixed, stored, and handled properly so that the baby does not get sick.

## What's in formula?

It's good to have an idea of what's in formula so that you know what you are giving your baby.

Commercial artificial milk for babies has been around since 1900. Early attempts to mimic breastmilk were disastrous. Apart from no one having any idea what the ingredients should be, poor bottle and nipple design, unhygienic practices and surroundings, and unhealthy water all contributed to a high infant mortality rate. During the 1900s, general improvements in the standard of living, better-designed bottles and nipples and the growing realization of the complexity of breastmilk helped make formula feeding safer.

Infant formula is made from either cow's milk, goat's milk or soya beans. Formula made from cow's milk has been around the longest, suits most babies, and is considered to be the safest. The cow's milk, goat's milk, or soy liquid is altered to overcome the inadequacies and risks involved if these substances are given to babies unmodified. Simply diluting them is not the answer as in their unchanged state they all lack many ingredients that are essential for a baby's proper growth and development. The protein, sugar, and fat content are in different proportions to those found in breastmilk, which makes them difficult for babies to digest.

The changes are made are designed to make the end product more like breastmilk; however, the variety of nutrient and immunological factors that are present in breastmilk are not found in formula.

Choosing a formula is often confusing as there are many brands manufactured by different companies. The differences between brands mainly center around the balance and types of fat, protein, and carbohydrate that are used. It does not matter which brand is chosen as there is no best formula. All infant formulas sold in the United States meet the relevant nutritional and quality-control standards.

## Features of formula made from cow's milk

**PROTEIN:** There is more than twice as much protein in cow's milk as human milk. A high proportion of the cow's milk protein is hard, lumpy protein known as casein protein. Breastmilk contains a high proportion of soft, more shredded protein known as whey protein which is easier for babies to digest. The protein in cow's milk formula is altered so that the proportion of whey protein becomes higher than the proportion of casein protein. Recently, "antibodies" have been added to infant formula. Unlike antibodies present in breastmilk, they are inert.

**CARBOHYDRATE:** Human milk has a higher sugar content than cow's milk, so extra lactose is added to formula. Lactose is a natural sugar found in animal milk. Lactose is not found in plants, so sugars such as sucrose, corn syrup solids, or a mixture of both are added to formula made from soya bean liquid.

**FAT:** The fat in cow's milk has a different composition to the fat in human milk, so formula contains a blend of vegetable and milk fat to get a fatty acid profile that resembles breastmilk. Long-chain polyunsaturates that are found in breastmilk but not cow's milk have been added to formula in the form of fish oil, evening primrose oil, and vitamin E in an attempt to mimic the long-chain polyunsaturates found in breastmilk.

Formula is also supplemented with vitamins and iron. Essential minerals are adjusted—including lowering the salt content of cow's milk.

## SOME FORMULA FACTS:

- Sweetened condensed milk, evaporated milk, and raw goat's milk are not for infant feeding and can harm your baby if used regularly. These products put babies at risk of vitamin and mineral deficiencies and health complications. Sadly, problems may not be noticed until the damage is done.

- The majority of formulas are made from a cow's milk base and these are recommended as the first choice. Formula made from soya beans or modified lactose formula should only be used for medically diagnosed conditions and, where possible, on a temporary basis only. These formulas have no advantages for most babies and should not be used indiscriminately as there are possible problems associated with their use.

- The price of different formulas and whether they are sold in pharmacies or supermarkets bears no relation to their quality or nutritional value.

- Changing the type of formula (that is, from cow's milk based to soy based) because your baby is unsettled, a fussy eater or has heat rash or hormone rash is a waste of time and rarely makes any difference to the baby or the rash. The small number of babies who do appear to have diet-related problems may benefit from a particular type of formula, but it's best to get advice from a health professional on what may be suitable. There is no evidence that soy formula provides protection from allergy. Babies who are allergic to cow's milk are often also allergic to goat's milk and soy milk.

- Specialty formulas appear with regularity on the market, mostly in response to identified normal anxieties that parents (mostly mothers) experience about their babies' eating behaviors. For example: fifty percent of toddlers are picky eaters, which is a normal developmental phase that unfortunately (and understandably) does cause a great deal of stress in many homes. In response to this, the formula manufacturers have come up with a toddler formula—an unnecessary product taking advantage of a common worry. Similarly, a thickened formula has arrived on the market to alleviate the concerns of the parents of vomiting babies (again about fifty percent of all babies).

  Be wary of using specialty formulas, especially for healthy babies with no identifiable medical conditions. They have not stood the test of time and arrive on the market hailed as the answer to various baby behaviors (crying, not sleeping, vomiting, and so on) only to disappear quietly a few years later after problems with their use has surfaced or after it has become apparent that they do not do what the manufacturer claims.

- Changing the brand of formula because of a cost advantage (when a particular brand is on special) is fine. If you change, take care when measuring out the scoops per ounce of water.

- Standard infant formula is for babies aged from birth to twelve months.

- Follow-up Formula is for babies aged from six to twelve months, however, the use of this formula is not necessary for most babies. It has no advantages over the formula they are already having. By twelve months of age, babies should be offered a variety of family foods including cow's milk and as soon as possible be drinking milk from a cup.

## Genetically modified formula

The use of genetically modified components in the preparation of infant formula has not been prohibited by government regulations. The constituents most likely to be affected are those of soybean origin, so some brands of soy formula will contain genetically modified components. Other constituents derived from soybean products such as lecithin are used in cow's milk formula, so potentially all formula may contain GM protein.

Some infant formula manufacturers have elected not to use GM components. If it is not stated on the label of the formula and you want more information, call the manufacturer's information number.

# Safe bottle feeding

If you start breastfeeding and then decide to wean, talk to your midwife, or, if you have left hospital, your nurse practitioner about the best way to do this. Gradual weaning is much more comfortable than stopping breastfeeding suddenly. Unless there's an emergency, there's no need to do anything quickly. The medication that was commonly prescribed to help with weaning is no longer used owing to risks associated with its use.

## A word about "sterilization"

Sterilization is somewhat of a nonsense word we use in relation to caring for babies' feeding utensils at home. Sterilization is operation theater technique where the aim is a complete absence of all micro-organisms. This is not only an impossible feat in the average kitchen but not necessary for the baby's well-being.

Cleanliness is next to godliness and is a vital component of bottle feeding and expressing and storing breastmilk. Thorough cleaning and disinfecting of equipment as well as close attention to handwashing to make sure any harmful bacteria are destroyed is what is required.

### HERE'S A BASIC LIST OF EQUIPMENT

- **4–6 large bottles**

  A large variety is available. Bottles are made of clear glass or polycarbonate (rigid plastic). Many bottle manufacturers offer different-shaped bottles and bottles with "anti-colic" devices. Decorations and odd-shaped-bottles make bottles hard to clean and odd shape bottles do not prevent gasor colic, so stick to plain bottles. Disposable feeding sets are also available.

- **Several nipples**

  Nipples are either made from latex or silicone. Latex nipples cost less, are softer, and are preferred by some babies. Silicone nipples are harder, cost more, but last longer. Less elasticity means they are liable to tear and that bits can break off, which makes them a possible choking hazard. Inspect them frequently by holding them up to the light. If they look faulty, throw them away.

Shape variations have no particular advantages (as in orthodontic nipples) unless your baby prefers that shape. There are no superior bottles and nipples. Some babies may prefer one system to another, but, in general, constantly changing bottles and nipples is a needless expense.

- **A knife for leveling the powder**

- **A bottle brush to clean the bottles and nipples**

- **Disinfecting equipment**

It's advisable to disinfect bottle-feeding equipment until your baby's immune system is mature enough to protect her against germs. If you live where there is clean water, clean surroundings and refrigeration you do not need to keep disinfecting after your baby is six months old.

Rinse everything in cold water straight after use. Before disinfecting, wash carefully in hot, soapy water. Rinse well again. Washing is important—disinfecting doesn't work if old milk is left on bottles and nipples. Give nipples and pacifiers an extra good scrub.

When you disinfect, choose between:

## (A) BOILING
Place utensils in a large saucepan.

Cover with water.

Bring to boil and boil for five minutes, adding nipples for the last two minutes.

Please take care when boiling equipment to avoid scalding yourself or other children. One way to reduce this risk is to allow the equipment to cool in the saucepan until it can be touched before moving it, and, as often as possible, to do your boiling when the children are not around.

Store equipment you are not going to use straight away in a clean container in the fridge.

Boil clean equipment every twenty-four hours.

## (B) STEAM STERILIZERS

Steam sterilizers are automatic units that raise the temperature quickly to the range that kills harmful bacteria. To use, place clean equipment into the unit, add water according to the manufacturer's instructions, and switch on. The unit switches itself off when the job is done.

## (C) MICROWAVE STEAM STERILIZERS

Sterilizing units for use in microwave oven are another option.

# Using formula

When formula powder or liquid formula is combined with water all of your baby's food and drink needs are being met. The finished product is only as good as the manufacturer claims if the formula is reconstituted properly.

## Here's some important information

- The strength of formula is designed to remain constant so that you never have to strengthen or weaken the mixture. As your baby grows, it is the amount that increases, not the strength.

- Always use the scoop that comes with the particular brand of formula you are using. Scoops are not interchangeable between brands. Never use half scoops of powder.

- If you use concentrated liquid formula, use equal proportions of formula and water unless otherwise stated.

- If you change brands of powdered formula, remember to check the number of scoops per ounce of boiled water. The proportions vary between brands.

- When in doubt, check with a pharmacist, nurse practitioner, or doctor.

# Making your baby's feedings

Prolonged boiling of water has been found to be unnecessary when making up formula. To prepare water for making up formula, the teakettle should be emptied, refilled with tap water prior to use, and brought to the boil and removed from the heat within thirty seconds of boiling.

Always allow the water to cool before adding the powder or liquid.

The preferred and safest method for making formula at home is in the bottle, one at a time, because:

- It reduces contamination.

- It reduces the amount of equipment needed.

- It reduces the possibility of mistakes when mixing the water and scoops of formula—if a mistake is made, it is only for one feeding.

- If you prefer preparing formula for a twenty-four-hour period, it is safer to prepare five to seven individual bottles than prepare the formula in a pitcher.

## To prepare the bottles

- Measure the amount of cooled, boiled water required into individual bottles.

- Using the scoop supplied with from the formula can, measure the required number of scoops into the bottles. Use a knife to level off each scoop.

- Seal the bottle with a cap and disc and shake gently to mix it.

- Store all made-up formula in the center back of the fridge where it is coldest, not on the door where it is warmer.

- Throw out any formula not used after twenty-four hours.

## To prepare formula in a pitcher

Many parents do prepare formula in a pitcher for use over a twenty-four-hour period. This is acceptable when refrigeration is available and as long as the correct proportions (scoops to ounces of water) are calculated.

- Double-check the proportions needed for twenty-four hours with someone else if you are unsure. If there is no one to ask, it is better to make up the formula one feeding at a time, in the bottle.

**115**

## Safe bottle feeding steps

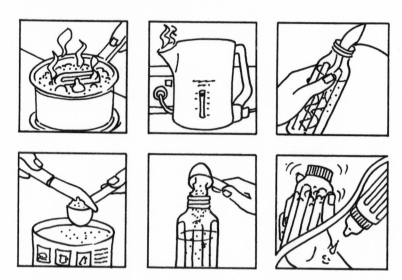

- Measure the cooled, boiled water into a pitcher with measuring levels marked on the side.

- Using the scoop supplied with the formula can measure the required number of scoops into the measured pitcher. Use a knife to level off each scoop. Avoid distractions when counting the scoops. Take the phone off the hook and turn off the radio. Have pen and paper handy to jot down the number of scoops you are up to if you are interrupted.

- Store the mixture in the center of the back of the refrigerator in either the covered pitcher or individual feeding bottles.

## Safety tips

- Always wash your hands and work surfaces before preparing formula.

- Put formula straight into the fridge as soon as it is made.

- Storing half-empty bottles for future use is risky as they quickly become contaminated once they have been heated and sucked on. Throw away the contents of used bottles after an hour.

- Check the expiration date on cans of formula and discard them if they are out of date.

- Discard any opened can of formula powder after one month.

- The safest way to transport formula is to take the cooled, boiled water and the powdered formula in separate containers and mix them when needed. If transporting prepared formula or expressed breastmilk it must be icy cold when you leave home and carried in an insulated pack to keep it cold. If you cannot heat the bottle when you reach your destination, it's quite all right to give it as it is.

- Never leave bottles warming for more than about ten minutes. Bacteria multiply rapidly in warm milk—this is a common cause of diarrhea.

# Giving the bottle

Giving babies cold formula is not at all harmful and at times may be safer than trying to heat it quickly (for example, in a microwave oven in a busy restaurant). Warming to room temperature is the generally acceptable way to give it, but if your baby is flexible about the temperature of her milk, it does make it easier for you when you are out and about.

Standing the bottle in warm to hot water is the traditional way (and remains the safest) of heating bottles. Bottle warmers are

Giving the bottle

convenient and safe as long as they have a thermostat control, but remember not to leave bottles warming in them longer than ten minutes. Microwaves are not recommended because of the safety aspects—babies end up with burned mouths because the temperature of the milk is misjudged or because of hot spots in the milk.

## Nipples and getting the formula to flow right

Initially it's often tricky getting the milk to flow just right. You may find you have to try several types of nipples before your baby is happy. To test the flow, hold the bottle upside down when it is filled with the milk mixture at room temperature—the milk should drip steadily. If you have to shake it vigorously, it is too slow and your baby will go to sleep before she drinks what she needs. The milk should drip easily at a steady rate without pouring out in a great stream. A little leakage at the corner of her mouth while she feedings is nothing to worry about; as she gets older, this will stop. If you have difficulty finding the perfect nipple always go for a faster nipple rather than a slow one.

# Feeding time

Before giving the bottle, always check the temperature of the formula by shaking a little from the nipple onto the inside of your wrist.

Make yourself comfortable, cuddle your baby close to you holding her gently and firmly. If she feels secure and cozy the feeding will be more enjoyable for you both.

Put the nipple against her lips. She will open her mouth and start to suck. Keep the neck of the bottle at an angle so that the neck of the bottle is filled with the milk mixture. When she stops sucking strongly or when she drinks about half the milk, gently remove the bottle and see if she wants to burp (see burping, page 95).

If she has gone to sleep, unwrap her, put her over your shoulder, rub her back, and stroke her head, legs, and tummy to wake her up. Wait until she is in an alert state before offering her the rest of the milk.

## How long does it take to drink the bottle?

This varies tremendously between babies, but roughly it is between ten and thirty minutes. Less than ten is too fast when they are young as they are not getting all the sucking time they need to feel contented. More than thirty is too slow for most babies and means they are probably falling off to sleep before drinking quite enough. Adjust the flow as best you can to suit your baby either by screwing the plastic attachment on the neck of the bottle tighter or by trying different nipples. As babies grow older, they take a lot less time to drink their bottles.

### Safety tip

It is dangerous to "prop" a bottle and walk away, leaving baby to manage on her own. The milk may flow too quickly and cause her to gag or even choke so that she can't breathe. As well, babies who feed a lot on their own are at greater risk of ear infections. Babies need to be held, cuddled, and talked to when they are fed.

# Bottle feeding twins

When one baby is asleep and one awake, you can nurse and feed. When they are both awake and hungry at the same time, change them both, give each one a cuddle, then sit them in either portable baby chairs or propped up together on a couch. Sit in front of them and feed one baby with one hand and one with the other. Make sure you are comfortable and not straining your back, neck, or arms while you feed.

Of course, hold them for feedings whenever possible, but when it's not, sit them close together and chat away while you give them their bottles. Don't worry if one drinks more than the other—twins are like any other two individual babies and may drink different amounts.

# Bottle feeding premature babies

When premature babies are very young and/or sick, the volume of milk is restricted and monitored closely, but by the time they go home they are ready to follow the same guidelines as for full-term babies. Premature babies do better with faster nipples or nipples that have a cross-cut rather than a hole.

# How much milk?

*(note: Number of feedings relates to the volume in the bottle, i.e. less volume, more bottles, and more volume, fewer bottles)*

| Age | Weight | Volume | Feeds |
|---|---|---|---|
| Birth to one week | 2½ oz per lb. of body weight. Increase daily. | 1–2 oz per bottle | 6–8 bottles every 24 hours |
| One to four weeks | 2½ oz per lb. of body weight | 2–4 oz | 5–8 bottles every 24 hours |
| Four to eight weeks | 2½ oz per lb. of body weight | 4–5 oz | 5–8 bottles every 24 hours |
| Eight to twelve weeks | 2½ oz per lb. of body weight | 5–7 oz | 5–7 bottles every 24 hours |
| Three months to six months | 1½ oz per lb. of body weight | 5–8 oz | 4–5 bottles a day plus food (3 meals a day by 6 months for lots of babies) |
| Six to nine months | | 4–6 oz | 2–4 bottles a day or drinks from a cup Eats 3 meals a day* |
| Nine to twelve months | | 4–6 oz | 2–3 bottles a day or drinks from a cup. Eats 3 meals |

*Babies who are breastfed and/or use cups rarely drink the volume of liquid consumed by babies who drink from bottles—this is not a problem.*

Bottle-fed babies, like breastfed babies, drink variable amounts and may have some feedings close together and others further apart.

**121**

Please remember there are many individual variations on these amounts and number of bottles. Information about the quantity for age on formula cans is a guide only and may not necessarily suit your baby. Many babies never drink the "required amount" for their age and size; others need more. Plenty of wet diapers, consistent weight gains that are not excessive, and a thriving, active baby mean all is well.

## FOR MORE INFORMATION

Chapter 15: The Crying Baby page 331 *(lactose intolerance, protein intolerance, gas, colic, and the relationship of formula)*

Chapter 14: Sleeping and Waking in the First Six Months, page 310

Chapter 24: Feeding Your Baby *(introduction of whole cow's milk, page 504)*

Chapter 9: Bottle Feeding Your Baby After the First Two Weeks *(early weaning, page 175)* chapter **eight**

# Breastfeeding Your Baby After the First Two Weeks

## *Your diet*

Sometimes so much is made of the mother's diet that women choose to use formula because they incorrectly believe they have to make unacceptable changes to their diet. Breastfeeding is a body function and like any body function works better if you are well nourished. Eating well helps you enjoy your breastfeeding and your baby more and helps your body adjust to the extra work.

On the other hand, women who live where there is never enough food manage to breastfeed well—so even when diets fall short of the ideal, your baby will still thrive. It is only in extreme cases that the mother's diet affects the quality of breastmilk. After all, breastfeeding ensured our survival 40,000 years ago when humans had very little in the way of food reserves. Let's dispel a few myths:

- You do not have to eat enough for two. Women's bodies seem to conserve energy when they breastfeed. As well, fat stores laid down during pregnancy provide extra energy. Regular meals are the best way to go, so try not to skip meals. Alternatively, frequent snacks throughout the day might suit you better until you are used to your new life and have worked out who is going to prepare the meals!

- You do not have to drink heaps of any sort of fluid, including cow's milk, to make milk. You will notice that you are often thirsty when you nurse, so drink what you need to, to relieve your thirst.

- There is no food or beverage that makes more milk.

- Baby rashes, baby poo, baby crying, and all the strange and wonderful things babies do in the first three months rarely have anything to do with what their mothers are eating. Eat your normal diet, experiment with food you don't normally eat—if you think it upsets your baby, don't eat it again for a while.

  Take no notice when well-meaning people around you suggest something you're eating is upsetting your baby or giving her a rash. Think about women from other cultures who have been eating spicy food and breastfeeding for thousands of years as you enjoy a chocolate after dinner.

# Feeding patterns

Breastfeeding is not like bottle feeding where the volume taken per feeding increases and the number of bottles every twenty-four hours decreases as the baby gets older. Most women need to keep breastfeeding six times or more every twenty-four hours to maintain the milk supply; however, the sucking time usually decreases, often quite dramatically, between six weeks and three months. Breastfeeding around this time becomes easy, often sensual and pleasurable without having to worry anymore about the all-important position. This pattern of breastfeeding continues until a reasonable amount of food from a spoon is going down (between four and seven months), at which time if you want to or if your baby decides to, you can start to decrease the number of breastfeedings.

# How to express and store breastmilk

Expressing isn't an essential part of breastfeeding, but being able to express your breastmilk is a very handy skill for a few different reasons, for example:

- When breastfeeding is delayed after birth.

- To relieve engorged breasts in the early days. Hand expressing helps soften the nipple and areola so that it's easier for your baby to get a good mouthful of breast.

- To remove a little milk before feeding if your supply is abundant and your baby is being overwhelmed by a sudden rush of milk.

- For your comfort if your baby refuses one breast or goes through a phase of breast refusal. (See breast refusal, page 161.)

- To remove a little milk if your breasts still feel lumpy and uncomfortable after a feeding.

- For times when you won't be around for a feeding—study, returning to work, or a night out.

Expressing by hand

Learning how to express can be messy and tedious, and, like whistling or riding a bike, some women find it easier than others. Many women breastfeed and never express. If you can't express much milk, it does not mean you have a low supply. Your baby can stimulate and remove the milk much more effectively than you can. Whichever expressing method you use, you will find switching breasts frequently increases the amount you express and relieves your fingers (if hand expressing) and arms. Switching frequently also lessens the chance of hurting your breasts by trying to express milk after the flow has slowed down.

**N.B.:** Expressing is different to breastfeeding. When breastfeeding, the baby is not rapidly swapped from one breast to another.

Expressing can be done by hand expressing, by using a hand pump, or by using an electric pump.

## Hand expressing

There are lots of good things about hand expressing.

- It's convenient and free.

- Skin-to-skin contact stimulates milk production more efficiently and makes the let-down easier.

Hand expressing seems awkward and slow in the beginning, but many women find it becomes easy and efficient with a little practice. When you express, the aim is to stimulate the let-down reflex, then, by putting pressure where the milk is stored (under the areola), removing the milk. Gentle pressure is applied to the areola, not the nipple or the breast.

Wash your hands before you start. There are a few different ways of hand expressing, and once you know the basics, you will probably find your own style.

Here's one way. Think of expressing as two separate actions.

**A) ASSISTING THE LET-DOWN:** Support one breast from underneath with the opposite hand. Massage your breast gently but firmly with your free hand. Use a circular motion similar to that recommended for self-breast examination, paying particular attention to the underneath part and the part along the side of your breast near your arm, as this is where most of the glands where the milk is made are located. After massaging, stroke the breast with a feather-light touch using all your fingers. Stroke from the top of your breast to your nipple.

This technique for helping the let-down is used for whichever method of expressing you are using.

**127**

If there is going to be a long time before your baby can go to the breast because she is premature or sick and you are expressing every three hours or so, thinking about your baby and looking at her photo can help stimulate your milk. A quiet place and some relaxation techniques help too.

**B) EXPRESSING THE MILK:** Until you get used to hand expressing, don't worry about collecting the milk. Practicing in the shower or bath is relaxing, or simply squirt the milk into a towel.

Support your breast in one hand. Place your thumb and first two fingers of the other hand on the edge of the areola—the thumb is above, the fingers below. When hand expressing, the aim is to move the milk along the ducts in the breast and empty the stored milk under the areola so that you use your fingers in the same way a baby sucks.

Here's the tricky part. Push your thumb and finger into your breast, then compress your thumb and fingers together. Repeat the action. Push in, compress, push in, compress. Rotate your fingers and thumb around the areola to express all the stored milk. Swap hands when the position of your thumb and fingers becomes awkward.

Avoid pinching or squeezing the nipple as this closes up the milk ducts and the milk won't flow—it also hurts!

Until you are used to hand expressing, it's easier to use a clean wide bowl held between your legs or on a low table to catch the milk so that both your hands are free; leaning forward means gravity helps the let-down. Have a towel handy. Later, when you can do it better, hold a clean container near your breast and express into it.

Expressing milk for storage takes twenty to thirty minutes in the early weeks. After your milk is flowing well, it takes less time. Try expressing each breast for five to seven minutes, three to five minutes, then two to three minutes. These times are just a guide—when the milk dwindles, change breasts. Never try and force milk out when it's not coming easily. Handle your breasts gently as putting pressure on them can cause bruising and discomfort.

## Expressing with a hand pump

Some women find it easier to express using a hand pump. Many types of hand pumps are available. Many women find the cylindrical piston hand pump that looks like a large syringe the easiest to use. Place the flat rim of the pump over the center of your nipple and press it firmly against your breast, holding it in place while you move the outer part of the pump backward and forward. If using other types, follow the instructions.

The technique for using a hand pump is similar to hand expressing. Use the same massage and stroking techniques to stimulate the let-down, arrange for privacy, and go slowly and gently. If the milk stops spurting, slightly altering the angle of the flat rim of the pump on the areola from time to time increases the flow of milk.

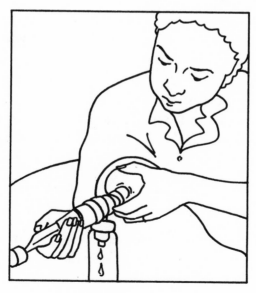

Expressing with a hand pump

## Expressing with an electric pump

Electric pumps are more efficient and less tiring when expressed milk is needed for any length of time. Electric pumps are also useful occasionally to increase the milk supply. Electric pumps are expensive to buy and may be rented to use at home from hospitals and breastfeeding accessory outlets such as Medela. When renting, you will need to buy the kit that goes with the pump (breast flanges, tubing and collection bottles). Kits cost $25–$100 and pump renting costs $1 to $3 per day.If you don't have anyone to show you how to use an electric pump, follow the instructions for use carefully to avoid infection or getting bacteria in your milk.

# *When is the best time to express?*

When to express depends on *why* you are expressing:

- When your baby can't go to the breast for a long time. If your baby is sick or premature, most of the time you will need to express about eight times every twenty-four hours. You can be flexible about the length of time in between—expressing does not have to be done every three or four hours. The more you express, the more milk you will make; however, it is also important that you look after yourself as well. Six hours of undisturbed sleep at night is good for you.

- Returning to full-time work. (See Work and Breastfeeding, page 438.)

- For times when you won't be there—regular absences for study, work, or voluntary work, or for occasional days away.

While they are fully breastfeeding as well, most women find it difficult to express enough for one feed in one expressing session, so don't be surprised if it takes several days to express enough for one feed. It is quite normal to only be able to express 1–1½ oz aday. Think ahead, express daily, and store the expressed milk in the freezer until you have enough so that you are not under pressure to produce enough milk for a feeding on Saturday morning before going out on Saturday night—very stressful! If you expect to have regular absences, it is a good idea to express and freeze milk daily.

**The best times to do this are:**

- After a feeding when there is likely to be extra milk available. Early morning feedings after you and your baby have slept are often a good time.

- In between feedings when you are pretty sure your baby is going to sleep for three or more hours—try pumping after she has been asleep for two hours.

- Any time when your supply is abundant and your baby fills up on one breast. Feed on one breast and express the other.

## How much to express?

A rough guide is 2½ oz per pound of body weight for each twenty-four hour period when babies are under three months. This may be anything from 2 oz. to 8 oz. depending on your baby's age and size. When it's for an occasional bottle, a rough estimate is fine.

FOR EXAMPLE:  0–4 weeks, 2–4 oz
4–8 weeks, 4–5 oz
8–12 weeks, 5–8 oz

If for some reason all your baby's feedings are going to be expressed breastmilk given in a bottle please refer to the section on bottle feedings for more information. When expressing for occasional feedings be kind to your babysitter and leave a little extra when you can, as babies can often drink faster from a bottle than the breast, then look around for more.

# Storing breastmilk

Breastmilk can be stored in plastic containers, plastic or glass bottles, or disposable, sealable plastic bags. Plastic bags take up much less space but need a label with volume as well as the date. Double plastic bags are more secure. If most of your baby's feedings are to be given in a bottle, avoid freezing her milk in a glass container, as there is some loss of antibodies when breastmilk is stored in glass.

Wash the containers, rinse, and disinfect them. After you express the milk, pour it into the prepared container and put it in the fridge. If you intend to freeze the milk, wait until it is cold, then pour it into another container in the freezer. Each time you express fresh milk, wait until it is cold, then add it to your frozen supply until you have enough for a feeding, then start a new lot. It's quite all right to keep adding fresh milk to frozen milk as long as you cool it first. This avoids lots of little packets of frozen breastmilk all over the freezer. Freezing breastmilk in ice cube trays is not practical once your baby is old enough to drink substantial amounts. Apart from that, a cube might go into a gin and tonic by mistake!

## Storage of breastmilk for home use

Expressed breastmilk looks quite interesting because it freezes in layers that may be different colors, and at times there appears to be little specks in it. This is normal, and as long as you have followed these guidelines for storing the milk, don't worry.

## HOW LONG CAN BREASTMILK BE STORED AND STILL USED?

The guidelines below are for healthy babies at home. If you are collecting and storing milk for a premature or sick baby in hospital, ask for advice from the staff in the nursery.

| Breastmilk | Freezer | Refrigerator | Room temperature |
|---|---|---|---|
| Freshly expressed breastmilk (in a sealed container) | • 2 weeks in freezer compartment inside refrigerator<br>• 3 months in freezer section of refrigerator with separate door<br>• 6–12 months in deep freeze (0°F or lower) | • 3–5 days (39°F or lower) Store in the back of the refrigerator on the top shelf where it is colder—not on the door. | • 12–24 hours (colostrum) 79°F or lower.<br>• 6–10 hours (mature milk) 79°F or lower. It is always advisable to use a refrigerator when one is available. |
| Previously frozen breast milk (thawed in refrigerator or under running water) | • do not refreeze | • 24 hours | • 1 hour |

**IN GENERAL**

- Use fresh milk whenever possible.

- Breastmilk has a good shelf life, but it is always advisable to refrigerate it soon after expressing when a refrigerator is available.

- Freeze milk that will not be used within two days.

- Use the oldest milk first; date the container at the time of collection.

- When adding cold, unfrozen milk to stored frozen milk, don't leave more than a week between additions.

# Using the stored milk

If the milk has not been frozen, stand the bottle in a container of warm water to warm it before feeding or give it as it comes. The person feeding your baby should always test the temperature of the milk by shaking a little from the nipple onto the inside of their wrist.

If the milk is frozen, defrost it gently. Here are two ways:

- Defrost just before feeding by running cold water over the container. Gradually increase the water temperature until it is warm to hot. Keep the container in the water until the milk defrosts. It's similar to the way you defrost frozen shrimp.

- Alternatively, you can prepare in advance by taking the frozen milk from the freezer and leaving it in the fridge until it defrosts. It must be used within twelve hours—if it hasn't fully defrosted when it's needed, use some warm water. This method has the advantage of having milk available instantly for a feeding, but it may be wasted if your baby doesn't use it. Breastmilk should never be refrozen.

Microwaves should never be used to defrost or heat breastmilk.

# *Is there enough milk?*

You may find yourself worrying if you have enough milk. Worrying about milk supply is one of the main reasons women stop breastfeeding, yet a lot of the time the worry is unfounded.

How can you tell if there is enough milk?

Mothers and those around them mistakenly think there is not enough milk at times. All is likely to be well if:

- Your baby has six to eight pale, wet diapers every day.

- She has a good poo every so often or at every feed.

- She grows steadily—which is easy to see as she grows out of her clothes, her bassinet, and fills up the space in her car seat. Weighing her from time to time also gives you an idea of how she is growing.

Here are some common reasons for believing there may not be enough milk. If all the signs mentioned above are present it is unlikely the following things are signs of not enough milk.

- **Your baby keeps turning her head and opening her mouth as if she wants to suck on something even after several good feedings:** This is called the rooting reflex and is present in all babies from birth, usually disappearing by three to four months of age. Babies do this when they are hungry, but they also respond like this when they are awake for any length of time, restless, overstimulated, bored, or overtired. Often wanting to suck on something is a sign of needing sleep, not food.

- **No sensation of a let-down:** Some women never feel a let-down; others find the let-down sensation fades or disappears as their baby grows older so not feeling a let-down is not a sign of low supply unless there are other indications.

- **Your baby is very unsettled a lot of the time:** The reasons why some babies cry a lot and have trouble falling asleep and staying asleep are complex and varied. If your baby is taking the breast well and growing and developing as she is meant to, it is unlikely her restless behavior has anything to do with your breastfeeding.

- **You can't express much milk:** Many women who breastfeed well can't express. Your ability to express isn't a reflection of how much milk your baby takes.

- **Your baby starts to suck her fists all the time:** Between eight and twelve weeks, babies' hands are never out of their mouths. Hands in the mouth is a normal part of their sensory/motor development and not a sign of hunger.

- **Your breasts change; they stop leaking, become softer and smaller, and the full feeling goes:** Breast changes like this are normal and happen between six and twelve weeks. Breastfeeding becomes easy and efficient; the fullness and leaking that happens in the early weeks is only temporary.

- **Your baby stops pooing a lot and only goes once every few days:** Most breastfed babies don't poo nearly as much after the first six weeks—a big soft poo less often does not mean your supply is low.

- **Your baby takes a lot less time at the breast:** Breastfeeding is a body function, and like all body functions, the more you do it the better you get. It's a bit like running around the park—after you've been doing it for a few months, it's much less tiring, you enjoy it more, and do it faster. As your baby grows, she becomes more skilled at removing the milk and your body responds, so you become an efficient team.

- **Your baby wakes a lot at night or suddenly starts waking a lot at night:** Nighttime waking is dealt with in detail in Sleeping and Waking, page 310 and The Crying Baby page 331. In general, unless there are obvious signs of not enough milk night waking in itself is not a sign that babies need more food.

## How do you know there is a problem?

Sometimes, of course, the feeling that your baby is not getting enough milk is correct. It is not clear-cut. Obsessions with weight gains in the past meant many women weaned when they didn't have to or want to, but if you are unsure of what is happening, weighing and measuring your baby is still the best guide. Weighing is best done with an experienced health professional who is as interested in breastfeeding as you are and can use the weight as a guide to work with you to resolve the problem—if one exists. Weighing is not a test to determine whether or not formula should be given.

### INTERPRETING WEIGHT

It's quite likely your baby is not getting enough milk if:

- there is a constant, gradual weight loss;

- she is still below her birthweight at four weeks or older;

- she keeps gaining less than one pound a month.

Other signs that *may* indicate there's not enough milk:

- a sudden change from a reasonably content baby to increased fussiness and more unsettled times;

- a sudden increase in the number of feedings, which don't seem to satisfy your baby as much as they used to;

- fewer wet diapers. You may also notice some diapers are damp rather than wet (it's difficult to judge diaper wetness with the latest hi tech disposables as they absorb fluid very efficiently);

- Infrequent poo is fine as long as there's a good big soft one when it comes. Infrequent green "splats" are often a sign of underfeeding.

When your baby is healthy and well, temporary underfeeding is rarely an emergency situation, but there are times when prompt medical attention is needed. It is unusual for these things to happen simply because of a low milk supply, but here are some signs something more serious is wrong:

- your baby becomes floppy and pale and won't suck;

- she has a fever;

- most of her diapers are dry;

- she has a sudden major weight loss over a short period.

## Why isn't there enough milk?

Here are the most likely reasons:

- **Difficult start:** If your baby is premature, sick, or jaundiced, your birth complicated, or your baby sleepy, you may find breastfeeding takes longer for everything to start working, so there may not be enough milk for a while.

- **Your position, your baby's position:** If your baby is not in the best position for breastfeeding, she can't suck well enough to make everything work as well as it can. If you are uncomfortable or ill at ease, your body can't respond, and this affects the amount of milk you make.

- **Not enough feedings:** If your baby doesn't take the breast often enough, your body doesn't get a strong message to keep making milk, so the amount of milk available is less than your baby needs.

- **Strategies for sore nipples:** Temporarily stopping breastfeeding or using a nipple protector can decrease the supply.

- **Hormonal changes:** Sometimes hormonal changes in your body alter the balance slightly, so less milk is made, for example, pregnancy or menstruation. Concerns are also often raised about the minipill interfering with the milk supply. In theory the minipill (which is progesterone only) should not diminish milk supply, unlike estrogen, which does. Two researchers in Australia have been unable to demonstrate in controlled studies that the minipill diminishes the milk supply; but to be absolutely sure, a study would have to be done with larger numbers of women over longer periods of time. Other researchers claim that the minipill demonstrates no consistent alteration of breastmilk composition, volume, or duration of lactation. Occasionally there are times in my work when I suspect that the minipill may contribute to fussy feeding and a diminished milk supply, but it is usually very hard to be certain whether the problem is caused by the minipill or other reasons. However, there are times when stopping the minipill seems to help increase the milk supply.

- **Smoking:** Smoking affects the milk supply for some women and not for others. When it does, the supply tends to start out all right but decreases as the baby grows. Lots of low milk supply difficulties can be solved, but if you smoke and your supply is low, the chance of increasing your milk to meet all your baby's food needs for any length of time is unlikely. Reducing the number of cigarettes you smoke to as few as possible, not smoking for the hour before feeding and not smoking while you feed reduces harmful effects. The relationship between smoking and low milk supply is unclear, but it is well documented. However, it must be emphasized that if you are a smoker who can't stop, all the advantages of breastfeeding are still there for your baby, so breastfeed for as long as you can (which may turn out to be a long time).

- **Illness:** If you or your baby becomes sick, you might find there is not enough milk. Again, this should only be a temporary situation until you recover. If your baby is sick and not sucking as often or as well, you need to express for comfort and to remind your body to keep making milk.

- **Lifestyle, stress, and/or exhaustion:** Lots of women find their breastfeeding works well even when they lead busy lives, get very tired, work outside the home, have stressful days, or come through a major upheaval. For others, breastfeeding is a fine balance and doesn't work well unless they adapt their lifestyle to breastfeeding. Lifestyle adjustments are often only temporary, but some women find that for the period that their baby is exclusively breastfed, they have to limit their activities, avoid major upheavals, and make sure they are always well nurtured and rested.

- **Breast reduction and other breast surgery** may hinder milk production.

- **The way the baby sucks:** Breastfeeding takes two, and occasionally the baby's technique just doesn't do what's needed to keep the milk flowing. The baby is usually healthy and well and sucks on a nipple quite happily, but when it comes to the breast, she nurses in a way that does not stimulate the mother's supply. This is sometimes temporary and by expressing to increase supply, use of a nursing supplement (see page 145), and a little formula, the problem can be overcome until the baby sucks more effectively. Occasionally it is impossible to resolve, and either expressed breastmilk or formula has to be given in a bottle.

- **Unknown:** It is very distressing when you and your baby are doing everything right and yet your baby does not thrive. This does not happen very often, but there are times when there does not seem to be a definable cause or solution for a low milk supply. Some researchers believe that a small number of women do not have the metabolic capacity to produce enough milk for their babies; however, to date there is little work being done to investigate the reasons for this.

- Apart from the possibility of underlying metabolic problems, the following things may play a part sometimes for some women:
  a) Unresolved grief for the loss of another baby (crib death, stillbirth, or a baby given up for adoption).
  b) A sudden emotional shock (such as the sudden death of a parent).
  c) Intense homesickness (having your first baby miles away from familiar faces and places).

It must be emphasized that these things do not mean breastfeeding won't work. Successful breastfeeding can be a beneficial healing process in times of emotional trauma, but occasionally the emotional trauma gets in the way of the breastfeeding.

## What do you do when there isn't enough milk?

Fortunately, there are things you can do to increase the amount of breastmilk your baby is getting without using extra food or weaning. Low supply is usually a *temporary* difficulty.

Occasionally it is a *longstanding* problem and the breastmilk has to be supplemented with formula or food from a spoon. This can often be done carefully so that breastfeeding continues.

Here's a general guide for a *temporary* low supply. Ask your partner and other family members around you to read this as well.

- Support and encouragement from those around you makes an enormous difference. Comments that constantly undermine your confidence don't help. For example, "The women in our family have never been able to breastfeed"; "Are you sure she's getting enough?"; "Your milk is too watery"; "Put her on the bottle—it doesn't matter."

- If possible, get help from someone who knows how to check your position and your baby's position during a feeding.

- Feed your baby whenever she's hungry or awake and alert. Try not to keep using a pacifier to extend the time in between feedings. Remember, she needs seven to eight breastfeedings every twenty-four hours.

- On the other hand, don't let your feedings go on forever in an attempt to give your baby "the hind milk." Endless long feedings are exhausting and aren't an effective way to increase your supply. Frequent feeding has to be balanced with rest and relaxation for you. As long as the position is right, ten to twenty minutes of effective sucking does the job.

- Always offer both breasts every feeding. Try to make sure your baby is offered the second breast when she is in an alert state. Change her diaper and tickle the soles of her feet to wake her up if she is asleep. If she still doesn't take the second breast, don't worry; offer both breasts again at the next feeding.

- Plan a few days of complete rest. See if you can arrange help with the household chores, as resting while everything around you is in a state of chaos is not very relaxing. Take your baby to bed. Feed her as much as you can while you watch television and listen to music.

- There is no special food that makes more milk, but if you stop eating properly, your body doesn't work as efficiently, so make sure you stay well nourished.

- Avoid strenuous exercise programs and dieting rigorously to lose weight.

- If you are using a nipple protector try as many feedings as possible without it; if you are giving bottles to rest sore nipples, try to let your baby take your breast again as soon as possible.

- Express to make more milk, but with caution. When there are difficulties with the position and your baby's sucking technique needs a little time to develop, expressing a few times a day after feedings can be useful. A full-service electric double pump is easier and more efficient. When the positioning is better and your baby's sucking is stronger, you can stop.

  If your baby's position at the breast is good and she sucks well, then let nature take its course. Frequent feedings and rest should solve the problem without expressing as well. Expressing to increase the milk supply is not always useful as it has a tendency to make a stressful situation even more stressful, which doesn't do a lot to help the milk flow. If expressing as well as feeding makes you tense and hassled, then it is unlikely to be of much benefit.

When low supply becomes a *longstanding* problem:

- Plan your life to get some rest. Perhaps reorganize the household chores so your partner does more. Can you think of ways to cut back on some of your activities for a week or so? Maybe going home to your mother is an option. Or, she might be able to come to you.

- If after a period of time you have to give some extra food because your baby is not gaining enough weight, start with a small amount of formula (1–2 oz) once or twice a day after a good breastfeeding. Continue to nurse frequently, rest, and make sure you are both comfortable at feeding time. A small amount of formula does not mean all is lost!

- An option instead of a bottle and nipple is a nursing supplementer. A nursing supplementer consists of a container similar to a bottle that contains either expressed breastmilk or formula that is worn in a pouch around the mother's neck. A piece of fine tubing that carries the milk from the container to the nipple is gently taped to her breast so that the end of it lies near the nipple. When the baby sucks at the breast, the milk is drawn through the tubing into her mouth at the same time as milk from the breast. For some mothers, use of a nursing supplementer helps while they build up their supply and keeps their baby at the breast. Nursing supplementers don't suit everyone. Some mothers find them difficult to use, especially in front of anyone; some babies won't suck with a nursing supplementer in place whereas others quickly get used to it and won't suck without it.

- Two types of nursing supplementers are available—the Medela Supplemental Nursing System and the Lact-Aid Nursing Trainer System. Contact Medela at 1-800-TELL YOU (1-800-835-5968) or http://www.medela.com. Contact Lact-Aid at 1.423.744-9090 or http://www.lact-aid.com It's essential to have a person experienced in using a nursing supplementer to help you when you start.

- From three months onward, babies can be supplemented with food from a spoon instead of formula in a bottle—an option that can work well when it seems unlikely the milk supply is going to provide all your baby needs. When your baby is not getting quite enough breastmilk and you have done all the best things to do to increase your milk, she can get extra food from rice cereal, fruit, and veggies. Trying food from a spoon instead of formula in a bottle means your baby still gets all the milk you do make because:

  a) It takes time to increase the amount she manages to eat from a spoon, which means she is still keen to take the breast. Large amounts of formula in bottles go down quickly, the baby loses interest in the breast, and bottle feeding takes over.

  b) Food from a spoon is not an alternative food source taken by sucking, so she eats from a spoon and sucks from the breast.

  c) The extra calories from the food help your baby gain weight, you gain confidence, and often the milk supply improves.

    Remember this is an option. It doesn't suit all mothers and babies when low supply is a problem, and your baby should be at least three months old before you try it.

# Not enough milk—summary

- Not having enough milk does not happen nearly as often as everyone thinks it does. Check carefully why you think there is not enough. If you can, talk it over with an experienced breastfeeding adviser.

## IF IT DOES SEEM TO BE A PROBLEM

- Check your position when you are feeding;

- Check your baby's position—she may need to be tucked in closer to you;

- Feed your baby seven or eight times every twenty-four hours;

- Always offer both breasts;

- Try to get some extra rest;

- Can you stop smoking or cut down?

- Delay taking the minipill for contraception;

- Expressing after some feedings may help.

## IF IT BECOMES LONGSTANDING

- Offer some formula (a small amount to begin with) or any expressed breastmilk you might have after two or three breast-feedings every twenty-four hours; OR

- A nursing supplementer might suit you and your baby; OR

- Give one bottle of formula or previously expressed breastmilk once a day in the evening. Give the appropriate amount for age. Let your partner give the bottle while you have a complete break. Continue giving seven or eight breastfeedings the rest of the time, taking care with positioning. Stop the supplements if your supply increases; OR

- Start food from a spoon when your baby is three months old. Continue breastfeeding. Slowly build up the food to two to three meals a day. Give the food after the breast and continue seven to eight breastfeedings every twenty-four hours.

# Lots of milk

Some women find they have so much milk it causes temporary difficulties. If you have lots of milk, you might find your breasts always feel full and leak all the time. Your baby will probably have big weight gains, poo heartily and everywhere, and may gasp and pull off the breast because the flow is fast at times. She is also likely to have some good vomits. Some of these things are distressing, but they are harmless. As your baby grows and the milk flow settles, you will find the leaking, pooing, and vomiting gets less.

## What can you do?

- At first, do nothing, as the milk flow often adjusts to the baby's needs quite quickly.

- If the milk flow continues to be abundant, try feeding your baby only one breast each feeding for a while. Put your baby back on the first breast instead of offering the second breast. For comfort only, hand express the breast your baby doesn't take—just express until the full feeling stops.

- Hand expressing a little milk just before a feed sometimes makes

**147**

it easier for your baby to manage when she goes to the breast.

- Sometimes changing positions helps. The underarm hold (see page 86) sometimes seems to stop the choking.

- You might find the leaking is embarrassing. Try using the nondisposable breast pads made from a soft fabric that allow moisture to pass through and keep your skin dry. Multi-colored tops are a good disguise.

- Remember, this is temporary and will not go on for the whole time you breastfeed. In the meantime, take pleasure in watching your baby thrive on all your wonderful milk!

For a small number of women, oversupply is a distressing situation that causes constant breast problems such as plugged ducts and mastitis (see page 150). The baby may also be very unsettled and become a fussy feeder, pulling away from the breast after only sucking for a short time. Like many breastfeeding difficulties, these things will usually resolve in time (it's unusual for oversupply problems to continue past three months). Here are some suggestions to manage:

- Try to feed your baby when she is sleepy on a softer breast and leave her on the same breast until it is fully drained (very soft). Hand express the other breast for comfort if you need to.

- Avoid skipping feedings until the supply has settled. If your baby starts sleeping longer than five hours at night, you may need to express at the time of the missed feeding, if you wake with painful, bursting breasts (it's very unfair when the baby lets you sleep and your breasts don't).

- Continue to make sure you follow the guidelines for positioning so that your baby can drain your breast efficiently.

- Check your breasts frequently for hard, painful, or red segments. Use massage and hand or pump expression to relieve the troublesome spot.

# Fast flow

Milk often spurts out when you let-down at the beginning of a feeding or halfway through. Babies find this upsetting when they are young and often choke and cry and pull off the breast. Fast flow is not necessarily associated with an oversupply of milk, so care has to be taken that any strategies used for a fast flow do not diminish the milk supply. If your baby is generally settled and you are not having the difficulties described in the previous section (see "lots of milk," page 147), just try hand expressing a small amount of milk before the feeding. You may also find changing the position from across your front to under your arm halfway through the feeding helps avoid choking on the second let-down. As your baby grows and the let-down intensity decreases, the problem corrects itself.

# Clicking noise when breastfeeding (the baby, not you)

Sometimes babies click while feeding. If your baby is thriving, the feeding is comfortable, and your nipples are not sore (apart from some discomfort for twenty to thirty seconds at the beginning of the feeding), ignore the clicking noise. If your nipples are hurting throughout the feeding, or if your baby is very unsettled and perhaps not gaining weight, the clicking in this instance is a sign that the position is not right. If possible, ask for help to check your feeding. If not, go back to the basic guidelines for positioning and go through them step by step. Changing position from front to underarm (twin style) might help.

## One breast bigger than the other

Some women find when they are breastfeeding that one breast is bigger than the other. It may be because the baby prefers one breast and sucks longer and more efficiently on that breast or because one breast just makes more milk. If this happens, it is much more noticeable in the first six to eight weeks and then tends to settle. At times the breast size will continue to be different for the whole time the baby is breastfeeding, but the breasts do go back to being similar after weaning—so if this is happening to you, don't panic about being lopsided forever.

## Plugged ducts

When you are breastfeeding, the milk is carried from the glands deep inside the breast to the front of the breast by a network of tiny tubes called ducts. If one of the tubes becomes blocked, the milk can't flow as well and you are likely to notice a lump that at first may not be painful. The lump is thickened milk. One or more can form at any time, but this is more common in the first three months.

### Why does it happen?
Something holds up the milk flow. Here are the usual causes for a plugged duct, but sometimes it is difficult to pinpoint a reason.

- If your baby's position at the breast is not quite right, the breast won't be well drained after a feeding so there's more chance of milk banking up in one of the ducts. Pain or discomfort throughout the feeding is a sign the position is not right. This should not be confused with the toe-tingling discomfort many women experience for the first thirty seconds before and after a feeding in the early weeks. (Opinions vary as to the cause of toe-tingling discomfort, but it is not due to positioning when the feeding is comfortable apart from the uncomfortable sensation at the beginning and end of the feeding.)

- Sometimes the way breasts are handled harms the ducts. Try not to grip them tightly when you feed your baby. Using a finger to hold the breast away from your baby's nose while she nurses is unnecessary when the position is correct. When you massage and express, try not to squeeze or slide your hands on your breasts.

- Tight bras or clothing putting pressure on breasts can stop the milk flow.

- If the normal pattern of your breastfeeding is interrupted, ducts may become blocked. Things like delayed or hurried feeding, going back to work, stopping night feedings, traveling, or giving up breastfeeding suddenly can contribute to problems with the milk flow.

What can you do if you feel a lump anywhere in your breasts?

- Nurse frequently and offer the lumpy breast first for two feedings in a row. Try changing the way you nurse. If you normally sit, lie down on your side. If you usually feed with your baby's body under your arm, try holding her in front of you. If you can do it so that you are both comfortable, feed her so that her chin points toward the lump.

- Massage the lump firmly with the same technique used for self-breast examination. It's important not to squeeze your breast or slide your hands down the breast. The lump may be painful and red. Sometimes it helps if the lump is massaged by your partner, lover, or friend with some nice oil.

- Massaging and hand expressing while sitting in a warm tub helps if the breast is still lumpy and uncomfortable after a feeding.

- Arm exercises similar to breaststroke movements also help.

- Make a point of putting your feet up and resting whenever you can, especially when your baby is sleeping during the day.

# Mastitis

Mastitis is a medical term for a red, swollen breast. If mastitis happens while you are breastfeeding, it is very painful and usually caused by bacterial infection. Up to ten to twenty percent of women develop a breast infection in the first few weeks of breastfeeding.

## Why does it happen?

- An abundant supply in the early weeks while the milk supply adjusts to your baby's needs.

- A plugged duct that doesn't resolve.

- From damaged nipples when bacteria enter the duct through a graze or a crack in the nipple.

- Mastitis is more likely to happen if you become ill or exhausted; smoking may also contribute.

Sometimes the cause is unknown. Mastitis can strike like lightning and is often mistaken for influenza, as sometimes at first there is only minimal breast tenderness and no sign of a blocked duct. When this happens, the breast symptoms do appear later.

## What are the symptoms?

- You feel hot, feverish, and depressed.

- Your breast may be red, swollen, and exquisitely tender.

- There are often red streaks on the sore breast.

With prompt treatment you may be able to avoid antibiotics through the use of warm packs, massage, rest, acetaminophen, arm exercises, and frequent breastfeedings.

Whatever you do, don't stop breastfeeding. Let your baby suck—your milk will not harm her in any way.

If this works, you will know because the influenza symptoms will go away and the pain will be gone from your breast.

On the other hand, if after six to eight hours there is no improvement and you feel very ill and depressed, you need medication.

Antibiotics are the most effective medication for treating infective mastitis and preventing the risk of an abscess, so visit your family doctor. The antibiotics will not harm your baby.

Continue frequent breastfeeding while you take them. Disregard advice to stop breastfeeding temporarily—this is wrong advice and can lead to added discomfort and unplanned weaning.

It is important to take a ten-day course of antibiotics. Take the whole course even though you will feel like a new woman in forty-eight hours.

A few women seem to get one bout of mastitis after another. Recurrent mastitis is very tiring, and the precise reason for the problem varies between women and for the same women between bouts. Finding the exact cause and fixing the problem so that the mastitis doesn't keep recurring is difficult, and different things may work (or not work) for different women. La Leche League International can be of great help in this situation as word-of-mouth remedies from women to women can often offer potential solutions unavailable from other sources.

# Breast abscesses

An abscess is a collection of pus (like a boil) that happens in a breast either because mastitis has not been quickly and effectively treated or because of an infection from cracked or grazed nipples. If it's because of damaged nipples, the abscess is likely to be near the nipple; if it is because of mastitis, it forms where the red infected area of the breast is. An abscess is very painful.

Breast abscesses are rare, but if one forms, medical attention is needed immediately. Treatment involves antibiotics and usually surgical drainage. Breastfeeding should continue. If for any reason you can't feed from the infected breast or it is too painful, express it until you can put your baby back to the breast.

If you have to go to hospital, see if you can arrange to take your baby with you or get help to express your milk regularly. Breastfeeding from both breasts during and after treatment is recommended, but milk often continues to leak from the incision following drainage of an abscess, which can be hard to deal with. Nevertheless, although it is messy and aesthetically a problem, there is no harm in it. If you continue breastfeeding, you may find the breast with the abscess doesn't produce as much milk with this baby as it did before the abscess appeared. Interestingly, research shows the bulk of the milk supply is found in different parts of the breast with each baby, so with another baby it is likely that the breast will function as if there were never been a problem.

# *Persistent sore/damaged nipples*

Most damaged nipples heal well in the first six weeks, but unfortunately some women find breastfeeding is not particularly enjoyable (an understatement some would say) for up to three months because of ongoing sore nipples and breast pain for which there may not be a solution other than time. If you reach a point where you cannot bear the thought of another breastfeeding, it is advisable to take your baby from the breast and express for a week before putting her back. Hand expressing is often advised in this situation but is unrealistic for many women who find it easier to use an electric pump or hand pump. Give your baby the expressed milk in a bottle. When your nipples (or nipple; it is often only one nipple that is a problem) are healed, start to put your baby back to the breast once or twice every twenty-four hours, slowly building up to full breastfeeding again. If possible, get help from a nurse practitioner or lactation consultant the first time you put her back to the breast.

Sometimes ongoing nipple soreness can be diagnosed as specific medical conditions, which means they can be helped by treatment. The range of conditions follow:

## CANDIDA ALBICANS (COMMONLY KNOWN AS THRUSH) OF THE NIPPLES

*Candida albicans* is a common infection caused by a yeast that is able to infect the deep organs of the body as well as the skin, and particularly affects mothers and babies. Nipples may become infected with *Candida albicans* in a number of different ways.

- *Candida albicans* infections occurring in women are common in the mucous membrane that lines the vagina. If this is present

**155**

when she gives birth, her baby will be born with the same infection in her mouth and digestive tract.

- *Candida albicans* can occur in a baby's mouth (called thrush when it's in the mouth) whether her mother has a vaginal infection or not.

- Women who are breastfeeding sometimes find the combination of their baby's sucking along with the constant dampness and friction of breast pads and bras leads to a yeast infection on the skin on the areola and nipple.

When the nipple and areola become infected by *Candida albicans* they become red, dry, and itchy, although just to confuse the issue, these signs are not always there. The nipples are painful before, during, and after a feed, and often suddenly start to hurt where previously they didn't. Sometimes there is a burning pain radiating up the breast from the nipples, especially after a feeding. It's important to treat the baby for thrush if the mother is being treated for a yeast infection of the nipples even if there is no sign of thrush in the baby's mouth.

A yeast infection of areolas and nipples may happen at the same time as cracked and/or painful nipples in the early weeks or suddenly develop at a later stage when there has been no history of damaged or sore nipples. A definite diagnosis is sometimes difficult, and I feel there is a tendency for yeast infections as a cause of sore nipples and breast pain to be overdiagnosed; however, there are times when the signs and symptoms are clear and they can be treated effectively with nystatin (which comes in oral drops). The treatment should be continued for a week. If the sore nipples or breast pain don't improve rapidly with the correct treatment it's reasonable to assume the problem is not caused by *Candida albicans*. (See Needle-Sharp Pain, page 102.)

## DERMATITIS

Dermatitis is caused by something irritating the nipple and areola such as creams, sprays, clothing, or soap that makes the nipple and areola red and sore. Women who have sensitive skin and suffer from eczema are more likely to develop nipple dermatitis.

Expose your nipples as much as possible, taking care outdoors if it's windy and/or sunny. Wear cotton near your skin. Be very careful about what you put on your nipples as lots of products are likely to make things worse, not better. A mild hydrocortisone ointment (ointment is better than cream on a moist surface) will relieve the inflammation if the diagnosis is definite.

Hydrocortisone will not help if the problem is caused by the way your baby is taking the breast.

## SMALL, WHITE BLISTER

Occasionally milk collects in a spot on the nipple, just under the skin, and looks like a whitehead. The skin around the spot is swollen and painful. As the collection of milk causes a blockage in the milk flow, there may be associated lumps farther back in the breast.

The discomfort doesn't last for long. Usually the baby's sucking removes the collection of milk, but if it is very painful, try having a warm bath or shower, then gently apply some pressure behind the spot and see if it will pop out. If it doesn't come easily or if it's very painful, leave it alone—your baby will eventually suck it out. If she doesn't, the most effective treatment is removal of the spot by a doctor or lactation consultant familiar with the procedure.

## WHITE NIPPLE

Sometimes a nipple looks white and moist. This is possibly something to do with the blood circulation to the nipple. Sometimes pain is associated with a white nipple, especially if the tip of the nipple is flattened after a feeding. When this happens, it is probably because the end of the nipple is being pressed against your baby's hard palate.

Try cupping your breast with your palm and fingers, your thumb lightly resting above the areola, and direct the breast squarely into your baby's mouth (see illustration). This makes it easier for her to extend the nipple past her hard palate.

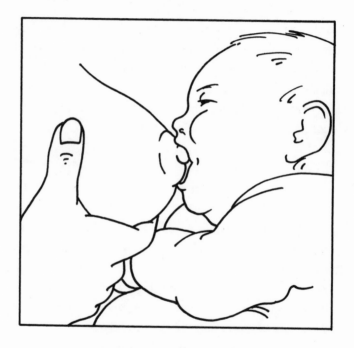

A white nipple is not always associated with painful feeding. When it is not, it is unlikely the position of your baby at the breast is a cause. A sudden sharp pain when the blood returns to the nipple after feeding is experienced by some women.

Sometimes a warm compress to the areola before and/or after feeding will prevent the reaction and alleviate pain.

Make sure your bra and clothes are not too tight, avoid disposable breast pads, and expose the nipple when you can.

Leave your bra off at night if it's comfortable to do so. Feeding your baby in a warm room and drinking a cup of tea just before the feeding improves circulation. Sucking on a white nipple does not hurt your baby.

# Breast pain

Persistent breast pain that is not related to an obvious condition such as mastitis or referred pain from damaged nipples is a problem for a small number of women. It is perhaps more common in women who experience troublesome breast pain prior to pregnancy or who have very sensitive skin. If you feel the pain is unusual, please see your family doctor. Here are some suggestions that have been found to be helpful:

- Reduce the caffeine in your diet. Apart from coffee, caffeine is found in many other drinks and processed foods.

- Reduce the salt in your diet. Again, check processed foods.

- Take vitamin B1 and vitamin B6 tablets daily.

- Wear a firm, well-fitting cotton bra day and night.

# Aching upper back and shoulders

Can be a problem for some women while they are learning to breastfeed, especially if there is an old injury or a past history of problems in that area. Take care to sit upright with your back straight. Try not to lean over your baby—bring her to your breast, not your breast to her. Use a firm pillow to support your baby.

A feeding pillow (My Brest Friend) is available for women who require postural and/or help with positioning their babies when they breastfeed. It is designed to support the back, neck, shoulders, and arms and is of great benefit to women with back and neck problems who are breastfeeding.

It is available by mail order 1-877-690-6117 or from http://www.babycenter.com.

Warmth around your upper back and shoulders helps (a shawl or soft blanket). Heat to your back and shoulders (a hot water bottle) after feeding is soothing. Back and shoulder discomfort gradually improves as you and your baby become more skilled in this breastfeeding business.

# Should I wean?

You may find yourself in a dilemma where you feel breastfeeding is the pits, but the thought of weaning also fills you with dismay. I find that most women get through this time as long as their babies are thriving and they have good support from family and a health professional. The problem will not last forever, and you will almost certainly be delighted that you carried on.

It is very difficult, however, to keep going when there is the added problem of a low supply that cannot seem to be resolved. In this situation you may need to talk to your health professional about combining breast and bottle feeding or slowly starting to wean.

# Combining breast and bottle feeding

Combining breast and bottle feeding is an option when, despite all efforts, there is not enough breastmilk. Many babies in this situation will happily take both. Even though the amount of formula may indicate that most of the feeding is via the bottle, there are still benefits from giving your baby the breast, before each bottle and perhaps at other times, such as in between feedings, for comfort. Give your baby ten minutes or so at both breasts then offer the bottle with the amount of formula required for your baby's age (see chart, page 121). Combining breastfeeding and formula feeding in this way can continue for as long as you are both happy.

# Nursing Strike (breast refusal)

Lots of normal, healthy babies have times when they refuse to go to the breast. You are probably unaware this happens and may find it an upsetting experience that can become somewhat of an ordeal for a while. The most common age for babies to refuse to nurse seems to be between two and five months. They are usually thriving and gaining weight well. It often happens out of the blue, although some babies who refuse the breast have always been fussy feeders.

## What happens?
When you try to feed your baby, she might suddenly cry, suck, pull off the breast, then keep crying or simply fidget and squirm and refuse to take the breast. You might find she refuses every feeding for twenty-four to forty-eight hours, then takes the breast again as if nothing has happened, or she might take some feedings well and refuse others. The on-again off-again feeding may go on for three weeks. Often the night and early morning feedings are fine, with each feeding during the day becoming more and more difficult. By evening everyone is very tense.

**161**

If this happens to you, you are bound to feel devastated, wonder what on earth you're doing wrong, and even lose confidence in yourself and your breastfeeding. Don't panic. Be aware that it is not your fault; it happens to lots of mothers; it is nearly always temporary; with the right advice and moral support, you can get through this dilemma and continue breastfeeding.

## WHY DOES IT HAPPEN?

Many reasons are suggested for breast refusal, and you may find one that applies to your situation, but most of the time I find a particular reason (that you can do something about) just can't be found.

Sometimes breast refusal happens because of the minipill (see Not Enough Milk, page 138, pregnancy, or menstruation. All of these things affect the hormone balance, which temporarily changes the taste of the milk and the amount of milk. If you are taking the minipill, the fussy feeding usually stops when your baby gets used to the taste and your supply improves. Some women do consider alternative contraception. Similarly, during pregnancy the fussiness is temporary and it is fine to continue breastfeeding when everyone is happy. If you menstruate while you are breastfeeding, you might find breast refusal occurs when a period is due and stops when it is over.

Not wanting to take the breast may be a sign your baby is not well. For example, a sore throat makes babies miserable and not happy to suck. Rare occasions crop up when refusing the breast is a sign of something more serious, so if your baby is floppy, pale, and not wetting her diapers please see your doctor right away. The let-down is often slower after the first three months, and your baby might get agitated and impatient waiting for the milk at some feedings. Babies adjust to this. Don't confuse breast refusal with a shorter sucking time or the age of distraction (three to five months). Breastfeeding is a body function, and the process becomes more and more efficient as time goes by. Your baby learns how to nurse very competently and your body responds, so the feedings become much shorter. You will find your baby continues to thrive beautifully. Try not to make her take the breast more often or for longer than she wants.

Three to five months is, as I've said, the age of distraction. Babies become fascinated with the world around them. Nursing is not as important as what goes on elsewhere. Even though they have days and days where it seems they don't nurse much, they continue to gain weight and look the picture of health. When this is happening, a quiet place at nursing time where there is nothing to look at helps.

## What can you do about nursing strike?

When the night feedings and early morning feedings are good, enjoy them. Your baby is almost certainly getting what she needs from these feedings. If you are worried about her health, have a medical checkup from someone you trust, so your mind is at rest.

Make sure there is enough milk if you suspect there may not be. Breast refusal is usually not related to not enough milk, but in this instance weighing and measuring your baby is the best way to be absolutely sure and to put your mind at rest. Extra rests for you, company from a calm person during the day, and a complete break from stressful situations helps.

### HERE'S A BASIC PLAN OF ACTION TO FOLLOW:

- Whenever your baby cries and refuses the breast, stop the feeding. Trying to make her take the breast makes things worse.

- Change tactics—go for a walk, hand her over to a calm person, or see if she will sleep.

- Whenever possible, pick your baby up and feed her when she is in a sleepy state.

- Avoid bottles and formula as much as possible. If your baby refuses the breast for twenty-four hours or if she is sick, you might need to use a bottle. Most times when breast refusal happens, extra fluids in bottles are not needed. Giving a bottle at this time may lead to weaning.

- Express for comfort and to keep the milk flowing if you need to.

Breast refusal is usually only temporary, lasting from two to three days to two to three weeks, but occasionally a baby cannot be per-suaded to return to the breast. The problem becomes permanent instead of temporary. This doesn't happen very often, but when it does, some of the pleasure of breastfeeding goes and weaning becomes an attractive alternative. It is important for you to have a nice time with your baby, so this is certainly reasonable in these circumstances.

## Juice, water, and vitamin drops

Your baby doesn't need daily water (even in hot weather), juice, vitamin supplements, or fluoride. Premature babies do need extra supplements for the first three to four months after birth as they do not arrive with stores of iron and vitamins.

Breastmilk contains all of the above apart from fluoride, which is not needed until the second year and only then if you live some-where where there is none in the water supply.

Some mothers do give their baby water in a bottle for a few rea-sons that have nothing to do with nutrition. Here they are—you may decide yourself if you think it's a helpful thing to do. When your baby is very unsettled and you've just done the twentieth feeding of the day, letting someone else give her some water in a bottle may give you a rest and break the unsettled cycle—if she'll drink it. Babies often won't drink water.

Regular drinks from a bottle might prevent potential difficulties caused by bottle refusal at a later date when it would be very useful for her to drink from a bottle.

# If you become ill

It's certainly no picnic when you are unwell and you have a baby or young children to look after. Mothers can rarely take sick leave.

When you are breastfeeding, the milk supply might be less than it is when you are well. Babies manage quite well when there is less milk for a while without anything alarming happening. Is your partner able to take time from work and/or go to your baby at night, change and settle her so that all you have to do is nurse her? When your partner is around or anyone else who can help, take your baby and go to bed. Your baby cannot catch coughs, colds, the flu, or a stomach bug through your breastmilk. Being breastfed protects her from these things to a large extent, especially gastroenteritis, but don't forget to wash your hands carefully before feedings and stick to all the rules of good hygiene.

Occasionally a medical condition arises and hospital admission is required. Make sure you tell your doctor you are breastfeeding as sometimes it's possible to take your baby with you. You may have to express or get help to express for a short time if you are not well enough to nurse so that someone else can feed your baby. If there is short-term use of problematic drugs, the milk can

**165**

be discarded until the drugs are out of your system and previously stored breastmilk or formula can be used for a while—there is no need to wean.

Staff in general hospitals are usually not familiar with breast-feeding, expressing, or the distress of weaning suddenly, especially when the mother doesn't want to, so ask someone to contact the nearest maternity unit, where there should be a nurse or a lactation consultant available who can help you and act as a spokesperson for you.

## Drugs and medications in breastmilk

It's wise not to take any unnecessary drug or medication while you are breastfeeding. This includes speed, cannabis, cocaine, methadone, and heroin (although in some countries women who use these drugs do continue to breastfeed under medical supervision). Alcohol is harmless in small quantities, but not in any great quantities, other than a small drink every so often. In relation to smoking please turn to page 140.

When it's necessary to take drugs for an illness or a medical condition, it's important to get the most appropriate drug and correct information about the possible effects on your baby. It's also important to take what you need in order to maintain your health or get better as quickly as possible. You also need to know if your baby will be temporarily upset, get diarrhea or be at risk of a yeast infection while you are taking the medication.

Drugs can cause problems either because they are harmful for the baby, or because they interfere with the body's ability to make milk.

It is now recognised that there are relatively few drugs that can't be taken while breastfeeding. Some drugs need to be monitored by checking the level in the milk, taking blood tests or watching carefully for changes in the baby's behaviour, for example sleepy behaviour, poor feeding, or screaming attacks. Unfortunately, many babies are weaned unnecessarily because the information available from pharmaceutical companies about drugs advises mothers not to take most drugs. This is base on legal considerations, not scientific knowledge. This means that women are sometimes not treated adequately or babies are removed from the breast unnecessarily. It's impossible in this book to provide detailed information on the risks and benefits of individual drugs. If you find yourself in doubt, the best people to check with are health professionals who use additional more accurate information than that supplied by the pharmaceutical companies, for example, breastfeeding-friendly pediatricians, La Leche League counsellors and lactation consultants. An excellent article on the topic can be found on http://www.askdrsears.com.

# Breastfeeding from one breast

When there is only one breast to feed from because of the removal of all or part of a breast, breastfeeding can still work well providing the remaining breast is normal. If you only have one breast to use, you may feel apprehensive about breastfeeding when you are doing it for the first time. Here are a few tips:

- Confidence is everything. Think about all the women who breastfeed twins. Encouragement from those around you and help when you need it from an interested breastfeeding adviser makes an incredible difference.

- Difficulties and problems that might arise when feeding on one breast are exactly the same as for women who feed from two breasts. The two most likely to worry you in the first four to six weeks are thinking you may not have enough milk and a sore nipple. The advice about these is the same whether you nurse with one breast or two.

# Feeding after implants or breast reduction surgery

Being able to fully or partially breastfeed after augmentation or breast reduction surgery varies a lot according to the way the surgery is performed, so it is best to decide to breastfeed and wait and see what happens. While an optimistic and positive approach is desirable, I am aware of the heartbreak involved when women are given completely unrealistic expectations by well-meaning breast-feeding enthusiasts. Some women do breastfeed well, but others only manage to breastfeed to a small extent. Nevertheless, they find the experience fulfilling, and not disappointing, as long as they haven't been led to hope for the impossible.

- Breast implants: As there is usually little disruption to the ducts or nerves in the nipple or breast, breastfeeding proceeds normally for many women who have had implants, but care needs to be taken to drain the breasts well, so let your baby have the breast frequently. Research suggests there may be problems related to breastfeeding after *silicone* implants. More research is needed to verify this. At this stage it seems wise to obtain further advice if you wish to breastfeed following breast implant surgery that involves the use of silicone implants.

- Breastfeeding following breast reduction surgery is also possible, and it never should be assumed that it won't work, but it is much harder to establish and maintain breastfeeding for any length of time. Most women who breastfeed following breast reduction surgery also use some formula. The formula can be given by bottle or a nursing supplementer (see page 144). When this is carefully done, breastfeeding can be maintained and often the use of formula stopped when food from a spoon is introduced.

# Jaundice and breastfeeding

(See Jaundice, page 196.)

# Phenylketonuria (PKU) and breastfeeding

Phenylketonuria is an inborn error of metabolism in which the baby cannot tolerate normal amounts of protein. The incidence of PKU in the US is approximately 1 in 15,000 births. Special milk and a diet supervised in a speciality metabolic clinic is essential, but it's important to know that breastfeeding can usually continue as well under supervision.

# Human Immunodeficiency Virus (HIV) and breastfeeding

Research around the world strongly suggests HIV, the virus that causes acquired immune deficiency syndrome (AIDS), is passed in breastmilk sometimes. It is still not clear why some babies are infected from breastfeeding and others aren't. Many women who are HIV positive breastfeed without infecting their babies; however, when formula feeding is a safe option, it is now considered wise for women who are HIV positive not to breastfeed. When formula feeding can't be done safely, it is best to breastfeed.

## Hepatitis B

Women who are Hepatitis B carriers may breastfeed safely once the baby has been immunised; immunisation is commenced straight after birth.

## Hepatitis C

There is currently no evidence that Hepatitis C is transmitted through breastmilk, and the Centers for Disease Control (CDC) recommends that women who are Hepatitis C carriers breastfeed, but that consideration be given to temporarily abstaining if the nipples are cracked and bleeding.

## Baby won't take a bottle

Many breastfed babies are understandably not keen on using bottles. Some babies obligingly drink from breast or bottle, which makes life easy, especially for times when mothers aren't there.

Others will drink some things from bottles and not others—for example, juice and not milk; expressed breastmilk but not formula, and so on.

A few make life interesting for their mothers by drinking from a bottle at some times but not at others and give no clue as to why or when they are likely to oblige or refuse. An appreciable number adamantly refuse a nipple and bottle no matter what's in it. Sometimes this happens even when the baby has been having regular bottles from a young age, so making an effort to head this off at the pass by giving a bottle a week from an early age doesn't work for everyone, but it can help.

Lots of women breastfeed and never use bottles. Bottles are not an essential part of baby feeding. Their main value is convenience, and the first thing to do is work out why you want your baby to take a bottle, then decide what your options are if she keeps refusing. Here are some reasons why you might want your baby to drink from a bottle:

- Pressure from those around you who tell you a few bottle feedings will make your baby sleep better at night (not a valid reason—it won't make any difference);

- A rest from the breast;

- Occasional times when you're not there (a night out, shopping, the dentist, and so on);

- Regular times when you're not there working, studying, and so on);

- You've gone back to work full-time;

- Early weaning because of breastfeeding difficulties or because it's your preferred option.

## What can you do when your baby refuses to drink from a bottle?

- Changing bottles, nipples, and brand of formula hardly ever makes any difference. When babies are ready to accept a bottle in general, any type of bottle or nipple and any brand of formula will be accepted. You might like to try a few different products, but it's not worth buying out the store.

- Try once a day, at the same time every day when your baby is hungry but not overtired and hysterical. Make sure it's several hours since her last breastfeed.

  Starting to give the bottle while she is half asleep might help.

- When possible, have someone other than you offer the bottle. Persist for as long as you or they can, even if it means trying on and off until the next feeding—if you succumb and give a breastfeed quickly, you are unlikely to get anywhere.

- Changing the position from the breastfeeding position helps. Try sitting your baby in a portable baby chair opposite you or feed her while you walk and talk to her.

## PAINFUL OPTIONS—THE LAST RESORT

If time is running out and it is essential that your baby uses a bottle, the only way left, unfortunately, is to not feed your baby until she is so hungry she takes a bottle. Naturally this is painful for you and your baby, but there are rare times when there is no other choice. Once your baby is happily taking a bottle it will be forgotten quickly—by her anyway! There are several ways of tackling this:

- As long as your baby is well and healthy try leaving her and the bottles with your babysitter. Obviously you need a skilled babysitter willing to give it a go. Grandmas are sometimes the answer. Fathers can also be invaluable for this as they are often more consistent and persistent so the baby responds.

- If this does not work, unfortunately the only other thing to do is to withhold the breast until she drinks from the bottle—this might take up to twenty-four hours and usually means weaning as giving some breast and some bottle simply won't work.

- If you do this at home please have someone with you for moral support and practical help. It is advisable to give your baby some fluid during the process, either from a cup, spoon, or dropper or go back to the occasional breastfeed if you have to.

## AVOIDING THE PAINFUL OPTIONS

When you are faced with this dilemma, it's a good idea to reassess things and work out how essential it is that your baby uses a bottle. A rest from the breast, occasional absences, and regular times when you're not there can be managed by using a cup, teaspoon, or dropper and letting your baby wait until you come home. Healthy breastfed babies can wait five to six hours for a feeding. You are likely to find your baby is not looking for a feeding nearly as often when you're not around. Alternatively, when your baby is very young, you might decide to take her with you.

Trying to make a well-fed, healthy, breastfed baby drink from a bottle when she doesn't want to so that she'll sleep better at night is a pointless, stressful exercise that will make no difference to her sleeping patterns, so ignore suggestions like this. Once your baby is old enough to eat food from a spoon, breastfeedings can be replaced with food and a cup. A breastfed baby never needs to be forced to use a bottle after five or six months of age unless there's some sort of unavoidable emergency (rare) or for nutritional requirements because the milk supply is very low and the baby refuses food and a cup.

## FOR MORE INFORMATION

Chapter 10: Early Worries and Questions *(heat rash, hormone rash, and so on, page 187, poo variations, page 213, vomiting, page 216, Infant Newborn Screening Test, page 198)*

Chapter 13: Growth and Development *(rooting reflex, page 296, hands in mouth, page 301)*

Chapter 9: Bottle Feeding Your Baby After the First Two Weeks, page *175*

Chapter 14: Sleeping and Waking in the First Six Months *(unsettled period, page 315)*

Chapter 15: The Crying Baby *(normal crying patterns, page 332)*

Chapter 16: For Parents *(contraception and the minipill, page 402)*

Chapter 18: Feeding Your Baby *(starting new food, page 425)* chapter **nine**

# Bottle Feeding Your Baby After the First Two Weeks

## *Weaning*

Weaning means stopping breastfeeding or expressing breastmilk into a bottle, and using other food and/or fluid instead. Infant formula is the best and safest substitute for breastmilk when babies are under nine months of age.

### Early weaning

Weaning is often accompanied by feelings that you may find are unexpected. There is a sense of loss and guilt. You may feel sad and depressed. Feelings like this are more intense in the first three months after birth. Unfortunately, many women who change from breastfeeding to formula are often made to feel they have to justify their decision to family and friends.

If your decision to wean is easy and a relief, these feelings

**175**

usually don't last long—it is perfectly normal to have a good cry.

If the decision to wean is difficult or your breastfeeding doesn't work out because of factors you feel were outside your control, the emotional aspects are greater and last longer. Don't dismiss them with "it doesn't really matter" or "I'll get over it." Crying helps and it is essential to talk things over with your partner or a sympathetic health professional.

## How to wean

Weaning is often referred to as "drying up the milk." This is an inaccurate term as it implies weaning means a complete absence of milk. In fact, many women find they can still express some milk months after they finish breastfeeding. What you are aiming for when weaning is not an absence of milk but avoiding hard, painful breasts, which may lead to mastitis.

The time it takes to do this varies from woman to woman. If lactation is not well established, weaning may only take a few days; if it is abundant, it's a good idea to plan on four to five weeks. Gradual weaning is the most comfortable way to wean for most women, both physically and psychologically. It also gives you a chance to think about things and perhaps combine bottle and breastfeeding rather than completely weaning (see page 160).

Start by missing one breastfeed, and replacing it with formula. When you do this, you will notice your breasts become quite tender. Continue to breastfeed as usual for the other feedings. When your breasts feel comfortable again, drop another feeding. See the table for a guide to when to substitute the bottle for breastfeeding. The feeding times on the guide are only approximate. Nurse at the times you normally do. Go to each stage when your breasts are comfortable. As your milk diminishes, you will need formula top-ups for some of the breastfeedings (a top-up is approximately 2–4 oz of formula offered after the breastfeed). Medication is not used to help the weaning process any longer as there are health risks associated with its use.

## Weaning straight after birth

Some women decide not to breastfeed at all. Resulting levels of discomfort and breast inflammation vary a lot from woman to woman. Engorgement and pain can be helped by oral analgesics and cold compresses or cabbage leaves placed on the breasts.

The use of cabbage leaves is somewhat controversial as there is no reliable research supporting their beneficial effects or any scientific explanation as to how they work. However, there is plenty of anecdotal evidence that the use of cold cabbage leaves reduces inflammation and pain. Cabbage leaves also reduce the milk supply, so care has to be taken if they are used for engorgement or oversupply not related to weaning.

### USING CABBAGE LEAVES

Thoroughly washed and dried cold cabbage leaves are applied to the breast and held in place with a bra. Fan the leaves around your breast avoiding any contact with the nipples. Change leaves frequently when they become limp and warm. When using cabbage leaves for weaning, continue using them for as long as they are needed for breast comfort. Obviously, do not use cabbage leaves if you think you may be allergic to cabbages or if the idea is distasteful. Stop using them immediately if you develop a rash or itchy skin.

## Sudden weaning after a period of breastfeeding

It is not always possible to wean gradually for a few different reasons. When stopping breastfeeding quickly, you may experience full, hot, painful breasts unless your milk supply is low or not well established.

## MANAGING SUDDEN WEANING

- Wear a well-fitting firm (not tight) bra day and night.

- Take analgesics (such as acetaminophen) when you need to.

- Apply cold compresses or cabbage leaves.

- Gently hand express three times a day for four to five days, twice a day for two to three days, then once a day if you need to. Whenever possible, hand express under a warm shower. You do not need to express much milk—the expressing is for comfort only.

- An intensely painful breast accompanied by illness and fever is a sign of an infection. See your family doctor as soon as possible.

Once your baby is having formula for all her feedings, you may have lumpy breasts for some time. As long as they are not painful or seem unusual, ignore them.

| TIME | STAGE 1 | STAGE 2 | STAGE 3 | STAGE 4 | STAGE 5 | STAGE 6 |
|------|---------|---------|---------|---------|---------|---------|
| 6 am | breastfeed | breastfeed | breastfeed | breastfeed | breastfeed | |
| | | | (+ top-up) | (+ top-up) | (+ top-up) | W |
| 10 am | breastfeed | BOTTLE | BOTTLE | BOTTLE | BOTTLE | |
| | | | | | | E |
| 2 pm | breastfeed | breastfeed | breastfeed | BOTTLE | BOTTLE | |
| | | | (+ top-up) | | | A |
| 6 pm | BOTTLE | BOTTLE | BOTTLE | BOTTLE | BOTTLE | N |
| 10 pm | breastfeed | breastfeed | breastfeed | BOTTLE | BOTTLE | |
| | | | (+ top-up) | | | E |
| 2 am | breastfeed | breastfeed | BOTTLE | breastfeed | BOTTLE | D |
| | | | | (+ top-up) | | |

Your hormones may take some time to return to normal. Some women begin to ovulate as soon as they wean, others find the return of ovulation and menstruation is delayed by several months. If you are taking the minipill (progesterone only), you should be aware that the chances of conceiving increase as the breastfeeding decreases, so it's advisable to use alternative contraception if you wish to avoid pregnancy. It is safe to start the combined pill (estrogen and progesterone) while your baby is still having some breastfeedings. The combined pill also helps diminish the breastmilk.

The decision to wean is yours. Try not to let anyone pressure you either way. If breastfeeding is important to you, try every avenue before you start weaning. The correct advice at a sensitive time can make the world of difference. Avoid hasty decisions. A nutritional emergency in a healthy baby that requires sudden change is very rare.

# Feeding patterns

As your baby grows, the amount of milk taken at each feeding increases and the number of bottles gets less. (See the chart on page 121.)

When your baby is emptying all her bottles, go to the next recommended amount. Remember there is a range of variation on amount of milk and number of feedings at any age. Giving your baby what she wants, when she wants it, works well most of the time but occasionally small problems arise that need a slightly different approach.

## Babies who drink too much

A number of babies seem perpetually hungry, rapidly increasing the amount they drink until they are having a lot more than what is recommended for their age and weight.

You might find that she drinks a lot between three and eight weeks of age, then the amount she drinks gets less and she doesn't seem as hungry. Alternatively, she might continue to want endless 8 ounce bottles without any sign of slowing down. What can you do?

- Check that you are making up the feedings correctly. If the formula mixture is too strong, your baby might be thirsty, not hungry. If the mixture is too weak, your baby is needing extra because she is hungry.

- Is your baby really hungry? Babies who don't sleep much want to suck a lot for comfort, not food. Settling techniques, instead of constant bottles, can help to cut down excessive feeding. Don't forget, crying, and sleeping difficulties in a baby are usually separate issues from feeding, whether the baby is breastfed or bottle fed.

- Sometimes starting food from a spoon at three months means less volume of milk and a happier baby.

## Babies who drink too little

Some babies are small eaters who are invariably healthy and developing normally but exist quite happily on half the recommended amount for their age and weight.

If your baby is like this, you are probably finding that once her immediate appetite is satisfied, she loses interest and starts to cry when you try to keep giving her the bottle. She may have been like this from birth or has gradually become more fussy as time goes by. When you're a mother, you can have a deep emotional investment in feeding your baby. If your baby fusses and doesn't drink what she's "supposed" to drink, it's very easy to start thinking it's your fault and feel anxious, guilty, and even angry. It's normal to feel like this, but unfortunately it adds to feeding-time stress. As well, you may be contending with people around you urging you to make her drink more, which doesn't help. What can you do?

- Check that the hole in the nipple is not too small.

- Check you are preparing the formula correctly.

- Look at your baby. Is she bright-eyed, alert, and vigorous? Is she having six to eight pale, wet diapers a day and having a good poo every so often? If so:
  a) Take it easy—accept that she is a fussy eater. You cannot make your baby drink when she doesn't want to.
  b) Try to have relaxed feedings. When she starts to cry and refuses the bottle, stop the feed, don't keep trying to make her drink when she is upset.
  c) Offer her the bottle three- to four-hourly as often as you can rather than little snacks every hour or so. Waiting until she's really hungry means she'll drink more.
  d) When you can, feed her when she is sleepy.
  e) Avoid endlessly changing the formula, the bottles, and the nipples. Whenever you make a change, you will notice that for a day or two things seem to improve, then go back to how they were. This tends to increase everyone's anxiety and makes things worse.

Babies who drink less may put on less weight. This is not a problem for your baby as long as she is well and keeps gaining around a pound a month. If she has no weight gain for a month or so or loses weight, a visit to a pediatrician is a good idea.

Starting food from a spoon early (around three months) usually doesn't make a lot of difference, as fussy drinkers are often fussy eaters, so you end up with double trouble. Occasionally a fussy drinker loves food from a spoon, which is a great relief for everyone because the amount she eats from a spoon makes up for what doesn't go down by bottle. If you try food from a spoon, make sure you give the bottle first, as one or two little mouthfuls of food may mean she drinks less from her bottle than usual.

# *Hard poo*

Generally babies who are having formula produce poo that is something like modeling clay or play dough in texture and is a khaki sort of color, but there are a few variations on the theme, so don't worry if your baby's poo doesn't quite fit this description. These babies tend to go only once every day or two.

Constipation is not *how often* your baby goes but what it's like when she does go. If her poo is hard and dry like a rock or small pebbles, it means she is constipated. Some babies having formula do get constipated for a while until their bodies adjust.

Some babies having formula do get constipated for a short time until their bodies adjust.

When your baby is having formula, it is nice to see a poo every day or so, as that's a way of keeping check of what's going on. If she hasn't been for several days or if she does a hard, dry rock, action needs to be taken. This occasionally happens in the early weeks if she has been having formula since birth. Because all formula varies slightly some babies may become constipated on one brand and not on another. In general, liquid formula (ready-to-use, ready-to-pour) is less likely to cause constipation than powder formula. This does not mean, however, that you have to use liquid formula, as constipation is not a problem for the majority of babies having powder formula. But if constipation becomes problematic changing to a liquid formula temporarily can help.

## What do you do?

- Remember modeling clay or play dough poo is normal—no need to do anything.

- Make sure you are making up the formula correctly. Formula that is too strong causes constipation—don't forget, water first then add the powder.

- First, try offering your baby extra drinks of cooled, boiled water a couple of times a day. This might help if she will drink it.

- Here is a plan for you to follow if extra water doesn't help:
  a) Put one small teaspoon of sugar into every bottle of formula until your baby does a good poo. When she poos, stop the sugar. Stop the sugar anyway after twenty-four hours—she will probably do a poo soon after the last bottle in the twenty-four-hour period. A little sugar is a good way to stimulate her bowel and get things moving and far better than resorting to medications and suppositories.
  b) After the sugar regime, give a little diluted prune juice every day for a while until your baby is pooing well.
  c) Prune juice is a fruit juice made from dried plums that has an ingredient that stimulates the bowel. It is available in the supermarket or alternatively you can make your own by gently boiling about twelve prunes in 1¼ cup of water; don't add sugar. When the mixture is a nice dark brown, strain off the water. Dilute it half and half with cooled, boiled water—try one ounce of prune juice with one ounce of water. This may be strengthened or weakened, or you may give more or less according to what you think your baby needs.

- Occasionally before you know it, a crisis situation happens and your baby is so distressed, immediate action is needed. If this

**183**

happens, it is necessary to give an infant suppository to bring quick relief. After the event, start one of the regimes suggested here or see your family doctor or early nurse practitioner for advice.

# Sudden bottle strike

If your baby suddenly refuses her bottle it might be a sign she is not well, especially when it is accompanied by floppiness, fever, diarrhoea or sudden unusual vomiting. Even when none of these symptoms are present see your family doctor to rule out a sore throat or an ear infection.

# Changing the formula

Formula is constantly changed, often at the advice of health professionals, but changing formula will rarely change your baby's health or behavior—it simply gives you something else to think about for a day or two. Changing the type of formula once may sometimes be warranted in special circumstances where there are clear indications for doing so (cow's milk-based to soy-based or low lactose, and so on) but constantly swapping *brands* is pointless apart from a cost advantage.

# Juice, water, and vitamin supplements

Full-term babies having formula need none of the above unless constipation is a problem. Formula contains adequate amounts of all nutrients including water. Premature babies are given supplements for the first three to four months after birth to make up for their lack of stored vitamins and iron.

## FOR MORE INFORMATION

Chapter 8: Breastfeeding Your Baby After the First Two Weeks *(hand expressing, page 126, mastitis, page 152)*

Chapter 16: For Parents *(contraception, page 402)*

Chapter 14: Sleeping and Waking in the First Six Months *("growth spurts" or the six weeks change, page 322, the unsettled period, page 315, options for settling, page 316)*

Chapter 18: Feeding Your Baby *(starting new food, page 425)*

# chapter ten

# Early Worries and Questions

*I could still remember how having a two-day-old baby makes you feel faintly sorry for everyone else, stuck in their wan unmiraculous lives.*

Marni Jackson, *The Mother Zone, Love, Sex and Laundry in the Modern Family*

Small things cause anxious moments for parents in the early weeks after birth. Most of these things are normal and have a simple explanation—or are easy to treat if treatment is needed. If you are ever unsure of what is happening, ask for help from your early practitioner nurse or family doctor.

## Baby skin

Babies rarely have a flawless complexion in the first three months, so don't be alarmed when your baby breaks out in a variety of rashes and blotches. Strange rashes and dry skin during this time are usually due to your baby's body adjusting to her new world and to hormones that are passed from you to your baby just before birth. They are unlikely to be caused by allergies, breastmilk or formula, your diet, or in fact anything you are doing.

## Dry skin

Most newborn babies have patches of dry, flaky skin ranging from barely noticeable to what looks like a shedding of the whole outside layer of skin. Dry skin on young babies is not a dry skin condition—it is the layer of skin that came in contact with the fluid inside the womb. A moisturizer helps the appearance of the skin, but eventually the flakiness disappears whether you use a moisturizer or not.

Peeling skin is common in the groin of newborn babies. It won't worry your baby at all, so don't confuse it with diaper rash. Peeling skin in the groin doesn't need treating, but if you would like to smooth on a soft cream until it goes, that's fine.

## Newborn rash

The newborn rash appears soon after birth and is a blotchy red rash that is all over the baby's body. Some of the blotches have a white spot in their center. The newborn rash is caused by things being next to your baby's skin that she is not used to such as clothes, undershirts, and diapers. It comes and goes and is more obvious when your baby cries. The blotches won't worry your baby and disappear quickly, so no treatment is necessary.

## Heat rash

Heat rash refers to those tiny red dots that are mostly over your baby's head and neck, but you may notice it anywhere on her body, especially where two lots of skin come in contact. The tiny red dots often join up to form red splotches. Heat rash is common in babies and toddlers up to the age of three, especially when the

**187**

weather gets hot; however, it appears in most newborns regardless of the weather while their bodies adjust to the relatively hot, humid environment after life in the temperature-controlled womb. As your baby's body sweats less and her skin gets used to having sweat on it, the rash fades. Overdressing sometimes contributes, but many babies of this age get heat rash no matter how they are dressed or what the weather is like. It does not cause itchiness or distress in young babies and does not need treating.

## Sweating

It is normal for babies to be sweaty little people. Their bodies overcompensate for their new environment, so you are likely to notice your baby's head gets very damp while she is feeding and that the sheet in her bed is quite damp at times when you pick her up. Sweaty heads and bodies are common up until three years of age.

## Hormone rash

Hormone rash is the rash commonly known as the "milk rash," which is unfortunate as the rash has nothing to do with your baby's diet. The exact cause is unknown but thought to be due to the high levels of hormones passed from mother to baby during labor, stimulating the oil-producing glands (the sebaceous glands) and causing pimples. Your baby's skin may feel crusty and there may be crust on her eyebrows, head, and ears.

Hormone rash and heat rash are usually around at the same time all mixed up together, and the combined effect can be a bit alarming when there's a lot of both. Unless it's very severe, which is unusual, it needs no treatment as it won't bother your baby at all—she's too young to look in the mirror! The rash disappears like magic at around three months, leaving behind the fine, clear baby skin you see in advertisements in magazines or on TV.

Neither of these rashes has anything to do with your baby's crying and sleeping patterns.

## Cradle cap

Cradle cap refers to the formation of crusts on the scalp, eyebrows, and behind the ears. The exact cause is unknown, but cradle cap is an oily skin problem, not a dry skin problem. The underlying cause can't be treated, so treatment of cradle cap involves softening the crusts as they form so that they can be painlessly removed. Crusts can persist on the scalp well into early childhood for some children, but for the majority of babies it stops happening between six and eight months, and often before.

Suggestions for softening and removing the crust are many and varied. Here are the ones I find easiest to use and most effective:

- For eyebrows and/or behind ears, try frequent applications of sa moisturising cream such as Moisture Therapeutic cream. When you're at home, massage a little into your baby's eyebrows and behind her ears every time you change her diaper so it becomes part of your routine. At bath time, wipe her eyebrows and ears gently with a cloth to remove the softened crust.

- For a crusty scalp, try petroleum jelly. This is very effective for babies who don't have much hair but trickier for those with a lot of hair. Massage some petroleum jelly into your baby's scalp before bed, leave in overnight, and wash out with soap the next day at bath time, removing any crusts that are soft enough to remove easily. You have to remove the crusts—they don't just float out. After the bath, brush your baby's head with a soft brush.

Make sure you massage the petroleum jelly into your baby's scalp, not her hair, and don't use too much or there'll be a terrible mess!

Cradle cap is a nuisance because it can't be prevented and time is the only cure. If it is mild and you don't mind the look of it, you needn't do anything—it is harmless. If a lot of crusts are building up, softening them and removing them regularly prevents a build-up, which looks unsightly and can get quite smelly.

## Bright red rash around the anus

Most breastfed newborns poo a lot, especially in the first six weeks. Lots of poo is quite normal, but you might find your baby gets a bright red rash around her anus. Occasionally there may even be a little bleeding. It is unlikely this rash will bother your baby, and once she stops pooing so much (around six weeks), the rash goes away. Until this happens, a good barrier cream helps protect the skin. Put a generous amount on the anal area at every diaper change.

## Baby impetigo

Occasionally newborn babies develop blisters or pimples filled with thin pus—usually on the lower part of the abdomen under the navel and/or in the diaper area. They burst and leave a raw area. The blisters and pimples are caused by a staphylococcus infection and spread if they're not treated, so see your family doctor. In the early stages they can sometimes be treated successfully by applying povidone-iodine (Betadine) or an antibiotic ointment, but often oral antibiotics are needed.

## Tiny movable lumps

Tiny, movable lumps are sometimes felt under the skin anywhere on a baby's body, including the head. They are harmless and are likely to be either a small sebaceous cyst or a lump caused by burst fat cells. Neither needs treating.

# Diaper rash

Diaper rashes don't happen because mothers do the wrong thing, although I'm sure many are made to feel this way when they ask for help to treat a rash.

*What sort of diapers do you use? How often do you change her diaper?* are all questions you're likely to become familiar with in the next year. Advice to stop using plastic pants or to leave your baby out of diapers for long stretches of the day and night is impractical and unnecessary and usually offered by "experts" who have never looked after babies for any length of time.

## WHAT IS DIAPER RASH?

Diaper rash is a general term that refers to the variety of red, blotchy, and sometimes spotty skin conditions babies get in the diaper area. Diaper rash may appear on the genitals, around the anus, on the buttocks, on the lower part of the tummy that is covered by the diaper, in the groins, and on the thighs. Sometimes the whole diaper area is affected and sometimes the rash may only appear on one of the above areas.

## WHAT CAUSES DIAPER RASH?

The combination of wetness, friction, and heat that is generated inside a baby's diaper makes the risk of a diaper rash ever present. The chafing and sogginess damage the protective layer of skin causing an area of rough, red, hot blotchiness. Once the skin becomes damaged, it often becomes infected. The most common infection in the diaper area is *Candida albicans*, which is a yeast. Most diaper rashes have a yeast infection as well as the original rash within seventy hours if the treatment to remedy the red bottom is not successful.

Diaper rash can also be caused by medication, viral diarrhea or occasionally when a new food is introduced into the baby's

**191**

diet. Sometimes rashes are caused by creams, washing powders, or disposable diaper liners.

No miracle cream or powder exists that prevents or cures all rashes. Frequent diaper changing helps avoid red bottoms, but some babies are prone to diaper rash no matter how often the diaper is changed and will not be free of diaper rash until they are out of diapers.

Claims are made by disposable diaper manufacturers, and supported by some dermatologists, that disposable diapers have a place in preventing and treating persistent diaper rash. Good-quality disposable diapers use modern materials that keep the skin dry, and as they are thinner than cloth diapers, they are less likely to result in overheating. However, I cannot say that in my work I notice any great difference between the incidence of diaper rash whether cloth or disposable diapers are used. Successful treatment of diaper rash is most likely when a correct diagnosis of the rash is made. So if your baby's bottom doesn't respond quickly to simple measures, it's a good idea to seek help from a nurse or doctor before buying out the drugstore.

## SOME GENERAL DIAPER RASH TIPS

Frequent diaper changing helps avoid prolonged skin contact with urine and poo and so minimizes wetness, friction, and overheating.

- Washing of the skin in the diaper area at every change to keep the skin scrupulously clean increases wetness, is irritating to the baby's skin, and wipes away the natural protective secretions. If you are not treating a diaper rash, routine use of a moisturizer to both clean and keep the skin supple is recommended. Use with a tissue to clean up after a wet or pooey diaper.

- If your baby has a rash and you are using a prescribed medicated cream, discard all other powders, moisturizers, or creams. When your baby is just wet, pat dry with tissue. If she does a poo, clean using a damp tissue, then pat dry. Use only the medicated creams for seven to ten days, or until the rash is gone. If the rash does not improve markedly in three days then let your nurse or doctor know.

- Pre-moistened baby wipes are convenient to use when you are out and about, but avoid them if your baby develops a diaper rash until the rash is better. Always pat the skin dry after using baby wipes as they leave the skin very wet, causing extra friction.

### DIAPER RASH IN THE FIRST THREE MONTHS

Diaper rashes in the first three months mostly cure themselves or respond to simple treatment. Newborn babies often have a heat rash in the diaper area and on the lower part of their tummy that is covered by the diaper. This usually clears quickly of its own accord. Cornflour or zinc and starch powder helps. When using powder, put some in a small plate, then apply with your fingertips rather than shaking it out of the container—your baby might inhale the powder.

Many red bottoms respond well to one of the barrier, healing creams available. When one of these preparations doesn't work, it often means a fungal infection is present and needs an anti-fungal cream to clear it up. When you use medicated creams, make sure there is no other cream or powder on the surface of the skin, as this stops the medicated cream from working.

## Red patches

Red patches are often present on babies' eyelids, between their eyes, on the bridge of the nose, or on the forehead and on the nape of their neck. Occasionally they are also on the nose or top lip. The official name for red patches is storkbeak marks, and they are caused by collections of tiny blood vessels, highly visible underneath babies' fine skin, which is half the thickness of adult skin.

Storkbeak marks fade slowly, taking up to a year to finally disappear, and are always much more visible when your baby cries.

## Birthmarks

Birthmarks come in a variety of colors and shapes. The common ones are listed below. Unusual birthmarks need a trip to a skin specialist to have a name put to them and to discuss the likely outcome.

### MOLES

Moles are brown marks, come in a variety of shapes and sizes, and often don't appear until the baby is six weeks old. Some are coffee-colored and look as if they are painted on; others are dark brown, some are raised, and sometimes they are hairy. Moles may be anywhere on the body and they are permanent.

### STRAWBERRY MARKS

Strawberry marks are very common and are caused by red blood cells escaping from the blood vessels. Strawberry marks are not present at birth but appear sometime in the first six weeks. They are bright red, soft swellings with often a blue appearance around the edges of the larger ones. After they first appear, they have a period of growth until the baby is about nine months old, then they just sit there until sometime late in the second year when they begin to disappear. Most strawberry marks completely disappear by three years of age. Strawberry marks surface anywhere on the body—sometimes in the most unlikely places like inside the mouth, eye, or on the genitals.

## MONGOLIAN SPOTS

Mongolian spots are caused by accumulations of pigment under the skin and look like bruises. Mongolian spots are harmless and found on the skin of babies who have olive or dark skin. They are present at birth but occasionally appear as late as three months. They fade during the first three years.

## Milia

Small whiteheads often found on babies' noses at birth are called milia. They are caused by blocked sebaceous glands and are usually gone by four to six weeks. Don't squeeze them!

## Blue patches and veins under the skin

Your baby's skin is very thin, so this makes the veins under the skin very easy to see. You may notice a blue vein across the bridge of her nose and small blue patches on her body. Fine baby skin is also the reason for the blue tinge around her mouth where there is an abundant blood supply and has nothing to do with gas—goodness knows where that piece of folklore came from. It's time health professionals stopped perpetuating the myth.

## Blue baby hands and feet

Blue hands and feet are nothing to worry about as long as your baby is otherwise well. Tiny extremities often feel cold even in a warm atmosphere and are due to an immaturity in your baby's circulation. You will find her hands and feet quickly turn pink again when she wakes up, cries, and moves around. Baby hands and feet are often very sweaty because the large numbers of sweat glands on the skin surface of the hands and feet are all overreacting to the new environment.

## Mottled skin

Mottled skin with a blue hue is quite normal and due to immature circulation of the blood. Premature babies frequently have very noticeably mottled skin.

## Hairy bodies

You may be astonished at the fine fuzz of hair on your baby's body, found mostly across her shoulders, on top of her arms, and on her back. Hairy ears are also common. Called lanugo, this hair grows while your baby is in the womb and usually disappears in the first four to six weeks after birth.

## Jaundice (yellow skin)

Jaundice means that your baby's skin and whites of her eyes look yellow. In most cases, jaundice in newborn babies is different from the jaundice children and adults get, which is usually related to illness.

A newborn baby is born with an overload of red blood cells that she needs while she is in the womb but doesn't need once she is born, so her liver starts working immediately to break down the red blood cells and excrete the leftover product, which is called bilirubin. Bilirubin is one of the breakdown products of blood and is normally processed in the liver, then eliminated from the body in the bowel motions and urine. For some time after birth, a baby's liver doesn't work as well as later, so the bilirubin builds up inside the baby's body and causes the yellow color on the skin and eyes.

In most babies jaundice is not harmful and the color fades by the end of the first week. Occasionally, however, the amount of bilirubin gets very high and the baby needs special treatment. As high levels are dangerous, care is taken to make sure the bilirubin levels are within a safe range. Bilirubin levels are checked by placing a special device on her skin, or, if a more accurate check is needed, by a blood test. Jaundice can be made to fade more quickly by placing the baby naked under a shining bright light with her eyes protected. The light breaks down the bilirubin in the skin and takes the load off the liver.

Some jaundiced babies who are breastfed remain a pale yellow for many weeks (up to twelve weeks sometimes). This sort of jaundice is harmless and *there is no need to stop breastfeeding*. Women are put through needless stress and inconvenience when they are told to take the baby off the breast for forty-eight hours and give formula. Ask for a second opinion if you don't want to do this, as the only reason to stop breastfeeding for forty-eight hours is to reassure the parents and the doctor that the jaundice is in fact breastfeeding jaundice and nothing more serious.

On rare occasions the jaundice is caused by something more serious such as an infection, a blood disorder, or a liver problem in which case the baby is cared for by a pediatrician. Again, breastfeeding can continue either from the breast or by giving expressed milk by tube, dropper, syringe, or bottle.

# Vitamin K

Vitamin K is offered routinely to all newborn babies to prevent a rare but potentially fatal bleeding disorder in the first six months. Vitamin K is best given by a single injection soon after birth.

# Infant newborn screening

## SPhenylketonuria (PKU) and breastfeeding

Phenylketonuria is an inborn error of metabolism in which the baby cannot tolerate normal amounts of protein. The incidence of PKU in the US is approximately 1 in 15,000 births. Special milk and a diet supervised in a speciality metabolic clinic is essential, but it's important to know that breastfeeding can usually continue as well under supervision.

## Hepatitis C

There is currently no evidence that Hepatitis C is transmitted through breastmilk, and the Centers for Disease Control (CDC) recommends that women who are Hepatitis C carriers breastfeed, but that consideration be given to temporarily abstaining if the nipples are cracked and bleeding.

Some babies having formula do get constipated for a short time until their bodies adjust.

When your baby is having formula, it is nice to see a poo every day or so as that's a way of keeping check of what's going on. If she hasn't been for several days or if she does a hard, dry rock action needs to be taken. This occasionally happens in the early weeks if she has been having formula since birth. Because all formula varies slightly, some babies may become constipated on one brand and not on another. In general liquid formula (ready-to-use, ready-to-pour) is less likely to cause constipation than powder formula. This does not mean, however, that you have to use liquid formula, as constipation is not a problem for the majority of babies having powder formula. But if constipation becomes problematic, changing to a liquid formula temporarily can help.

## Infant Newborn Screening

There is a range of rare medical disorders in babies that can be identified early by taking a sample of blood from the baby shortly after birth via a heel prick. Diagnosing these disorders soon after birth before symptoms develop allows for early treatment, and gives babies the chance to grow and develop normally or, in cases where there is no cure for the disease, to greatly improve their quality of life by starting treatment early. Mandatory testing for Phenylketonuria, Congenital Hypothyroidism and Galactosemia is a requirement in all states. Mandatory testing for other disorders varies from state to state. Apart from state mandatory screening, tests are also available for a wide range of additional disorders. Please ask your pediatrician or family doctor for more information about US National Screening and what is appropriate for your baby, as some tests are relevant only for selected groups. It must be emphasised that very few babies test positive, but identifying these disorders early in life is an important preventative measure.

# Heads

Your baby's head is about a quarter of her total length, so you will probably think it looks enormous in proportion to the rest of her body. The bones of her head are not joined together firmly at birth, so her head can shape or mold to fit through the birth canal during labor. This means babies who are born the usual way (head-first through the vagina) often have odd-shaped heads for a while—especially noticeable when there's no hair!

Babies who are born by cesarean section or who come bottom-first usually have more rounded heads.

Sometimes babies' heads have swollen areas caused by pressure from labor. When it is just the skin involved, it is called a caput. Swelling caused by a caput disappears in a few days. If the bone also becomes swollen, it is called a cephalhematoma and takes longer to disappear. About twenty percent of cephalhematomas take up to twelve months to disappear—this is nothing to worry about and again is much more noticeable on bald-headed babies.

Your baby's head has two spaces where the bone is missing, called fontanelles. The fontanelle at the back of the head closes quickly and is often not noticed by parents. The fontanelle at the front of the head is diamond-shaped and fairly visible in most babies, so parents are aware of its existence and are sometimes nervous about touching it or washing their baby's head. You won't hurt your baby by touching the soft spot or by washing her head as the space in the bone is covered by very tough material. The size of the fontanelle varies tremendously from baby to baby and can close any time from three to eighteen months. It is quite normal to see the fontanelle pulsating and, at times, sunken. A sunken fontanelle is not a sign of impending illness in a healthy baby unless there are other signs and symptoms that something is wrong.

The joints in your baby's head are movable to allow her head to adjust to the birth canal during delivery. This is called molding and is the reason why babies' heads are bumpy and sometimes a funny shape. Strange shapes usually right themselves during the first few months.

## Lopsided heads

Many babies' heads grow in what appears to be a lopsided way. Head shape is a common concern for many parents, particularly as the incidence of flatness at the back of babies' heads appears to have increased with the practice of placing babies on their backs to sleep as recommended to reduce the risks of Sudden Infant Death Syndrome.

Here is some basic information, but I must emphasize that if you are concerned about the shape of your baby's head, please see your pediatrician or family doctor, who will advise you if you need to see a specialist doctor. It sometimes takes an expert to differentiate between the causes of lopsided heads. The vast majority of asymmetrical or flat heads either need no attention or simple changes as to how the baby sleeps or is held.

There are four main reasons why babies' heads look lopsided. Occasionally the flattening or asymmetry will be a combination of one or two of the following:

- The joints of your baby's head are movable to allow her head to pass through the birth canal during birth. This is called molding and is the reason why newborn heads can look lumpy and bumpy and have a funny shape. Strange shapes due to molding usually right themselves during the first few months.

- Some heads are lopsided because the bones of the skull are soft, and when babies sleep continually on their backs, the part of their head they sleep on flattens. To be certain that the back of the head doesn't flatten too much, turn your baby's head to the right for some sleeps and to the left for others as often as you can, until she is old enough to move around and change the position herself.

- The joints of the skull (called suture lines) gradually join and become fixed by around six months of age but are not solidly fused until late in childhood. When one of the suture lines joins more quickly than the others do, the head looks asymmetrical (lopsided). The flattening that occurs due to this process is most common on the right side of the back of the head. Most of these asymmetrical heads improve by themselves. A very small number may need surgery to correct the shape or to allow for proper brain growth.

- Sometimes the head looks lopsided because the baby holds her head constantly to one side while looking to the other (see below).

# Holding head to one side

Parents are often aware that their baby constantly holds her head to one side while always looking to the other, especially noticeable around three months when the baby has good head control. This is called torticollis and varies from a mild degree of asymmetry, which is common, to a severe degree, which is not nearly so common. In the past, surgery was often performed in late childhood to correct torticollis because the significance of a baby constantly holding her head to one side was not understood. Nowadays a severe degree of torticollis is almost always fully correctable with early diagnosis followed by exercises and muscle stretches under supervision of a physiotherapist.

The exact cause for torticollis is unknown but is thought to be a combination of the position of the baby in the womb, some damage to the neck muscle during birth, and a lack of blood supply to a small part of the neck muscle pre-birth.

### MILD DEGREE

Opinions vary as to whether any treatment is needed, but a visit to a pediatric physiotherapist is useful to assess the movement of your baby's neck and to get some information on a few simple exercises and things to do to encourage your baby to hold her head to the other side and look the other way.

### SEVERE DEGREE

A severe degree may be caused either because the baby has a very tight muscle in her neck or because a lump is present in the muscle. The lump is called a "sternomastoid tumor" and is usually not present at birth but appears some time later. It gets bigger for a while, then disappears at about six months. Physiotherapy treatment is the same for both and consists of exercises and muscle stretches as well as advice about the best ways to carry and lie your baby to enhance the benefit of the stretching exercises.

# Hair

Your baby may be born with a thick crop of hair or she may have almost none. Thick hair tends not to fall out while fine, wispy hair falls out in patches and is gradually replaced by a new lot. Babies who sleep on their back can have a shiny bald patch on the back of their head for a long time.

It may take months or even years for hair color to become apparent.

# Eyes

Eye color is a fascinating topic of conversation. Eyes that go brown stay brown, so if this happens early, you know what the color will be. All other colors can change, and it may take up to a year or longer to know what the final color will be. Green eyes are unusual in the first year, so it may take even more than a year before the color is obvious. I have seen very blue eyes go brown as late as nine months.

Red streaks are often seen in babies' eyes and are due to tiny blood vessels bursting from pressure during birth. They disappear in a few weeks and are nothing to worry about.

Young babies sometimes look endearingly cross-eyed because their eye muscles are not strong enough to keep them straight (not a sign of gas). Cross-eyes are usually fleeting, not constant, and stop happening at around six months of age. If it is constant or persists beyond six months, the eyes need checking by an ophthalmologist or an optician.

The whites of babies' eyes look colored, usually a bluish hue, and often stay this way until the age of two or three years. This is because the sclera (the tough white covering) is half the adult thickness for a couple of years and the blood vessels behind the sclera are easily reflected.

## One eye looks bigger than the other

You might think one of your baby's eyes looks bigger than the other—lots of parents ask about this! Generally, if you look closely at photographs of anyone, you will notice eye size is not identical and that most people of any age have a slight variation in the size of their eyes. It seems to be more noticeable in babies and is often because one of the eyelids falls a little lower than the other, adding to the impression that one eye is bigger than the other. A mild droopiness of one eyelid is very common and usually fixes itself in the first year.

## Foreign body in eye

Babies occasionally collect a small foreign body in their eye such as a speck of dust that just seems to sit there, not causing any irritation or distress the way it would in an adult's eyes. The best way to remove it is to float it out by squeezing some water from a saturated cotton ball over the eye. If this doesn't work or if your baby is distressed, see your family doctor.

## Tears

Tears can be present when your baby cries as early as four weeks or might not appear until nine months.

Your baby can see clearly from birth and will be very interested in human faces, especially yours. Babies are near-sighted, so as well as staring at your face, you will notice she is attracted to light and movement.

# Blocked tear duct (discharging eye)

About half of all babies experience a discharging eye some time in the first three months after birth. Because it is so common, parents are not given a clear explanation of what the cause and possible consequences of sticky eyes are.

Most sticky eyes in young babies are caused by a blockage in the ducts that drain the eye. Sometimes the eye just waters without crustiness or discharge, but often there is a yellow discharge that is worse when the baby wakes after sleep.

Discharging eyes in babies are usually a plumbing problem, not infectious, and don't harm the eye, so don't confuse this with the highly infectious conjunctivitis that older babies and toddlers sometimes get (usually from rubbing mucus from their noses into their eyes during the course of a cold).

## WHAT SHOULD YOU DO?

Wash the eyes when they need it. Use one clean cotton swab for each wipe. Start near the nose and gently wipe out. Dry the eye in a similar manner. You don't need to buy sterile, normal saline from the drugstore—tap water is fine.

Breastmilk is also a useful fluid to clean sticky eyes with. If the eye is very swollen and crusty, and washing can't keep it in check, antibiotic drops or ointment are needed. Drops are easier to put in the eye, but they increase the watery effect, which sometimes causes dermatitis around the eye or on the baby's cheek. Ointment is harder to administer but marginally more effective. The antibiotic ointment or drops clear away the discharge and make the eye more socially acceptable but don't unblock the duct, so the eye often continues to water even after antibiotic treatment. If antibiotic treatment is used, it is limited to a week, as blocked tear ducts can take a few months to resolve and it is not necessary to continue to use antibiotics for the entire time they are blocked. On very rare occasions the blockage is so extreme that oral antibiotics and attention from an ophthalmologist are required.

Mothers are often advised to massage the tear ducts. Massaging involves pressing gently but firmly on the inside of the top of the nose where the two small ducts from the eye meet the duct that runs down the inside of the nose. For this to have any effect at all, you need someone to show you how to do it.

Massaging tear ducts several times a day is something mothers find difficult to do because their baby objects and they end up feeling guilty about not following instructions. Stop feeling guilty and don't worry about massaging your baby's tear ducts. After many years of observing lots of blocked tear ducts, I have come to the conclusion that massaging the ducts rarely makes any difference. The tear ducts unblock spontaneously regardless of antibiotic treatment or regular massage. Most ducts clear by six months of age if not before. A few older babies need the duct probed by an ophthalmologist to clear the blockage. In an adult or older child this is a simple outpatient procedure, but as babies can't lie still, they need a general anesthetic. Probing the duct is left as late as possible but usually done around twelve months of age when the blockage is still easy to fix.

# Ears

Sometimes baby ears fold forward or look creased and out of shape because the ear tissue is very soft. It's best not to try sticking the ear back as doing this makes no difference, is uncomfortable for your baby, and irritates her skin—most ears correct themselves in time, but if you are unduly concerned about the way an ear sticks out, have a consultation with a pediatric plastic surgeon.

After a while you will notice your baby's ears secrete a lot of wax. This is quite normal—it's the way the ear cleans itself.

# Noses

Babies breathe rapidly, often irregularly, and at times sound as if they have a blocked nose. As they cannot blow their nose or clear their throat, and their tiny airways are very narrow, normal mucus and milk accumulates, which makes their breathing sound weird to adult ears. Inhaling the dust in the air is another reason babies sound blocked up and noisy when they breathe. If your baby shares your room, you'll find the way she breathes very noticeable in the middle of the night. Noisy breathing accompanied by strange squeaks doesn't mean your baby is at risk in any way or she has an allergy. Ignore it if you can—there is no need to use drops or any device to extract things from your baby's nose.

# Continual noisy, rattly breathing

A small number of babies who are otherwise healthy have continual noisy, rattly breathing that doesn't cause distress for the baby—only the mother who has to live with constant comments from well-meaning people around her. The reason for the noisy breathing is a temporarily "floppy" voice box. When the vocal cords tighten sometime in the first two years, the noisy breathing stops.

# Hoarse cry

Parents sometimes notice a hoarseness present when their baby cries and feel guilty for letting their baby cry for ten minutes. In fact, babies are prone to a certain amount of hoarseness because the tissue on the area below their voice box is susceptible to swelling when they are young, which makes them sound hoarse at times when they cry. In a well baby this has no significance.

# Sneezing

You are probably aware that your baby sneezes a lot. Baby sneezing is due to dust in the air, and sneezing is a good way for her to clear her nose.

# Hiccups

Adults find hiccups uncomfortable and tedious, but babies don't seem to mind them at all. A top-off at the breast or some tap water helps if your baby's hiccups are worrying you, but there's really no need to do anything. By the way, hiccups aren't caused because of the way you are feeding or burping your baby!

# Sucking blisters

You might notice small blisters on your baby's top lip. These are called sucking blisters and are normally present when babies are getting all their food from sucking. Sucking blisters are a natural condition that does not cause discomfort.

# White tongue

Babies do not make a lot of saliva until they are eight to twelve weeks old, so they frequently have milky-looking tongues when they are very young because there's not a lot of saliva to clean the tongue. When they are having formula, the white tongue looks quite thick.

White tongue and sucking blisters are often confused with thrush. Thrush in a baby's mouth appears as patchy, white spots on the inside of the lips and cheeks. The patchy spots cannot be removed by wiping. Thrush rarely causes babies discomfort unless it is left untreated for a long time and gets to the inflamed, bleeding stage. If you are unsure whether your baby has thrush or not, see your practitioner nurse or pediatrician doctor.

# White spots on gums

Raised, white pearly spots are sometimes seen in the roof of babies' mouths and on their gums where they are often mistaken for teeth. These small cysts tend to pop out on the side of the gum, are not related to teeth in any way, and are not the reason why your baby is going through an unsettled stage. Raised white spots appear on and off during the first year and disappear as mysteriously as they arrive.

# Tongue tie

Tongue tie refers to a condition where the baby's tongue is attached to the floor of the mouth rather than floating free. Mild tongue tie is very common, tends to correct itself, and is unlikely to cause any problems with sucking, eating, or talking. Babies or children with more severe tongue tie who have difficulties with sucking, eating, or talking may need surgical release of the tongue after careful evaluation of the anatomy by a pediatric surgeon. Severe tongue tie needing surgical intervention is rare and more likely to be found in families where there is a history of the condition.

(See tongue tie and breastfeeding, page 102.)

## Lumps in the jaw

You may feel lumps under the skin on your baby's jaw or cheekbone. These are due to fat cells bursting during labor and are more likely to present after a birth with forceps. The lumps are harmless and disappear in a few weeks.

## Lumps like small peas on the back of the neck

Small, movable lumps behind a baby's ears or on the back of the neck are common and normal. They are enlarged lymph nodes and are not significant unless they are large, tender or warm to touch, in which case see your pediatrician.

## Lots of saliva

Between eight weeks and twelve weeks, you are bound to notice that your baby starts to have a very wet mouth with lots of bubbles.

"Teeth!" everyone around you exclaims, but constant dribbling from the age of three months is unrelated to the growing of teeth. All babies froth and bubble from this age whether they grow their first tooth at three and a half months (earliest apart from the rare baby who is born with a tooth) or seventeen months (the latest).

Eight to twelve weeks is the time the human body starts to make saliva. Babies don't know how to swallow their saliva and sit around with their mouths open all day, so it all falls out! When your baby learns to shut her mouth and swallow her saliva (sometime around the age of fifteen months), the dribbling stops.

# Bodies

## A dimple at the base of the spine

This is called a sacral dimple and looks like a tiny hole the size of a pinhead in the center of your baby's back just above her buttocks. Close examination will reveal it isn't a hole but a dimple. Sacral dimples are very common and most grow out in time.

## Fingernails

Staff in maternity hospitals advise mothers to bite, peel, or file their baby's fingernails; this is fine when your baby is very young, but after the first week, feel free to cut them with a pair of scissors. Buy a small pair of blunt-ended scissors, wait until your baby is relaxed, gently pull away the skin from behind the nail, and cut the top off the nail. When you are not used to cutting baby fingernails, it's a bit scary at first, but you'll be amazed at how quickly you become good at it.

## Toenails

Baby toenails look as if they are ingrown as they are very short and embedded in the nail bed. Toenails grow up and out during the next three years, so there is no need to worry about this.

## Blisters around fingernails and toenails

Sometimes the skin around the fingernails and/or toenails becomes red and swollen and may form blisters. This doesn't bother the baby and can usually be treated by dabbing on some Betadine. Occasionally more severe infections need antibiotics.

## Scratching

Small babies scratch their faces, and it's impossible to cut their nails short enough to prevent this from happening. Mittens aren't a great idea as babies prefer their hands free and the scratches heal very quickly. Most scratching stops when the baby's movements become a little more coordinated, usually around three months of age.

## Grunting

You are probably amazed at the strange noises your baby makes, especially as you lie awake in the middle of the night unable to sleep as snuffling, snorting, squeaking, grunting, and groaning sounds fill the air. Grunting seems to be the one that bothers most parents as there is the fear there is a blockage or that their baby is in some sort of pain and needs treatment. All babies make noises in the night and all babies grunt to some degree, some more than others—premature babies do it all the time!

## Red, swollen breasts

The same hormones, passed from mother to baby at birth, which cause the hormone rash, also cause enlarged breasts in many babies (boys and girls). It may happen to one or both breasts and varies from being hardly noticeable to extremely obvious. Occasionally the breasts excrete a little milky fluid. They will take six to eight weeks to go back to normal, are not uncomfortable for your baby, and rarely need treatment.

## Umbilical cord

Your baby's cord will eventually shrivel and fall off. The time it takes to do this varies from a few days to three weeks, occasionally longer. After the cord falls off, expect a little discharge and bleeding to come and go for up to three weeks. If needed, clean the navel with a cotton ball and water. Cord infections are rare, but a very strong smell and shiny, puffy red skin around the navel is an indication all is not well. See your pediatrician.

## Navels that stay moist

Sometimes a collection of cells, called a granuloma, remain after the cord has fallen off. Until these cells die, a continual, sticky discharge keeps the navel moist. The discharge is usually not a sign of an infection and won't harm your baby but may irritate the skin around the navel and cause a red rash. Granulomas can persist for several months. Your family doctor can touch the granuloma with some silver nitrate, which helps it dry up, but don't be tempted to do this yourself as there are rare times when a granuloma is a sign of something more complicated.

## Bowel movements

The first movement your baby passes is called meconium and is a greenish, black sticky substance that gradually changes until the amazing, unpredictable array of bowel movements start to appear.

Mothers are often amazed at the number of times their baby does a poo in the early weeks. It's quite normal when you're breastfeeding to feel as if you are putting food in one end only to have it immediately returned from the other. Frequent runny poo doesn't mean your baby has diarrhea or your milk is too sugary or rich.

You may find your baby's bowel movements vary a lot. They can be bright yellow (like pumpkin), seeded dark yellow (like French mustard), dark green and mucus-like, or a lovely lettuce green. None of these variations are significant in a healthy, thriving baby.

Breastfed babies generally poo many times a day in the first six weeks. This gradually decreases in the second six weeks until some only do a big poo every so often. Every so often may be once every two or three weeks. When your baby is only having breastmilk and no other food or fluid, this is absolutely nothing to worry about. Don't compare it to adult bowel habits and feel you have to do something to make your baby go if she is in this sort of a pattern.

A breastfed baby who doesn't poo much in the first six weeks may not be getting enough milk, although this is certainly not always the case. The best way to check is to weigh your baby and get an idea how much weight she has been gaining weekly since birth.

Babies who have formula usually do dark, sticky poo that looks like modeling clay.

### BLOOD IN THE POO

Occasionally an otherwise healthy baby passes a mucus-like blob of blood in her poo. This can happen whether the baby is breast-fed or having formula, and although it is rarely a sign of anything significant, you should always check with your pediatrician. Unless it persists or unless other symptoms are present, your baby should not need treatment or investigation.

## Cracking joints

Many parents notice their baby's joints crack, most noticeably the knees and shoulders. Clicky hips may need treatment (see below), but cracky knees and shoulders are quite normal.

# Clicky hips

A clicky hip means that the hip joint can be moved around easily. Most new babies have clicky hips at birth because the ligaments around the joint are loose, which means the head of the thigh bone moves out of place easily. The ligaments are loose because they have been softened by the same maternal hormones that also cause the temporary hormone rash and enlarged breasts. Clicky hips due solely to stretched ligaments are also temporary, improve rapidly, and need no treatment.

## DEVELOPMENTAL DYSPLASIA OF THE HIP

This means the head of the thigh bone does not fit properly into the socket because the socket is shallow. It doesn't happen very often, but when the socket is shallow it is important the treatment to form a deep socket for the head of the thigh bone to fit into is started as soon as possible.

Congenital dislocation of the hip (CDH) can be diagnosed by a skilled health professional moving the baby's legs in a special way to see if the thigh bone can be moved out of the socket. It is tricky and sometimes X-rays or ultrasound is used when CDH is suspected or a baby is in the high-risk group for CDH. Early diagnosis is vital to prevent lifelong problems. The modern treatment is usually a Pavlik harness, which holds the hips at right angles to the body and stops the baby stretching her legs out, so a deep socket is formed for the head of the thigh bone to fit into. The harness is worn for about three months and is a highly successful way of treating CDH. The use of double diapers for treating either clicky hips or CDH is no longer recommended, because it promotes hip extension which is not a good position for normal hip development.

# Feet

Baby feet often turn in and out in a funny fashion. Most of the time this is because of the way the baby lies in the womb. These are called postural deformities and always correct themselves either spontaneously or with simple exercises or the use of a plaster for a short time.

A club foot points downward and inward and is usually a structural deformity where the foot has limited movement. It needs immediate attention from birth. Treatment is long-term and involves physiotherapy, splinting, and possibly surgery to get a more normal foot position.

## Vomiting

It is normal for healthy babies to vomit and regurgitate their food. Some do it a lot, others only occasionally. Sometimes it is quite dramatic and will frighten the life out of you as your baby returns milk in a great gush from both nose and mouth. If the milk is returned straight after a feed, it comes up the way it went in. If it comes up sometime later when it is partly digested, it is lumpy and a trifle smelly. About half of all babies vomit enough to worry their parents and complicate normal living, whether it's a great gush or continual splats of curdled, partly digested milk with its own distinctive aroma, often deposited on a shoulder. Almost all babies bring up some milk along with a burp in the middle or at the end of a feed. Unlike adult vomiting—which is associated with nausea, bad food, or the possibility of serious illness—vomiting in healthy babies is generally not associated with any of these things. It is thought to be a mechanical problem. The valve at the top of the stomach does not close properly, so when the stomach contracts (a normal function of the stomach), some of the food shoots up and out. This valve doesn't start functioning efficiently in some babies until they are a year old. This is a simple explanation of something still not clearly understood; there are certainly other factors involved that remain unknown.

The vomiting may start soon after birth or may not start until your baby is nearer to three months. It is often an on again, off again sort of thing—just when you think it's over, it starts again. A small number of babies have problems associated with reflux vomiting or regurgitation, such as heartburn, lung problems, and, only very occasionally, poor weight gains. (See esophageal reflux, page 344.)

All these things need special attention; however, the majority of reflux vomiters are happy vomiters who have no ill effects from their vomiting, apart from the constant aroma and mess, which doesn't bother them at all. Needless to say, being vomited on all day does not do much for mothers' self-esteem and it is a great relief when it stops happening at about a year, or sometimes even sooner. Here are a few tips:

- Reflex vomiting happens equally to breastfed and bottle-fed babies. Most families with more than one baby will have one baby who is a vomiter, nearly always a happy vomiter with no other complications.

- No treatment exists that is outstandingly successful, so if your baby is otherwise happy and well, there is no need to worry or do anything. Weaning or changing to a soy formula is a pointless exercise. The smell of breastmilk returned is far more pleasant than formula, and soy formula smells the worst.

- There is no evidence that consistent thickening of feedings works; happy vomiters are better off without it.

- Don't change your feeding to accommodate the vomiting. That is, there is no need to nurse less often or for shorter periods, or to dramatically cut down the amount if you're bottle feeding. It is not your method of feeding or your technique that is making your baby throw up, so feed away as if it wasn't happening.

• Early introduction of food from a spoon makes very little difference; it just means there is interesting colored vomit instead of white, especially if your baby eats avocado.

## SHOULD THE MILK BE REPLACED AFTER A VOMIT?
If your baby seems content, don't worry about replacing the milk. If she seems to be hungry or wanting to suck some more, put her back to the breast or give her another 2 ounces of formula.

Vomiting can be caused by other illnesses such as pyloric stenosis, an upper respiratory tract infection, a urinary tract infection, or gastroenteritis. These illnesses do cause other signs and symptoms such as fever, significant weight loss, sniffles and mucus, loss of interest in feeding, dry diapers, or diarrhea. Always have vomiting investigated if you are unsure of the cause.

## BLOOD IN VOMIT
Healthy babies who vomit blood are usually breastfed babies whose mothers have sore nipples. The color of the blood can vary from pink to dark, almost black. When the nipples are cracked and bleeding, the reason for the blood in the vomit is quite obvious, but sometimes there may be no visible signs of a bleeding nipple, just soreness. This does not hurt your baby, but you will need some help with your breastfeeding.

## Pink urine
There may be times when you change your baby's diaper that you find a pink stain on the diaper. This is harmless, not blood but a substance called urate, often present in the urine of young babies until the kidneys become mature enough to filter it out.

Urates can be present in a healthy baby's urine as late as three months of age.

## Transparent crystals in urine

If you see tiny balls of clear white jelly in your baby's urine and she is wearing a disposable diaper, it is the filling that is used in disposable diapers to absorb moisture. It is harmless.

## Genitals

The genitals of both boys and girls often look larger than life, which is partly due to hormones and partly due to the birth process (particularly babies who are born bottom-first).

### BOYS

It's quite common for a baby boy's scrotum to have fluid in it, which makes the scrotum look large and swollen; this is called hydrocele. As the fluid is gradually absorbed, the scrotum subsides—it may take several months.

Normally there are two testes in the scrotum that are quite easy to feel. Testes travel from the abdominal sac into the scrotum during late pregnancy. If the opening through which they travel doesn't close off, one of the testes can appear and disappear from the scrotum, especially when the scrotum is exposed to the cold. Eventually the opening from the abdominal sac closes and the testicle remains in the scrotum.

Occasionally one or both of the testes never descend and so are never felt in the scrotum. If the testicle doesn't descend into the scrotum after one year of age, surgery is performed some time between one and three years. The operation involves bringing the testicle into the scrotum and securing it there. Penises come in a variety of shapes and sizes. If you are worried about the size or shape check with your family doctor.

**CIRCUMCISION:** In most baby boys a piece of skin, known as the foreskin, covers the tip of the penis. Surgical removal of the foreskin is called circumcision. The number of routine newborn circumcisions in the US has steadily declined in recent years as more parents question the procedure; however, it remains a controversial issue with adherents on either side of the debate.

Those against routine circumcision on healthy males (and I am one) view the procedure as an unnecessary, painful operation with some risk and no benefit. Unless it is medically required (rare) circumcision always has been and still is primarily for cultural, religious or aesthetic reasons. And as more boys are left intact in Western societies, the aesthetic reasons. like fashion, will fade.

However, if you want your son circumcised talk it over with a few people so you are clear about why you want it done. Things like cleanliness, a matching set with father or to avoid future problems are not valid reasons.

If you decide to go ahead find a pediatrician who uses a local anaesthetic as despite rumours to the contrary circumcision is painful. Your baby should be full-term, healthy, gaining weight and not jaundiced. After the circumcision your doctor or nurse will instruct you on caring for the penis. A lubricant is applied to prevent sticking to the diaper, the swelling and scab resolve within a week. After healing it is normal for the tip of a circumcised penis to look bluish in colour.

Uncircumcised penises need the same care as the elbow—none. The foreskin should not be pushed back. It will retract eventually of its own accord, often around three years of age. Forcing the foreskin back before it is ready causes pain, bleeding and scarring, which may cause damage that results in a circumcision having to be done.

## GIRLS

Baby girls occasionally have a small amount of bleeding from the vagina, caused by the withdrawal of some of the maternal hormones they receive at birth. When you part the labia, you will see a white discharge around the vagina and inside the labia. This is a normal secretion—you do not have to clean it. If the labia can't be parted on a baby girl of any age, check with your pediatrician. The labial skin on babies is often paper thin, so the edges of the labia adhere to each other. Estrogen cream applied regularly for a few weeks thickens the skin, helping it to separate, but it is not used until the baby is over 12 months.

# Minor medical problems common in the first three months

## Hernias

A hernia in a young baby happens because a special structure needed by the baby when she was growing in the womb doesn't close off the way it is supposed to after birth. One of the internal parts of the body then bulges through the opening. The two most common places this happens are the navel and the groin.

### UMBILICAL HERNIA (NAVEL)

An umbilical hernia is a soft swelling on the navel that becomes noticeable when the cord drops off. Some are small; others are almost alarmingly large.

If your baby has one, you will notice when she is quiet the navel is flatter than when she cries, at which time the bulge pops out looking like a red balloon. Gently pushing it shouldn't hurt your baby and makes a squelchy sound.

An umbilical hernia is caused by an abnormal opening between

**221**

the abdominal wall and the abdomen that is present before birth to allow nourishment to pass to the baby by the umbilical cord. Sometimes it does not completely close as it is supposed to after birth, and a small part of the intestine protruding through is well covered with skin and tissue, so the condition is usually harmless and rarely needs treatment. In time the tummy muscles grow close, so the bulge decreases slowly and goes away, usually by the age of three years, if not before.

Rare conditions do exist where an umbilical hernia is partially or fully strangulated. More rarely, abdominal protrusions in young babies can be a sign of an abdominal defect that needs urgent repair; however, unless these abnormalities are present, even large umbilical hernias are usually left untreated.

Applying adhesive bandaging or binding to the navel causes a rash, is uncomfortable for the baby, and makes no difference in the bulge.

## INGUINAL HERNIA (GROIN)

An inguinal hernia appears as a lump in the groin. The swelling often comes and goes according to whether the baby is sleeping or crying. It's a good idea to check for the presence of a lump in the groin if your baby is having sudden screaming attacks for no apparent reason, especially if your baby is premature, as inguinal hernias happen to premature babies more often than full-term babies.

This kind of hernia is caused by an abnormal opening between the abdominal wall and the groin that is present before birth to allow the passage of the testicle into the scrotum. The opening is present in boys and girls (even though girls don't have testes or a scrotum) and normally closes a month before birth, which is why an inguinal hernia is more common in premature babies.

Unlike an umbilical hernia, an inguinal hernia always needs an operation to prevent complications. This is because the opening through which the intestine protrudes is small and the muscles in the groin tight, so the blood supply to the intestine may be cut off. Even if the lump can be pushed back or doesn't cause distress, it should be repaired as soon as possible. It may repeat on the other side, so both sides are repaired. Surgery is very successful and involves one or two days in the hospital.

# Head colds

Colds are not common in the first six to twelve weeks because the antibodies mothers pass to their babies protect them to some extent. Remember, sniffling and sneezing in the first three months is not a sign of a head cold unless there are other symptoms. Head colds are caused by viruses that damage the mucous membranes of the nose and throat. This is what causes the runny nose, the sore throat and eyes, the cough, and sometimes a headache and fever.

Complications from head colds such as ear or chest infections are more common in babies and young children than in adults. As well, the extra mucus generated by a cold seems to hang around forever, even after the cold gets better.

There's not a lot you can do to prevent your baby from catching a cold. Breastfeeding helps, but breastfed babies can still catch colds. It's difficult to keep a spluttering toddler with a streaming nose away from her baby brother or sister, but you can ask friends and relatives with head colds not to come too close.

## HERE ARE SOME HEAD COLD TIPS

Head colds without a fever are rarely helped by any of the various medications commonly suggested. The decision whether or not to use antibiotics can be difficult. Most head colds are caused by viruses, so antibiotics (which fight bacteria) are unlikely to do a lot. Antibiotics can cause diarrhea and yeast infections, so their use often complicates head colds in babies rather than having any beneficial effect. Babies with head colds aren't helped much by drugs that dry up the mucus. Some have a sedative effect that is best avoided, especially in babies under six months. Constant use of medicated nose drops increases the mucus and may damage the lining of your baby's nose—which leads to other problems later—however, used occasionally, they can help if your baby is too blocked up to feed properly.

If your baby is sleeping and eating as well as can be expected given that she is somewhat miserable and uncomfortable, there is no need to medicate. Noisy, bubbly breathing is acceptable as long as she is not struggling to breathe. It's normal for a baby with a head cold to do poo that contains mucus and to have a few mucus-filled vomits too.

Unfortunately there is no magic potion that makes colds get better quicker. Treatment always involves relieving the symptoms. If your baby has a badly blocked nose, here are some helpful hints:

- Try a vaporizer. Despite the fact, recent research shows a vaporizer makes very little difference, lots of the parents I talk to find a vaporizer helps.

- A little Vicks dabbed onto the sheet in your baby's crib, well away from her mouth, will help her to breathe more easily. It's best not to put it directly onto a young baby's skin and to test a small amount before rubbing it onto the chest of an older baby.

- Weak saline nose drops can be used freely to wash out her nose. If you use medicated baby nose drops, try to only use them occasionally before a feeding if her nose is so blocked that she can't suck. Once the worst of the cold is over (about a week) and your baby can suck reasonably happily again, stop using them.

**224**

If your baby has a head cold with a fever, use one of the baby acetaminophen preparations to bring the fever down. A fever is a temperature reading of over 98.6°F. Dress her lightly, give extra breastfeedings or other clear fluids, and use the acetaminophen three- to four-hourly until the fever subsides.

Coughing accompanying a head cold is usually caused by the mucus trickling down the back of your baby's throat. If there is a lot of coughing, check with your doctor to make sure there is no chest infection. If her chest is clear, try some of the suggestions for blocked noses. Cough suppressants shouldn't be given to babies.

It's wise to consult your doctor if you are worried or if she has a fever when she is under three months. Other symptoms that need medical attention are breathing difficulties or wheezing and feeding problems in young babies who suddenly refuse to suck.

## Bronchiolitis

Bronchiolitis is an infection caused by a virus that babies can get and is similar but not the same as an attack of bronchitis in adults. It often occurs in epidemics, especially during the winter months. The virus causes coughing, wheezing, and cold symptoms, and the younger the baby the more potentially serious the condition, especially if the baby was born prematurely. An attack of bronchiolitis can range from being mild to severe. No drugs are available to destroy the virus, so antibiotics are not appropriate, and treatment involves making sure the baby's breathing is adequate and that the baby is eating enough to stay well nourished.

Mild cases are treated at home while moderate to severe cases need admission to hospital, sometimes to an intensive care unit. Drugs may be used to improve the baby's breathing.

Bronchiolitis usually gets worse for three to four days, stays the same for another three to four days, then starts to get better, taking about two weeks for full recovery. The cough is the last thing to go. An attack of bronchiolitis does not mean the baby will become an asthmatic later on.

# Medicating babies

A wide range of baby medications is available, and large numbers of healthy babies are given some sort of medication before they are three months old. Most of the time the use of medication is inappropriate, not needed, and doesn't cure the problem.

## Why are drugs used so much?

Part of the delight and frustration of babies is their mystery. They can't talk and tell us what the matter is or how they feel, and unfortunately part of the way we look after babies is to regard everything they do as a curable medical condition, even when what they are doing is related to their behavior, not their health. Parents become very anxious when their baby is either not well or does puzzling things (like crying a lot), and often, on the advice of a health professional, use some sort of medication in the hope of a miraculous cure or a change in their baby's behavior.

Most of the time, the commonly used drugs or herbal remedies have little effect on the health and behavior of otherwise healthy babies. At best they are a waste of money—at worst some may be harmful, particularly when they have a sedative effect.

There are times when medication is vital because of a chronic or serious health problem, and this should be taken care of under a doctor's supervision and monitored regularly; however, giving well babies drugs is often unnecessary, so here's a few things to think about before you do:

- Try to think through why you are giving the drug. Is it for a clearly defined physical symptom or is it because of the way your baby is behaving? For example—a fever is a clearly defined physical symptom. Grunting, getting red in the face and drawing up the legs is a normal way for babies to behave. These are not clearly defined physical symptoms of a medical problem.

- If you are advised or prescribed medicine for your baby, ask the following questions: What's in the drug; What are the possible risks and side effects; What condition are you treating and how does the drug work; What are you hoping to achieve by giving my baby this drug; What are the chances of a positive response; Is this drug really necessary?

- Read the label. Find out what is in the medication. Generally, medication that contains a single drug is preferable to those that combine several.

- Give the medication from a dropper or a teaspoon—not in your baby's bottle or in her food.

As your baby grows and you learn more about her normal development and behavior, you will become more confident and manage without relying on unnecessary medication, especially when you have seen her through one or two minor illnesses.

## When to call the doctor

Often new parents don't have a doctor, as having a baby usually happens at a time in life when people are generally well and have no need of medical care. Once a few babies start to arrive, however, a doctor you know and trust is a very worthwhile investment. Lots of doctors have special areas of interest that they have given extra time, attention, and study to, so look for one who has an interest in pediatrics and family medicine.

Deciding when to take your baby to the doctor because she is unwell or behaving strangely is a dilemma for most new parents (and often for those not so new). A few guidelines follow.

There are often times when a baby has slight behavior changes or mild symptoms that do not need urgent attention. Frequently the problems resolve themselves quickly or you find out they are not problems at all but normal features of babyhood.

Babies in the first twelve months have a whole range of interesting strange habits that adults try to interpret, often coming up with quite inappropriate conclusions. Similar strange actions and habits are common to all babies and are usually reflexes, part of normal development, or a baby's way of practicing skills. For example, playing with and pulling ears is one of these actions and not a sign of teething or an ear infection.

If your baby is thriving, active, and wetting and pooing normally, it's unlikely there's anything wrong, but always seek help when in doubt. Sometimes situations do arise that need immediate medical attention. Here they are:

- A sudden loss of interest in feeding, especially when it's a young baby who won't suck.

- A constant high fever that doesn't respond to acetaminophen and taking off some of the baby's clothes. Any fever in a baby under three months.

- Sudden vomiting and diarrhea.

- Persistent screaming—crying around the clock.

- Difficulty breathing.

- Any abnormal discharge, especially from the ears.

- A convulsion or fit.

- Any strange posture or unusual eye or body movements.

- A sudden outbreak of a strange rash you can't identify.

- Any unusual swelling or lump, especially if it is painful to touch.

- Loss of interest in surroundings and/or abnormal sleepiness or floppiness.

- Thick, smelly urine.

## Helping your doctor to help you

Find out about house calls and what service is available for off hours.

If several things are worrying you about your baby, make a list before you see your doctor. Try to give her or him a clear message about the problem without introducing a whole range of irrelevant issues. Ask for a clearer explanation, if you don't understand something.

Second opinions are useful, but if you keep shopping around, no one will be directly responsible for your care and you may not get the best help when you really need it. Give your doctor time to get to know you and your baby so that she or he can give you individual care suited to your needs.

Finally, babies and young children often behave in quite unpredictable ways that are well within the normal range. They also get funny things wrong with them when no one really knows what the matter is. Don't push your doctor for a diagnosis and medication for the sake of it. If she or he is honest enough to admit they don't know what's wrong, respect this honesty. Far too many normal babies and children are put through a barrage of unnecessary invasive diagnostic tests and given inappropriate medicine because of pressure from parents for a precise answer when there is none.

# chapter eleven

# Daily Care

*If you were an Eskimo baby*
*You'd live in a bag all day.*
*Right up from your toes*
*To the tip of your nose*
*All in thick cosy furs tucked away.*

Lucy Diamond, "An Eskimo Baby,"

*The Book of a Thousand Poems*

Unless you are used to handling small babies, you are likely to feel awkward and a bit nervous for the first few weeks when you dress and undress your baby, change her diaper and bathe her. Feeling like this is normal. Your baby is blissfully unaware that you are learning and you will be amazed how quickly you become efficient at babycare skills.

## Changing the diaper

If you are using cloth diapers it really doesn't matter which of the folding methods you use as long as the diaper goes on firmly and does what it's supposed to do. The same size cloth diapers fit your baby until she no longer needs them. Adjustments are made to allow for her size as she grows by the way you fold the diaper. You will need to use double cloth diapers at night once your baby starts sleeping longer. Most brands of disposables last all night without leaking, but if there are problems, try poking holes in one diaper with a fork, put it on, then put a second one over the top.

## How often?

Expect to use eight or more diapers every twenty-four hours. Diapers need changing once or twice at most feeding times and at other times when your baby is awake.

There's no need to change your baby before a feeding when she's ravenous unless there's a leaky mess. Likewise, if she's been changed before and during a feed it's fine to put her down without changing her again. If your breastfeedings are close and frequent, don't worry about changing her every time you nurse—just put her on the breast and put your feet up.

## What do you do?

Take off the used diaper using the front of the diaper to wipe off any poo still on your baby. Fold the diaper so the poo can't fall out and put it to one side. Gently wash her bottom, front and back, with damp tissues or tissues and a hypoallergenic moisturizer such as Moisturel lotion, paying attention to wiping in between creases. To clean the back part, lift her legs, holding both ankles together in one hand with a finger between her ankles, and raise her bottom slightly.

After washing, pat dry. Apply cream or powder if you are using any. Put on a clean diaper. If you are using disposables, wipe your fingers clean of any cream; otherwise you'll have trouble getting the adhesive tabs to stick. The part of the disposable diaper with the tab goes to the back; the part of the diaper the tab adheres to goes to the front.

Girls do not need the labia separated to clean inside. Boys should never have their foreskin pushed back.

Dress your baby and leave her somewhere safe while you deal with the used diaper. Whether you use a cloth or a disposable scrape the poo off the diaper into the toilet before either soaking it or putting it in a plastic bag and throwing it out.

Don't forget to wash your hands.

# Dressing and undressing

Make sure the change table or dresser you are going to use to dress and undress your baby is flat, firm, stable, and the right height for you to work comfortably. It's much easier to use a change table or a dresser than to use your lap or bend over a bed.

When dressing or undressing you'll probably find it's the top half that's the trickiest until you become more skilled.

## Undressing

Leave the diaper till last. Undo all the snaps. Gently slide her legs out of the stretchy or pull off any leggings. Roll the stretchy to shoulder level and gently pull the sleeves over and off each arm. If your baby has a separate top, stretch the neck of the garment after your baby's arms are free and remove it carefully from *front* to *back* over her head so that it doesn't touch her face.

## Dressing

Put the diaper on first. Once again, stretch the neck of the garment and this time, going from *back* to *front* pull it over her head so that it doesn't touch her face, supporting the back of her head raising it slightly as you go. Guide your baby's arms through both arm holes into the arms, then her legs into the bottom half. Do up all the snaps.

Dressing, undressing, and bathing young babies is complicated by the way a lot of them cry and appear to be very distressed while it's all going on. After the contained life in the womb where there were limits to their movements and a relatively unchanging environment, even small changes to their bodies and their world will worry them until they become accustomed to new sensations and feelings. Lying naked on a change table must feel a bit like falling off a cliff to young babies as they have no knowledge of the extent of their new boundaries.

By three months, most babies don't mind having their diapers changed and love having a bath. Dressing and undressing is also much easier at this age.

If your baby cries a lot while you are attending to her care when she is young, try to stay calm and do what you need to do. It's a normal way for babies to behave and doesn't mean you are doing something wrong. Individual babies' responses to diaper changing, bathing, dressing, and undressing vary enormously. If your baby cries at these times and your friend's baby doesn't, it doesn't mean anything is wrong.

Here are a few tips to help:

- Pick clothes that are easy to put on and take off. For example, front snaps, stretch or expandable fabric.

- Avoid buttons and bows. Most families are given at least one beautiful outfit that is invariably difficult to get a baby in and out of, especially when the baby is in full crying mode. This doesn't mean you can't ever use it, but save it for a special occasion.

- Have three or four easy changes ready.

- When dressing a crying, hungry baby, don't worry about minor details. Get the basics done, then do up buttons and straighten collars while she's feeding.

- Sometimes young babies are calmer and easier to dress and undress while lying on their tummy.

# *Bathtime*

Bathing grows into a happy time that becomes lots of fun for you both, but in the early days you might wonder when the fun is going to begin! Lots of new mothers find bathing difficult at first. When you get used to handling a slippery baby and your baby starts to enjoy her bath, things improve dramatically.

If you find bathing stressful during the first six weeks, only bathe your baby once or twice a week. Just cleaning her face and bottom are quite adequate the rest of the time.

On the other hand, if a deep relaxation bath helps a baby who cries a lot, then bathing twice a day is fine. It's all right to bathe your baby before a feeding, after a feeding, or in the middle of a feeding. You will soon work out what suits you both best.

There are many ways to bathe babies. Here is one way.

## First, a few safety reminders

- Make sure the room is warm with no drafts.

- If you use a sink, take care that your baby doesn't bump against the faucets or burn herself on the hot faucet.

- Always put your hand on your baby before turning away.

- Wrap her up and take her with you if the phone rings, or if you can, let it ring.

- Put cold water in the tub first, then add the hot. Mix the water before putting your baby in and test the temperature by dipping your elbow in. The water should feel warm to the touch.

Prepare everything before you begin. You need diapers, diaper fasteners, pins, plastic pants, jumpsuit or nightie, cotton balls, and soap or a liquid baby bath preparation. Useful but not essential is a mois-

**235**

turizer, petroleum jelly, Q-tips and your favorite diaper cream. You also need two towels or one towel and a hand towel. Here we go!

- Undress your baby. Leave her diaper on. Swaddle her snuggly in a towel. Wash her face with damp cotton balls or a washcloth. Pat dry.

- To clean her ears, smear a little petroleum jelly on a cotton ball, shape it into a point, then wipe firmly inside her ear, lifting out any accumulated wax. Poking cotton swabs into her ears or nose is dangerous and never necessary.

- Wet your baby's head, then soap it with soapy palms. Use a mild soap. Tuck her under one arm, hold her head over the tub, and rinse it well. Babies usually enjoy this part. After her head is rinsed, lie her back on the table and dry her head gently but briskly with your other towel.

- Next, unwrap your baby and remove the diaper. Wet her body with your hands and gently massage in some soapy water or a moisturizer. This is when she is likely to cry. Gently turn her onto her tummy if it makes things easier.

- Now it's time to put her into the bath—here's how to pick her up. If your hands are slippery or soapy, rinse and dry them before you put your baby in the tub. One hand supports her head, neck, and shoulder. The palm of your other hand supports both legs below the knees. Use your forefingers to separate her ankles. Lift and gently place her in the tub.

- Once she is in the tub keep supporting her head and neck. You will find she will float in the water. Use your free hand to rinse off any soap or just to gently splash water onto her body. Unless your baby has an ear infection (very unusual at this age), it doesn't matter if her ears are under the water when you bathe her.

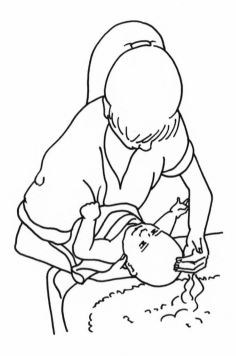

1. Wet your baby's head, then soap with soapy palms.

2. Lift and gently place her in the tub.

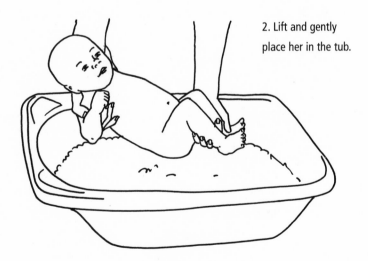

**Two bathing steps**

- When you are ready, lift her out of the tub the same way you put her in. Pat dry, especially behind the ears, between her fingers, under her arms, under her chin, and in the groin area. When she is dry, apply some moisturizer if you want to.

- Dress her. Remember, diaper first!

Another variation on the baby bath is the deep relaxation bath. The deep relaxation bath can be used to help babies relax and sleep.

The water is deep and warm (100°F). You lift your baby into the deep bath and hold her on her back in the water. Her head rests on your wrist while your other hand supports her legs with your forefingers between her ankles.

Move her backward and forward through the water. After a few glides, turn her over onto her tummy, supporting her head on the inside of your wrist. Babies usually relax in the deep, warm water. Some fall asleep; others kick and move about. It is easy to hold her as she is supported by the water.

Keep baby in the water as long as the water stays warm. When you lift her out, leave her on her tummy. Place her on a dry towel and pat dry.

Like any practical procedure, bathing is difficult to do from written instructions only. The deep relaxation bath is easier if you get someone to show you. Ask your friends who have babies how it is done.

If the deep relaxation bath bothers you, don't feel pressured by well-meaning advisers into feeling it is essential for your baby—it is an option to use if you would like to. Babies also enjoy a shower with their mother or father. A mat in the shower is essential to avoid falls.

## Massage

After your baby's bath, if you are both happy and relaxed, try some baby massage. Baby massage is gentle touching using long, firm, smooth strokes. Baby massage is beneficial at any age, so wait until you feel confident about handling your baby if you are a bit nervous during the first six weeks. Baby massage is not for everyone, so don't feel it's something you have to do if it's not your scene. It is not the definitive answer to baby crying and sleeping problems, but it helps calm babies and it can be very enjoyable for parents and baby alike. Baby massage is never very successful when your baby is very tense and crying a lot or any time you are rushed and feeling anxious or trying to keep an active toddler amused as well. The best time is after a bath as long as she is not hungry. Like all skills, baby massage takes time to learn.

### HERE'S A VERY SIMPLE METHOD
Lie your baby on her tummy. Using a little almond oil or some moisturizer and water, rub your hands together. Stroke your baby's back using a hand-over-hand motion, gradually moving downward, stroking her buttocks and legs right down to her toes. Initially, this is enough to start with, especially if turning her onto her back makes her cry, which is quite likely when she is very young. As time goes by and you both become more relaxed, turn her over and continue stroking her tummy and the front of her legs.

If you are interested in baby massage and wish to learn more, try one of the many books or videos available that demonstrate this traditional art.

## What to wear

Trying to work out what clothes to dress your baby in so that she won't be too hot or too cold might cause you some concern. Try not to worry too much. Once again, you'll find as your baby grows you'll quickly get used to working out how much to put on or leave off.

### Here is a reasonable guide

- **Summer:** a cotton body suit; a cotton nightgown, or short-sleeve, short-leg stretchy; sun hat if out of doors; diaper; socks; at bedtime, a cotton receiving blanket, and cotton mesh blanket if required.

- **Winter:** one or two shirts or a bodysuit; a warm nightgown or a long-sleeve stretchy; a warm jacket or sweater; leggings or socks, hat if out of doors; at bedtime, one or two flannelette cuddlies and one or two blankets.

Obviously concessions have to be made for air-conditioning and heating (including in cars) and extremely hot or cold climates. As long as your baby's chest, tummy, and head are warm to touch, she is comfortably clothed. Hands and feet normally often feel cold, so they are not a good guide to her body warmth. A good way to check is to put the back of your hand on her tummy; a warm tummy means all is well.

An overheated baby gets very red in the face, sweats profusely, and will probably cry vigorously—although a certain amount of sweating and heat rash is normal for all babies and not related to being overdressed.

## Out and about

Facing the great outdoors can seem quite daunting in the early weeks after birth, and it's easy to be overcome with dread at the thought of going anywhere when you start to think of the effort involved. While you are learning the best way to do the shopping, manage public transport if necessary, and keep appointments, life before baby suddenly seems very much easier. Despite a few improvements in recent years, our society is generally not at all considerate to the needs of mothers trying to negotiate their way around with little ones in tow. Many women tell me they start to understand for the first time the problems disabled people experience in their daily lives, especially those trying to get out with twins, triplets, or a couple of babies close in age.

You will find practice makes perfect, and the more you go out the more efficient you become at planning how to get where you are going and what you need. Start with simple excursions and build up to more ambitious ventures as you gain confidence. Having a baby bag always packed with the basics makes outings easier. In your bag you need four or more diapers, disposable baby washcloths and your favourite diaper cream, cotton balls and tissues, a few soft, gauze weave diapers for mopping up, an extra pacifier (if you are using a pacifier) and safety pins. And an all-purpose baby blanket that can be used as a changing sheet, a cover or to put on the floor so your baby can lie on something familiar and clean.

A lot of women are extremely nervous when they first start to drive with their new baby in the car seat on the back seat of the car. Driving anxiety passes, so don't let it put you off going somewhere in the car. If you are worried because you can't see your baby in the capsule attach a mirror to the headrest on the back seat so you can keep an eye on her.

Breastfeeding while you're out is often easy, but unfortunately women breastfeeding in public are still given a hard time in some places. Wear a two-piece outfit with a top that can be lifted from the waist. If the thought of nursing in public bothers you, before you go, check about for a private site to nurse. If you are bottle feeding, the safest way to transport formula is to take the cool, boiled water and the powdered formula in separate containers and mix them when needed. If transporting prepared formula or expressed breastmilk, it must be icy cold when you leave home and carried in an insulated baby bottle pack to keep it cold. If you cannot safely heat the bottle when you reach your destination, it's quite all right to give it as it is.

Some mothers plan their outings around their babies' eating and sleeping schedules; others just go when they are ready. Either approach is fine. There's no need to go rushing out every day, but you will find that you and your baby are much happier at home and with each other if you spend some time each week out and about.

## Take care in the sun

Babies should be kept out of the sun. Babies do not need daily sun kicks to get Vitamin D. A few minutes of indirect sun is more than enough to ensure adequate Vitamin D synthesis. Apart from this diet can amply supply your baby or toddler's vitamin D needs by way of breastmilk, formula as well as the calcium and vitamin D fortified foods that are available for older babies and toddlers.

In America it is recommended that sunscreens be avoided for babies under six months of age because there isn't enough evidence to date that sunscreen absorbed through a baby's thin skin is danger-free. It is fairly easy to keep young, immobile babies away from the sun by providing light covering with a receiving blanket to exposed parts of their bodies. When you are in the car use shades on the car windows rather than draping something over the car seat.

As your baby grows and is more exposed to the outdoors, it is vital to keep her covered, ideally by a tight-weave T shirt with a collar, long pants and a hat that provides shade over her face, neck and ears. A sunscreen should be applied to the exposed parts of her body once she is over six months. Sunscreens play an important role in sun protection, however, the most important line of defense against sun damage is to avoid unnecessary exposure by covering up as much as possible when in the sun and avoiding sun exposure from 10AM to 3PM. This is important for all of us but especially during the first three years of life when the skin is very thin.

A sunscreen may be applied sparingly to exposed parts of babies' and toddlers' bodies when they are in the sun. Sunscreens have a place in protecting your baby's skin, but the most important line of defense against the sun for all of us, but particularly for babies, is to avoid unnecessary exposure and to always cover up as much as possible when in the sun.

## About sunscreens

Some sunscreens work by absorbing ultraviolet radiation, others work by reflecting the ultraviolet away and may be less likely to cause allergic reactions to the skin. Sunscreens have a sun protection factor (SPF) that ranges from 4 to 30. The higher the SPF, the longer the sunscreen protects. A 30+ SPF gives babies the most effective protection. Sunscreens that protect against both ultraviolet A and ultraviolet B are called broad spectrum, and a baby's skin needs this protection. Specially formulated baby and toddler sunblocks are combinations of ingredients thought to be less allergenic and so less likely to irritate a baby or toddler's skin.

The chemical PABA is a sunscreen additive that causes problems for sensitive skin so it is not in a number of sunscreens. Some sunscreens have an alcoholic base that may sting a baby's skin.

### IN SUMMARY, WHEN CHOOSING A PRODUCT FOR YOUR BABY

- Read the label carefully;

- Use 30+ sun protection factor;

- No PABA;

- Non-alcoholic base;

- Water-resistant base;

- Broad-spectrum base.

Many brands are available that comply with these recommendations, so don't go to the added expense of buying a baby sunscreen if the one you have already fits the bill. Always do a skin test by applying a small amount on your baby's forearm—if there is no itch or sting within a few hours, the product is safe to use.

# Care in hot weather

Healthy babies do not suddenly dehydrate when the weather gets hot (think of all the babies around the world who live in very hot climates) as long as a little care and commonsense is used. The fontanelle on all babies' heads pulsates, so there are times when it looks depressed or sunken—this is normal.

## Hot weather tips

- Keep your baby out of the sun during the dangerous hours. The sun's ultraviolet light is at its most intense between the hours of 10 am and 2 pm (11 am and 3 pm in areas where there is daylight saving).

- Dress your baby in light, cool clothing—when out of the sun, an undershirt and diaper is all she needs. Use cotton cuddlies for wrapping.

- Never ever leave your baby in a parked car no matter what the weather!

- Use a fan (not directly on your baby) in the room where your baby sleeps (unless of course you have air-conditioning).

- Well-fed healthy babies (breastfed or bottle fed) do not need to be constantly offered extra water or juice in hot weather. If it is very hot and you think your baby is thirsty, by all means offer some water, but don't get worried if she doesn't drink it. If you are breast-feeding, offer extra feedings—there's plenty of water in breastmilk.

# Where should she sleep?

Doubtless, no matter where you choose to put your baby to sleep, someone will tell you it's not right. Thirty years ago, sleeping with babies was frowned upon, ten years ago the family bed was pro-moted by many as the best place for a baby to sleep, and nowadays it's hard to find universal agreement on any one place. It may take you some time before you work out what suits you all the best. Try not to be pressured by something you read or by other people's opinions into doing something you're not happy with.

There are several safe options—here they are:

## Separate bed—sharing your room
### ADVANTAGES

- Great emotional security for you knowing your baby is close.

- It's easier to do the night feedings as your baby is close by.

- It may be the only option if you have limited space—having the baby share your room may be preferable to the baby sharing the toddler's room when the baby is very young.

## DISADVANTAGES

- Noisy breathing, grunting, sucking fists, hiccuping, and wriggling are all normal for sleeping babies, and your sleep may be disturbed even when your baby is asleep.

- Babies over four months are much more likely to call for room service when they wake in the night if they share the room with their parents and may continue to do so indefinitely.

## Sharing your bed

It is quite safe for babies to share their parents' bed as long as the parents are not smokers, drunk or drugged, or use a water bed. However, recently doubts have been raised by some research that suggests co-sleeping may increase the risk of Sudden Infant Death Syndrome (SIDS). As much more research to confirm or deny this is still needed, the decision to share the bed with their baby must be left with parents. For more information, contact the Sudden Infant Death Association in your state.

## ADVANTAGES

- Great emotional security to know your baby is close to you. Some women sleep better when they sleep with their babies.

- Breastfeeding can take place when you are in a sleepy state, which means you get more rest.

- It is cosier in the winter months.

- Certainly an option with a very young baby who is unsettled at night. Some newborns settle much better in their parents' bed than in their bassinets, which means everyone gets more sleep.

- Sleeping with your baby can be a great aid to getting breast-feeding going and keeping it going.

## DISADVANTAGES

- The majority of parents in our society don't like sleeping with their babies and toddlers. Generally speaking, our standard of living gives us the opportunity for space in our daily living and we become accustomed to this. Sharing the bed with babies and children involves a degree of discomfort and irritation that most people find intolerable.

- You might find you can't relax and sleep for fear of rolling on your baby.

- The baby's noises might keep you awake.

- Not all babies who are crying and unsettled automatically sleep better once they are in their parents' beds. Some continue crying anyway—if your baby is like this, it might be easier to settle in her own bed.

- You'll find the bed sharing goes on indefinitely unless your baby sleeps mostly in another bed by three months of age. The arrangement is rarely voluntarily ended by the child until she is quite old (three to five years). Deciding to change the arrangement before your baby or child is ready involves approaches a lot of parents find painful. There is rarely an easy answer, so if you think sharing your bed with your baby is going to worry you in the future, only do it when she is very young, to maximize your sleep.

## Own bed—separate room

Some recent research suggests that babies are less at risk of SIDS if they sleep in the same room as their parents for the whole of the first year. Much more research needs to be done to ascertain whether sleeping alone in a separate room is a risk factor or not, so again the decision must be left to the parents.

## ADVANTAGES

• You might sleep better undisturbed by baby noises.

• You have some privacy and space.

• There's less likelihood of a sleep problem when your baby is over six months, and if it does occur, it is easier to deal with if your baby is used to being in her own bed in her own room.

## DISADVANTAGES

• You might find separate nighttime accommodations impossible to handle emotionally until your baby is much older and past the time when she is at greatest risk of SIDS (over six months).

• Night feeding is less convenient, especially during winter, and less economical if heaters are used at night.

• Occasionally the number of breastfeedings at night may get to be less than needed to keep a good milk supply going in the early weeks.

# Sleeping positions

The sleeping position of the baby is one of the four factors recognised that may contribute to reducing the risk of SIDS. Statistical evidence suggests babies are more at risk when they are placed on their tummy to sleep. At the time of writing, the recommendation from the Sudden Infant Death Association is to lie all babies on their backs from birth.

# Swaddling or wrapping

Swaddling or wrapping babies is a method that has been used by many cultures for centuries to help babies sleep. It makes them feel secure and prevents them from waking themselves up with their startle reflex. Swaddling doesn't suit all babies, and as there is no medical reason to swaddle healthy, full-term babies if your baby doesn't like being wrapped and it doesn't help her to sleep, forget about it.

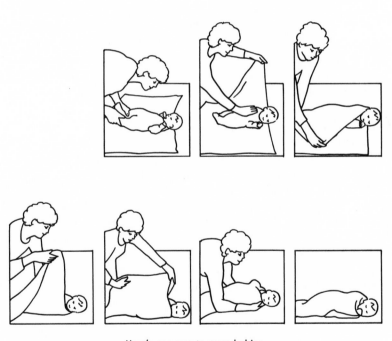

Here's one way to wrap babies.

# Lotions and creams

A guide to the basic lotions and creams you may need in the first three months follows:

| Heads | Bodies | Bottoms |
|---|---|---|
| Wash with simple soap | OPTIONS FOR THE BATH<br>• Nothing<br>• Baby bath lotion<br>• Almond oil | OPTIONS FOR CLEANING<br>• Damp tissues<br>• Moisturel lotion<br>• Disposable wash cloths*<br>*avoid using if rash present |
| TO SOFTEN CRADLE CAP CRUSTS<br>• Vaseline, or if severe ask your pharmacist to make up:2% Acid Sal/2%Sulphur in a hypoallergenic moisturizing cream. Apply overnight—wash out the next day | MOISTURIZER<br>A hypoallergenic moisturizer (e.g., Moisturel lotion) | SOOTHING BARRIER HEALING CREAMS<br>A variety are available—e.g. Desitin, A&D cream, Lansinoh. |
| CRUSTY EYEBROWS<br>Apply a little hypoallergenic moisturizer (e.g. Moisturel cream) to eyebrows at each diaper change | RED SKIN BETWEEN SKIN SURFACES<br>e.g. back of elbow joint, under chin, back of knee joint, under arms, groin area<br>• Zinc and starch powder<br>• Destin powder<br>• Cornflour | RED ANUS AND/OR A RED GENITAL AREA<br>(including bottom)<br>—choose from<br>• Desitin<br>• Butt paste<br>• A&D<br>• Triple Paste |
| CRUSTS BEHIND EARS<br>Apply a little Moisturel cream behind ears at each diaper change | SUNSCREENS<br>Not for babies under six months, see page 243 | YEAST INFECTION<br>(diagnosis required)<br>• Topical antifungal cream |
| HEAT RASH AND HORMONE RASH<br>Do not treat | HEAT RASH<br>No need to treat under three months | HEAT RASH UNDER DIAPER THAT DOESN'T CLEAR SPONTANEOUSLY<br>• Zinc and starch powder<br>• Destin powder<br>• Cornstarch |

The number of creams and lotions available for babies' bottoms, heads, and bodies is overwhelming. Skin peculiarities in the first three months tend to be transitory and generally do not need much treatment.

A word about moisturizers. Moisturizers are not essential but an appropriate moisturizer has a number of uses, for example, as a soap substitute, for newborn peeling skin, for massaging your baby, for cleaning the diaper area and for treating crusty eyebrows and ears. Moisturizers are designed to retain the natural moisture of the skin, not to add oils to the skin. Choosing a moisurizer can be difficult because of the unlimited array available to buy. Here are some tips:

- Avoid expensive moisturizers with additives such as fragrances, vitamins, herbal extracts, honey, milk, and so on. Not only do they cost a lot more but also the claimed health benefits of the additives are unproven and may irritate new baby skin.

- One moisturizer is sufficient. You do not need different moisturizers for the face, hands and body. Moisturizing lotion is good for cleaning the diaper area, for massaging and in the bath. Moisturizing cream is thicker and useful for small areas such as crusty eyebrows and ears and dry skin patches.

- Look for an all-purpose hypoallergenic inexpensive moisturizer that has ingredients to help the skin retain it natural water (petroleum and glycerin). Moisturel products fit the bill, but there are many other brands as well.

## FOR MORE INFORMATION
Chapter 12: Safety *(for safe use of change tables, page 261, diaper buckets, page 257)*

**FURTHER READING**

*Baby Skin*, by Nelson Lee Novick MD, Clarkson Potter Publishers, New York, 1991.

# chapter **twelve**

# Safety

*I knew a Cappadocian*
*Who fell into the ocean*
*His mother came and took him out*
*With tokens of emotion.*

A. E. Houseman, "I Knew a Cappadocian"

A higher standard of living, improved preventive health care, better health education, and major advances in medical technology have all helped reduce the baby and child mortality rate.

It is sad to note, however, that while the preventable causes of death and disability have largely been eliminated, our young are still at risk from preventable injuries. Injury is the leading cause of death for children under fifteen years. The cost in cash terms to a community is estimated at millions of dollars a year. The cost in anguish, pain, and disability can never be measured.

Why do such accidents keep happening to our little ones? It's not because child safety is ignored. Excellent child safety information is available in books via the media and as part of parent education programs. Our hospitals have enthusiastic, knowledgeable staff available for advice and education. Laws are passed in the interest of child safety—for example, the mandatory use of child restraints in cars and bicycle helmets.

It's not because parents don't care. Wanting to keep our babies safe forever is a very strong instinct, so it's hard to understand why so many children die or need medical attention as a result of unintentional injury.

The greatest number of deaths and injuries occur in the one-to-four age group and are caused by motor vehicle/pedestrian accidents, drowning (the most common), choking, suffocation, falls, burns and scalds, poisoning, and electrocution.

As well as these specific causes, accidents happen for two important general reasons. People believe accidents to be fate or something that happens to someone else. Many parents take it for granted that they will know how to protect and care for their babies and children. In fact, child safety depends a lot on acquiring knowledge, recognizing potential hazards, planning ahead, and budgeting for safety items as they are needed. Very few adults understand or appreciate baby and child development before they have their own babies. Unless an effort is made to learn about development, parents are not always aware of the potential hazards their babies and children face living in an environment primarily designed for adult comfort rather than child safety.

Babies and children develop dramatically from birth to age five. Children between one and five years old are at greatest risk of injury, and home is the place where they are most likely to come to harm.

Babies in their first year are also vulnerable and need your protection, so it's worth taking a little time to plan a safe environment for your baby before the birth. As well, learn all you can about baby development as you go so that it's easier to understand the things babies do at various ages that are likely to lead to unintentional injuries.

Specific hazards relating to development and ways of avoiding injuries is looked at in each section of the book. This section gives you a general guide to making your home safe as well as looking at the special safety needs of babies in the first three months.

## The risk of injury is increased when:

- Either parent is unwell but especially when the mother is unwell;

- The baby cries excessively or the toddler is extremely active and never sleeps;

- There's great excitement caused by visitors, a new baby, and so on;

- There's a change of environment such as holidays, moving, or visiting;

- There's nowhere safe for the baby to play;

- The baby equipment doesn't comply to safety standards;

- The parents have unrealistic expectations of baby behavior and no understanding of normal baby development.

# Making your home safe

Once your baby arrives, you have much less time for housework, repairs, and shopping. The excitement, tiredness, and stress can also make you more vulnerable to injuries during the early months, so it's a good idea to think about repairs and changes before your baby arrives.

## Kitchen

- Replace electrical appliances and cords if they are old or you doubt their quality. Short or curly cords are much safer than old dangly cords.

- Make sure you have plenty of hand towels for quick drying of wet hands before using electrical appliances. A good supply of pot holders makes handling hot dishes and pots safer.

- Do you know what to do if a pan catches fire on the stove?
  a) Smother the fire with a damp cloth or lid; and
  b) Turn off the burner.

**NEVER**
  a) Throw water over the flame, or
  b) Attempt to remove the pot.

- Always keep a close eye on boiling fat or oil and never leave the kitchen while using boiling fat or oil.

- Overloading electrical sockets is dangerous. Lighting and appliance switches should be located well away from faucets.

- A non-slip floor is always advisable, but especially in the kitchen. It's a good idea to get into the habit of wiping up spills immediately.

- Replace tablecloths with placemats.

- Always turn the handles of your pots and pans inward. Get into the habit of using the rear burners before the front ones.

- Make sure your stove is well anchored to the wall or floor.

- A lid on your kitchen garbage helps prevent disease and, after your baby becomes active, helps prevent exploratory ventures into the trash and the possibility of her inhaling something.

- Keep knives and sharp tools out of reach—the same for matches and lighters. Plastic bags are a great hazard for babies and children so store them well out of reach too.

- Keep all detergents, bleaches, dishwashing detergent, and household cleaners locked up. If they are normally kept in a cabinet under the sink, install a child-resistant latch on the cabinet door.

- A dishwasher with a safety lock is strongly recommended.

## Bathroom

- The hot and cold faucets should be clearly marked.

- Never use electrical appliances or heaters near the bath or shower. Store and use all electrical appliances in a room other than the bathroom.

- Use a non-slip mat in the tub and on the bathroom floor.

- Install a child-resistant cabinet for medicines, aerosols, hair products, and so on.

- Remember to keep the toilet lid closed. Bathroom cabinets installed above the toilet are hazardous—toddlers love to climb onto toilet seats and open bathroom cabinets.

- Diaper pails full of liquid are a potential disaster because mobile babies could pull themselves up on them, tumble in, and drown, so if possible, keep them in the laundry or somewhere out of reach in the bathroom.

- Store scissors, razor blades, and any other sharp objects out of reach.

- Being able to open the bathroom door from the outside means no one gets locked in. Installing a privacy lock is a way of keeping privacy while maintaining access in case of an emergency.

# Laundry

- As in the kitchen, keep all cleansing agents, chemicals, and dangerous equipment in cabinets with child-resistant latches.

- Keep the washing machine and dryer closed at all times; again child-resistant latches are a good idea.

- A childproof lock on the laundry room door ensures unsupervised babies or children stay out.

# Bedrooms
## YOUR BABY'S ROOM

- Check and bassinets are safe and stable. Don't place that cribs or bassinets near windows with dangers such as hanging venetian blind cords or curtain ties—these are dangerous.

- Install bars and safety locks on bedroom windows to ensure that windows do not open more than 4 inches (100 mm). This will stop little ones from falling out. Leave the area around the windows free of furniture. Close and lock ground flees windows at night.

- Low-power night lights in your room, the baby's room, and the hall make it safer when you attend to your baby at night.

- A child-resistant lock or handle to your room and/or the baby's room will prevent smaller children from making unsupervised visits to the baby.

- Use child-resistant plugs.

## YOUR ROOM

- Store medications, perfumes, makeup, scissors, earrings, pins, cuff links, coins, and breakables away in a safe place.

- Safety catches are simple to install on the window in your bedroom. Don't put anything near your window that a toddler can climb onto.

## Halls, living room, and stairs

- Keep all doors, passages, and stairs free of obstructions.

- Arrange storage for vacuum cleaners and any other major electrical appliances.

- Use child-resistant plugs on all electrical outlets.

- Avoid slippery floor coverings, loose rugs, or highly polished surfaces.

- Special fire guards should be used in front of all fires. The guard should be firmly fixed to the floor or wall.

- Consider installing safety glass if you have large areas of low-level glass. Glass doors should be made more obvious by attaching a colorful motif to them at child and adult eye levels.

- Remove small, fragile, or breakable items until your youngest child is about five years old.

- Precious possessions, musical equipment, televisions, and videos should be kept as high as possible. Store tapes, records, and discs well out of reach.

- Alcohol is a poison for a child. Store alcohol and cigarettes well out of reach.

- Indoor plants should be non-poisonous, and you might find it easier keeping indoor plants outside until your baby is past the eating dirt stage.

• Loop curtain and blind cords out of reach as they are strangulation hazards.

## Pets

Pets who are used to a free run of the house need reeducating.. If you can change their habits before the birth, you will avoid potential hassles. Always supervise children with pets until they are old enough to know how to behave around animals.

## Treating your home for pest control

If you treat your home for pest control, find out the chemicals being used, and which may be harmful to babies and children. If possible, arrange to be out of the house when the treatment is being done and to allow some time for airing before being inside again. Always ask if there will be anything left behind (pellets, etc.) and where they are going to be left.

## For overall house safety

• Install a smoke detector;

• Lower the hot-water temperature to 50°C;

• Install a safety switch or a mains-operated circuit breaker.

Babies from birth to three months old are not very mobile, but you need to be aware of certain safety measures for even this young age group.

"When eyes are off, hands should be on" is a vital safety rule. It's amazing how quickly babies wriggle off change tables, slip under water, or roll off a bed.

## IF YOU ARE USING A CHANGE TABLE, MAKE SURE

- It is stable and will not collapse while you are using it;

- The sides are raised so that your baby can't roll off;

- It's the right height for you to work comfortably;

- The changing surface is strong, easy to clean, and there are no gaps or spaces near the changing surface that your baby's head or limbs can get caught in;

- You never leave her unattended on the change table. A strap to keep your baby in place is useful, but she still shouldn't be left unattended even when secured with a strap;

- Everything you need is within reach.

## Bottle and pacifier safety

- Bottles shouldn't be propped and left. If something needs your attention in the middle of a feeding ask for help, or, if it's not urgent, delay what needs doing until after the feed. If you have to answer the phone or front door, take the bottle with you.

- When buying a pacifier, go for a good-quality brand rather than a cheap one.

- Never dip the pacifier in sugar water or honey. There are potential risks of botulism poisoning from giving babies honey in their first year, and dipping pacifiers in sweet encourages a habit that may be difficult to break. Pacifiers dipped in sweet things eventually lead to black teeth.

- Never use anything, for example, a rolled-up diaper, to hold your baby's pacifier in place as she will be unable to spit out the

**261**

pacifier if she has trouble breathing and may suffocate.

- Attaching the pacifier to your baby's clothes with ribbon or string is a strangulation hazard. You also risk cutting off the blood circulation to her finger or hand if the ribbon or string gets wrapped around her finger or wrist.

- Keep pacifiers clean by giving them a good scrub, then boiling or steaming for a couple of minutes.

- Inspect your baby's pacifier regularly and replace it when necessary.

- Adults should not suck pacifiers before placing them into their baby's mouth. It does not clean the pacifier. Sucking the pacifier, in fact, is a potentially dangerous practice that can introduce a range of bacteria into the baby's mouth and gut which can cause health problems.

## Portable chairs

- Make sure the baby chair has a broad base so that your baby can't push back and topple over.

- Always secure your baby with the harness—the best harness is one that covers shoulders, waist, and crotch.

- Baby chairs can move off a table top amazingly fast propelled by nothing more than a baby's gentle movements, so the floor is the best place—don't forget to remind everyone the baby is down there! Keep a close eye on other children, pets, and adults carrying hot drinks or food.

# Cribs and bassinets

- Buy a crib certified by the Juvenile Products Manufacturers Association (JPMA).

- Place the crib or bassinet away from windows, heaters, and electrical outlets.

- Always remember to keep the crib sides up.

- Never use hot-water bottles or electric blankets for babies or toddlers.

- Remember to take your baby's bib off before you put her to bed.

- Remove plastic coverings from mattresses and dispose of immediately—don't use them to protect the mattress. Any plastic is dangerous—keep all kinds of plastic bags and film away from babies.

# Strollers and carriages

- Buy a good quality stroller certified by the JPMA.

- Make sure the brakes work properly. Test without the baby inside. When you buy, check that the safety harness has both shoulder, waist, and crotch straps and that they can be adjusted to be used effectively, even when your baby is very young. Babies falling from strollers is a very common occurrence, and it is often because safety harnesses are inadequate.

- Don't overload the stroller or carriage when your baby is in it. Try to avoid hanging shopping bags from the handles.

- Always fit and adjust the safety harness correctly.

- When you change the position of the carriage or stroller make sure your baby's hands or fingers can't get caught.

- Take care when using the carriage or stroller on escalators.

# Car safety

Cars are almost an extension of the home these days, and your baby is likely to spend several hours every week in the car. Here are some safety points:

- Never leave babies or toddlers alone in cars, especially in hot weather. When you leave the car parked, make sure the buckles and seats are covered as babies may be burned.

- Remove any loose objects or sharp-edged toys from the car before making any trip.

## Using an infant car seat (restraint) or a convertible car seat

- Always put your baby on her back. Never swaddle her in a receiving blanket before putting her in the seat. If blankets are needed, adjust the harness first then cover her.

- Adjust the crotch strap of the harness first, then adjust the shoulder straps until they are firm. The harness shoulder straps should be level with or above the baby's shoulders. Make sure your baby's arms and legs are not caught under the straps and the harness buckle clicks when it is done up. Remember to change the slots for the shoulder harness as your baby grows.

- The rear center position is the safest place for the car seat but this has to be weighed up against potential back strain for the mother getting the baby in and out of the car, so the right-hand side near the curb-side door is a reasonable option. Always take your baby in and out of the car by the rear curb-side door.

- When your car seat is in the rearward-facing position, make sure it is not resting on the back of the front seat as this interferes with the safe functioning of the seat.

- If you are using an infant (non-convertible) seat make sure the handle is in the down position once the seat is placed in the car.

- When you are on a long trip stop and give your baby a break from the car seat every couple of hours—when she is awake. Infant car seats have been designed to carry babies in cars. They are not intended to be used as bassinet substitutes. Try to avoid leaving your baby in the car seat for long periods.

# Other general safety tips

- Avoid holding your baby and drinking a hot drink at the same time. Ask friends to put their hot drinks somewhere safe when they hold your baby.

- Smoking and holding a baby is also a health and safety hazard. Give up smoking or if you can't, don't smoke or allow others to smoke near the baby.

- Powder is useful for some skin conditions. When using powder, put a small amount into a dish, then apply with your fingertips. Don't shake the powder vigorously into the air—your baby might inhale some.

- Cotton swabs need never be used. Cotton balls are quite adequate for noses, ears, and bottoms.

- Check clothing, especially bootees and socks, for loose threads that might cut off circulation or strangle your baby.

- If you give your baby medication, check what it does, what's in it, possible side effects, and the correct dose. Always read the label. If you have any doubts, don't give it.

## Toy safety

- All rattles, shakers, and stuffed animals or dolls should be free of small parts that could be chewed or pulled off and swallowed.

- There should be no sharp edges or harmful ingredients.

- Choose toys appropriate for your baby's age. Toys for toddlers may be dangerous for babies. Check labels, especially when your baby receives a toy as a gift.

- Throw away broken or grubby toys.

- Take care with the packaging. Babies often enjoy the packaging as much as the toy, so throw away any plastic and check the box for sharp bits or staples.

## Babysitter safety

It may be some time before you feel you can leave your baby, and obviously you will feel much more comfortable if you can leave her with a grandparent, family member, or a trusted friend when you do take the plunge. If you use an agency, make sure it is one recommended to you by someone whose advice you respect. Inexperienced teenagers are not the ideal babysitters for young babies.

**266**

- Show the babysitter how to use equipment such as the stove, heaters, and so on.

- Make sure she knows where your emergency list of phone numbers is (see below).

- Always leave your phone number and address and the phone number of a reliable friend or relative in case she can't locate you.

- Your babysitter also needs to know, in writing, what to do in an emergency and where the first aid kit is kept (see below).

- Leave your babysitter a reliable flashlight.

## Emergency numbers

Have a list of important numbers near the phone:

| | |
|---|---|
| POLICE | FAMILY DOCTOR |
| POISON CONTROL | 911 (SEE PAGE 501) |
| AMBULANCE | NEIGHBOR |
| FIRE DEPARTMENT | RELATIVE |
| NEAREST HOSPITAL EMERGENCY ROOM | PHARMACY |

# Your first aid kit

## DRESSINGS

Bandages in various sizes
Gauze squares for cleaning wounds
Non-stick pads that won't stick to wounds and cause bleeding and pain when removed
Adhesive tape
Triangular bandages to use for slings
Cottonwool swabs
Sticking plaster

Clean non-fluffy cloth or clean plastic film to cover burns until seen by a doctor

## CREAMS, LOTIONS, MEDICATIONS

Antiseptic solution

Calamine lotion

Saline eye wash for foreign bodies in the eye

Spray for treating stings

30+ sunblock cream

Paracetamol tablets and liquid with child restraint lids

A bottle of ipecac to induce vomiting only if you live more than thirty minutes from medical assistance. Ipecac should only be used on advice from a doctor or a poisons information centre as it is dangerous to use it for some poisons (for example, kerosene). Ipecac needs replacing every three years.

## FIRST AID EQUIPMENT

Safety pins of various sizes

Scissors with one sharp end and one blunt end

Tweezers

Disposable gloves

# Immunization

Immunization saves the lives of millions of adults and children world wide by preventing a number of serious infectious diseases that, prior to the development of safe vaccines after 1945, killed or disabled huge numbers of young children.

High levels of childhood immunization in a community protect not only the children who are immunized but those vulnerable others who are too young to be vaccinated, the rare baby who can't be vaccinated and those few who do not respond.

Immunization procedures, recommendations and vaccines are constantly being revised and it is impossible in a book to keep the information absolutely up to date. The information provided here is based on the best information available at the date of publication. If you are ever in any doubt about aspects of your baby's immunization please talk to your pediatrician, nurse practitioner or family doctor.

## What is the difference between vaccination and immunization?

Most people use the word vaccination and immunization inter-changeably but technically the meanings are slightly different. Vaccination is the term used to describe the process of giving the vac-cine (by injection). Immunization, on the other hand, is the term used to describe both getting the vaccine and then becoming immune to the disease. Immunity follows most vaccinations but not always.

## How does immunization work?

When bacteria and viruses make you sick, your body's immune system fights off the disease by making antibodies that either kill the bugs or render them harmless. Sometimes these antibodies con-tinue to protect your body from the disease long term (for example, measles) or the effect wears off more quickly which means you can become infected again (for example, whooping cough). Of course catching a disease also exposes you to all sorts of complications from the disease, including death and disability, so this is not the best way to acquire immunity.

## What is in vaccines?

Vaccines contain a small amount of a particular bacteria or virus that are scientifically changed so that they will not cause disease but will

**269**

make your body produce antibodies to protect you from the disease. Vaccines also contain a small amount of preservative or a small amount of antibiotic to preserve the vaccine and some vaccines contain a small amount of an aluminium salt, which helps produce a better immune response. Vaccines in America no longer contain thiomersal—a mercury containing preservative—however it is wise to check as some vaccines containing thiomersal may still be in the system.

## How quickly do vaccines work?

Protection from an infection does not occur immediately after immunization, because the normal immune response takes several weeks to work. Since this artificial immunity may wear off after a while, it is often necessary to get booster shots to build long lasting protection. For example, a baby who receives one or two doses of the combined diptheria-tetanus-pertussis vaccine (DTaP) is not totally protected against these diseases.

## How effective are vaccines?

Most vaccines are not totally protective and become less protective if national immunization rates fall. Illnesses are usually shorter and less complicated in vaccinated babies.

## Why do babies and toddlers need so many doses?

Babies and toddlers have immature immune systems that do not work as well as the immune systems in older children and adults, therefore more doses of vaccines are needed in the first five years of life to protect against the most serious infectious diseases of childhood. In the first two months of life, babies are protected from most infections by antibodies that are transferred from their mothers during pregnancy. As these antibodies wear off, the risk of serious infections rises so the first immunizations must be given before this happens.

# Are vaccines safe?

No vaccine is one hundred percent safe but the unpleasant side effects they sometimes cause are relatively minor and reversible. Serious adverse reactions to vaccines are not only extremely rare but are significantly less common and less severe than the diseases the vaccines prevent.

To date there is no conclusive scientific evidence supporting links between vaccination and HIV/AIDS, allergies, asthma, Sudden Infant Death Syndrome, autism or multiple sclerosis.

These days, even babies who are not immunized because of parental choice are more protected than those of years past because many diseases no longer exist and because the unimmunized have healthy lifestyles and diet.

# Benefits and Risks

Unfortunately immunization is now often viewed as a controversial procedure rather than an important step in helping to raise healthy children, and there are a growing number of people who have reservations about immunization.

This has happened because:

- Following the success of immunization programs we now have generations of children who have been protected from infectious diseases, so many parents today don't understand what a serious threat diseases such as diphtheria, polio and whooping cough was to babies and toddlers of previous generations. Or that the diseases will reappear if national immunization rates drop below certain levels.

- The small but influential group of activists who oppose immunization are very vocal, present their arguments with a great deal of fervor and provide good media copy. Part of their appeal is due to the fact that historically health professionals, public

271

health officials and associated agencies have not always dealt respectfully and honestly with valid parental concerns about the safety of vaccines. One of the positives about the anti-vaccine activists is that they have pushed health professionals and government agencies to take parental concerns seriously, answer questions and improve vaccine safety.

• Recently two safety lapses have contributed to distrust about immunization.

• One was the use of a preservative, thimerol, that contained mercury in a dose that was more than twice the safe amount recommended for young children by the Environmental Protection Agency. This was not altered until eighteen months after the issue first surfaced.

• The second was the vaccine-associated polio caused by the oral polio vaccine that causes eight to nine cases of vaccine-associated paralytic polio a year. Despite the fact that since 1979 the only cases of polio in the US were caused by the oral vaccine it was only in 1999 that the Centers for Disease Control and Prevention (CDC) switched back to the injectable vaccine that cannot cause polio.

• Unfortunately the age when immunization is given coincides with the time in early childhood when SIDS and brain damage caused by seizures is most likely to happen. This means that there is a chance that either of these things might happen as an *unrelated* event following immunization or the slight possibility the vaccination will bring on a problem that was about to happen anyway.

• The parents of the small number of babies who have or appear to have serious damage as a result of immunization will have strong concerns about the process for babies in general.

## Finding out the facts

I regularly speak to parents who justifiably feel they need more information beyond the "be wise, immunize" platitudes of the past, before they are prepared to undertake a procedure that they feel may risk the health of their babies. The dangerous downside of the anti-vaccine activists is that their claims are not based on objective scientific interpretation of data. Their theories do not stand up when measured against this criteria. When looking for information make sure you use reliable sources that use current, verifiable and scientifically credible sources (see Further Reading at the end of this chapter). Be aware, too, that official sounding names such as National Vaccine Information Center and Parents Requesting Open Vaccine Education are *anti-vaccine* networks.

## Homeopathic Vaccines

Homeopathic "immunization" has not been proven to give protection against infectious diseases. They are not put through the stringent safety tests the recommended vaccines have to undergo to make sure they work and are safe.

The Council of the Faculty of Homeopathy, London, issued a statement in 1993 that reads: "The Faculty of Homeopathy, London strongly supports the conventional vaccination program and has stated that vaccination should be carried out in the normal way, using the conventional tested and proved vaccines, in the absence of medical contraindications."

# *Vaccines and the diseases they prevent*

## Hepatitis B (Hep B vaccine)

Hepatitis B is a serious viral disease that causes acute and chronic liver damage. Babies who get this disease may only have mild symptoms or even none at all, however many of these babies will carry the virus and in adult life be able to pass it to other people. Hepatitis B is transmitted by infected body fluids—blood, saliva, semen. There are only three likely ways a baby or toddler will become infected:

- Through blood transfusion (rare today as all blood is carefully screened for this).

- Babies born to mothers with Hepatitis B are at high risk through blood exposure during birth.

- By continued, close contact with an infected person.

Hepatitis B can also be spread are by sharing of syringes, sexual contact and contaminated instruments such as those used for tattooing and body piercing.

Although the risk of babies and toddlers catching this disease is very small the American Academy of Pediatrics and the CDC recommend Hepatitis B immunization during infancy for the following reasons:

- To avoid the small risk of infection from a casual contact or unknown source

- To reduce the incidence of Hepatitis B in the country as a whole and eventually eliminate it. This goal is easier to accomplish by immunizing during infancy.

### POSSIBLE SIDE EFFECTS OF THE HEP B VACCINE:

Most side effects of the Hep B vaccine are minor and disappear quickly. They may include soreness at the injection site, mild fever, nausea and joint pain.

# Combined diphtheria, tetanus and whooping cough (DtaP vaccine)

## DIPHTHERIA

Diphtheria is caused by bacteria found in the mouth, nose and throat of an infected person. Diphtheria causes a membrane to grow around the inside of the throat that leads to severe respiratory illness. The poison (toxin) produced by the diphtheria bacteria can spread throughout the body and cause serious complications such as paralysis and heart failure. Diphtheria is now rare in the United States.

## TETANUS

Tetanus is an often fatal disease caused by bacteria in soil and manure that enters the body through a wound that may be as small as a pinprick. The toxin attacks the nervous system causing breathing difficulties and painful convulsions. Because of immunization tetanus is now rare in the United States although it still occurs in adults who have not been immunized.

## WHOOPING COUGH (PERTUSSIS)

Whooping cough is a highly contagious bacterial disease spread by coughing and sneezing. It causes severe coughing spasms and vomiting and is most serious in babies under a year of age. Complications include convulsions, pneumonia, coma and permanent brain damage. Around one in every 200 children who catches whooping cough will die from it. A more pure form of the whooping cough vaccine (acellular) is now available which has eliminated the number and severity of the reactions some babies suffered with the previous vaccine (whole cell).

This vaccine is also available minus the whooping cough component (DT) and as tetanus on its own.

## POSSIBLE SIDE EFFECTS OF THE DTAP VACCINE

The recommended (acellular) DTaP vaccine has few side effects. Some babies may have a mild fever and redness, soreness and swelling at the injection site. Mostly these will settle without treatment but acetaminophen can be given if necessary.

## HAEMOPHILUS INFLUENZAE TYPE B (HIB VACCINE)

Hib was the most frequent cause of life threatening infection in children under five before the introduction of the Hib vaccines in the 1980s. It is not related to influenza. It can cause meningitis, swelling of the throat, which can block breathing (epiglottitis), pneumonia and joint infection. Both meningitis and epiglottitis can develop quickly if left untreated and rapidly cause death. Despite the decrease in the incidence of Hib it is still prevalent especially in children under the age of two.

## POSSIBLE SIDE EFFECTS OF HIB VACCINE

Hib vaccines are very well tolerated with only five percent of babies having mild swelling and pain at the injection site.

## POLIOMYELITIS (POLIO) (IPV VACCINE)

Polio is a gut virus that causes fever, vomiting and muscle stiffness and can effect nerves and cause permanent disability. It can also paralyse breathing and swallowing muscles and lead to death. Due to immunization there has not been any naturally occurring cases in the U.S. since the 1970s. OPV (oral live vaccine) has recently been ceased and replaced with the new inactivated injectable vaccine (IPV) because of the risk of vaccine-induced paralysis with the OPV (one in 2.5 million doses, see page 272).

## POSSIBLE SIDE-EFFECTS OF IPV VACCINE

There are very few side effects from IPV. Mild symptoms such as headache and muscle pain may make a small number of babies fussy for a short time.

## COMBINED MEASLES-MUMPS-RUBELLA (MMR VACCINE)

Measles, mumps and rubella (German measles) are all serious viral diseases that still occur in America.

## MEASLES

Measles is a serious, highly contagious viral illness that causes fever, rash, runny nose, cough and conjunctivitis. Complications following measles can be very dangerous and include pneumonia, brain inflammation and a rare serious illness called subacute sclerosing panencephalitis (SSPE) that occurs in children several years after a measles infection. SSPE is a disease that rapidly destroys the brain and results in death, it develops in about one in 25,000 cases of measles. Only several hundred cases of measles occur each year in the U.S.

## MUMPS

Mumps is a viral disease that causes fever, headache and swelling of the salivary glands. Serious complications in children are rare. Outbreaks in the US occur but there are less than 1000 cases per year.

## RUBELLA

Rubella is a highly contagious mild viral infection that causes a slight a fever, swollen glands, joint pain and a rash. It is extremely rare for babies and toddlers to have serious complications from rubella, but it can cause birth defects if the mother becomes infected with the virus in the first twenty weeks of pregnancy. The best way to protect against rubella is to make sure *all* women are immunized before pregnancy, and to immunize *all* children.

## POSSIBLE SIDE EFFECTS OF MMR VACCINE

Five percent of children receiving the MMR vaccine develop a fever and sometimes a rash five to twelve days after immunization. Children who develop this rash are not infectious to others. Occasionally the mumps component causes mild swelling of the salivary glands about three weeks after the immunization. More serious reactions are rare and pose less of a risk than getting these diseases.

## MMR AND AUTISM

There is no conclusive evidence to date to support the alleged link between the MMR and autism. Two expert panels, one convened by the American Academy of Pediatrics and one by the National Academy of Sciences found that autism cases did not increase with the increases in the percentages of children who received the MMR vaccine.

## CHICKENPOX (VARICELLA VACCINE)

Chickenpox is an acute contagious disease caused by a virus. The infection in healthy children is generally mild with fever and itching with a rash. The disease in adults tends to be more severe with a higher incidence of complications. Babies born to mothers who contract chickenpox from five days before to two days after birth are at risk of an overwhelming infection with a thirty percent fatality rate.

Chickenpox has always been viewed as a common and harmless childhood illness that was part of everyday life however 1 in 60,000 deaths occur from chickenpox, almost all of them in previously healthy children and adults. It is also a very uncomfortable illness that requires a week at home to recover. The chickenpox vaccine may also protect against shingles, a very painful form of adult chickenpox.

## POSSIBLE SIDE EFFECTS FROM THE VARICELLA VACCINE

Some soreness and swelling at the injection site. Three to four percent of children receiving the vaccine develop a rash within three weeks of the vaccination. The rash is not infectious.

## PNEUMOCOCCAL DISEASE (PCV VACCINE)

Pneumococcal disease is an infectious bacterial disease that causes meningitis, blood infections, pneumonia and sinus and ear infections. It is the leading cause of bacterial meningitis in the U.S. About 200 children die from pneumoccal disease each year.

The pneumoccal vaccine (PCV) gives immunity against seven strains of the pneumoccal bacterium that cause most of the serious infections in children, however, there are other causes of meningitis that this vaccine will not protect against. Contrary to a popular misconception it will not prevent *all* ear infections as bacteria other than the pneumoccus cause many of the ear infections in childhood. The vaccine does decrease the number of ear infections by about 15%, and significantly decreases the number of ear infections caused by the pneumoccocal bacteria that are resistant to antibiotics which makes many ear infections easier to treat. The main purpose of this vaccine is to protect against serious infections such as meningitis and blood infections.

### POSSIBLE SIDE EFFECTS FROM THE PCV VACCINE

Soreness and swelling at the injection site and a mild fever.

### HEPATITIS A (HEPATITIS A VACCINE)

Hepatitis A is a viral infectious disease, passed by touch or in contaminated food. Poor hygienic practices by infected people is the main way the disease is spread, for example, inadequate washing of hands after a bowel motion. This vaccine is only recommended for use in selected states and regions, and for certain high-risk groups; consult your local public health authority.

## INFLUENZA (INFLUENZA VACCINE)

Influenza is recommended annually for babies over six months with certain risk factors such as asthma, cardiac disease, sickle cell disease, HIV, diabetes and can be administered to others wishing to obtain immunity. See your pediatrician or family doctor for more information.

| | |
|---|---|
| At birth: | Hep B#1 |
| Two months: | Hep B#2, DTaP, Hib, IPV, PCV |
| Four months: | DTaP, Hib, IPV, PCV |
| Six months: | DTaP, Hib, PCV |
| Twelve months to fifteen months: | Hep B#3, Hib, MMR#1, Varicella, PCV |
| Fifteen months to eighteen months: | DTaP, IPV |
| Four to six years: | DTaP, IPV, MMR#2 |

**Standard recommended childhood immunisation schedule United States, 2001**

## GETTING THE SHOTS—COMMON QUESTIONS

**Can more than one immunization be given at the same time?**
Yes. The vaccines recommended for routine use in babies and children can safely be administered at a single visit as long as they are given in separate syringes and in different parts of the body, for example, one in each thigh. There are ways of reducing the number of shots. Ask your pediatrician, family doctor or nurse practitioner about the combination Hib/Hep B vaccine and about using the brand of Hib vaccine that only requires three shots, not four. It is advisable however to stick to the schedule rather than spreading the shots out over too many visits. This does not cause problems for your baby, avoids unnecessary expense and inconvenience and makes it easier to keep track of the schedule and make sure no shots are missed.

## WHAT ABOUT PREMATURE BABIES?

Preemies should be vaccinated according to the recommended schedule from the actual date of their birth, not the expected date of birth.

## IS VACCINATION COMPULSORY?

All states require proof of vaccination before children can enter school; most private schools and daycare centers also require proof of immunization before they will accept your child. However not all schools and centers require every shot.

Medical exemptions to vaccination will allow entry to schools, for example leukemia, cancer or AIDS. And all states except Mississippi and West Virginia also accept religious exemptions. In some states qualifying for an exemption from vaccination is a complicated process that may require hiring an attorney.

## WHAT ABOUT LOW COST OR FREE VACCINES?

You can get low-cost or free vaccines at U.S. public health service clinics. To find one near you call (800) 232-2522. Every child up to 18 years of age who is enrolled in Medicaid, who lacks health insurance, or whose health insurance does not cover vaccines is eligible. All American Indian and Alaskan Native children are also eligible.

## SIDE EFFECTS

Many babies do not have any side effects to their immunisation. When they do the symptoms are usually mild—local reactions such as soreness, redness, itching or burning at the injection site for one or two days. Systemic reactions include fever, rashes, drowsiness and general discomfort that may make the baby irritable and unsettled for one or two days. About five percent of babies experience fever, rash, cold symptoms and/or swelling of the salivary glands (under the jaw) five to twelve days after the MMR. And around three to four percent will get a rash up to three weeks after the Varicella vaccine.

Rarely, a baby may become pale, floppy and unresponsive between one and twenty-four hours following immunization. This frightening event is called a hypotonic episode and happens to only a miniscule number of babies nevertheless it is extremely frightening if your baby happens to be one of the miniscule number. It is usually associated with the pertussis (whooping cough) vaccine but is much less likely now the acellular vaccine is the standard vaccine. A hypotonic episode can happen with other vaccines suggesting that the pertussis components are not the only factors contributing to such an event.

Follow-up studies show that all babies fully recover from hypotonic episodes and do not have repeat episodes with subsequent vaccines.

## TREATING SIDE EFFECTS

- If necessary give a dose of acetaminophen (Tylenol). The dose is 7mg per pound (15mg per kg) and the dose can be repeated in four hours. Acetaminophen is not a sedative but it has a mild sedative effect on some babies the first few times it is used. Never exceed the recommended dosage.

- Give extra fluids

- If side effects following immunization are severe and persistent, for example, a fever higher than 103°F, high pitched and prolonged crying, or if you are worried for any reason contact the pediatrician, family doctor or your nearest hospital.

# Vaccine Adverse Event Reporting System (VAERS)

VAERS is a system for reporting injuries suspected of being caused by vaccines. In the rare event your child has a vaccine-associated injury, or even if you think a medical problem your child has might have been caused by a vaccine, ask your doctor to file a VAERS form. You can also report a vaccine reaction to VAERS yourself. The toll-free information line is 1-800-822-7967.

## National Vaccine Injury Compensation Program

This is a federal program that offers compensation for the care of anyone believed to have been injured by vaccines. For more information call toll-free at 1-800-338-2382 or go to:http://www.hrsa.gov/bhr/vicp.

## Contraindications to immunization

Instances when immunization cannot be given are virtually non-existent, but unfortunately sometimes health professionals are nervous about being blamed for times when babies do experience adverse reactions and may unnecessarily delay or withhold immunization.

## None of the following are reasons to postpone or omit immunization

- A simple febrile convulsion or a pre-existing neurologic disease.

- A family history of convulsions or SIDS

- Asthma, eczema, hay fever, runny nose, snuffles or allergies

- Treatment with antibiotics

- Treatment with inhaled cortisone or cortisone cream

- Recent or imminent surgery

- If the baby is being breastfed

- If the mother is pregnant

- A history of jaundice following the birth

- Cerebral palsy, Down's syndrome or autism

- Contact with an infectious disease

**When you take your baby to be vaccinated, alert the doctor or nurse if your baby:**

- Has a major illness and/or a high fever that day

- Has ever had a severe reaction to any vaccine

- Has any severe allergies

- If she has had an injection of immunoglobulin or a whole blood transfusion in the last three months.

- Has had an immunity lowering disease, for example, leukemia, cancer, HIV/AIDS. Or if she is having treatment that lowers immunity, for example, steroids such as cortisone and prednisone or radiotherapy and chemotherapy.

- Has a medical condition that affects the brain or spinal cord

# SUMMARY OF THE MAJOR SAFETY HAZARDS AND PRECAUTIONS BIRTH TO 3 MONTHS

*Most safety hazards remain throughout early childhood. The chart emphasizes specific hazards associated with developmental stages at this age.*

| Age | Developmental stage | Safety hazards | Precautions |
|-----|--------------------|----------------|-------------|
| 0–8 weeks | little motor control—may lift head when on tummy | SUFFOCATION BY:<br>• plastic bags<br>• propped bottle<br>• pacifier held in position by a rolled-up towel<br>• tight clothing around neck | • remove plastic covering from mattress<br>• safe use of pacifier<br>• check baby clothing |
| 0–8 weeks | | BURNS AND SCALDS:<br>• bath water too hot<br>• hot drinks spilled on baby | • check water temperature before putting baby into tub<br>• don't handle hot liquids and baby at the same time |
| 0–8 weeks | | HEAT EXHAUSTION:<br>• baby left in car on a hot day | • open all car windows<br>• never leave baby alone in a parked car |
| 8–12 weeks | may roll over | FALLS:<br>• from change table, couches, and beds<br>STRANGULATION:<br>• head caught between crib bars | • never leave baby in a parked car<br>• never leave baby unattended in elevated position<br>• make sure gaps between rails on cots are between 2⅜" wide |
| 8–12 weeks | holds given objects for short periods | INJURY:<br>• babies of this age are unaware of what they are holding and have no control over their fine motor skills | • do not give sharp or breakable objects to baby to hold |

## FURTHER INFORMATION
The National Network for Immunization Information
66 Canal Center Plaza Suite 600
Alexandria, VA 22314
Telephone: 877-341-6644
http://www.immunizationinfo.org

National Immunization Program Website
http://www.cdc.gov/nip
National Immunization Hotline
(800) 232-2522

Consumer Reports has an excellent article on vaccination on their website: http://www.consumerreports.org/baby/report09.html

Another website that is an excellent source of supplemental factual information on the topic of immunization is:

http://www.geocities.com/issues_in_immunization/about_this_website.htm

# Growth and Development

*So far as I can see,*
*There is no-one like me.*

E.V. Rieu

Watching your baby grow and develop is such a miracle you are bound to find it one of the most joyful aspects of having a child. The rate at which babies grow and develop often causes confusion because of the wide variation in age for achieving a lot of the milestones and because what is a delightful stage for some parents is stressful for others. For example, the toddler years may be a joy for some while others find a certain nightmarish quality about the antics that go on during this time.

Constantly hearing how dreadful the next stage will be from well-meaning friends can get a bit annoying at times. Remember, every parent's experience is different at every age and stage of their baby's development, so try not to listen to tales of doom about future stages.

Despite the normal variations in baby and toddler milestones, you will find there is a basic pattern common to all babies. They smile before laughing, hold things before reaching out and grabbing, and usually sit before walking. Babies often achieve milestones, then forget about them temporarily. It's not unusual for them to repeat actions like waving, clapping, rolling, or making talking noises over and over again only to stop suddenly for a while. As long as they continue to grow and learn new things, this is nothing to worry about.

# What is growth?

Growth refers to an increase in size. This is easy to gauge by measuring weight, length, and head circumference. Most babies who are given the right food grow as they are meant to. Normal growth in healthy babies is quite obvious as they move from bassinets to cribs and from restraints to car safety seats.

Health professionals use prepared charts for assessing height, weight, and head circumference. These charts are called percentile charts and represent measurements of babies and children of a certain population (for example—all babies in America in a certain year). As normal variations in height and weight are considerable, the results are drawn on a graph in measurements of a percentage in order to allow for all the variations. The lines on the graph represent the fifth, tenth, twenty-fifth, fiftieth, seventy-fifth, ninetieth, and ninety-fifth percentiles. Most babies' weight and length fall somewhere between the fifth and ninety-fifth percentiles. Allowances have to be made for premature babies.

## Understanding the charts

If your baby is in the fifth percentile for height and weight, it means ninety-five percent of other babies her age are heavier and taller than she is. If your baby is in the ninety-seventh percentile, three percent of other babies her age are heavier and taller than she is. Both measurements are within the normal range.

Sometimes the concept of percentile charts is hard to grasp. Here's another way: imagine your baby in a room full of other babies her age. If she is in the third percentile, most of the other babies in the room would be bigger than her, but if she is in the ninety-seventh percentile, she would probably be one of the biggest babies in the room.

Percentile charts are useful as they are a visual way of understanding your baby's growth as well as seeing the wide range of measurements that are normal. Your baby will follow her own growth pattern, which depends a lot on family characteristics. Comments from onlookers such as "what a big/small baby" are nearly always false perceptions based on unscientific observations. If someone's comments alarm you, ask your nurse practitioner or pediatrician to plot your baby's measurements on a percentile chart. Ask to see the chart, and if you don't understand it, ask for an explanation. It doesn't matter which percentile your baby is in as long as growth is consistent and height and weight are in reasonable balance. (See percentile charts on page 602).

Interestingly, by the time they are three years old, only a small number of babies are in the same percentiles they start out in. Head circumference can also be charted on the percentile chart. Babies' heads are measured because their rapid growth in the first year makes it easy to check that they are growing at the right rate.

# What is development?

Development refers to your baby's ability to learn all the skills she needs to enjoy a good quality of life. To a large extent, development comes naturally to healthy babies who have plenty of love and attention. Development includes things like movement, language, toilet training, and play. We tend to take all these functions for granted, but acquiring them is amazingly complex.

Developmental achievements are referred to as milestones. Milestones are grouped under the following headings:

# Gross motor

- Involves control of large muscles. These skills enable babies to sit, walk, and run.

# Fine motor

- This refers to the ability to control small muscles. These skills enable your baby to manipulate so that she can hold a rattle, pick up objects, and eventually scribble with a pencil all over your walls.

# Vision

- Vision is the ability to see near and far and interpret what is seen.

# Hearing and speech

- Hearing is the ability to hear (receive) and listen (interpret).

- Speech is the ability to understand and learn language.

# Social behavior and play

- These skills enable your baby to learn socially acceptable behavior. Examples are eating, communication, and personal relationships.

A number of factors may affect growth and development. Some cause delay, which may be temporary or sometimes permanent, while some may advance babies in certain areas.

## Genetic influences

- Genetic influences can have quite significant effects on growth and development. Small, thin parents are likely to have small, thin babies. A father with a large head may have a baby with a large head. Special talents such as musical and sporting abilities often appear through generations.

## Prematurity

- Any baby born at less than thirty-five weeks (compared to forty weeks for a full-term baby) needs an allowance made for prematurity. For example—if birth was at thirty weeks, ten weeks is subtracted from the baby's age from birth in recognition of the fact that she is likely to attain her milestones up to ten weeks later than a baby born at forty weeks.

- By the time most premature babies reach their fourth birthday, four out of five have caught up with their peers, and many catch up long before this.

## Illness and/or prolonged hospitalization

- If your baby has to spend any length of time in hospital, development may be temporarily delayed.

- Babies who have major surgery may be late acquiring a few specific skills. This usually rights itself once they are back in their own surroundings. A long debilitating attack of diarrhea or the flu can delay milestones temporarily.

**291**

## Environmental and emotional deprivation

• When home is a place where a baby has plenty of love, stimulation, and attention, as well as the opportunity for a wide variety of play, a delay in growth and development is very unusual. Delay can happen when there is no love, an unstable, unsafe environment, and "no one cares if you grow or if you shrink."

## Babies born with problems

• A small number of babies are born with specific problems that will greatly affect their growth and development. Babies with conditions such as Down's syndrome, spina bifida, cerebral palsy, and so on need special help with their development so that they can live the best quality of life possible.

# Growth 0–3 months

Average birthweight is around 7 pounds (3175 grams) but healthy newborns can weigh from 5 pounds (2608 grams) to 10 pounds (4535 grams) or more. In general, boys tend to be a little heavier than girls, although there is great variation within this overall trend.

Weighing babies is just one way of checking on your baby's general well-being and by no means an essential part of her care. First babies seem to be weighed much more frequently than subsequent babies, who survive just as well.

Weighing is a useful guide for:

- Working out whether the breastmilk supply is low.

- Working out whether unsettled behavior in babies under six months is due to hunger or other factors.

- Adjusting the diet of a baby who is underweight.

- Adjusting the diet of a baby who is overweight.

Constantly weighing your baby under the supervision of an unsympathetic health professional can cause great stress, especially if you are breastfeeding for the first time. Weekly weighing is not necessary unless you feel like it or there are specifically defined medical reasons for doing so.

Work out some sort of weighing routine that you feel comfortable with or completely if you don't feel like it. It's advisable to weigh your baby on the same scales when possible as different scales give different results.

## Weight gains in the first three months

Your baby loses about ten percent of her birthweight in the first three to four days. This is caused by loss of extra body fluid, passing meconium (her first poo), and a limited food intake. She will probably regain her birth weight by the time she is ten days old, if not before.

Some babies need extra time to start gaining weight, so don't panic if the weight is a little slow, especially if you are breastfeeding. As long as your baby has good muscle tone, is vigorous, sucking well, and has six to eight pale, wet diapers, relax and carry on. From two to three weeks onward, babies gain anything from 5 ounces to 1 pound (150 to 450 grams). Weight and length never mean as much taken on their own as they do taken together and plotted on a percentile chart so that an overall pattern of growth can be seen.

## Length

Average length at birth is between 19 inches and 22 inches (48 cm and 56 cm). You will almost certainly find a discrepancy between the birth measurement and the next visit soon after birth at your pediatrician's office. Measuring babies accurately needs two people and the right equipment, which may not be available at birth, so don't worry if it appears your baby has shrunk or turned into a giant on the second measuring.

During the first three months, your baby will grow about 5¼ inches a month. Length increases in spurts every few weeks, so weekly measuring frequently shows no growth. Measuring every three to four weeks is much more rewarding.

# *Reflexes*

It's a good idea to know a little bit about baby reflexes. Apart from being interesting, it helps explain some of the strange things babies do. Some of the settling techniques suggested for restless babies relate to some of these reflexes.

What are they?

Reflexes are automatic responses to nerve stimulation, and a number are present in new babies. Some you will be familiar with as they persist to a lesser degree throughout life, such as jumping in response to a loud noise; sneezing; gagging; yawning; coughing; blinking.

Other reflexes are peculiar to babies and disappear at various times in their first year. Many of the things your baby does happen because she doesn't have control over many of these reflexes; however, recent research suggests some baby reflexes are accompanied by voluntary, intentional movements. Turning the head and seeking for the breast, taking the breast, and sucking are thought to be examples of this.

The three main reasons for baby reflexes are:

## a) Survival and protection

Certain reflexes are needed for life outside the womb, so that babies can obtain nourishment and breathe. Reflexes involved in obtaining nourishment are the rooting reflex, the sucking reflex and the swallowing reflex. (These are explained on page 296.) An example of two reflexes involved with breathing are yawning and the way a baby automatically turns her head to one side to breathe when placed on her tummy. Examples of protective reflexes are blinking, gagging, and coughing.

## b) For living life in the womb

Crawling and walking reflexes are directly related to life in the womb. Babies use their feet to push off the side of the womb as they move about inside the womb during pregnancy, so after birth if pressure is applied to the soles of their feet, they respond by stepping or crawling. These reflexes have nothing to do with later crawling and walking and are gone by four weeks.

## c) Primitive reflexes

I find the most fascinating reflexes are those thought to be related to early humans. These are called primitive reflexes.

Grasp reflexes in hands and feet are there in memory of an age where it was necessary to clutch onto fur. Your baby will demonstrate the grasp reflex by closing her fingers over your forefinger if you put it in her hand. She will also grasp anything else that comes in contact with her palm such as your long hair, the chain around your neck, the side of the tub, or her father's hairy chest.

Touching the soles of her feet will make her toes curl.

Grasping fingers and clenched fists start to lessen after three months. The grasping toes don't disappear until she can stand alone.

Another primitive reflex is the Moro reflex. Any jarring or sudden change in your baby's balance will make her throw out her arms and legs. The Moro reflex is very strong for two months and gone by three to four months.

Here are some other reflexes you are bound to notice:

## Sucking

The sucking reflex is a powerful one. Not all the sucking your baby does relates to hunger and food. Babies frequently suck on objects even when they are not hungry, especially when they are overtired or upset. This is called non-nutritive sucking and appears to be an inborn, natural thing that babies do to relieve distress. Some babies need to do this more than others. The sucking reflex is replaced during the first few months of life as voluntary sucking takes over when objects are placed in the baby's mouth.

## The rooting reflex

When your baby's cheek is touched either on purpose or accidentally, she will turn her head in the direction of the touch and open her mouth to suck. Parents often mistake the rooting reflex for a sign of hunger. Your baby does do this when she is hungry, but she will also behave like this lots of times when she is awake and stimulated, whether she's hungry or not. The rooting reflex is very strong for three to four months and may be present for up to a year.

## The startle response

Noise, a sudden movement, or your baby jerking herself awake makes her fling out her arms and legs, cry, and get quite upset. These reflexes often make it difficult to settle young babies because they keep waking themselves up, which is why some settling techniques involve wrapping or holding your baby firmly to help her get into deep sleep.

## The quivering lip

Sudden noise, movement, or change of your baby's posture often starts the bottom lip quivering, which in an older child or adult indicates emotion or cold. The quivering bottom lip in a young baby is another reflex and not indicative of either of these things; it is due to external stimuli such as being undressed or disturbed.

## The gag reflex

Gagging is an automatic response to stimulation of the lower part of your baby's throat. It is our bodies' natural defense to unsuitable things going down the throat and persists throughout life, but the gag reflex is very exaggerated in babies compared to the gag reflex in adults. It can be quite significant in older babies who gag a lot when they are given finger food or lumpy food—parents often mistake this for choking.

# Development: newborn to six weeks

## Gross motor

When your newborn lies on her tummy, you will notice she lies with her arms and legs curled up because of the way she has been lying in the womb. If she was born bottom-first, her legs will not curl up as much.

Most newborns lift their heads while they are on their tummies and turn their heads from side to side if only for a second. They do this to gain their balance.

If you lie your baby on her back and pull her gently toward you, her head will fall back behind her body. This is called head lag and is why it's important to support your baby's head when she is being held, fed, or bathed.

**297**

# Fine motor and vision

• **Fine motor:** Your baby grasps objects that come in contact with the palm of her hand.

• **Vision:** Your baby is able to see from birth. Young babies are near-sighted, so brightness and movement will attract your baby's attention, and faces and eyes are the things she focuses on best. Hold your face close to her face, move it slightly from side to side, and watch how she follows you with her eyes. Do it any time after birth when she is relaxed and alert.

# Hearing and speech

• **Hearing:** Your baby is able to detect a loud noise and respond with a startle reflex (a jump) from birth, but you will find her response is not there for every sudden loud noise. When she is sleeping deeply, crying, distracted, or feeding, a sudden noise will often make no impression whatsoever. You may find when you try to make her jump by clapping or banging a door, there is no response, so don't worry the life out of yourself by continually trying to test her hearing. After a few weeks, you will start to notice she does respond to noises such as an adult coughing or sneezing, keys rattling, or a dog barking.

Newborns respond selectively to different sorts of sounds. A soft noise such as a "whooshing", music, or a lullaby can soothe and calm your baby while a loud, jarring noise has the reverse effect. She will also stop crying at times to listen to your voice.

Every year approximately 24,000 babies are born with significant hearing impairment, and the American Academy of Pediatrics wants every parent to know that early detection of hearing impairment is crucial for optimum language development. Every newborn should have their hearing tested. The cost for an accurate test is around \$30–\$40, covered by state funding or most insurance carriers. In most states, hearing testing is now mandatory.

- **Speech:** Until your baby starts to coo and make other noises from about six weeks, crying is her only vocalization, although not her only form of communication. She does have other more subtle ways of communicating such as grasping your finger, staring intently at your face, and coming off the breast when she wants to, but crying is the form of communication you're likely to be most aware of in the early weeks. The amount and duration of crying is highly variable between babies. Some babies cry infrequently and only then for an obvious reason; others confuse and bewilder everyone by crying for long periods of time for reasons impossible to work out.

## Social behavior and play

Many of your baby's reflexes are outside her control, but you will notice there are times when her response to things is intentional. Research in the last twenty years shows that newborn babies are capable of responding purposefully and making choices. Responding to your voice and being comforted by rocking, sucking, cuddling, or skin-to-skin contact are all examples of this. Your baby is aware of differences between tastes—from a very young age babies frequently reject water but drink breastmilk or formula eagerly.

# *Development: six weeks*

## Gross motor

By six weeks, your baby has noticeably more head control, so you will find you don't have to support her head as much when you lift and hold her.

## Hearing and speech

- **Hearing:** Sudden noises will make your baby jump, although there are still times when she doesn't respond.

- **Speech:** Between five and eight weeks, she will start to make beautiful gurgling, cooing noises when you talk to her. The first responsive noises babies make are magical sounds.

## Social behavior and play

- Along with the cooing noises, the first smile appears—and what a moment that is! A small number of babies smile as early as ten days. People love to refer to early smiling as gas. A non-communicative grimace, which is very common for babies to do especially when they are sleeping, is not a smile (nor is it gas); but when your baby looks at you and smiles in a way that is definitely communicative, ignore suggestions of gas—it is a smile! The average age for the first smile is between five and eight weeks.

# Development: three months

## Gross motor

At three months, your baby has almost full head control with sometimes slight head lag when you pull her toward you from a sitting position. If she doesn't mind lying on her tummy, she will prop herself up on her arms and crane her head around, practicing her balancing and getting a grand view of the world. When you hold her standing on a firm surface, she may bear her weight, sometimes sagging a bit at the knees. Lots of babies love to stand and bear their weight from as early as eight weeks. If your baby does, you will not cause her any harm by letting her stand as much as she wants to (as long as you have the patience to hold her—some babies like to stand all day). It is a myth that early weight bearing causes back problems or makes babies bowlegged, so ignore comments suggesting this.

## Vision and fine motor

- **Vision:** By three months, babies can't get enough to look at. Between three and five months you might find feeding becomes tricky because of the way your baby is constantly distracted by everything around her.

  Human faces and eyes still hold the most interest, especially yours. She will now follow your movements around the room.

- **Fine motor:** At around this time you will notice your baby's fists and fingers are never out of her mouth. Continually putting her fists and fingers into her mouth is part of your baby's sensory motor development and not a sign of teething or hunger. Nor is it a bad habit you have to do something about. There's no need to put mittens on as it's important for your baby to have access to her fingers.

  All babies do this to some degree, replacing fists and fingers with objects when they are old enough to deliberately grasp things to put into their mouths. They have an in-built internal drive that motivates them to explore and find new stimuli so that they can learn about the world around them. As well as this, three to four months is the age babies start to do things intentionally. When your baby sees her hands drifting past her face, she puts them into her mouth on purpose and keeps repeating the action, at times frantically pushing her fists so far in she makes herself gag. The everything-in-the-mouth stage remains constant throughout the first year and gradually decreases during the second year.

When you place a rattle in your baby's palm, she will grasp it and wave it aimlessly, not really knowing she's holding it. Eventually it just drops out of her hand spontaneously without her being aware that it has gone. She will not look for it. Hand-to-eye coordination enabling babies to know they are holding something and to deliberately put objects other than their hands in their mouths starts between four and five months.

Sometime between three and four months your baby will start to clasp and unclasp her hands and to look at them a lot.

## Hearing and speech

- **Hearing:** Your baby now responds more consistently to loud noises. In fact, being super-sensitive to loud or sudden noises is normal for a lot of babies this age (especially the noise of the vacuum cleaner). She also gets excited at the sound of approaching voices or footsteps.

- **Speech:** The cooing quickly becomes constant vocalization (talking noises), which has a delightful musical sound.
  Chuckling and laughing start at around three months.

## Social behavior and play

Three to four months is a magical age. When your baby wakes, she probably makes lots of tuneful noises now instead of crying, particularly in the mornings. Most babies of this age really enjoy their baths—although if your baby doesn't, it doesn't mean anything is wrong. She will love to be tickled, played with, talked to, and sung to.

# Variations in milestones

Developmental milestones are geared to about the middle fifty percent of babies. They do not allow for the two extremes of the developmental scale, which are still normal. Try not to worry yourself needlessly by comparing babies or expecting a milestone to happen the day your baby turns a certain age.

Normal variations are greatest in the gross motor area. Here are the commonly noticed variations in the first three months.

- **Rolling:** From four weeks to nine months. Involuntary rolling can happen from as early as four weeks, so never leave your baby on an elevated surface and walk away.

- **Head control:** Some babies develop strong head control very early; others still have wobbly heads that bob forward at three months.

- **Supporting weight when held on a flat surface:** From eight weeks to nine months.

- **Smiling:** Ten days to eight weeks.

- **Responsive cooing noises:** As early as a few weeks to eight weeks.

- **Tuneful talking noises:** From seven weeks to three months.

# Stimulating things to do

Parents today are bombarded with ways to provide optimum development. Many find the feeling that they should be constantly involved in stimulating activities, flashcards, musical appreciation, swimming lessons, and baby gym overwhelming, especially when there don't seem to be enough hours in the day to do the necessities let alone endless activities.

Remember, your baby is part of your family. Being part of a family involves times for housework and maintenance, personal time for each family member, and times when everyone is together. A healthy baby given the proper food in a loving home will grow and develop at her own rate as she is meant to. Extra activities are great when you have the time and money or when they provide a social outlet you both enjoy, but there are lots of simple things you can do that are not greatly time-consuming and do not cost much.

Here are some suggestions for the first three months:

- Walking: It's fine to prop your baby up as soon as she is taking an interest in the world at large. Just make sure she is secure and not able to fall out when you go over a bump.

    At home she will like looking at mobiles hung about 12 inches (30 cm) from her crib. Make sure the mobile is always out of your baby's reach. Mobiles can be changed from time to time.

- From as early as two to three weeks, your baby can sit in a portable baby chair so that she can see what's going on around her.

- Lots of babies enjoy lying on some towels on the floor without their diapers on.

- A selection of inexpensive toys that your baby can start to learn to reach for helps her hand-eye coordination. Things that squeak or make an interesting noise are popular as are dolls with realistic faces and wobbly toys that bounce back when swiped at.

- Your face, your eyes, your voice, and your touch are the most important learning and entertaining things for her.

## A word about tummy time

Mothers are frequently advised that it is important to give their babies regular time on their tummies in order to ensure optimum development. Some experts believe that regular tummy time strengthens back and neck muscles, encourages head control and coordination, and is a great aid in helping the baby to learn to crawl. The emphasis on tummy time has recently increased with the recommendation that babies be placed on their backs to sleep from birth to decrease the risk of SIDS. There is now concern that there are increased numbers of babies with a flatness at the back of their heads due to sleeping on their backs, and tummy time is being recommended to help the temporary head flatness.

Tummy time is not a problem for mothers who have babies who enjoy time on their tummies. But many, if not most, babies protest heartily after half a minute, which causes their mothers great distress.

Encouraging babies to enjoy tummy time involves lying down with your baby face to face, talking to her, and amusing her while she lies there. The aim is to try to extend the time each day.

## IS THIS REALLY NECESSARY?

In my opinion the answer is no for the majority of healthy, normally developing babies who will learn to crawl, walk, and otherwise develop as they are meant to.

The world is full of examples of perfectly developed babies who are kept wrapped for the first years of their lives. For example, a study found that Navajo Indian babies who had been kept more or less immobile in cradleboards throughout most of their first year walked at exactly the same age as Western babies raised in capital cities.

Some babies with specific disabilities or born prematurely need a variety of guided activities to enhance their development, which may include tummy time, but this is not necessary for most babies.

Temporary head flatness caused by sleep position rights itself once the baby is moving around during the night and sitting up either alone or supported. See page 200 for more information about the head shape issue.

Do not let me discourage you if you want to spend time each day encouraging tummy time. On the other hand, avoid letting it become a motherhood stress test.

# Toys

Toys are very much related to your baby's development. In the first three months, toys and activities are centered around stimulating your baby with sounds and small movements. Here are some suggestions for the first three months:

- Rattles squeakers, and shakers.

- Mobiles: Your baby will like to look at a mobile from a very young age. Black and white geometric shapes with pictures of faces create great interest.

- A pull-the-string music box hung out of reach keeps young babies interested and can help them settle.

- One or two soft, washable toys for company.

- Between eight weeks and three months, your baby starts to look straight ahead, opens her hands some of the time, and starts swiping at things, so a toy frame with dangling bits and pieces is a suitable toy at this age.

- Clear, colorful pictures around the walls create interest. It's fun to walk around the room with your baby having a conversation about the things and people in the pictures.

You don't have to have wall-to-wall toys at any age. Babies and toddlers do better with a few at a time, and no matter how ideal the toy, their attention span is limited, so they will become bored with anything after a period of time, which varies from baby to baby. Try not to have too many unrealistic ideas of the entertainment value of toys. A few well-chosen items that suit your baby's age and stage of development are essential, but there is no toy on the market that will keep any baby entertained for hours every day or replace getting out of the house whenever possible or being played with by parents or brothers and sisters.

# Developmental summary: 0–6 weeks

## Gross motor

- lying on back—head goes to one side

- pull to sit from lying—head falls back

- when held sitting—back curves a lot

## Vision and fine motor

- pupils react to light

- follows a face one-quarter of a circle

- can see from birth—near-sighted

- hands usually closed

- grasps a finger placed in palm of hand (involuntary)

### Hearing and speech

- startled by a sudden noise
- coos and smiles by six weeks

# Developmental summary: 3 months
## Gross motor

- lying on back—head stays in the midline
- pull to sit from lying, little or no head lag
- when held sitting, back curves slightly
- lying on tummy usually lifts head
- when held standing—may support weight, likely to sag at the knees

## Vision and fine motor

- visually very alert
- follows a face and eyes half a circle
- plays with hands—fists constantly in the mouth
- holds a rattle if you place it in her hand but is unaware she has it

## Hearing and speech

- sudden noise distresses
- vocalizes tunefully

## Social and play

- usually enjoys bath

- loves to be talked to and played with

### FOR MORE INFORMATION

Chapter 8: Breastfeeding Your Baby After the First Two Weeks *(breastfeeding, low supply, page 138, breast refusal, page 161)*
Chapter 14: Sleeping and Waking in the First Six Months *(startle reflex, page 314, crying patterns, page 315)*
Chapter 15: The Crying Baby *(crying patterns, page 332, weighing, page 345)*
Chapter 24: Feeding Your Baby *(gagging, choking, page 499)*
Chapter 12: Safety *(toys, page 266)*

### FURTHER READING

*From Birth to Five Years—Children's developmental progress*, Mary D. Sheridan, revised and updated by Marion Frost and Ajay Sharma, Routledge (Import), 2nd Edition, 2001.

*Touchpoints—The essential reference guide to your child's emotional and behavioral development*, T. Berry Brazelton, MD, Perseus Pr, USA, March 1994.

*The New First Three Years of Life*, Burton L. White, Simon & Schuster, USA, 1995.

chapter **fourteen**

# Sleeping and Waking in the First Six Months

*Sister Peters says that newborn babies mostly sleep well. It is*
*only when they get home they start bawling their heads off.*

Elizabeth Jolley, *Cabin Fever*

We are now moving into the trickiest area in the world of babies—
that of baby behavior. Behavior describes what the baby does or
doesn't do without making value judgments about her character
now or her character in the future.

Crying, waking, and sleep mostly relate to baby behavior and
not to the more tangible things you will keep hearing about like an
inexperienced mother, food, or medical conditions. The term
behavior is not used as a way of describing babies as "good"
and/or "bad." "Good" and "bad" are meaningless labels based on
adult concepts that we persist in giving humans at an age when
they have not yet developed any control over their behavior. A lot

**310**

of the ways that babies behave relate to them adapting to a new environment by doing what they have been programmed to do for the last 40,000 years to ensure their survival.

A range of behavior is observable and common to most babies which is what much of the advice given to mothers about crying, waking, and sleeping is based on, but it is vital to understand that:

- Babies are unpredictable.

- Frequently, clearly defined reasons to explain why the baby's doing what she's doing do not exist, so there are no guaranteed solutions all of the time to difficulties with sleeping, waking, and crying.

Information about babies' sleeping and waking often leads parents to believe there is always an answer to making babies sleep and stop crying and only one set of correct guidelines to follow. Unfortunately, experts in baby care often think they have to solve problems and provide answers when there are none, often giving mothers quite unrealistic goals. The word *should* seems to be used a lot. For example: "your baby should be sleeping through the night"; "in the day your baby should be up for one and a half hours then should sleep for one and a half hours"; "when your baby wakes after twenty minutes she should be put back to sleep" and so on. The mother ends up feeling hopeless when the advice doesn't work and usually assumes it's something she's doing wrong or she has a "bad" or sick baby. Most of the time, just knowing what's normal, how long a particular way of behaving is likely to last, and that not that much can be done to change what's happening is the most helpful approach for the mother and her baby.

Looking at all the safe options rather than attempting to diagnose, cure or make healthy babies behave in a certain way is the approach I use. Giving a diagnosis or one definitive answer is

**311**

limiting and traps parents. Providing options allows them to make choices and enables them to care for their babies in their own way.

# Let's look at sleep first

Babies have to learn to sleep; sleeping for long stretches on their own is not something that comes naturally, and some learn to do it quicker than others. Babies are all different, so the individual range of sleeping and waking they do varies considerably.

The way we sleep whether we are babies or adults is quite complex and consists of various stages ranging from being awake to dreaming to light non-dreaming to deep non-dreaming. Dreaming sleep is called rapid eye movement sleep (REM).

## Here is a simple description of the stages of sleep

- Non-REM sleep varies from stages of drowsiness to very deep sleep. When woken from very deep sleep, we are slow to respond and confused.

- During REM sleep there is increased brain activity. If we are woken from REM sleep, we become quickly alert.

- Brief wakings occur at various times between stages of sleep. During the night the average sound adult sleeper wakes briefly up to nine times a night, returning quickly to sleep a lot of the time unaware of waking, so there is no such thing as "sleeping through." "Sleeping through" is a term used to describe the way a baby sleeps who no longer disturbs her parents during the night. The baby who "sleeps through" does in fact wake throughout the night but puts herself back to sleep without waking her parents.

When young babies are in REM sleep, they twitch, breathe irregularly, sometimes grimace (not a sign of gas) and flicker their eyelids. When they are in non-REM sleep they lie very still. Breathing is much more regular with an occasional sudden movement or startle, which is enough to wake some babies and start them crying.

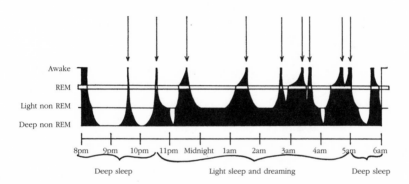

**Each arrow represents the number of times we briefly
wake in the night (babies and adults)**

How we sleep

REM sleep takes up to fifty percent of a baby's sleep cycle compared to twenty-five percent in adult sleep cycles. During the first three months, babies go into a REM sleep cycle when they first fall asleep. By three months of age, this is reversed, and the first stage of sleep is non-REM, which continues through life. The entire sleep cycle (that is, passing through the various sleep stages) takes fifty minutes in a baby compared to ninety minutes in an adolescent. Some researchers believe that the increased amount of REM sleep in young babies may be an important factor in brain development.

Just looking at baby sleep cycles alone, without even thinking of the usual reasons given for erratic sleep (hunger, too hot, too

**313**

cold, gas, and so on), gives us some very good reasons why babies have such irregular sleeping and waking patterns:

- The increased amount of REM sleep means they wake more easily and are often alert and ready to go when they do wake, and mothers usually find it's very difficult, if not impossible, to get their babies back to sleep.

- As young babies go to sleep via REM sleep, it takes longer for them to pass into non-REM and deep sleep, so there are times when helping them go to sleep is also difficult.

- Jerky movements or the startle reflex may wake them suddenly out of deep sleep; this can happen after only an hour's sleep. Again, getting them back to sleep is difficult.

- The brief waking from one stage of sleep to the next brings babies fully awake. Until they learn how to put themselves back to sleep every time, it is normal for them to cry some of the time when they wake in between sleep stages.

## How much sleep do babies need?

I don't think anyone knows for sure; the range for healthy newborn babies varies from nine to eighteen hours every twenty-four hours. Some babies either do not seem to need much sleep or cannot sleep more than nine hours every twenty-hour hours. This makes them harder to live with as they tend to get overtired, which makes them ornery, but it does not harm them in any way.

Rather than look at what "should" happen, I think it's much more useful to look at what does happen with most babies' sleeping and waking patterns in the first three months.

# Sleeping and waking variations in the first three months

## The first two to three weeks

Many babies start out eating and sleeping in very regular patterns. When they cry, it's easy to work out what the matter is, and everyone around the mother says "what a good baby." For most of them, this doesn't last long, and by week three, they are starting to behave quite erratically—sleeping less and crying more at times when no one can work out what the matter is.

## After three weeks

### THE MOST COMMON SLEEPING AND WAKING PATTERN

One five-to-six-hour sleep (if you're lucky, during the night), a couple of three-hourly sleeps, several two-hourly sleeps, and up to five or six hours of catnapping, interspersed with wakefulness and crying.

### THE UNSETTLED PERIOD

Eighty percent of normal, healthy, well-fed babies have one session of unexplained crying every twenty-four hours. This usually starts to happen around three weeks and continues until they are eight to twelve weeks old. The session of crying behavior lasts from one and a half to five hours. It's often in the evening but may happen at any time. The other common time is the unsociable hours just before dawn. I call this the unsettled period.

**WHY DOES IT HAPPEN?** No one really knows because the baby can't tell us. When your baby is feeding well and sleeping well most of the time, apart from the unsettled period, accepting it and working out ways to manage until she changes is more important than trying to figure out exactly why it is happening. The unsettled

**315**

period is rarely anything to do with breastfeeding, the brand/type of formula, or burping techniques, although fond relatives will almost certainly keep talking to you about gas and a little pain. When such a high percentage of healthy babies behave like this, one can only assume it is a normal response to the dramatic change of their environment from the womb to the world, as well as an inability to sleep at this time. They become stressed and overtired and are unable to either get to sleep or enjoy being awake.

## WHAT CAN YOU DO DURING THE UNSETTLED PERIOD?

Here are the options to think about until the unsettled period stops happening (at about three months, if not before).

**OPTION 1. GIVE UNLIMITED BREASTFEEDINGS:** Babies often look hungry when they are unsettled because they seem to want to suck all the time, so some women just keep breastfeeding their babies until they eventually settle. Peace is achieved for a while whenever the baby is at the breast. The frequent breastfeeding does not harm the baby in any way, but some women find the constant feeding exhausting and notice in the long run their babies fuss and cry whether they are fed a lot or not.

Babies having formula should not be offered unlimited amounts of formula during the unsettled period as bottle-fed babies cannot adjust the volume of milk the way breastfed babies can and may just keep drinking whatever they are given. At best this makes them throw up and at worst makes them overweight. As hunger is not the cause of the unsettled period, try not to offer formula more than every two and a half to three hours; keep to the amount your baby usually drinks at other times.

**OPTION 2. LIMIT THE FEEDINGS, TRY OTHER SETTLING TECHNIQUES:** Keep to your normal feeding pattern instead of breastfeeding continuously. Give your baby one feeding, offer a top-off an hour later (if you're breastfeeding), then wait the usual two and a half hours before the next feeding.

Instead of feeding:

- Wrap, rock, and pat: Try swaddling your baby firmly, put her to bed, and rock the bassinet while you pat her bottom. If she goes to sleep, she is more likely to stay asleep than if you put her to sleep at the breast or in your arms and then put her down. (See helping-to-sleep tips, page 328).

- Keep her next to you (or give her to your partner) in a sling or front pack for as long as it is acceptable to you (or your partner). When the unsettled period is in the evening, handing the baby over to someone other than the mother helps. Some women find it upsetting when their partner walks in and calms the baby fairly quickly. This happens because an unavoidable level of stress builds up between the baby and her mother when the baby is unsettled, so another person who has not been with the baby all day can often break the stressful cycle. When the father is the one at home all day, the same thing happens to him, so don't feel it's something you're doing wrong or that your baby doesn't like you.

- Try a bath: It doesn't matter if she's already had one that day. If she's been very unsettled and you haven't fed her for a few hours, a bath and a feeding often do the trick—sleep descends.

- Pacifiers: Using a pacifier helps some parents and some babies. Not all babies will take pacifiers and there are some negative aspects to their use (see page 57), but if giving your baby a pacifier brings some much needed relief, go ahead.

**317**

## OPTION 3. LIMIT FEEDINGS, ALLOW SOME CRYING (THE BABY, THAT IS, AND MOTHER TOO IF YOU FEEL LIKE IT):

Leaving babies to cry is never easy. Some parents find it easier than others and most parents find it easier when it is not their first baby.

There is much confusion surrounding the concept of control crying—the idea of leaving your baby to cry for a while when she is having a long session of fussy behavior during her unsettled period and can't get herself to sleep and stay asleep.

I prefer not calling it control crying when babies are under six months, as that implies a regime or method that aims to get a permanent, predictable response within a certain time. I don't think that it is possible or even appropriate to attempt to teach babies much less than six months to sleep by leaving them to cry as a planned strategy day in and day out. It is true that sometimes these regimes appear to work quickly with very little crying involved (probably because the baby was going to settle anyway, not because of the particular control-crying strategy). However, it is equally true that there are many times when the baby cries endlessly and the mother gets more stressed trying to put the regime in place. Unlike some people, I do not believe that control-crying regimes are necessarily harmful for younger babies, but there are too many times when they do not go according to plan and so create stress for the baby and anxiety for the mother.

In general, I find that responding promptly to young babies' crying as often as possible in the first six months is the best way while parents and babies are finding their way. This strategy will eventually get the same results, often more quickly and with less pain, than trying to comply with a control-crying regime (modified or otherwise).

I am not suggesting, however, that it is necessary for the mother to wear herself out with constant rocking, patting, breastfeeding, and walking the floor. Nor am I suggesting that every parent has to leave their baby to cry when they don't want to. Rather, I believe that allowing a healthy, well-fed baby to cry at times is a safe option in a loving home. Depending on the baby, most parents find that it is impossible to avoid some crying sessions each day and that there are times when leaving the baby to cry for a while is preferable to the other options.

**SUGGESTIONS FOR LETTING A BABY CRY:** Keep to your normal feeding pattern.

Leave her up for half an hour to an hour after the feeding, sitting in a portable chair, or on the floor without her diaper on, or hold and cuddle her. After this, give her a top-off (if you are breastfeeding), then put her to bed and give five to ten minutes of comforting (rocking, patting, and so on), then leave.

Go back into the room every ten minutes or so and do a little more rocking and patting or pick her up if you want to—calm her and put her down again. In between visits, get on with whatever needs doing to take your mind off the crying. If the crying is really upsetting you, pick her up and go back to either of the other options, but try to wait twenty to thirty minutes because she may go to sleep. Some mothers find that when they let their babies cry on and off for a couple of hours, then give them a bath and a good feeding they fall sound asleep and stay asleep; the unsettled period only lasts two and a half to three hours instead of the five- or six-hour stint that happens when babies are kept up and walked, rocked, and patted and breastfed for hours at a time. Tolerating some baby crying does help develop better sleep patterns for a number of babies.

**WHAT ABOUT WHEN THE UNSETTLED PERIOD IS IN THE MIDDLE OF THE NIGHT?** It's not easy. Letting babies cry in the middle of the night is usually quite an unrealistic suggestion and not particularly useful when they are under six months old, so you either stay up and walk the floor, rock and pat, or go back to bed and take your baby with you. If you don't want your baby in your bed for the next few years, make sure she's back in her own bed by the time she's three months old. When you are up a lot at night, you have to try and catch up on sleep in the day, and I know this is difficult, especially if there are other children, but at this stage of your baby's life it is easier to change your sleep habits than to try to change hers.

## THE CATNAPPER

A number of babies never sleep soundly for three to four hours at a time. After twenty minutes they stretch luxuriously and become instantly alert as if waking from eight hours sleep! Many babies can be taught to sleep through the night after six months, but I have never found a way to make babies who don't sleep much in the day sleep more or longer. If your baby catnaps and is otherwise reasonably content and feeding well, it's best to accept the fact that her daytime sleeps will be short and frequent rather than longer and fewer. Trying to resettle babies who catnap after they wake is difficult and needs a lot of persistence as well as being able to tolerate a fair amount of crying, with every likelihood nothing is going to change. Most mothers decide it's a pointless exercise. Babies who catnap usually sleep well at night.

## THE DAYTIME SLEEPER, NIGHT WAKER

Quite a few babies sleep very well in the day and wake every couple of hours through the night. If your baby does this in the early weeks, there's a good chance she may reverse the pattern herself by the time she is a month or so old. It's usually worth waking babies for feedings every three and a half to four hours during the day from about three weeks of age rather than letting them sleep six hours. This will help them to start to learn the difference between night and day.

## BAD DAYS

Everyone has bad days with babies and toddlers. Bad days happen when a chain of events lead to everything in the day going from bad to worse, with a nightmarish quality descending by evening. The first bad day you have with your baby will come as a shock, particularly if things have been running smoothly until now. Your baby may sleep lightly, wake early, feed poorly, and cry a lot no matter what you do.

**WHAT DO YOU DO?** Don't panic—a bad day is exhausting and stressful but rarely a sign of anything major.

If you feel you need to, ask someone you trust (nurse, practitioner, pediatrician) to check your baby to make sure she is well. A vigorous baby with good color and six to eight pale, wet diapers is likely to be just fine despite the fussing and crying.

During the day, get out of the house with your baby if possible. Staying at home and listening to the crying makes everything seem worse. Even sitting in your pediatrician's waiting room can make things seem better. Alternatively, reassurance from a sympathetic friend or your mother helps a lot, especially if they are able to take over for a while.

Bad days always end eventually. Everyone has at least one in the first few weeks and several in the first three months.

## THE SUDDEN MAJOR CRYING EPISODE

A sudden crying episode that appears to come out of the blue for no apparent reason is quite common in healthy babies at any time in the first year but is more likely to happen in between two and six months. The baby is quite happy one minute and inconsolable the next, and it is often difficult to calm her.

**WHAT CAN YOU DO?** Stay as calm as you can. The more agitated you get, the more your baby will cry. Sudden crying episodes last up to four hours and all you can really do is see it out. A bath helps. Often after a bath and a feeding, sleep will descend.

If your baby is otherwise well and it doesn't keep happening or go on for lengthy periods (more than four or five hours), a sudden crying episode is usually not a sign of anything significant. If in doubt, see your pediatrician.

### THE SIX WEEKS CHANGE (SOUNDS LIKE THE MENOPAUSE)

Some babies, whether breast or bottle fed, go through a change around six to eight weeks where they are more wakeful (therefore cry more) and want to feed all the time. When this happens, it may last about two to three weeks. For a number of years this has been called a growth spurt and while such an explanation is certainly reassuring, I'm not at all convinced that it is the reason for babies' behavior around this time. Other researchers feel it has to do with a big leap in the baby's mental development, enabling her to learn a new set of skills that changes the way she perceives the world, causing confusion and bewilderment.

Whatever the reason, an unsettled few weeks is certainly observable in an appreciable number of healthy, well-fed babies around this time. Like a lot of things to do with babies, it's unclear because the baby can't tell us and all we can do is hazard a guess. If your baby changes around this time, remember it's normal and temporary. Give extra feedings and cuddles until it passes.

## Night waking under six months

Most babies wake at least once in the night, cry, and won't go back to sleep without attention. This is something that is better to accept than try and change when your baby is under six months of age.

As previously mentioned, sleeping through really refers to the stage when babies start to put themselves back to sleep in the night without waking their parents. The age at which they do this varies tremendously, and because this is a common topic of conversation between families, mothers often think something is wrong when their babies are still waking at night.

It's important to remember your baby's waking habits at night have nothing to do with your ability as a mother or your baby's development. Sleeping through is not a developmental milestone like walking, sitting, smiling, and so on.

## Night sleeping and waking variations

- Baby takes a late evening feeding (between 8 pm and 11 pm) and an early morning feeding (1 am to 4 am). Roughly sixty percent of babies stop needing one of these feedings between six and twelve weeks.

- Some babies continue to wake and need attention once a night (between 1 am and 4 am) indefinitely.

- Other babies need no attention for eight hours or longer from as young as eight weeks, then suddenly start calling for room service again once or twice a night at about four months.

- About twenty to thirty percent of babies continue to wake and cry every three to four hours through the night, indefinitely.

Some babies do sleep between eight and twelve hours permanently from about six to eight weeks of age. *What's their secret?*

## HERE ARE THE USUAL STRATEGIES PARENTS TRY, TO ENCOURAGE UNDISTURBED NIGHTS IN THE FIRST SIX MONTHS

- **Waking the baby between 10 and 11 pm for a feeding to avoid getting up at 2 or 3 am.**

  It's worth a try, but the results are extremely variable. For example, some babies are difficult to wake, don't eat well, and still wake at 3 am. Others wake quite happily, eat well, then stay awake for the next two hours! A few wake happily, eat well, go back to sleep, and still wake at 3 am. Many parents I talk to find this strategy makes things worse, not better, so don't persist if you find this is the case. Try to go to bed earlier (at least a few evenings a week).

- **Replacing feeding with rocking, patting and pacifiers.**

  Babies under six months can't really be 'trained' to sleep longer, so this strategy usually means everyone gets less sleep. Occasionally giving the pacifier instead of feeding may bring instant, sustained sleep, but chances are you'll be up and down all night replacing the pacifier.

  A feeding is usually the best way to settle babies at night when they are under six months, so don't hesitate to start feeding again at night if necessary.

- **Giving extra food.**

  It is often suggested that giving extra food in the day or the evening helps babies stop waking at night. Sometimes this appears to do the trick, but the relationship between food and babies' night waking is extremely unpredictable. If you wish to try food from a spoon as a way to encourage undisturbed nights, wait until your baby is three months old and try not to see it as the magic answer, as ninety percent of the time it isn't.

Starting one bottle of formula as a top-off in the evening to improve the nights does work sometimes when you're breast-feeding, for an unfathomable reason, even when there is obviously plenty of breastmilk. Nutritionally it's not necessary for your baby when you have plenty of breastmilk, so whether to try or not is up to you.

Generally speaking, giving extra food whether it's formula or food from a spoon is not going to make any difference unless the baby is not getting enough to eat and is hungry, and even then it may not change anything. I see many instances where an underfed breastfed baby who sleeps all night starts waking again when given more food.

When your baby is still waking a lot at night after six months, strategies can change if it is a problem for you. See Chapter 28, page 542.

# Routines and spoiling

It's unfortunate the word *spoil* is still used often when we talk about babies and how to look after them. Spoiling is a negative word that suggests a spoiled baby will grow into an unpleasant child who no one likes.

When parents are worried about spoiling their baby, it implies babies can deliberately make parents do what they want them to do by acting in certain ways. Conflicting advice from lots of people who are all sure they are right makes it difficult for a new mother to know whether she is spoiling her baby or not; if she is, does it matter?

The term *spoiling* shouldn't be used when we talk about babies, especially in their first year. A baby is too young to try to make her parents behave in a certain way by thinking through the results of

**325**

her actions; for example, "If I cry a lot, they'll pick me up."

Living with the way a young baby eats, sleeps, and cries is one of the hardest things parents have to learn to adapt to. Some babies obligingly fall into a regular eating pattern and learn to sleep on their own very quickly. It is often assumed these are "good" babies with efficient mothers, but in fact these babies just happen to adjust to our way of life a little faster than others. This does not make them grow up to be better people.

The eat-and-sleep babies whose parents proclaim proudly "we don't even know we've got her" are in the minority. Perpetuating the myth that this is how babies are meant to be causes new mothers a great deal of anxiety.

Generally, working out how best to meet a baby's needs either by trying to organize a flexible routine or simply not bothering with a routine is one of the trickiest areas of babycare. Years ago, experts' advice centered around a rigid eating and sleeping routine that involved letting the baby cry for long periods if she didn't happen to fit in with the schedule. Today's experts tell us just as strictly to always pick your baby up so that she'll feel secure and loved, and to meet all her needs promptly, feed her whenever she cries. This is often at odds with advice from the older generation—don't pick the baby up all the time or you'll spoil her. No wonder new parents feel confused!

Trying to make a baby behave in a certain way by imposing a set of rules on her before she has developed any control over her behavior makes life unnecessarily miserable for the baby and her family. During the first six months of a baby's life, a routine is more for adult convenience rather than something that is essential for a baby's well-being. Routine becomes more important later. Toddlers and children need stability and routine for security and safety.

So it's much better to take a reasonably relaxed approach if you can and try not to get yourself in a knot about four-hourly feeding and sleeping regimes. A baby's natural instinct is to be held and breastfed more or less continuously. It does not come naturally to babies to be fed larger amounts less often and put somewhere on their own to sleep, although this is what fits in best with our very structured way of life. In many cultures babies are given the breast constantly while permanently attached to their mothers. This probably avoids a lot of the hassles mothers go through in our culture trying to work out how to make babies cry less and sleep longer but is not a practical approach for life with a baby as we live it. Patience and flexibility are needed while our babies learn to fit in with our way of life.

During the first six months, it may seem at times that the days and nights with your baby are chaotic, but you will find as the months go by a pattern emerges that tends to become more consistent in the second six months.

If a routine is important to you, it is much easier to gradually structure eating, sleeping and waking cycles over a reasonable period of time. When possible, stick to a consistent way of doing things even when your baby doesn't sleep much. If you keep changing her feeding, bathing, and sleeping routines, her sleeping and waking cycles will remain unpredictable and irregular.

On the other hand, if routine doesn't matter at all to you, just do what you feel comfortable with.

All babies and families are different. Babies thrive just as well in families where they are guided into a flexible routine as they do where there is no routine at all, as long as their homes are safe, stable, and loving.

# Summary of sleeping and waking: 0-6 months

There are ways of encouraging babies to sleep, but remember there are no guaranteed solutions all of the time to the problems of crying and sleeping, so don't feel inadequate when you can't help your baby to sleep; baby experts don't know the answers a lot of the time either.

There are times in the early weeks when parents may have to change their routines (mother sleeps in the day, father cooks the dinner and maybe sleeps in another room for a while), as at this time it is impossible to change the baby's routine.

## Here are some helping-to-sleep tips

• Abolish the words good, bad and spoil from your baby vocabulary and encourage those around you to do the same.

• Look for options rather than solutions.

• Make sure your baby is not hungry. Hunger does not play a major role in wakeful babies, but if you're breastfeeding, a quick check of your baby's weight tells you if there's enough milk; a one-off clothed weight is sufficient. Little or no weight gain over several weeks is an indication she might be hungry. If you're bottle feeding, make sure you're making the formula up the way it's supposed to be made.

• Is your baby ready for sleep? From three weeks on, babies start to have regular times when they are happy to be awake. This time increases as they grow older. When they are ready for sleep, they start to cry or grunt and suck their fists. Their movements become jerky and they lose eye contact.

- Babies sleep better on a firm mattress. There are no particular mattresses that are more advantageous than others in relation to SIDS.

- The following things are options, all of which work some of the time. Some of them are unacceptable to some families, some of them are not possible because of family lifestyle, and some may lead to hassles later, but they are all safe.

> Breastfeed your baby to sleep;
> Rock and pat your baby to sleep;
> Sleep with your baby;
> Try wrapping your baby firmly so that she can't wake herself up when she startles;
> Carry her in a sling;
> Give her a warm bath;
> Play some soothing music;
> Go for a walk;
> Give her a pacifier.

Unfortunately, if babies only ever learn to associate sleep with these things, it often means they don't know how to sleep unless these things are present. For example—when a baby goes to sleep on the breast or in her mother's arms, she will often wake again soon after being put into her crib and it is very difficult to help her back to sleep. Once she is up again, she gets tired very quickly, starts to cry, goes to the breast again, falls asleep, is put into her crib, only to wake again a short time later when the cycle is repeated. The reason this happens is because the baby goes to sleep under one set of conditions, and when she wakes briefly, as she passes from one sleep stage to the next, is immediately aware her environment is different, so comes fully awake and starts to cry instead of slipping into the next stage of sleep.

As time goes by, mothers find it more and more difficult to carry out these routines. So another option is to put your baby down awake and let her cry to sleep sometimes. Like all the other options, sometimes this works and sometimes it doesn't, but letting a well-fed, tired baby cry before sleeping can be an aid in helping her to learn how to sleep. Try leaving her for up to twenty to thirty minutes sometime during the day or the evening, following the guidelines on page 316.

## FOR MORE INFORMATION

Chapter 5: Choosing Baby Products *(pacifiers page 57)*
Chapter 12: Safety *(pacifiers page 261)*
Chapter 28: Sleeping and Waking Six Months and Beyond *(teaching to sleep, page 543)*
Chapter 11: Daily Care *(where to sleep page 245)*
Chapter 19: Common Worries and Questions *(thumb sucking page 455)*

# chapter fifteen

# The Crying Baby

*Babies can cry without learning, as far as I know, yet*
*they have to learn to make all other sounds.*

Kate Llewellyn, *The Mountain*

All babies cry. You may find listening to your baby cry is one of the hardest parts of being a parent. From your baby's point of view, crying is an essential part of her survival and not something she does to irritate or upset you.

## Why do babies cry?

Baby crying has helped the human race survive; it is a vital way of communicating. It's the most obvious form of early communication but not the only one. Young babies send out communication in other more subtle ways. They gaze intently at an adult face, coo, smile, grasp a finger, and indicate when they don't want food by not sucking or pulling away. Mothers respond to all these things and take great pleasure in many of them. Crying, however, is the most powerful way babies have of communicating when they are very young and to some extent during the whole of their first year.

Parents are often unprepared for the crying, believing that as caring people who are only too happy to do the right thing and meet all their baby's needs their baby will not cry. They find it shattering to discover that a certain amount of crying is normal for all babies and for some babies that amount is a lot.

Parents, understandably, start to think it would be much easier if their baby's main way of communicating was not by crying, but crying is the main way babies have of letting their protector know they need something.

A lot of the time what they need is obvious and easy to provide. Obvious causes of crying are things like hunger, overtiredness, thirst, feeling too hot or too cold, loneliness, overstimulation, being undressed and bathed, or being alarmed by a sudden noise.

Babies also cry when they are in physical pain. An accident, an injection, or a circumcision are clear-cut reasons for distress we can all understand. Medical problems such as an inguinal hernia or a bowel obstruction are other painful experiences. It's very upsetting when a baby gets sick, but, once diagnosed, the problem can be treated; knowing something can be done always brings a sense of relief.

When there is no obvious cause, mothers, fathers, and even health workers feel helpless, hopeless, and distressed, especially when the crying goes on for a long time. I'm sure the baby feels pretty miserable too.

# Patterns of crying

The age and times of day babies cry tend to fall into patterns that can be identified.

From birth to three weeks, many babies sleep a lot; the crying periods don't last long and are easy to resolve.

From three weeks onward, things may change, sometimes dramatically. Babies tend to cry more and sleep less. The crying, unsettled behavior can roughly be divided into three groups:

- Explained crying is expected crying and the cause is obvious. It is easy to do something that calms and settles the baby such as feeding, changing, or gently rocking. Sometimes a bath, a walk, or, if it's in the middle of the night, taking the baby to bed is what's needed.

- Unexplained crying is unexpected crying for a reason that is hard to find. Unexplained crying for a short period every twenty-four hours is normal for about eighty percent of all babies.

- A small number of babies (about twenty percent) cry a lot for large parts of the day and night, so instead of having one session of crying they have several that go on for a long time. These babies sleep poorly, wake early, cry, and draw up their legs a lot. Days stretch into weeks and into months, with no change. There are bad days and worse days, rarely any good days, until things slowly start to change between three and six months. This sort of crying in healthy, loved, protected babies remains to a large extent a mystery and is what this chapter of the book is about.

Glance at the titles in the baby book section of any bookstore. You will always find a number of books offering the definitive reasons, cures, and ways to help babies who cry a lot. I can only add my point of view to what's already circulating. Like all information related to crying babies, my approach will help some and not others. I do tend to write more about what doesn't work rather than what does because despite the constant flow of literature and research for the last one hundred years, no causes or treatments have been identified that have made any significant difference to helping crying babies who appear to be otherwise healthy. Ideas change, new theories replace old, but the babies keep crying.

If your baby cries a lot, it is important to be aware that:

- The majority of crying babies are healthy babies who do not have a clearly defined, treatable medical problem.

- There is not an easy, single answer that suits every baby who cries excessively.

- Crying babies invariably grow into delightful older babies and toddlers.

- This period of your baby's life is something you have to go through together. Practical help, support, and understanding help a great deal, but beyond a certain point, parents are on their own.

I hope the following chapter contributes to your understanding of these babies and helps you and your baby through the crying.

# How does excessive crying affect the family?

Even though in the sum total of a baby's whole life this is a tiny part, living with a baby who cries excessively can have a profound effect on the parents, their relationship, and family life. Most people are astounded at how much time any baby takes up even when things are going well. If the baby spends a large amount of time every day crying and unhappy and apparently not responding to all the love and attention she is getting, the mother becomes physically and mentally exhausted.

## Mental exhaustion

Feelings of guilt, loss of confidence, and loss of self-esteem may come from within or may be triggered by health professionals, partners, grandparents, or the neighbour. Women whose babies cry a lot often become isolated simply because even if they can accept the crying, others can't.

A mother with a crying baby may feel disappointed when a much loved beautiful baby doesn't meet everyone's expectations— not a good baby. Disappointment might turn to anger as the mother tries harder and harder and becomes more and more exhausted.

This is a pretty grim scenario and of course not everyone experiences all of these feelings all of the time, but it is quite normal for a mother in this situation at times to wish she had never had the baby and for both parents to see life before the baby as quite pleasant.

## Physical exhaustion

Women find so much time in the day is spent with the baby that there is little left for anything else and the house becomes chaotic. Well-meaning advisers tell mothers to forget about the housework, knowing they themselves would find it stressful living in a mess. It would be more useful to offer practical help.

A constantly crying baby causes a physical response in some women. Chest pain, sweating, palpitations, nausea, or light-headedness are all common. Add to this sleep deprivation and often an inadequate diet—is it any wonder women working under these conditions are in a state of physical exhaustion!

## Relationships

Relationships are certainly tested in ways they never were before the baby arrived. Sex and social life tend to become non-existent. Couples who previously lived in harmony argue over the best way to look after the baby (pick up, let cry, share the bed, separate room, medicate, don't medicate, stop breastfeeding, keep breast-feeding, change the formula, and so on and so on).

Some fathers blame the mother; some ignore the mother's distress and feel sorry for the baby. Others become helpless and hopeless, insisting on their right to sleep, so the mother starts to feel she is dealing with two crying babies, not one.

Another man might want to share the responsibility and give as much support and comfort as he can, only to find the mother shuts herself and the baby off from him. He starts to feel useless and switches off.

Constant crying is doubly difficult when there is no one to share feelings or help decide the best options. Sole parents with no one often find they end up using medication or leaving the baby to cry, even when they don't want to do this. There just seems to be no other solution.

A constantly crying baby is likely to give any relationship, good or bad, somewhat of a battering. In general, good relationships stay good after a baby arrives and bad ones tend to get worse—the baby only emphasizes how good or bad the relationship is. This is magnified for the twenty percent of parents who have a baby who cries a lot in the first three to six months; however, many relation-ships emerge stronger and a new bond forms between the couple.

## *What can be done?*

1. **Rule out hunger and feeding problems.** Very few crying babies cry because they are hungry; the reason for the crying is rarely that simple, but it is important to make sure. If your baby is cry-ing a lot and you are breastfeeding, weighing the baby is the most reliable way of checking the likelihood of hunger. A one-off

clothed weight is sufficient. Little or no weight gain over several weeks is an indication she might be hungry. If weighing reveals hunger is the cause of the crying, giving extra food will help your baby to be more settled.

- **Breastfeeding:** Check your baby is in the best position to feed well. Worrying, unexplained crying in a healthy breastfed baby who is gaining weight well is rarely a breastfeeding problem. It is suggested that excessive crying in some breastfed babies happens because the baby is only getting the foremilk, which means she is getting too much lactose (the sugar found in milk) and that changing the way the mother breastfeedings solves the problem. If the mother is feeding for relatively short times at each breast, she is told to leave the baby on the first breast until the baby decides to come off before offering the second breast. Note that research shows it is not possible for babies to consistently consume only low-fat foremilk. I have not found altering breastfeeding patterns makes any difference to an unsettled baby's behavior and often raises unnecessary doubts in the mother's mind about her ability to breastfeed and the quality of her milk at a time when that's the last thing she needs.

  Excessive crying happens equally to breastfed and bottle-fed babies, so weaning does not mean the crying stops. Some women manage better by weaning, but think everything through carefully before you take this step if breastfeeding means a lot to you.

- **Bottle feeding:** Make sure you are making the formula the way it's supposed to be made. When babies are crying a lot, it's always tempting to keep changing the bottle, the nipple, and the brand and type of formula, but this rarely makes any lasting difference. In general it's best to stick to a cow's milk-based infant formula suitable from birth.

2. **If you are concerned about your baby's health, have her checked by a pediatrician to rule out the possibility of a clearly defined medical condition.** Persistent crying occasionally does have an obvious underlying medical cause that is possible to diagnose accurately. When this is the case, the medical cause can be successfully treated, which brings an end to a lot of the crying.

## The main medical causes

### INGUINAL HERNIA

A hernia in the groin can become clamped off by the tight muscles in the groin. This is called strangulation, causes intense pain, and should be operated on as soon as possible. A similar thing can happen to baby boys who have an undescended testis, although this is rare.

Note, a squashy lump on the navel that pops out when the baby cries is an umbilical hernia. Umbilical hernias are very common, rarely cause pain, and are unlikely to be the cause of constant crying.

### INTESTINAL OBSTRUCTION

When a baby cries a lot, parents are often worried that something is wrong inside because their baby turns red and draws up her legs when she cries (see page 341 for an explanation about this). Several medical conditions can cause intestinal obstructions in babies, but:

- they are very rare;

- babies born with these conditions are nearly always diagnosed soon after birth;

- the other main type of intestinal obstruction (intussusception) is more likely to occur between three and twelve months and is usually a clear-cut diagnosis;

- crying due to intestinal obstruction is accompanied by weight loss, pallor, a sudden change in the baby's poo and an alarming change in the baby's behavior. Turning red, grunting a lot, and drawing up their legs is normal behavior for most babies and not a sign of pain.

## URINARY TRACT INFECTION

A small number of crying babies do turn out to have urinary tract infections. Once treated, the baby is much happier. Testing of a crying baby's urine is now routine. Other signs apart from the crying might be thick, smelly urine with obvious discomfort when the urine is being passed by a very irritable baby who might also have a fever.

## BABIES BORN WITH PHYSICAL OR MENTAL DISABILITIES

Most of these problems are diagnosed at birth or soon after. Unfortunately some are less obvious, and it may be many months before parents know exactly what is wrong.

For example: cerebral palsy—minor degrees of cerebral palsy are difficult to diagnose and can cause tense, crying babies; deafness can cause crying, unsettled babies; undiagnosed heart conditions can also be a cause of irritable babies who do not eat well and gain weight poorly.

All these things are rare and unlikely to be the cause of your baby's crying, but because they do exist and are sometimes overlooked, make sure your baby is checked by a pediatrician.

## COMMON INFECTIONS

Illnesses such as head colds, viral diarrhea, bronchiolitis, sore throats, or ear infections are either obvious causes or easily diagnosed and can all contribute to a crying baby. When the baby recovers, the crying behavior settles whereas the healthy, crying baby cries on.

Viral diarrhea, sore throats, and ear infections are a much more common cause of explained crying in older babies and toddlers and are not seen very often in babies under three months of age.

## THE FOLLOWING THINGS DO NOT CAUSE PERSISTENT, UNEXPLAINED CRYING IN HEALTHY BABIES

Teething; cradle cap; heat rash or hormone rash; frothy or loose poo in a healthy breastfed baby; constipation in a bottle-fed baby; thrush; diaper rash.

Having ruled out hunger and the possibility of an underlying illness, there remain the myriad theories and unproved diagnoses with their accompanying treatments that parents quickly become familiar with as they try to find an answer. Writing about every theory and suggested cause is a book in itself, so I will look at the major themes in use at the current time to explain and/or treat crying babies under two groups—medical and non-medical.

# Medical approach

Unlike the previous medical conditions, these medical conditions are not clear-cut, so the treatment may not be wildly successful. The majority of babies who are treated for the following conditions probably haven't got what it is they are being treated for.

Apart from finding the few babies who have the diagnosed condition and so benefit from the treatment, the other advantages of the medical approach are:

- It helps the mother to feel better and stop blaming herself for her baby's distress.

- Medication often has a valuable placebo effect. A placebo effect refers to a positive result achieved by a non-medical remedy or a harmless medical remedy prescribed for a non-existent condition. The placebo effect should never be ridiculed because no one knows for sure why some babies cry so much in the first three to six months. If harmless remedies and simple diagnoses help parents through a critical period, the placebo effect should be encouraged. By understanding that a placebo effect exists, parents are also more aware of the limitations of medications and remedies.

- It gives the mother a concrete plan of action instead of vague reassurances.

The medical approach also has disadvantages:

- It can give parents unrealistic expectations of results.

- A medical diagnosis not properly explained is very worrying for some parents—they think their baby has a serious long-term illness, which is not the case.

- Searching for a medical cause can start a merry-go-round of medication and feeding changes, which in themselves start to cause problems, so it becomes more and more difficult to work out what is going on.

- A medical diagnosis often precipitates unnecessary weaning for breastfed babies.

- Occasionally the medication suggested is unsafe.

The main medically based theories as to why babies cry a lot are all centered around the baby's gastrointestinal tract (the gut).

They are as follows: colic; allergy/food intolerance; esophageal reflux; lactose intolerance.

The persistent belief that healthy babies who cry a lot have gut problems has been shown over and over again by observation and research to be incorrect most of the time. Despite this, health professionals, who agree it's highly unlikely to be the cause of the baby's distress, continue to diagnose and treat something they themselves think is non-existent a lot of the time.

Why? Partly because of the baby's and parents' distress when there is no explanation, partly because of the time factor (it's quicker to diagnose and medicate than spend a lot of time counseling and comforting), and partly because medication is easily available whereas practical help and resources to help distressed families aren't.

A diagnosis of a problem in the gut is nearly always based on the way the baby behaves, not on medically proven symptoms. All babies turn red in the face and draw up their legs at times when they cry. This is an automatic reflex that can be observed in all babies whether they cry excessively or not. It is usually because they are generally distressed, not because they have pains in their bellies. Similarly, an adult stamping his or her foot when upset does not mean he or she has a pain in the foot. The longer babies cry and the less sleep they have, the more distressed they become and the more they repeat this action. Adults quite inappropriately project their own intentions or reasons for actions or behavior onto babies and so confuse this with adult behavior that would indicate a pain in the gut. These medically based theories started from this premise.

## Colic/Gas

Colic and gas are the most frustrating of all the medically based theories as they really are an inaccurate way of describing what the baby does rather than what the baby has. Parents, however, are led to believe that the word *colic* is a diagnosis of a medically proven condition and so conclude treatment and a cure are just around the corner.

Colic is a general term that means acute paroxysmal pain. Nowhere else in medicine do we use the word *colic* without describing the site of the pain—example, renal colic, biliary colic or menstrual colic. Calling excessive crying in a healthy baby *colic* implies a severe pain in the stomach or bowel similar to that experienced by an adult who eats a bad oyster or who has a bowel obstruction. This doesn't make sense when we are referring to a normal baby who is having the correct food. The word *colic* as a diagnosis for a baby's crying really means "This healthy baby is crying a lot and we don't know why."

The myths surrounding babies and gas are second only to those of "teething."

Burping and passing gas are normal functions of the human body from birth to death, and all babies fart very loudly and very well from the moment they arrive. Some babies do appear to show discomfort associated with eating, digesting, and pooing by responding to these normal body functions by squirming, grunting, turning red in the face, and sometimes crying. I believe this is more a psychological response to the new sensation of all these things happening to their bodies, not physical pain or discomfort the way adults understand it. When babies are generally distressed, overwhelmed, and overtired, they are much more sensitive to these internal body movements, and exhausted parents looking for answers tend to see these responses as the cause of their baby's crying.

Helping your baby to burp when she is wriggling, squirming, and unsettled by holding her over your shoulder or lying her across your lap and applying some pressure to her back may relieve her distress sometimes, but overall burping techniques make very little difference to the behavior of crying babies.

**343**

## Esophageal reflux

Because reflux is such a common word used in baby circles, most mothers today are aware of it. It is frequently given as a diagnosis for babies who cry a lot. What is meant by the term gastro-esophageal reflux?

Gastroesophageal refers to the way the food in the stomach leaves the stomach at its top end and enters the esophagus. The esophagus or gullet is the swallowing tube attached to the top part of the stomach. It is normal for humans of any age to reflux some gastric content regularly into the esophagus, especially after meals, so it is confusing to use the word *reflux* to describe a medical condition in a baby without specifying exactly what the problem is.

For most of us, the reflux action that takes place between the stomach and the gullet does not cause any problems. The reflux action is more pronounced in babies because the valve that lies between the gullet and the top of the stomach does not work as efficiently in their first year as it does for the rest of their lives.

Poor coordination of the movement of food between the esophagus and the stomach also contributes to reflux problems in babies. It's still not clearly understood why some babies never vomit, some vomit all the time and are happy, and others vomit and scream and are miserable. None of the variations have anything to do with the mother's care of her baby.

When difficulties arise from this reflux action, they can be divided into specific problems.

**CONSTANT VOMITING:** Almost half of all babies throw up to a degree that makes parents anxious and complicates normal living. Apart from the vomiting, the baby is otherwise well, happy, and gaining weight. Unfortunately the constant aroma and mess is never ending and being vomited on all day does little for a mother's self-esteem. Vomiting often increases at around eight to

**344**

eleven months when many babies are crawling. They are horizontal to the floor at this time and heave themselves around, leaving multicolored puddles as they go. The vomiting eventually stops at about a year for all but five percent. A combination of an upright position and improved functioning of the valve between the stomach and the esophagus helps stop the flow. (For more on vomiting, see page 216.)

## LUNG PROBLEMS

A tiny number of babies who vomit a lot draw some of the stomach contents into their lungs. This causes coughing, wheezing, breathing difficulties, or pneumonia. If these problems keep happening, medical care is needed by a specialist doctor. Lung problems due to reflux vomiting are more common in very premature or sick babies.

## WEIGHT LOSS

A small number of babies who vomit excessively and who have heartburn are reluctant to drink because of associated pain. These babies develop anorexia, do not thrive, and need specialist attention. However, weight loss related to reflux vomiting is not common, so other reasons for weight loss should always be investigated before diagnosing failure to thrive caused by reflux.

Steady weight loss in a breastfed baby who has reflux vomiting is more likely to be because the milk supply is low than because of the vomiting.

Limiting a bottle-fed baby's intake to try to stop the vomiting will also cause weight loss. Babies who vomit but are otherwise happy should be fed as normal regardless of the vomiting. Reducing their intake reduces their weight.

## HEARTBURN

When unsettled, crying babies are diagnosed as having reflux, the person making the diagnosis usually means the baby is crying all the time because the stomach contents are irritating the gullet, causing heartburn. The condition is unpleasant and painful, so it's no wonder babies who suffer from heartburn are miserable a lot of the time. Vomiting may or may not accompany heartburn.

Occasionally the heartburn is so severe the gullet becomes ulcerated and bleeds, and the baby may vomit blood. Again this needs treatment from a specialist doctor.

Unfortunately, trying to diagnose reflux heartburn in babies is very difficult. The only symptoms are behavioral (that is, crying, wakefulness, breast or bottle refusal, back arching and so on) and there is a wide range of baby behavior in the first three to six months which, although worrying, does not necessarily indicate a medical condition warranting drug treatment.

Various invasive procedures can be used to diagnose troublesome gastroesophageal reflux in babies but none of them are so definitive that they are appropriate for all crying, unsettled babies.

It is recognized among health professionals that lots of reflux heartburn diagnoses are inaccurate guesses, and quite a number of babies are committed to unnecessary diagnostic tests and drug therapy as a result of this.

## TREATMENT FOR REFLUX PROBLEMS

Simple treatment involves positioning the baby when she sleeps so that she lies uphill and trying to feed her in a tilted or upright position, which is difficult in the early breastfeeding days but can be done once the breastfeeding is well established and there is less chance of nipple damage. Frequent small feedings are generally better tolerated than large infrequent feedings when the baby has heartburn.

A range of medications is used. (See next section.)

Very occasionally surgery is performed. It is only considered when there is no doubt about the diagnosis and there are continual complications that put the baby at risk and cannot be solved any other way.

## Allergy and food intolerance

Allergy to protein, which may be cow's milk or soy milk protein, is a possibility in one to three percent of babies. Research yields very conflicting results about the incidence of excessive crying being caused by allergy or food intolerance.

### WHAT IS AN ALLERGY?

An allergy is an adverse reaction of the body to antibodies that are not normally found in the body.

The reaction is caused by a foreign substance being introduced. The substance may be food or something found in food. It may also be medication, dust, smoke, insect bites, or pollutants. It's often a difficult process determining what allergic people are allergic to.

Allergic symptoms may be rashes, excessive mucus, abdominal cramps, diarrhea, swelling or vomiting. The symptoms range from being so subtle that they are attributed to a "difficult" personality to, rarely, anaphylactic shock where the airways constrict and the throat and tongue swell, which severely impairs breathing and is potentially life-threatening.

### WHAT IS INTOLERANCE?

Intolerance describes an adverse reaction some people have to certain substances but does not involve the production of antibodies. The symptoms of intolerance are rashes, migraine, irritable bowel, nasal congestion, asthma, nausea, abdominal cramps and diarrhea, lethargy, and limb pains.

The whole subject of allergy and intolerance becomes very confused when we look at it in relation to a baby who cries a lot in the first three to six months. Vomiting, rashes, sniffly breathing, lots of loose poo, and behavior that suggests pain but may not be pain are all normal features of healthy babies, and most of the time cannot be classified as disorders.

There is an unfortunate tendency for many health professionals to either blame everything babies and children have or do on allergies or refuse to acknowledge allergic problems exist at all. The reality lies somewhere in between. A small number of crying babies may benefit from treatment centered around allergy or intolerance.

Here are the usual suggestions:

- **IF THE BABY IS HAVING A COW'S MILK-BASED FORMULA, CHANGE TO A SOY-BASED FORMULA**
  This occasionally makes babies happier, but some babies who have an intolerance to the protein in a cow's milk-based formula also have one to the protein in soy-based formula. Some babies have an intolerance to soy milk but can tolerate cow's milk-based formula. Specialist formulas based on cow's milk, which have had the components treated so that it is easier for the baby to digest, are more likely to help a baby who is truly allergic or intolerant of cow's milk protein or soy milk protein. It must be emphasized that studies have repeatedly shown only a tiny number of crying babies respond to changing a cow's milk-based formula to a soy-based or specialist formula.

- **IF THE MOTHER IS BREASTFEEDING, TRY AVOIDING A RANGE OF FOOD TO PREVENT TRANSFER OF ANTIGENS TO THE BABY**
  When your family has a history of allergy or intolerance, there is a much higher chance your baby will be the same, and the

chances are doubled if both parents suffer from allergy or intolerance.

If this is the case and your baby is crying a lot, it may be worth eliminating milk and milk products from your diet and perhaps avoiding wheat, fish, and peanut products if you are breastfeeding. Some women who are breastfeeding are prepared to go further and, under the supervision of a dietitian, try a strict elimination diet. This eliminates naturally occurring salicylates and other substances that are known to cause adverse reactions.

In very rare instances, babies can have a major reaction in response to a food protein (usually milk) passed through the mother's breastmilk. For the majority of breastfeeding women who have a very unsettled, crying baby, the stress involved with strict specialty or elimination diets is disproportionate to the results achieved. The majority of crying babies spontaneously become much more settled between three and four months regardless of what they or their mothers eat.

In my work I have found that meddling with the mother's diet tends to be unsuccessful and often adds tension to an already stressful situation.

## Lactose intolerance

It is often suggested to mothers with crying babies that their babies are lactose intolerant, and they may be told to wean and use a low-lactose formula or to change to a low-lactose formula if they are bottle feeding. Like most of the other strategies used to try to help unsettled babies, diagnosing and treating healthy babies for lactose intolerance is mostly guesswork on the part of the person making the diagnosis and makes very little difference to how the baby behaves. It is particularly upsetting when the breastfeeding is going well for mothers to be told to wean and use formula because of lactose intolerance. Always ask for another opinion if you are told

**349**

to do this and note that lots of explosive, frothy poo is normal for healthy breastfed babies in the first six weeks and not a sign of anything being wrong.

## WHAT IS LACTOSE INTOLERANCE?

Lactose is a sugar that only occurs in the milk of mammals, including humans. Babies of all species produce an enzyme called lactase while they are receiving milk that helps digest the lactose. Once weaning occurs, lactase is no longer produced in any animals apart from humans. Not all humans continue to produce lactase. People from Asia, Mediterranean countries, the Middle East, and some Australian Aborigines do not produce lactase after weaning, which means their gut may be unable to digest the lactose found in milk products or products made from milk. It is very unusual for people from a Caucasian or Anglo-Saxon background not to produce lactase. People from this ethnic group rarely suffer from a genetic lactose intolerance.

It must be emphasized that babies from ethnic groups likely to be lactose intolerant tolerate breastmilk very well, and any problems with lactose only start after four years of age. Genetic lactose intolerance present from birth has only ever been identified in a tiny number of babies. Breastmilk has a lot of lactose, which has been there for 40,000 years; it is an important ingredient that helps in brain development.

Apart from a genetic lactose intolerance (the failure of the body to produce lactase), a temporary lactose intolerance can occur following gastroenteritis. The gut is damaged, lactase production is stopped, and gas, nausea, and diarrhea keep recurring if milk products are given. Again, interestingly, breastmilk is tolerated well by babies in this situation despite the fact it is high in lactose.

There is also evidence to suggest that some young babies may become temporarily lactose intolerant if their mothers drink milk

**350**

which then is passed in the breastmilk to the baby and temporarily damages the gut. This does not happen very often.

## Medication

Medical diagnoses are usually accompanied by medications. It's tempting for both parent and health professional to believe relief will come from medication, but there are problems when we medicate babies for crying even when we call it colic, reflux or gas.

- Most of the time the diagnosis and reason for medicating is guesswork because signs and symptoms are not clear and we can't ask the baby what's happening.

- There is a consistent high failure rate—that is, the baby's behavior doesn't change for any length of time. Parents find every time they try something new (change the formula, start medication, stop medication, and so on), the baby settles for a day or two, then goes back to crying a lot again.

- One difficulty in assessing whether medication works is that research shows a placebo effect of between twenty and thirty percent (see page 341).

- Medications can cause other problems such as heartburn, allergic reactions, vomiting, constipation, rashes and even increased irritability, which makes it more difficult to help the baby. And, over the years, most popular wind, gas, and reflux medications have been discovered to carry risks far outweighing any possible benefits for the babies. For example, drugs contain atropine, alcohol, dicyclomine, and cisapride (see following page).

- Drugs that consistently stop the baby from crying usually have a sedative effect rather than doing something that eases the baby's gut. They work on the baby's central nervous system, not on the digestive system, and parents are often unaware of this. Sedating healthy babies who cry a lot seems a risky business and not in the baby's best interest.

Unfortunately situations happen where daily living becomes intolerable because of a continually distressed, crying baby. Life with a crying baby usually becomes intolerable because the mother is not getting any practical help and support and is left alone day after day with her crying baby. Sedatives are resorted to as a way of easing an intensely stressful time, not because the baby needs them. It is safer for a healthy baby to cry than be sedated.

Here are the main drugs used for babies who cry a lot:

## Colic/gas

Colic and gas medications for babies create a profitable market. New ones appear all the time making extravagant claims about curing babies' gut problems. History reveals that this is not a new practice. Various miraculous potions have been concocted and sold to parents for at least two hundred years, often with the blessing of the medical and pharmaceutical professions. Think things through before you waste your money or buy something potentially harmful to your baby. Potions marketed as "herbal" or "natural" need just as much scrutiny as any others.

### NON-SEDATIVE

### SIMETHICONE DROPS (FOR EXAMPLE, MYLICON DROPS)

Simethicone is an anti-flatulent that, in the case of babies, purports to work by joining up all the small bubbles in the intestine so the large bubble will be passed! The recommended dose is given before each feed. Safe to use.

**GRIPE WATER:** Gripe water has been around for a long time. Traditional gripe water consists of dill oil, sodium bicarbonate, water, sugar and alcohol. The alcohol mildly sedates some babies the first few times it is used, and babies like the sweet taste. There are a variety of gripe water recipes available in the U.S, many without the alcohol and sugar. Always check the contents before buying. If you use traditional gripe water, limit the amount your baby has. Too much sodium bicarbonate (a salt) puts a strain on your baby's kidneys.

**HERBAL TEAS:** The use of herbal teas for babies is no longer recommended because a lack of quality control in the manufacture of herbal teas makes them unsafe because other herbs, weeds, or seeds may be present.

## HERBAL GAS PREPARATIONS (OFTEN ALSO CALLED "NATURALA"): These are found in lots of health food shops and pharmacies and contain a variety of different herbs. Parents often report a miracle change in their baby's crying after using one of these preparations; unfortunately the change is usually only temporary. Always find out what is in the mixture—occasionally quite dangerous sedatives are used in "natural herbal mixtures."

### SEDATIVE EFFECT
Some gas and colic medications contain drugs that work on the baby's central nervous system, thus calming the baby. Although they are promoted as reducing colicky behavior by easing spasms in the muscles lining the intestines, it is probably the effect on the central nervous system that calms the baby, not the anti-spasmodic effect.

### DICYCLOMINE (BENTYL, DI-SPAZ, FORMULEX, LOMINE):
Preparations containing dicyclomine have warnings on the labels not to administer them to babies under six months—yet it's the first

three to four months when babies are commonly diagnosed as having gas and "colic."

Until 1986 preparations containing dicyclomine were used freely for crying babies. Preparations containing dicyclomine were at times quite successful in stopping babies from crying so much, but mostly there was an improvement for a few days, then a return to the pre-dicyclomine crying.

As these preparations were freely available and as parents were hardly ever fully informed about all aspects of colic, it meant mixtures containing dicyclomine were frequently overused and abused. Excessive use can cause drowsiness, a decrease in urine output, constipation, and heartburn. Preparations containing the drug were declared unsafe for babies under six months. Looking objectively at all the medications given to healthy, crying babies, dicyclomine is not as potentially dangerous as some others that have no warning.

The problems associated with the use of dicyclomine are similar to those of any medication given to healthy crying babies. Much guesswork is involved, so it's risky to use any medication unreservedly hoping for something positive to happen. The risks are increased when the drug being used depresses the baby's central nervous system.

If you do use a preparation containing dicyclomine:

- Be aware of its limitations. It is not a miracle cure for crying.

- Use strictly as directed. When you reach the maximum dose, stop using it and dispose of it down the sink or the toilet.

### SEDATIVES

The following drugs are sedatives. They work by putting your baby to sleep, not by treating a pain in the tummy.

**PHENERGAN:** Phenergan is an anti-histamine that has a tranquil-lizing effect, so the baby gets very drowsy and aloof or alternatively extremely excited and irritated. It should not be used on babies under six months.

**PHENOBARBITONE:** It is unfortunate that preparations containing drugs such as atropine and phenobarbitone are still being pre-scribed for healthy, crying babies often without the parents being aware of what it is they are giving their baby. Phenobarbitone is a barbiturate that depresses the whole nervous system and causes abnormal deep sleep. It is also dependency producing, which means babies who are taken off it suddenly may convulse.

Phenobarbitone has a place when used for babies suffering from drug withdrawal (born to substance-addicted mothers), babies born with severe birth trauma, and occasionally for other specific medical problems. It is inappropriate to use it for healthy babies who cry a lot. Never use mixtures containing this drug.

**A WORD ABOUT ACETAMINOPHEN AND IBUPROFEN:** Tempra and Tylenol are examples of acetaminophen. Motrin, Advil, and Pediacare Fever are examples of ibuprofen.

Acetaminophen is a medication for babies when they have a fever or are in pain (following surgery). Acetaminophen is not use-ful for crying babies when the cause of the crying is unclear. Parents often resort to a dose of acetaminophen when they can't think of anything else to do. Doing this occasionally is okay, bear-ing in mind that paracetamol has a mild sedative effect on some babies the first couple of times they have it.

Ibuprofen is an anti-inflammatory drug that is also used for symptoms of fever and pain in babies, toddlers, and children. Both acetaminophen and ibuprofen are equally efficient in reducing fever and pain. Like acetaminophen, ibuprofen is not appropriate for healthy, crying babies when the cause of the crying is unclear. The safety of both drugs depends on them being used correctly. A multitude of acetaminophen preparations is now available with a variety of strengths and doses, so it is important to calculate and measure the dose correctly according to the manufacturer's instructions. If in doubt, check with another person.

Neither acetaminophen nor ibuprofen should be given more than once every four hours, and it is not a good idea to keep repeating the dose when you don't know exactly why you are giving it. For example, for crying or teething.

## Reflux

### REFLUX VOMITING

**THICKENED FORMULA (FOR EXAMPLE, ENGAMIL AR):** Parents who are using formula are often told that thickening the formula will help alleviate vomiting in their otherwise healthy babies. Suggestions include small amounts of rice cereal or cornstarch. Some formula companies make thickened formula specifically for vomiting babies. The rationale behind thickening feeds is to make the milk settle in the stomach so it doesn't flow up and out so easily. Very little evidence exists to show that the use of thickened feeding alleviates heartburn, so thickening milk does not have a useful role in making babies with heartburn happier. It is a strategy for the happy vomiter (see page 216) and, as it does seem to decrease the volume of vomiting, has the potential to make the parents of vomiting babies happier. As the baby is happy anyway, the use of thickened milk is more for social reasons rather than health. Thickened milk often makes babies constipated and, as it is difficult to thicken breastmilk, the notion of thickening feedings may also contribute to unnecessary weaning. Because of its very limited use I do not recommend this strategy.

**METCLOPRAMIDE (FOR EXAMPLE, REGLAN):** This is a drug used for the control of nausea and vomiting and is occasionally still prescribed for reflux vomiting in babies. However, it is now viewed as ineffective, and, as there are possibilities of significant side effects, it is no longer recommended.

## REFLUX HEARTBURN

**ANTACIDS (FOR EXAMPLE MYLANTA AND MAALOX):** Mylanta provides a protective coating for the esophagus. It does not stop babies from vomiting. Mylanta should be given after the feed unless pain prevents the baby from eating, in which case it can be given before. Dosage should not exceed seven times every twenty-four hours. If symptoms improve, the dose may be reduced after a week or two and then used as necessary.

**MOTILITY MEDICATION (FOR EXAMPLE PREPULSID, CIS-APRIDE):** Cisapride tightens the loose valve at the top of the stomach and so helps stop partly digested food from flowing into the esophagus and irritating it. It relaxes the valve at the bottom end of the stomach so that the food passes more easily through to the small intestine and hastens the passage of the food through the gastrointestinal tract. Cisapride causes stomach cramps in some babies.

Current research has cast doubt over the effectiveness of cisapride and has highlighted a risk of sudden death in some babies caused by the medication's effect on the electrical activity of the heart (thought to affect about one in ten thousand babies). The risks are greater for premature babies, who should not be given cisapride during the first three months. The use of cisapride has now ceased in most special-care nurseries in many maternity units throughout the world and some children's hospitals have elected not to use the drug for babies. The risk for full-term babies appears

357

to be small but in view of the fact that the drug does not reduce crying it seems pointless to take the risk, small though it may be.

**ACID BLOCKERS:** Acid blockers, for example Zantac, Pepcid, and Tagamet reduce the acid content of the gut, thus minimizing the irritating effect of regurgitated food on the esophagus. They appear to be safe and effective, but it is important to be as sure as possible that the condition exists before using these drugs. When the condition does exist, acid blockers appear to be the most effective medication. A side effect of acid blockers in a tiny number of babies is a raw red rash that may be present on the face or neck (from dribbling) or in the diaper area.

## Non-medical approach

The non-medical approach to excessive crying suggests that most of the time when babies cry a lot it is not caused by an organically defined condition; rather, it is the way the baby is responding to her new environment.

Certainly non-medical reasons are only theories or someone's point of view, but so are most of the medical theories as to why some babies cry so much. Many parents find the non-medical approach helpful as it avoids diagnostic tests, experimental medication, and meddling with feedings. This approach looks at ways to help parents adapt to the baby and what she's doing rather than trying to stop or "cure" it and involves looking at all the options parents may try and changing them when they don't suit. Like the medical approach, the non-medical approach may not stop the crying, but it helps the mother feel better about herself and her baby and gives her confidence to carry on without feeling the need to get on the medical roundabout.

Here are some non-medical reasons why some healthy babies cry a lot.

## Sleep

I believe an inability to get to sleep and go back to sleep (unrelated to any other factor) is the major cause of distress and crying in healthy babies. Learning to sleep is one of the tasks young babies need to learn. Learning to sleep involves:

- Learning how to "hold themselves together" to get to sleep. This is difficult for some babies—not able to get to sleep, they are unable to enjoy being awake. Their movements become jerky, they do not make eye contact, and as they become more and more agitated, their crying builds to a crescendo.

- Learning how to go back to sleep when suddenly woken from light sleep and dreaming sleep (REM). As mentioned previously, babies have long periods of REM sleep from which they are easily woken. The reasons for waking might be normal body functions (for example, a poo behind the anus is a strange sensation to a baby as is passing gas until she gets used to how it feels) or things relating to baby behavior such as the startle reflex. Once awake, the baby cannot get back to sleep, starts to cry, and eventually ends up crying uncontrollably, becoming more and more tense.

- Learning how to go back to sleep following the normal, brief wakings in between sleep stages instead of coming fully awake and crying.

## Frustration from overtiredness

Babies are only able to stay happy and awake for relatively short periods. The less sleep they have, the more crying there is likely

**359**

to be. For many crying babies it is the lack of sleep causing the crying, not the crying causing the lack of sleep—a situation that is difficult to change until the baby is able to sleep more and longer.

## Low sensory threshold

A number of all healthy babies respond in an exaggerated way to light, movement, noise, and their own normal body functions (burping, startle reflex, intestinal movements, passing urine or having a poo). Babies like this eventually also have trouble sleeping until their systems get used to the overload of sensations and movements. It is thought babies who have difficult births or sick premature babies are more inclined to have low sensory thresholds, but this is not always the case.

## The temperament of the baby

The role of the temperament of the baby comes up time and time again. A small amount of evidence exists that excessive crying may relate to a "difficult" temperament but I have a problem with this approach and do not use it in my work.

Apart from the fact that seeing the baby as difficult might mean a medical problem is overlooked, suggesting that a baby who has only been on the planet several weeks is difficult when we don't know the reason for her distress is somewhat of an insult to a small person at this stage of her life when we have no idea what sort of a person she will be. One of the things I have learned about being a parent is to be patient and wait for the end of the story.

## Other contributing factors

When a baby is very unsettled and crying all the time, everyone unfortunately starts to look for someone or something to blame. Blaming is destructive, not constructive, and great care has to be taken when assessing the possible role the following factors play so that they are not used to make mothers and fathers feel guilty and to blame for the predicament the family is in. I am mentioning them because I do think in some crying baby situations they play a part, and acknowledging them sometimes means they can be changed or help can be obtained from other members of the immediate or extended family. Here they are:

- building extensions to the house;

- moving;

- money worries;

- a major career change;

- visitors who stay a long time;

- relationship problems;

- an unsympathetic partner;

- isolation and loneliness suffered by the parent at home the most with the baby (usually the mother);

- great emotional stress suffered by one or both parents;

- ill health of one or both parents;

- unrealistic expectations of life with a baby.

Non-medical options for babies who cry a lot center around helping the baby not cry so much and helping the parents live with the crying. All of these things help some of the time, but there is no single option that consistently works all the time for every crying baby. Of course any of these can be done as well as using medication if the baby has been given a diagnosis and treatment.

Most of these options have already been described in Chapter 14, so please refer to that section if you want more detail.

- A pacifier: Distressed babies often need to suck a lot, not from hunger but to relieve their distress. The breast can be used for comfort if the mother is happy to do that.

- Calm handling: Sharp, jerky movements signal distress, which makes the baby more alarmed. Wrapping her firmly in a flexed position and avoiding overstimulation by lots of different people helps.

- Carrying the baby in a sling.

- A deep relaxation bath sometimes works wonders.

- Letting the baby cry is quite all right when there is nothing else to do, especially when the parents feel worn out and tense. Well-fed, tired babies often sleep well after crying when left for a short time. I suggest twenty to thirty minutes. Parents shouldn't hesitate to pick up their baby anytime they think they should, but there needs to be a balance between constantly picking up and putting down and allowing the baby a reasonable time to get to sleep.

- Gentle rocking, patting, music, or going for a walk are all soothing techniques that have been used for thousands of years to calm babies.

# Getting help

## Health professionals

Unfortunately a lot of health professionals don't get top marks when it comes to helping and supporting families with crying babies. Apart from the fact that there are always unhelpful people in any group of professionals, there are other reasons why this appears to be so:

- Parents caring for a crying baby often expect a miracle answer to safely stop their baby from crying. Such an answer doesn't exist.

- Health professionals who deal a lot with healthy, crying babies often just get bogged down in the sheer numbers of difficulties with unsettled babies and take the tack that in the long run the difficulties resolve whether they spend a lot of time with the mother and baby or not. Some health professionals lose interest and look for the quick answer.

- Many parents never give the health professional feedback. They see a health professional once, never think to tell him or her the treatment didn't work, and go on to the next health professional. Consequently some health professionals just keep dishing out the same old recipe, not really knowing whether it makes any difference to the baby's crying or not.

- Health professionals who have large numbers of clients to see may not be prepared to spend time counseling and comforting a mother and her crying baby once they are confident the baby is healthy and getting the right food.

When looking for professional help, the challenge is to find someone you trust to be the major adviser. It is quite reasonable to get a few different opinions, but you need one person who is flexible; someone you like and trust and feel confident with; knowledgeable enough to give you an objective summary of what you are being told so that you are fully informed; support-ive—this means he or she supports you in whatever action you take even if he or she doesn't agree with it (providing it doesn't pose risks for the baby).

The major health professional may be a nurse practitioner, a family doctor, a pediatrician, a psychologist, or a social worker.

## Other help

Unless you have a miraculous response from seeing a health professional, changing your diet or your baby's formula, or by giving medication, you will have to live with the crying.

I have used the word *parents* a lot in this chapter rather than *mother* to recognize that fathers as well as mothers have crying babies. I also recognize that men are sharing the ups and downs of parenthood more evenly than was the case in the past, but it still must be acknowledged that it is often the mothers who are caring for and spending the long, often lonely hours with the baby. Fathers have avenues of escape not available to the mother, and the crying baby remains primarily a woman's problem.

Practical help is vital, and it is sad to see how few women in our society looking after a crying baby receive any. I am sure there would be far less diagnosing and medicating of healthy babies if more consistent, easily available help and *company* were available for women who need it during the first three to six months after birth. It's amazing what a difference it makes just having someone else in the house who's just there even if they are not directly helping with the baby.

When practical help and company are not available, the following ideas provide limited help if you can arrange it:

- Do you have a trusted friend or family member who doesn't overload you with endless advice and who doesn't see anything odd about a baby who cries a lot who will mind your baby and give you a break on a regular basis?

- Can you arrange help with the housework? Can you pay someone for a while? What about asking one of your relatives who keeps burbling on about gas to do the shopping or the dishes or something practical instead? Can you put on some head-phones and let your baby cry while you clean up? You will feel much better and chances are your baby is going to cry anyway whether you walk the floor with her or clean the house. If you can restore order, you will feel better, more in control, and she may go to sleep.

• Send for your mother if this is appropriate. Go to your mother if she is a tower of strength who doesn't mind a crying baby around the house.

• Try to work out what makes you feel better then *do whatever you feel the need to do until your baby is calmer.* For example, frequent trips to see your healthcare professional (the right one won't mind). Look for support groups or mothers' groups in your area. Try the local newspapers, parenting publications. Check with your local hospital, community organizations, churches or synagogues, libraries and childcare co-operatives. Don't forget La Leche League for support and companionship. Talking to sympathetic friends on the phone can be a great help.

# Managing angry feelings

At some time or another every parent feels angry or irritated with their baby or with the situation they are in, which directly relates to the fact that they have a baby. Babies bring a lot of pleasure, but they also bring frustrations. A baby disrupts adult lifestyle and lim-its the mother's independence. It also throws up, cries a lot, and does not sleep at the most inconvenient and unpredictable moments. Angry or irritated feelings may range from a fleeting sen-sation to feelings so intense the parent feels he or she could easily do something they might regret. As the mother is probably the one with the baby most of the time, she is likely to experience this feeling more intensely and more often than the father.

When the baby is crying for a large part of every twenty-four-hour period, angry feelings are normal. So are negative feelings about the baby from time to time. It's important to blow off steam to someone, and men should allow their partners to express feelings of anger and to say rude things about the baby without showing shock and horror. Lots of the women I see say all sorts of nasty things from time to time, then feel much better because they have been allowed to say them. Nearly all the time these feelings are transient and the parent has no intention of acting upon them. The feelings go away when things improve.

Nevertheless, there may be times when you feel out of control and that there is a chance you might hurt your baby. Put the baby in her crib in her room and go as far away as you can. Call someone immediately: your mother; your partner; your nurse practitioner; casualty at your nearest children's hospital or local hospital; the nearest child abuse prevention service. And don't feel embarrassed to get help.

# Can having a baby who cries be prevented?

Probably not. Until we know more about the precise reason why some babies are so unhappy during the first six months of life, it is difficult to predict exactly what may or may not contribute.

Care during pregnancy and changing some negative lifestyle habits might help, but there will always be a considerable number of crying babies born to parents who take every care and a number of easygoing babies born to parents who are very careless about their personal habits. It sometimes seems very unfair, but remember, by taking care and providing the right environment, you are giving your baby a wonderful life and future that extends way beyond crying difficulties in the first six months.

## Care during pregnancy

Eat plenty of fresh food, cut down on takeout and refined food. Take steps to avoid food you have problems with. *Stop* smoking—research does show a higher incidence of babies who cry excessively in homes where one or both partners smoke. Avoid alcohol and drugs. Try learning relaxation techniques. Even if these things don't make a difference to how much your baby cries, you will manage better. Looking after yourself and your body also removes an element of guilt, which makes you less stressed.

## The non-crying baby of non-Western cultures

Observations and anecdotal stories suggest babies in non-Western cultures don't cry the way babies in Western cultures do (perhaps none of them suffer from reflux?). I'm never too sure how useful this information is to a woman gallantly doing her best for her crying baby. Suggestions to care for babies here the way they are cared for in peasant communities are for most women in our community unworkable.

Constant references to the non-crying baby of non-Western cultures suggests a superior style of mothering Western women can't quite achieve—so no wonder their babies cry a lot! I find this approach not at all helpful and quite damaging to our women's self-esteem.

It does appear that in some other cultures the work of motherhood is not left entirely up to one person the way it is here, so a baby who cries a lot can be handed around to many relatives. Our society also

**367**

elevates pregnancy and childbirth to unrealistic heights, then leaves women on their own to struggle with the task, making them wonder what they are doing wrong when at times it all seems too much.

However, many things about being women and mothers in our society are wonderful. Few of us would care to live the way women do in other communities, so let's stop making our women feel guilty about their education, their independence, their lives, and help them care for their babies the way they want to in the context of our culture.

## Last hints to help you through

- Try not to blame your baby; try not to blame yourself. This time is part of your life story together. Think how you will laugh about it when she is twenty-one.

- When you can, try to look ahead and make some plans for an optimistic future so that you don't feel completely bogged down in the present. Talk about holidays, perhaps schooling, and some nights out when the baby is calmer.

- Partners, work together! It is vital. The mother shoulders most of the burden, so father, please support her approach. Organize shift work on the weekends. Don't blame each other.

- Try whatever you think is reasonable. You will not spoil your baby by picking her up all the time, nor will you damage her by letting her cry.

- Never do anything that is suggested that causes you added stress, major inconvenience, or goes against what you feel is right. Remember you are in charge, not the health professionals or anyone else who feels inclined to tell you what to do.

# Some crying baby stories

*My baby was terrible. He screamed all the time and was never happy when he was awake. It started out as gas and I tried all the gas things, none of which helped. Gripe Water was the only one that helped a little bit. He kept getting worse especially after feeding. I only breastfed for a few days.*

*I went to a pediatrician who diagnosed reflux. After that, we started Mylanta and thickening the milk and started early solids. This made a slight difference, but he was still very difficult, and it went on until he was six months old, at which time he ate more than he drank and seemed to improve.*

*I was very tired and depressed and got very run down and sick. I couldn't enjoy him because he was so unhappy. I didn't realize babies could be so unhappy! I hadn't had much experience with babies, and other babies I had known before I had my own always seemed happy.*

*It put a strain on my relationship with my husband because I was always so tired, the baby took up so much time. I felt my husband wasn't understanding enough. Getting practical help with my baby was difficult because he was so hard to look after—no one wanted to mind him or help me.*

**SUGGESTIONS:** Accept all help; prepare for the possibility of a crying baby during pregnancy; try not to take too much advice from friends and never compare babies.

*My baby cried constantly. I tried to do everything I could to pacify him, but I couldn't. I was reassured by health professionals he was normal and I accepted that. As long as you get confidence from somebody that you're doing the right thing and not hurting the baby, you're okay—I managed.*

**369**

*I let him cry, shut the door, and put the radio on. As long as they're crying, they're fine—it's when they stop that you worry.*

*My husband was very supportive and took him for lots of long walks. He was a baby who constantly wanted to be on the move.*

*I did not medicate. I tried to stay calm and not get fed up. I did not get depressed.*

*It stopped at four months and it was a great relief when it did— heavenly in fact. He's been wonderful ever since. I felt like weaning because I felt it might help, but he thrived on my milk, so I didn't, and I'm pleased I didn't wean.*

**SUGGESTIONS:** Go for lots of walks; talk about it to a nurse practitioner; make sure you've done everything, then leave the baby to cry or take her for a walk.

*From about six to seven days, he started to scream from early morning to 5pm and often at night as well. He didn't just cry, he would scream; his body was like a brick. He'd arch backward. Occasionally I could rock him to sleep, then he would wake again.*

*I saw the early childhood nurse every week until he was eleven weeks old. We tried Mylicon and Mylanta, but nothing made any difference, although everything worked for a little while.*

*I was breastfeeding and had sore nipples and one episode of mastitis; however, despite everything, his weight gains were good.*

*At eleven weeks, I consulted a pediatrician. I continued to breastfeed but started to complement with a soy formula on the advice of the pediatrician. As well, treatment for reflux was started. I kept him upright as much as possible. This seemed to help.*

*By sixteen weeks, he was much better. He was fighting the breast so much I weaned at this time, but he fought the bottle as well.*

*I struggled on for another month, at which time he was on three meals a day and whatever he would drink. By then, although he never slept in the day, he did sleep at night.*

*By six months, he had stopped screaming.*

*How did I feel? Mentally I felt inadequate and as if I was not doing a good job. I felt that I should have been able to manage. I felt that people were talking about me and that it was never going to end. I felt that having a baby was the biggest mistake of my life. I got very depressed and put on a lot of weight. My husband was available and supportive and never blamed me, but it definitely put a strain on the marriage. I kept wondering why all my friends' babies were happy and easygoing and mine wasn't. Why me?*

*Through it all I did have a special feeling for him even though there were times I thought I hated him. No one is ever prepared for how much a baby can cry. Now I love him to pieces. He turned into a fantastic toddler and many of my friends' easygoing babies have turned into holy terrors.*

**SUGGESTIONS:** It's vital to have your husband's and friends' uncritical support. I found the nurse practitioner helped. In the early weeks, the nurse practitioner helped with the breastfeeding. Overall, none of the medication helped, however, Mylanta seemed to when he was four months old in conjunction with keeping him upright. The worst advice for me was to leave him to cry.

*The first week was okay, then at two and a half weeks she started to cry a lot. The worst time was from 7 pm to midnight. We couldn't settle her—we tried everything. I tried Gripe Water, warm water, Mylicon Drops, and Mylanta. The medication made no difference. We tried baths, car rides, and long walks.*

*I became exhausted and tearful, but not really depressed. Not knowing what to do, I blamed myself. My husband found it difficult because he had to get up early for work, but he didn't blame me and our relationship didn't suffer as we worked together.*

**371**

*I decided to go to my mother's place for a while. My husband wasn't keen as he thought we could work it out ourselves. While I was at my mother's place the baby was wonderful, no crying. After three days I went home refreshed after lots of sleep. At home she started crying again, but I found I could put things into perspective so I managed much better. I tried to get her to sleep in her crib rather than in my arms as often as I could. A nurse told me to strictly schedule her feeds, but I found that didn't work for me. I decided to breastfeed her whenever. And to keep her in bed with us at night. Around four months she gradually stopped crying so much.*

**IN HINDSIGHT:** Medication didn't help and was a waste of money. Nobody told me to "follow" the baby, so I nearly went mad trying to follow everyone's advice, none of which seemed to suit me or my baby. Support for the mother is vital—before you have a baby, you have no idea how hard it can be.

### FOR MORE INFORMATION

Chapter 6: Breastfeeding Your Baby For the First Two Weeks *(weighing babies, page 87, foremilk and hindmilk, page 88, burping, page 95)*
Chapter 7: Bottle Feeding Your Baby for the First Two Weeks *(what's in formula?, page 106, making the milk, page 114)*
Chapter 10: Early Worries and Questions *(hormone rash and heat rash, page 188, 187, medicating babies, page 226, growing teeth, page 210)*
Chapter 5: Choosing Baby Products *(pacifiers page 57)*
Chapter 14: Sleeping and Waking in the First Six Months *(unsettled period, page 315, settling techniques, page 316)*

chapter **sixteen**

# For Parents

*A mother, father and baby are in the most vulnerable
state of human existence, looking after the future of the
world. They need space, time, emotional support and economic
security. They need so much . . . And they have a right to it.*

Norma Tracey, *Mothers and Fathers Speak on the Drama of Pregnancy,*

*Birth and the First Year of Life*

## *Take care of yourself*

### *The first week after birth*

During the first week you may have a few concerns and minor discomforts, so here is some useful information.

* **Vaginal blood loss:** May be heavy for the first four days,
becoming thinner and lighter after this. The color changes in
the first ten days from red to pink-brown and then becomes a
creamy white. The creamy white discharge may continue for
up to six weeks. It is also normal to have some light bleeding
and spotting for up to six weeks. Because of the risk of infection, tampons should not be used until after the first six to
eight weeks (a small number of women menstruate at this
time).

- **Afterbirth pains:** Are more commonly felt by women who have had previous pregnancies. The pain is caused by a hormone called oxytocin that causes the uterus to contract, and discomfort may be experienced for three to four days. Use a hot water bottle for pain relief taking care not to burn yourself or your baby. For severe pain, acetaminophen is safe to take while breastfeeding.

- **Stitches:** Stitches often feel very tender for the first week or so depending on the extent of the tear or the episiotomy. Most heal quickly, the worst of the discomfort fading in three or four days. The stitches usually dissolve in seven to twelve days. If it is taking longer and you are feeling uncomfortable, it's a good idea to ask your midwife or family doctor to have a look and remove the stitches. Avoid using talcum powder and creams until the stitches have dissolved and the area is well healed. Any pain should have disappeared after two weeks. If your stitches are still painful after this time, see your family doctor.

- **Hemorrhoids:** Are swollen veins just inside the anus and can be very painful and even bleed. They are usually temporary, subsiding without any major treatment, but are troublesome for up to three months for some women. In the first forty-eight hours, cold packs give some relief. Hemorrhoidal ointment is available as well, but be careful not to get the ointment on your stitches. It is important to avoid constipation by drinking plenty of fluids and adding extra fiber to your diet.

    Sometimes it is necessary to take a fiber supplement such as Metamucil.

- **Contact your midwife, maternity hospital, obstetrician, or family doctor immediately for any of the following:**

Increased bright red bleeding;

Fainting or dizziness;

A painful, hot, red area in the lower leg;

A temperature of 100.4°F (38°C) or higher for more than two hours;

Burning or difficulty passing urine;

Painful breasts and a temperature above 99.5°F (37.5°C).

- **Postnatal check**

    See your midwife, family doctor, or obstetrician for a general check of your breasts, uterus, and cervix at around six to eight weeks after the bleeding has stopped—don't worry about a small amount of spotting.

# Those tired feelings

Mothers find they are often very tired during the first few months after birth. Why? Your body worked hard to give birth, and even though initially you feel exhilarated and excited, it takes a while to recover physically, especially while you adjust to night feedings and the normal anxious moments that accompany looking after a new baby. If you had a cesarean section or any birth complications, the recovery takes longer. Doing unfamiliar tasks and using muscles not usually used is tiring until your body adjusts. Always putting your baby's needs before your own and not being able to get other things done because your baby interrupts you makes you tired too. If on top of all this your baby is unsettled and cries a lot and is awake a lot at night, the constant lack of sleep will leave you feeling very tired. Breastfeeding difficulties may arise, which also contribute to fatigue.

# How to help yourself

Remind yourself that time spent with your baby is more important than anything else. Allow yourself time to settle her. Try to lie down at least once a day when she is asleep instead of finding another job to do.

In only a few short months she will be sleeping longer at night and having fewer feedings during the day, and all this will be behind you. A lot of breastfeeding problems can be solved or overcome in the first four to six weeks. When this happens, you feel a lot less tired.

Remember, you and your baby come first. If you make it clear, others will get the message. Rather than ask your visitors if they want tea or coffee, suggest they help clean up or feed your baby while you have a shower.

Switch off all advice from well-meaning friends and relatives. Practical help from those who want to do something will do a lot more to relieve fatigue than endless suggestions.

Sit down to do chores whenever you can—for example, when you are folding clothes, diapers or preparing meals. Put your feet up when you nurse or feed your baby. Can you learn to relax? If you can, it is very helpful as a fatigue buster. Use one of the tapes and the simple suggestions on page 11, or go back to the relaxation techniques you learned at your childbirth education classes.

Try to eat sensibly. It doesn't have to be a formal meal three times a day. Simple food such as fresh fruit and yogurt, fresh whole-wheat rolls and salad, cold chicken, frozen meals, or take-out is fine. If your partner, lover, or friend prepares a meal when he comes home, that's even better.

# *Your body*

Accept how you look for the moment. Your figure will go back to normal and you will fit into your clothes again. In the meantime, wear clothes that are comfortable and bright and make you feel happy. Exercise lifts your mood and makes you feel lighter all over. After the birth, a physiotherapist or nurse will show you how to do some recommended exercises without hurting yourself. Ideally it's great to do these exercises, but most of the women I talk to find they are too overwhelmed or too tired to set aside time each day, even if it is only ten minutes, so if you're not doing your postnatal exercises, you're not alone.

If you are conscientious about exercise, keep to gentle routines for the first few months. Light yoga that concentrates on passive stretches is excellent. Make sure you have a qualified instructor.

If you find it hard to fit exercises into your new life, just try walking and pelvic floor exercises.

Walking and babies go together. Start slowly and gradually increase the distance.

Pelvic floor muscles support the vagina, uterus, bladder, and bowel. Exercising pelvic floor muscles helps your body recover from the birth and prevents stress incontinence. Stress incontinence means that when you cough, sneeze, or jump up and down, a small amount of urine is passed. You don't have to set aside a special time for pelvic floor exercises. They are easy to do when you are resting, feeding your baby, or anytime. Here's what to do:

- Squeeze and hold the muscles around the urethra (where the urine comes out), your vagina, and your anus as if you are trying to stop yourself from passing urine. Hold for three seconds, then relax. Do this three times.

- Don't tense your thighs or tummy or hold your breath. Don't

**377**

overdo it. Start a day or two after birth and build up to fifteen to twenty-five a day, doing about five at a time.

Pelvic floor exercises are something recommended for all women throughout life, so after the first three months, start increasing the number you do. Do as many as you are able to before the muscle tires. The minimum aim is for 150 pelvic floor exercises a day!

Look after your back. Changes that happen to your body during pregnancy and extra strain on your abdominal muscles mean back problems are common after birth. The extra physical work also makes backache more likely. You are most vulnerable in the first six weeks, so avoid lifting laundry baskets full of wet clothes or heavy diaper buckets.

Make sure change tables and bassinets are the right height so that you can look after your baby without bending over all the time. When you feed your baby, get into a comfortable position with good support for your back. Ask for help when you need it, specially to empty the baby tub, or carry groceries.

If your back becomes painful, physiotherapists, chiropractors, and osteopaths offer treatment and exercise, but look for someone familiar with childbirth and postnatal care.

# *Your head*

Expect postnatal drift—not being able to concentrate or remember things is quite normal. Let yourself drift for a while. Take one day at a time; just attend to your immediate needs. Postnatal drift gradually disappears, although most of my friends and I think we still have it twenty years later!

As well as postnatal drift, it's common to have a wider range of emotions than you normally do. Many women find they burst into tears easily, feel elated one minute and depressed the next. Sometimes you might feel cross and irritated over things others see as unimportant. Feelings like this are a normal response to being tired and the stress and excitement that follow any major change in life. Here are a few suggestions to help you if you are feeling a bit strange:

- Admit it's rotten sometimes. Have a good cry when you need to. You are under no obligation to float in a constant rose glow.

- A partner who shares the work as well as the joys makes an enormous difference to handling roller-coaster feelings.

- Think about making contact. The first step might be talking to other mothers in the grocery store. Get in touch with members of your childbirth education class. Perhaps you made a friend while you were in hospital—call her! Join La Leche League International.

- If you feel your emotions are out of control, it's important to talk to someone like your doctor, or your nurse practitioner. Constant anxiety and depression can be helped.

- Take time for yourself whenever you can. Having someone stay with your baby while you get your hair cut, take a bath, or simply stare into space makes a lot of difference in how you feel.

# Relationships

Think about your relationship with your partner. You and your partner have to get to know each other all over again as parents, which takes some thought and effort from both of you. It's very easy to disappear into the mother-and-baby world and lose touch. Your baby is important, but so is your partner. Your partner needs to have access to you and the baby and needs to talk to you about how he feels. Keep in contact with friends and relatives. Your range of friends will change as you start to have more time with people with babies and less with those without. Speaking with other people who have babies is important for moral support and reassurance.

Arrange to go out without the baby when you can—even if it's only for an hour or two, it gives your relationship a great boost.

# Bonding

The popularization of the bonding theory in the seventies and eighties makes bonding seem like the super glue that holds mother and baby together without which irredeemable damage is predicted for the baby.

Advantages have emerged as a result of the emphasis on bonding. It has helped make it possible for women to have as natural a birth as possible; it has changed inhuman, illogical practices in maternity hospitals and helped more women establish breastfeeding successfully. But it gives many women the feeling that there is a critical period where she and her baby must bond or all is lost. As well, there is no mention of a father in all this, so the weight is completely on the mother to get it right or else . . .

Bonding is falling in love with the baby during pregnancy or at birth, but the normal range of feelings covers strong feelings of instant support to numb indifference. When you're in the latter group, it does not mean you are abnormal or that your baby will be deprived in some way if it takes time for your relationship to grow. I talk to a number of women who are never really comfortable with babies, but who find as their babies grow and become "people" their relationship blossoms.

No evidence exists that premature or sick babies or babies born by cesarean section suffer emotional deprivation because their mother didn't bond or bonded late. When things are difficult in the beginning, worry and distress might overshadow your feelings of love for a while, especially if your baby cries a lot during the first six months, but you will find the mysterious bonding will gently arrive as the weeks go by.

However, if you are ever seriously worried about your feelings for your baby, talk to your practitioner or your doctor so that you can identify what the problem is and find out where to get help.

# Conflicting advice

When you're a new or not-so-new, mother one of the hardest things you invariably find you have to deal with is the constant conflicting advice you get from everyone you come in contact with, whether it's a health professional or someone in the supermarket.

Conflicting advice is a blessing and a curse. It's a blessing (believe it or not) because it allows for the many variations in human nature and experience and provides for flexibility; it's a curse because it raises doubts at a time in your life when you are likely to be very vulnerable, unassertive, sleep-deprived, and unable to count to ten let alone work out whose advice you're going to take.

Advice comes from two sources—non-professional experts and professional experts. The mother who is doing all the work is rarely viewed as an expert, and usually the assumption is made that she knows very little and everyone else knows lots.

Non-professional experts are friends, family, neighbors and a whole range of people you hardly know like the man on the bus and the woman in the bank. Their advice is usually unsolicited and based on what they did with their own babies.

Professional experts are people such as practitioners, nurses, general practitioners, pediatricians, a range of specialist doctors, social workers, psychologists, physiotherapists, dietitians, occupational therapists, lactation consultants, midwives, obstetricians, counsellors who belong to voluntary groups such as La Leche League International, staff who work in childcare centers, preschool teachers, and pharmacists, to name a few. Their advice is based on their academic qualifications, their professional experience, which varies according to what training they have undertaken, their hands-on work, and scientific research.

Having this extraordinary range of people around is the main reason there is so much conflicting advice. Modern-day care of mothers and babies is very fragmented, and you are likely to be in the hands of a different expert every step of the way, as well as for every different problem that might arise. Other reasons for conflicting advice include tradition, fashion, scientific research, and the fact that babies are a mystery and can't tell us what is wrong or how they feel.

## Conflicting advice is here to stay—what can you do?

Understand that everyone is different and advice that suits one person may not necessarily suit another.

Unsolicited advice from non-professionals is usually given with the best intentions in the world. You'll probably find yourself doing it once your baby is older and you're feeling experienced enough to offer a few tips to friends about to have their first. Smile and say thanks and forget about it unless it's something you think is useful.

Conflicting advice from health professionals is harder to deal with, especially in the early months. Try to avoid seeing a million different people and find one person you trust.

Here are a few hints on dealing with advice from experts—remember if you're feeling confident and have no problems, you're the expert. Don't worry about the health professionals. Consider these things with regard to advice:

- Is it practical and realistic in relation to your life? Have you been offered some options?

- Is it safe?

- Does the person giving you the advice have any commercial interests that may influence the advice?

- Does the person have a lot of hands-on experience? Quite a lot of written information is done by people who do not work in the field.

- Does the health professional reject out-of-hand advice from other "experts" or is he or she happy to help you work out what's right for you?

- Is the advice conflicting or simply a variation on a theme, and does your health professional help you to see the difference? What most mothers are looking for is guidance, not instructions.

- Does your health professional make you feel confident and good about yourself and your baby? If not, find someone else.

- Don't assume health professionals know everything—they don't. You are in charge, and as the weeks go by, you will regain your assertiveness and confidence and learn to trust your own judgment.

# *For grandparents*

Rather than get into the complicated and diverse dynamics of family life and the role of grandparents, I thought I would just mention the main bones of contention I hear about each day in my work. With any luck this might help you and your parents avoid some of the irritations that pop up between generations during the first year with a new baby.

Grandparents are often led to believe that everything about babies and what you do with them has dramatically changed—it hasn't. Society has changed, and the fact that the baby is your child's, not yours, is a change, but babies and what we do with them hasn't changed much at all (in any of the important ways).

The things that I notice grandparents see as big changes in babycare are all pretty minor, but for some reason they often become major points of difference, causing unnecessary tension for many families. When this happens, it is unfortunate, as the birth of a new baby is potentially a time of great pleasure, bringing with it a new lease on life for the older generation and a fresh sense of family for everyone. Here's some information and a few tips:

- Grandparents don't have to provide solutions. Support and practical help are what's needed. Constant suggestions as to why the baby is doing what she's doing undermine a mother's confidence—it's better to accept the baby the way she is and avoid labels like "good," "spoiled," "naughty," and so on.

- There are many options for looking after babies, and your child might choose different options to the ones you chose. For example, she might be breastfeeding whereas you bottle fed, she might pick the baby up and sleep with it whereas you were more into routines and babies sleeping in their own room. Alternatively, she might be prepared to let her baby cry, something

you would never have done, and so on. Accepting and supporting her choice without a lot of comment is important.

- Solids (that strange name we give to the mush babies first eat)
are not usually started until four months or even later now. Giving babies food other than milk before four months has no
advantages for most babies and causes problems for some.
Cow's milk in bottles is now not recommended until nine to
twelve months.

- Babies, whether breastfed or formula fed, don't need extra
water, juice, or vitamin supplements.

- Breastfed babies usually can't be fed every four hours. Flexible
feeding times are needed, which means there may be times
when the baby is nursing frequently. Let your daughter do it in
peace without constant reference to the number of feedings the
baby has had.

- Plastic pants over diapers do not cause problems.

- Babies don't automatically start "sleeping through" at eight
weeks. If they do, it's a bonus. Apart from letting them cry all
night (not recommended), there is no safe way of teaching
young babies to stop waking at night.

- Teething causes nothing but teeth (see page 450).

- Blue around the baby's mouth does not mean she has gas (see
page 195).

- Regular weighing of healthy babies is not necessary unless the
mother wants to do it.

- Older babies often suddenly start to perform when one of the
grandparents comes near them. It is normal for babies between

nine and twelve months to become very wary of strange faces and places, but why it's so often a grandparent is hard to say. It's not permanent, nor is it personal or caused by anything you are doing wrong. If it happens to you, try to take it in your stride, stay calm, and don't overwhelm the baby with too much attention. For more information, refer to stranger awareness and separation anxiety on page 585.

# Health professionals you may come in contact with

## Pediatrician

A pediatrician is a doctor who has had, in addition to four years of medical school, three years of speciality training in pediatrics (the care of babies, children and adolescents). It has become the norm for many parents in the US to routinely consult pediatricians, some for up to several years after the births of their babies. Since pediatricians only see children, they are probably more familiar than family doctors are with normal childhood development, health and behaviour although this is not necessarily the case. Many routine childcare matters can be satisfactorily dealt with by a family doctor who sees lots of children or a pediatric nurse practitioner (who will probably give you more time on routine baby care matters). Or, if it's a breast-feeding problem, a lactation consultant is a good choice. Pediatricians are advisable for medical problems that require special knowledge and skill in pediatrics.

## Speciality Pediatricians

Includes a range of pediatricians to cover every part of your baby's body from head to toe, for example, pediatric gastro-enterologist, pediatric neurologist, pediatric orthopedic surgeon and so on . . .

## Family Physicians (Family doctors)

A family physician has three years of specialist training after four years of medical school in a broad range of areas that includes psychiatry, internal medicine, obstetrics and gynecology.

## Pediatric Nurse Practitioners

Many pediatric and family medical practices employ nurse practitioners who are registered nurses with additional qualifications in their speciality areas, in this case pediatrics. The nurse can help you with feeding and nutrition, well-baby checks, developmental assessments, counseling and a range of specific baby and child problems such as rashes, vomiting, crying, temper tantrums, toilet training and sleep. A nurse practitioner is likely to devote more time to non-medical matters (for example, normal sleep problems) than a doctor will.

## Lactation Consultants

A lactation consultant has an international qualification in human lactation (and often additional breastfeeding credentials as well). Lactation consultants are often health professionals (nurses, doctors or psychologists) but may be people from any background who have the qualification. Lactation consultants may work in hospitals, as private practitioners or as part of the team in a pediatric practice.

A lactation consultant can help you get breastfeeding off to a good start (if you feel you need this help) or help you with any breastfeeding problems that may arise.

To find a lactation consultant, talk to your pediatrician, nurse practitioner, the staff at the hospital where your baby was born, or a La Leche League Leader.

## La Leche League International (LLLI) Leaders

LLLI is a wonderful resource for all mothers, including women whose breastfeeding doesn't work out but still have an interest in lactation. The League's expertise, publications, monthly meetings and local volunteers can give breastfeeding women the confidence they need to breastfeed successfully.

La Leche League volunteers are called "Leaders." They are women with a personal experience of breastfeeding and special training in helping other mothers. League Leaders are available by phone for confidential counseling and breastfeeding information. La Leche League has a strict code of ethics which means all counseling is confidential and mothers or babies with possible medical problems are advised to contact a doctor.

## Licensed Clinical Psychologists

Psychologists help parents understand why their babies do the things they do and some parents find their approach useful for specific baby and toddler problems. Psychologists are also able to help with personal or relationship problems.

## Licensed Clinical Social Workers

A licensed clinical social worker can give you support and counseling to help you adjust to your new role. She or he will look at your problem in the context of your family and social situation, and will have a detailed knowledge of the community resources available for you to use.

# Your other children

If this is not your first baby, a lot of the things you agonized over the first time around will pass you by. One of your main concerns this time will be how your first baby adjusts to the newcomer. As well, parents often wonder if they can possibly love another baby as much as the one they already have; sometimes even feeling guilty that they are having another baby, especially when the first child's behavior regresses, sometimes alarmingly, in the first three to six months. If you get an attack of the guilts, bear in mind that learning to live with others in a family is a vital, even essential, part of human development. Most families have more than one child and parents have no trouble spreading their love around many children.

A great deal has been written on this topic, and I find the parents I see are very conscientious about preparing the first child; even with the best will in the world, however, things can still be a bit difficult for a while. Difficulties in adjusting are temporary, and it does take some children a little longer to accept changes in the family than others. The age when it seems hardest for children to adjust is from fifteen months to about three years. After the age of three, a child has more autonomy and is much more sure of his place in the world and your affections. He is also able to look after himself to some degree and has diversions such as friends and pre-school. This doesn't mean it's a mistake to have children close, but the closer they are, the higher your levels of energy and tolerance need to be to handle the hard work when they are little.

Here are some suggestions for getting your first child ready for the big event in his life.

- Make any changes well before the baby arrives. It's a good idea to sort out sleep problems, bottles, pacifiers, potty training, bed-

**389**

rooms, and starting pre-school before your baby is born, but do it well in advance. If you don't get around to it, it's best left until at least six months after the birth.

- Talk about families and how they usually have more than one child. Use your own or your partner's as an example.

- Wait until your pregnancy is obvious before telling him about the new baby, but make sure you tell him before anyone else does. Let him feel the baby, and talk to him about babies and what they do, as well as telling him some funny, positive things he did when he was a baby. Help him understand that the baby won't be an instant playmate because babies can't walk, talk, and so on.

- Expand his life outside the home. Organizing a social life for him means he has other houses to visit and places to go. It's also a way of showing him he's different from the baby.

- Plan the arrangements for his care well in advance so that he knows what's happening, and, ideally, knows and loves who-ever is responsible for his care.

- Show him the hospital or the birthing center where you will have the baby (unless you are having a homebirth). Tell him you will be gone only for a short time and he will be able to visit. Let him help you pack your bag. When he's not looking, put in a couple of surprises for him to find when he visits.

## After the birth

Things often get off to a smooth start until the first child realizes it's a permanent arrangement, at which time negative behavior is likely to surface. Most negative behavior in children at this time is not directed against the baby but against the huge adjustment that has to be made, so your child might be very loving to the baby and pretty horrible to you.

Try to keep to your first child's normal routine as much as possible, and any time you can spend with him without the baby helps enormously. When you can't do something he wants to do, try not to make the baby the excuse too often. Fathers can help a lot by minding the baby while you do something with the older child or by doing something interesting with the older child when you are busy with the baby.

Encourage friends to include your older child when they visit and bring presents. If he is old enough to understand, prepare him for the fact that babies attract a lot of attention—remind him that he did when he was a baby. Let him know he can sit with you if he is feeling lonely or jealous.

Expect changes in your first child's behavior. His concentration will be affected by the change in his life. He may be more clumsy than usual, so make sure his environment is safe. Young children don't understand concepts of sharing and cooperation, so ignore as much negative behavior as is reasonable and give him lots of attention for positive behavior.

Help him not to feel guilty about jealous feelings by talking to him about feelings, how strong they can be, and the best ways of handling them. Accept and even suggest that while the baby is a considerable nuisance at the moment, eventually he and the baby will be friends and will do lots of things together.

Avoid situations where your older child may hurt the baby as it will make him feel bad.

Try not to leave the baby's belongings all over the house under the first child's nose. Don't talk about the baby in ways that could hurt your child's feelings by saying things like "thank goodness we have a girl this time" or "she's a much easier baby" and so on.

It's unrealistic to expect your older child to automatically love the new baby; this will happen in time. Encouraging the idea that the baby likes him will help him feel special to his new sister (or brother).

Last but not least, remember you are only human, and looking after babies and young children is one of the hardest things anyone can do. Blowing your stack sometimes or finding it difficult to manage more than one is completely understandable. Don't agonize over it or waste time feeling guilty. As time goes by, it all gets easier; sometime between three and seven months, the first jealousy passes and your first child will forget what life was like when he was the only one.

## Postnatal depression

Many improvements have occurred in recent years in recognizing and helping women suffering from depression following the birth of a baby.

Thank goodness the views of fifty years ago have been challenged and found wanting. The widely held belief then was that postnatal depression was a sign of mental illness in women who rejected the role and normal responsibilities of motherhood!

This change of ideas means that women who are depressed feel less threatened and are more likely to seek help. Publicity about postnatal depression, many excellent books, education of health workers, and input from feminists have all contributed to a larger number of women feeling able to admit they need help and getting sensitive, effective treatment. Unfortunately, despite these positive advances, the reluctance of many women to ask for help, as well as the lack of resources to provide help for every woman who needs it for as long as she needs it, means we still have not come far enough.

I have never been happy with the term "postnatal" depression. Postnatal is a misleading term in many ways because it implies a condition that occurs directly after the birth of the baby. The term doesn't encompass the women who start to feel depressed further down the track when the excitement and novelty of the baby wears off and when much of the support they started out with is gradually withdrawn. In my work I find most women have some degree of depression in the first two years after birth, which, for a few, continues on and off until their children are at school or they are back at work. The label "postnatal" depression also has a tendency to make women feel abnormal when they are reacting in a normal way to situations where they are under a great deal of physical and emotional stress.

Like many mothers, you may find that you feel tired and down for some time after the birth because of the lack of unbroken sleep, the responsibilities of being a mother twenty-four hours a day, and the natural worry of your baby's well-being. Many women today are perfectionists in the workplace and have learned not to make mistakes. The unpredictability of babies, the trial and error that comes with caring for them, and the slow realization that there are not always answers to every problem can be an enormous adjustment that may take six to twelve months to come to terms with. Distinguishing between baby blues, the normal mixed feelings that come with adjusting to life with a baby, and what is known as postnatal depression is an important part of getting the right help if it is needed.

## The baby blues

As many as seventy percent of women experience the baby blues to some degree. They are likely to affect you within a week to ten days after the birth and are strongly associated with hormone imbalance. It can be an emotional and weepy time. The baby blues usually don't last long, and don't interfere with your sleep, your appetite, or your ability to function and care for your baby. Occasionally the baby blues can be prolonged and traumatic and herald the onset of major depression, but some women find they are a much needed emotional release.

## Postnatal psychosis

Postnatal psychosis can be a severe form of postnatal depression but is more commonly a different type of mental illness that occurs once or twice in every one thousand births. It is a disorder that requires prompt intervention, as left untreated there is a high risk of maternal suicide (and less commonly infanticide). With prompt recognition and correct treatment, postnatal psychosis has an excellent prognosis with full recovery in a few months.

## Mild depression (sometimes called postnatal disillusion or postpartum adjustment)

I am using "mild" here as a way of distinguishing one form of depression from another, not to minimize the impact of the depressed feelings. It is common for women at home with small children to suffer from mild depression. The risk of this happening is higher if the woman has a history of depression, but many women who do not have a history become depressed during the early years of their children's lives. If it happens to be the father at home, then he is at just as much risk of becoming depressed as the mother. Most depression suffered by people at home with young children seems to be caused by the demanding nature of the job—occupational depression.

Why does this happen? Looking after a baby can be lonely, constant, and unacknowledged work. It's often stressful because of concerns about the baby's feeding, crying, and sleeping patterns. A lack of personal spending money, fatigue, and a sense of being unappreciated and unrecognized for the job all contribute. Coming to terms with the fact that the baby care is not going to be shared equally with their partners is also a significant factor for many women who had expectations of this before the birth.

Mild depression like this tends to come and go at various times in the first two or three years and is often exacerbated by things such as particular developmental stages the baby is going through, sleep problems, baby illnesses, or financial or relationship problems. Mild depression is so common that it is thought by many to be a normal part of adjusting to parenthood and a natural consequence of being at home with babies and toddlers when there is very little in the way of company and support.

This is not to suggest that this is how motherhood should be. The fact that such feelings are viewed as normal is more an indictment on a society that rationalizes the miserable experiences of so many in such a way.

The perception that such feelings are the load we mothers have to bear does not make them any less unpleasant or distressing. Nor should it deter you from seeking help if you feel yourself sinking.

Mild depression usually responds to one-on-one counseling with the right person, company (joining in groups), solving baby sleeping and feeding problems, moving on past trying developmental stages, and, for some women, going back to work—even just half a day a week makes a great difference.

## Serious depression (usually called postnatal depression)

About ten to twenty-five percent of women suffer depression more severely during the first months after birth, although it sometimes takes them a lot longer to identify the problem. The causes for this are innumerable, and as well as all the occupational and adjustment reasons previously mentioned, other causes may include:

- A family history of depression or a previous history of mental health problems and emotional difficulties.

- Women who do not have a close relationship with the father of the baby are more susceptible as are women who do not have a circle of friends or relatives they can confide in and express negative feelings to.

- Women who live a highly organized lifestyle and who are used to being in control may be more at risk.

- Disappointment and feelings of failure following a forceps birth or a cesarean section sometimes play a part.

- A constantly crying baby.

- Life events such as moving and relationship difficulties can also be contributing factors.

- The role hormone balance plays is unclear, but it seems unlikely it plays a major role in postnatal depression. Hormone imbalance does not account for the number of women who become seriously depressed months after the birth.

- Women who have a biological vulnerability of feeling highly emotional under stress.

The causes of depression vary for every woman. Some women spiral into depression when none of the above are present in their lives. Other women may experience all these things yet not suffer from serious depression. Postnatal depression affects women from across the whole spectrum of society—the poor, the middle class, the educated, the uneducated, the disadvantaged, and the wealthy.

## WHAT ARE THE SYMPTOMS OF SERIOUS (POSTNATAL) DEPRESSION?

Here are the recognized warning signs:

- Feeling out of control.

- Low confidence, low self-esteem—a sense of loss of self.

- A continued inability to get anything done and the feeling of being a prisoner unable to leave the house.

- Feelings of frustration, anger, and resentment that do not go away. Women I talk to often mention feeling envious of women without babies or women who have older children.

- Alternatively, feelings of numbness.

- Physical symptoms such as constant headaches, palpitations, sweaty hands, sleeping difficulties (even when the baby is sleeping well), or loss of appetite.

- Constant feelings of guilt and shame.

- A fear of going crazy.

- Frightening delusions and fantasies about harming herself or her baby.

- Panic attacks.

## WHAT CAN YOU DO?

It is important not to try to carry on in the hope that the distressing symptoms will go away. The first step on the road to recovery is to tell someone. Discuss your feelings with your family doctor, a nurse practitioner, or a good friend. If you feel you do not get the help you need, try someone else.

The right health professional will:

**397**

- Accept you the way you are and not try to keep cheering you up.

- Respect your confidence.

- Let you express exactly how you feel.

- Help you with any baby sleeping, crying, or feeding difficulties or put you in touch with someone who can.

- Give you all the options available to you in the area where you live—there is no single avenue of help that suits everyone, so you need to know what's available and how it will help.

## Options for help

- Sympathetic one-to-one counseling from a skilled health professional who can help you help yourself is a vital first step. Self-help ideas are things like learning to nurture yourself, learning how to take a break, and setting long-term and short-term goals. With the help of the counselor you can slowly regain a sense of self and start to take control of your life again.

- Many women find joining a postnatal support group where they can talk to other women in confidence who are having the same experience helps a great deal.

- Reading books on the subject is helpful for you and your partner. Those mentioned at the end of this chapter provide guides for self-help.

- Your partner requires support and information too. Men often try to solve the problem quickly but end up feeling unappreciated and depressed as well. Your partner needs to understand what you are going through is not his fault and the power to fix the problem does not lie with him. Listening, accepting how you feel, and supporting whichever road to recovery you are taking are ways he can help, as well as sharing the tasks of caring for the baby and running the home.

- At times psychiatric help and drug therapy is appropriate. Some women may not like this idea, but psychiatrists skilled in the area do not load women up with unnecessary medication and in fact often do not medicate at all after consultation. Medication takes the edges off the symptoms but is not effective as a quick fix on its own and should always be used in conjunction with counseling and the other supports mentioned above.

Recovery is slow and takes two to twelve months, sometimes longer. A lot of patience is needed from you and your partner, as well as commitment from your health worker, because time is part of the recovery process. Although recovery can take a while, the result is positive for most women.

Obviously, given a choice, no one would choose to suffer from what is known as postnatal depression, but many women (and men) acknowledge that in hindsight positive things do come from the experience. By working through the pain of depression, they learn more about themselves and about relating to others, which has the potential to give a new, positive dimension to their lives.

# Sex

Sex has gone through a cycle of never being talked about to being talked about constantly. Pressure from magazines and the electronic media urging us all to be forever sexy makes many couples feel abnormal if they are not performing by a set time after birth.

Some literature suggests it is normal for women to be wildly sexual as a natural progression of birth and breastfeeding. A number of women do feel like this, but if you don't, it doesn't mean anything is wrong.

This look at sex is not intended to be comprehensive. It aims to let you know there are wide variations in the way women and men feel about sex after the birth of their babies. Of course, wide variations exist at any time, not just after childbirth.

You may be surprised to find out that several surveys have shown the following:

a) The arrival of a baby tends to change a couple's sex life in ways that are seen as negative. For example: many couples don't enjoy sex for up to two months after the birth; a lot of couples have sex much less frequently than before the pregnancy for a year or longer after the birth; at least half of all women are less interested in sex after the birth than they were before the pregnancy, and this may last for six to twelve months. Often this gives way to a new depth of sexuality and greater ease in having orgasms than before the birth.

b) Couples who pick up where they left off are the exception rather than the rule. Everyone needs to start having sex again at their own pace. No magic moment or demarcation line sets the right time. Variations cover as wide a range as three weeks to twelve months.

Here are some common reasons why you might not feel like making love for a while:

• That tired feeling again! Exhaustion makes sex seem like another demand that's not much different from cooking the dinner at the end of the day.

**400**

- Interruptions. Babies are unpredictable about their waking, sleeping, and eating habits and it takes quite an effort in the first couple of months to use time you do have for yourself for sex when you'd sooner sleep.

- Discomfort following birth. Stitches following a tear or episiotomy, hemorrhoids, or the aftereffects of a cesarean section are all going to influence how a woman feels about having sex.

- Breastfeeding. Data about how breastfeeding affects women's sexual behavior is conflicting. Some women enjoy sex in a whole new way while they are breastfeeding and others experience a decrease in libido until they wean or menstruate again. Estrogen levels are low while you are breastfeeding, so the chance of the vaginal wall becoming thinner, less elastic, and drier is likely. A lubricating gel may be necessary.

- Psychological. Many women have a fear of the unknown, not knowing what happened "down there." If you're worried, get a mirror and have a look to reassure yourself all is normal. Gently rotating two fingers in your vagina will give you an idea of any tender spots.

- Some women feel embarrassed about their bodies for a while. Everything from breasts to vagina seems to leak or flop, which makes them feel decidedly unsexy.

- Sharing the bed or bedroom with a strange third person takes time for many couples to get used to.

## What to do

- Wait until you are both ready. It usually takes the woman longer to feel like having sex, but sometimes it is the man. Often both feel like it at the same time.

- Communication is vital. If communication was good before the baby arrived, it is likely to remain good or reestablish in time. If communication was poor, solving any problems, sexual or otherwise, is much more difficult.

- Practical help for the mother is probably going to help her feel more like having sex than watching an erotic video will. This includes time away from the baby, relief from household chores, and the opportunity to catch up on some sleep.

- When one or both of you are chronically unhappy, marriage guidance or family therapy helps. A dramatic change in the sexual relationship that is not resolved in the first year after birth may be a sign the relationship has deteriorated, with both of you suffering guilt and anger over a variety of things. Ongoing lack of interest in sex can be a sign of depression in some women.

- If things are not good, get help from a third party. The longer you wait, the harder it is to change anything, and it is not worth living in misery for years or ending a relationship that could be successful.

    Ask your early nurse practitioner for information about sexual counselling, marriage guidance, or family therapy.

- Women should always seek advice if pain is still experienced deep inside or anywhere around the vagina six months or later, after childbirth.

## Contraception

If you wish to space your children over a period of time, you do need to think about contraception soon after the birth if you are having a sexual relationship. Here are the most common family planning methods. *You will need more detailed information on them before use.* Contraceptive advice and written information is available from your family doctor or nurse practitioner.

## Barrier methods

- **Condoms and spermicide:** These are particularly useful in the early weeks and while your baby is being breastfed.

- **Diaphragms:** Do need refitting. Wait at least six weeks before refitting, then have the size checked again after three months. Diaphragms must be left in place in the vagina for eight hours after having sex.

## Natural methods

- **Exclusive breastfeeding:** *This means breastfeeding without the use of pacifiers, bottles, or any other food.* If you are breastfeeding in this way it is reliable contraception as long as you have not started to menstruate, you nurse frequently and your baby is fed at night. Only a small chance of conceiving is possible if you follow these guidelines, but if another pregnancy would cause you problems, other contraception is advisable. If you do use breastfeeding as a contraceptive, you are at risk of conceiving once you menstruate, once your baby sleeps through the night, or once you start formula or food from a spoon.

- **Abstinence:** Abstinence until breastfeeding finishes or until conception is planned is probably practiced far more than anyone realizes. Abstinence means no penis-in-vagina sex; it does not mean no sex at all. Kissing, touching, oral sex, and cuddling are all ways of showing affection.

- **Withdrawal:** Withdrawal means the penis is withdrawn before ejaculation occurs. Withdrawal is not at all reliable but is cheap and readily available.

- **Rhythm, temperature, or mucus method:** Combination of all three is the most reliable. The aim of these methods is to know when ovulation is likely to occur and avoid having sex at these times. If this is your choice for contraception, you and your partner need to attend a family planning center that teaches natural family planning.

## Hormones

- **The progestin-only pill:** The progestin-only pill is a small dose of progesterone which is not harmful to your baby and should not interfere with breastfeeding. Some women who are breast-feeding report that when they take the progestin-only pill their babies refuse the breast and/or there is less milk. If you find you have difficulties breastfeeding or with excessive bleeding, changing to another brand of the progestin-only pill sometimes helps. If not, other contraception has to be arranged.

  The progestin-only pill works by thickening the mucus around the cervix, which makes it difficult for sperm to pene-trate. It is a very satisfactory form of contraception when combined with the added protection of breastfeeding.

  If you wean or if you are only breastfeeding once or twice every twenty-four hours, you need to think about other contraception. It's safe to take the combined pill (see below) and keep breastfeeding once or twice a day, although the estrogen in the combined pill decreases the milk supply.

  The progestin-only pill's contraceptive effect is best between three and twenty-one hours so try to avoid having sex for three hours after taking it or within three hours of the pill being due. Therefore, the best time to take it each day is midday or very early in the evening.

Make sure it's the same time each day.

- **The combined pill:** The combined pill, known as the "pill," consists of both estrogen and progesterone and stops ovulation. It is not recommended for women who are breastfeeding, not because the drug harms the baby but because the action of the estrogen interferes with the milk supply. If you wean and wish to take the combined pill, start right away. You do not have to wait until you menstruate. Diarrhea, vomiting, and some antibiotics can affect the pill's absorption, so extra precautions might be needed.

## Intrauterine device (IUD)

IUDs are an effective method of contraception and suitable for some women. An IUD can be fitted by your doctor eight to ten weeks after birth. IUDs do not affect lactation, but there is a slight risk of damage to the womb if a woman is breastfeeding.

## Sterilization

Sterilization of either father or mother is not usually recommended until the youngest baby is twelve months old. Making such a decision before twelve months is often influenced by a crisis, emotional stress, or a lifestyle change. Many people feel differently a year later. Sterilization of a woman is by tubal ligation, and for a man, a vasectomy. These procedures can be reversed, but they should be considered permanent contraception.

# Returning to paid work and childcare

Many women now work outside the home when their children are young for a variety of reasons, the main ones being:

- They have no choice owing to relationship problems or real financial need.

- They believe they have no choice because of social and economic pressure related to a high standard of living that has come to be seen as the norm over the last fifty years.

- Work brings self-fulfillment and career opportunities. It is unfair that men have unquestioned access to career and family while women have always had to choose. Most professions are structured, so a woman's advancement abruptly takes a plunge if she takes time out to have babies and then spends three or four years at home with them. A small number of couples are now arranging their professional working lives so that one parent is always at home with the baby. And a tiny number of couples are reversing roles.

- It is difficult for women (or men) to have to depend on another person's income.

- Life at home caring for babies and small children is often lonely because of the way our society is structured. It can be depressing because full-time care of young children at home by their mothers is overidealized and undervalued, making women at home feel that their work is worthless.

A combination of the above factors is involved for many women. In an ideal world, we would all do what suits us best. There are women in the workforce who would sooner not be there and there

**406**

are women who are at home who would love to go back to their other job.

The main solution offered in America for these dilemmas of our times is childcare and a diverse range of childcare provisions have increased dramatically in the last couple of decades. Informal childcare undertaken by friends, relatives and babysitters has always been around and still is, but services that range from nannies who care for babies in their homes, to daycare nurseries, to home-based daycare are now available for most families. Despite difficulties finding places in suitable geographic areas and the financial burden involved, the majority of parents seeking childcare usually find it.

Childcare has been viewed through rosy glasses for quite some time. A growing social, emotional, and economic investment in childcare means that we all want it to be all right, so the benefits have been emphasized.

The benefits center around the right of women to have the same access to careers and economic security as men, and the social benefits to the children—many of whom enjoy the interaction with other children. Some research shows that daycare experience helps children to become self-reliant, to learn to share and cooperate, and to have a larger view of the world. In families where there are extreme social problems, daycare is a vital way of relieving parent stress and keeping the family unit together.

The negatives have been suppressed due to fear of making parents feel guilty and because of the seemingly insurmountable difficulties of other options being made available in this country so that parents can combine parenthood with employment. The biggest negative impact is on babies and toddlers who spend long hours in daycare under the age of two.

Concerns about daycare for children under three have been raised by a number of people such as psychologists Penelope

Leach and Steve Biddulph. Two respected researchers, Edward Zigler from Yale University and Jay Belsky formerly from the Pennsylvania State University, both previously staunch proponents of childcare, have reversed their positions on daycare after closely observing daycare experiences of children under two for over a decade. Negatives center around the lack of one-on-one care by an adult who has a parent-like commitment to the baby or toddler, the increased possibility of a deprived childhood in a place where there is no privacy, no escape, no place of one's own, and a thirty percent increase in childhood illnesses.

It is still too early to know whether children who spend the first two years of their lives in full-time daycare will end up with more problems, social or otherwise, than those cared for at home. Chances are, most will not, nor should the prospect of this possibility be used to scare the wits out of parents. Until we know more, I see the main issue being about the quality of life children experience at this time in their lives, which in daycare centers is far from ideal. Parents themselves often admit this as do many of the staff who work at the centers. Prospective parents need to be fully informed so that they are in a position to make the best decisions for themselves and their babies. Blanket approval and bland reassurances about childcare in the first two or three years are not particularly helpful. Parents who have no other choice but to use daycare should be aware of the negatives so that they can lessen their impact as much as possible.

Many parents do have other options that they may not even consider if well-meaning health professionals keep telling them daycare is as good as or even better than care at home.

By planning ahead, it's often possible to work out ways to minimize daycare for children under two.

Here are some ideas:

**408**

- Lifestyle expenses can often be arranged to allow for one parent to be at home for twelve to eighteen months.

- Part-time work should be negotiated whenever possible.

- Don't assume daycare for nine hours a day, five days a week is the only option if finances dictate an early return to work. Sometimes parents can arrange their work so some of the care can be shared between them. If there is a choice between three days in daycare and care spread between daycare, grandma and father, choose the latter.

- One-on-one care at home is preferable to daycare, so if this option is affordable, employ a nanny. Some parents find sharing a nanny between two families is a good compromise.

- Whenever possible be prepared to change arrangements or find other care any time things are not working out.

- If the need to return to employment is based on career opportunities and self-fulfilment rather than a financial necessity, try to hold off full-time work for eighteen months. It may be unfair that it is usually the mother who has to make this choice, but the trade-off in terms of peace of mind and the child's quality of life is worth it.

## Getting organized

If you are returning to work sometime in your baby's first two years, it is important to lay the groundwork for a smooth operation. Finding good-quality childcare is a top priority and should be organized as soon as your pregnancy is confirmed.

## Commercial Childcare services available

Childcare services range from nannies who will care for your child in your home, licensed daycare nurseries, and home day care (family day care). Some parents make private arrangements with a babysitter or relatives who may be untrained but reliable and caring.

When you are choosing, be guided by the cost, the caregiver's ability to be warm and affectionate, the safety and cleanliness of the surroundings, the number of babies or children per caregiver and the caregiver's qualifications. Check what arrangements are made if the caregiver is sick and whether the same person will be there most of the time to care for your baby.

Try to arrange several times when you and your baby can be with the caregiver before you go back to work.

## Problem times

Babies and toddlers have lots of minor illnesses, especially when they are in care with other children. As they grow older, this is less frequent, but it is very common in the first two years.

Mothers in paid employment do get very tired, as few ever seem to get enough help to manage two jobs, either from their partners or their employers.

So, as well as arranging childcare, try and establish a network of friends and family who are prepared to help out in times of emergency.

Have a good talk with your partner so that you can make definite arrangements about sharing tasks—for example, picking up and delivering your baby to daycare, getting up at night, sharing care when your baby is sick, and sharing the housework evenly.

## Childcare when one parent is at home

The impression that childcare has untold benefits and no disadvantages has been so widely accepted that many parents have come to believe that even if childcare is not needed for work reasons, babies and toddlers should be in childcare anyway for "socializing." If you are concerned about this, be assured that, contrary to what everyone would like to believe, babies and toddlers are not well adapted for social groups. While they are fascinated by other babies and toddlers, they are far too young to spend long hours every day socializing. The normal social interaction that goes on between families and friends is all the socializing they need. By age two or three (depending on the child), most children are ready for some limited time in a group setting for educational and social purposes.

This is not to say that children under three cannot be left for short periods in group care or with other caring adults. Parents, especially mothers, need a break and time and space to attend to their own needs. Babies and toddlers often enjoy such a change too, but if they don't, they are unlikely to suffer when they are not left for long periods.

# Other odd occurrences

## Hair loss

Sudden hair loss is a distressing experience for a number of women. It's upsetting because it comes out in handfuls and seems like baldness is inevitable. The mother feels as if it's excessive, but it is usually not noticeable to others. It happens from two to three months after birth and is not related to breastfeeding, so don't wean! The exact mechanism is unknown but thought to be related to the major upheaval the body goes through at this time.

Sometime after eight months, the hair loss stops, and twelve months after the birth, new, thick hair starts to grow. Beware of myths and wrong diagnoses. It is not happening because of stress, nor do you need hundreds of dollars worth of naturopathic dietary supplements or an expensive course of hair-loss treatment. It bothers me when mothers are talked into expensive, unnecessary remedies that make no difference.

## Wrist and arm problems

Wrist and arm problems during pregnancy and the first year after birth happen to an appreciable number of women and to a large extent are unrelated to their previous occupations. Some women find painful wrists and arms most distressing and debilitating. The discomfort experienced may mean they are unable to pick up their babies and have difficulty sleeping.

Problems with wrists and arms can start at the end of pregnancy or appear for the first time six to twelve weeks after the birth and continue for up to a year, when they nearly always resolve spontaneously. Many women suffer mild forms of wrist and arm problems and never mention it.

The discomfort is usually diagnosed as carpal tunnel Syndrome and/or tenosynovitis according to precise symptoms. Carpal tunnel syndrome occurs when a major nerve in the wrist is compressed, in this case thought to be due to excessive fluid. Tenosynovitis is inflammation of a tendon in the arm.

The underlying cause in pregnancy and the first year after birth is unknown, but the old scapegoat hormones may play a part and the condition is aggravated (not caused) by the physical work involved in caring for a baby. Treatment should be conservative as, unlike carpal tunnel syndrome and tenosynovitis in the rest of the population, it resolves itself when it happens as a result of pregnancy and birth.

When looking for help, it's important to find a doctor or hand specialist who is familiar with this phenomenon. This can be difficult; despite the fact that it is not uncommon, very little is known about wrist and hand problems relating to pregnancy. Splinting of the wrists in neutral or slight extension day and night, diuretics, anti-inflammatory drugs, or cortisone injections are the usual medical offerings. Most of the women I talk to manage with splints and massage once they know the problem will go away, but it does take some endurance; if you are finding life unbearable, cortisone injections do relieve the symptoms quite dramatically and are safe to have if you are breastfeeding. Needless to say, help with physical chores makes a lot of difference. Surgery is rarely required, so seek a second opinion if surgery is suggested.

## Night sweats and hot flushes

These symptoms are related to breastfeeding and are experienced to some degree by a number of women. The symptoms are quite separate from fevers and chills caused by mastitis, which is sometimes a bit confusing. Mastitis symptoms are similar to the flu, whereas night sweats and hot flushes happen to women who are otherwise well.

The uncomfortable feelings are due to low estrogen levels. Low estrogen levels during breastfeeding are normal and essential for efficient lactation. It is thought that the low levels of estrogen can cause blood vessels to become unstable (sometimes narrow, sometimes wide), which causes the sweating, the hot flushes, and sometimes palpitations.

Not much can be done. The symptoms are aggravated by heat, alcohol, obesity, caffeine, and hot food. They do not last for the entire time you breastfeed. A dramatic improvement usually happens by twelve weeks, if not before.

# Sudden infant death syndrome (crib death)

Sudden Infant Death Syndrome (SIDS) is something none of us like to think about, but we do; naturally, the time we think about it the most is when our children are babies. Because of my work, I am very much aware that parents worry about SIDS, as the subject is frequently mentioned when I talk to them. I also come into contact with families who have suffered the shocking event that is SIDS, and as I write, I am thinking of them and the pain and grief they suffered and are still suffering.

It is normal to think about SIDS after the birth of your baby and at times during the first year or two. It seems at every age and stage of development there is something there to potentially cast a shadow over the joy children bring. Certainly it is hard to find a parallel for the sudden and unexpected death of a healthy baby, but as the years go by, there is the fear of "stranger danger" and the adolescent years bring the worries of car accidents and misuse of drugs and alcohol. These worries are part of being a parent, which we tend to be unaware of until we have a baby. Accepting they exist, taking whatever sensible precautions we can and getting on with life is also part of learning to be a parent.

If you find yourself thinking about SIDS, it's better to talk about it with your partner, family, friends, or health worker than to keep apprehensive thoughts to yourself.

## What is Sudden Infant Death Syndrome?

SIDS happens when a healthy baby is put to sleep and found dead sometime later. This can happen anytime in the first two years of life, but eighty percent happen in the first six months, with the greatest number occurring between one and four months. It nearly always happens during sleep. There is no specific reason, it is no one's fault, and the cause of SIDS remains a mystery.

Research into the cause of SIDS is constant, and many theories have evolved, some rational and others in the realm of the ridiculous. Hundreds of suggested causes have been disproved. It is likely there is more than one factor involved.

Because the cause remains unknown, advice to parents focuses on evidence from research and statistics. The research is analyzed

**414**

carefully and updated on a regular basis, so the recommendations for baby care are changed from time to time according to information arising from new data.

It is important to be aware that the cause of SIDS is still to a large extent outside the parents' control and that any babycare recommendations are to do with reducing the risk, *not* removing the unknown cause. The current recommendations are as follows:

- **PUT YOUR BABY ON HER BACK TO SLEEP FROM BIRTH**

It has been found that the risk of SIDS is increased if babies sleep on their sides or tummies, so it is recommended that they be placed on their backs to sleep from birth.

Concerns about an increased risk of babies inhaling or regurgitating their milk when sleeping on their backs has been shown to be unfounded. Back sleeping in this regard is just as safe as side or tummy sleeping.

When your baby moves from the bassinet to the crib, use a firm, close-fitting mattress, with no pillow or crib bumper.

Many older babies (five months onward) roll all over the place during the night, and it is unrealistic to expect parents to somehow manage to keep them off their tummies when they start to do this. It is not necessary at any age to buy a device to keep your baby on her back. One of the problems that inevitably arises out of the recommendations made in relation to reducing the risks of SIDS is that there will always be corresponding commercial attempts to use these recommendations to sell baby products. Be aware of any inaccurate claims of these products. If in doubt, check with a recognized SIDS authority for information about baby products (*see Resources, page 594*).

- **MAKE SURE YOUR BABY'S HEAD REMAINS UNCOVERED DURING SLEEP**

Tuck your baby in securely so that she can't slip under the bedding. Make up the bassinet or crib so that her feet are at the foot of the bed. Do not use continental quilts or pillows in the first year.

- **KEEP YOUR BABY IN A SMOKE-FREE ENVIRONMENT**

The risk of SIDS is increased if the mother smokes during pregnancy. The risk is doubled if both parents smoke. Babies exposed to tobacco smoke after birth have an increased risk of SIDS.

**FOR MORE INFORMATION**

**FURTHER READING**

*This Isn't What I Expected: Overcoming Postpartum Depression,* Karen Kleiman, Valerie Davis Raskin, Bantam Books, 1994, USA.

*Overcoming Pospartum Depression and Anxiety,* Linda Sebastian, LPC, 1998, U.S.A.

*Breathe Easy: The Friendly Stop-Smoking Guide for Women,* Susannah Hayward, Penguin Book, U.K., 2000 (available from http://www.amazon.com.uk)

part **two**

# 3 TO 6 MONTHS

# chapter seventeen

# Equipment

## *Child safety seat*

A child safety car seat is fitted to either side or the middle of the
back seat by using a rear anchor bolt and a seat belt and can be
transferred between cars. Your baby is restrained in the seat by a
six-point webbing harness.

If you have an infant (non-convertible) backward facing seat,
your baby needs to move from it to a child car seat once she
weighs 20 pounds (around six months for a lot of babies). You do
not have to wait until she can sit on her own before you do this.
Many babies do not sit alone until they are around nine months
and well over 20 pounds. You can use the reclining position to
help support your baby's head if necessary.

If you have a convertible seat, turn it around to its forward-fac-
ing position once your baby weighs 20 pounds.

# *Walkers*

A baby walker is a device on a frame with a seat that allows a baby who can sit alone to propel herself around using her feet and toes.

Not only are baby walkers a non-essential item, but over-whelming evidence relating to injuries strongly suggests the supply of walkers should be prohibited.

Walkers are very popular, and I can understand why when I talk to parents who use them. Walkers have wonderful entertainment value—babies love them. And if a mother happens to have a baby (or twins) who never sleeps, the time her baby is in the walker may be the only time she gets to do other things.

But walkers do not teach babies to walk nor do they provide them with any sort of beneficial exercise. The use of baby walkers has no developmental advantages for babies. The only positive feature they have is their entertainment value and the fact that their use gives mothers a break, which has to be weighed against the following:

- The extraordinary number of high walker-related injuries. In the U.S. since 1973, at least 34 babies/toddlers have died from injuries associated with baby walkers. In 1999, more than 8,800 toddlers aged 15 months and under were treated in hospital emergency rooms for walker-related injury. The greatest number of injuries is to the baby's head; other injuries include fractures, burns and scalds and broken front teeth. Nearly eighty percent of babies who suffer baby walker injuries are being supervised at the time of the incident and over half of the caregivers are in the same room as the baby.

- When babies are propped up in a walker, their bodies tend to stiffen and they push back with their feet, which encourages them to walk on their toes and strengthens one group of muscles more than another. The resulting posture is not part of natural walking and can delay walking. Walkers do not help babies develop their balance the way playing on the floor does. In healthy babies the developmental delay is short-lived and much more likely to occur when babies are left in walkers constantly for long periods.

It is not easy keeping active babies happy all day, especially when they don't sleep much, and I sympathise wholeheartedly with mothers who find using walkers preferable to listening to the whining. However after looking at the injury statistics and the very limited use a walker has, I cannot recommend their use. If you never use one, you won't miss it. If you do decide to go ahead here are some tips for safe use:

- Make sure the walker you choose meets the American Society for Testing and Materials (ATSM) voluntary and mandatory standards, which require that baby walkers must be either too wide to fit through standard doorways or have features, such as a gripping mechanism, to stop the walker at the edge of a step. Also look for the "Meets New Standard" label.

- Wait until your baby/toddler is weight-bearing before you use the walker. Weight-bearing means that when you hold her standing with her feet flat on a hard surface she bears her weight well on both feet without her legs buckling. Most babies do this by six months but some take longer (up to nine or ten months). A delay in weight-bearing is not a major problem in healthy baby who is developing normally but use of a walker unnecessarily delays weight-bearing even longer; in turn this delays pulling up, cruising around the furniture and walking.

- Keep your baby within view at all times

- Keep your baby away from hot surfaces and containers

- Eliminate dangling appliance cords

**421**

- Make sure to keep your baby away from toilets, swimming pools, and diaper buckets full of water.

- Limit use of the walker to around thirty minutes a day to minimize injury risks and to allow your baby the full range of movement needed for optimum development.

# Baby jumpers, battery-operated swings, and baby exercisers

Again, these products are non-essential items and have no advantages for baby development. Nor have they any exercising benefit. They are entertaining, offer babies new sensations, and give mothers the opportunity for a break, which is never to be sneezed at. Unlike baby walkers, their use is self-limiting as babies tire of them in a fairly short period. The risk of injury is minimal and development unaffected when used for healthy full-term babies. They are not recommended for premature babies or babies who have been unwell, as these babies need playing with in ways that enhance their development, and this equipment does not offer the best opportunity for this to happen.

# Stair gates and safety gates

Once your baby starts to get mobile, gates are useful to block off doorways of rooms such as kitchens, bathrooms, laundry rooms, and the tops and bottoms of stairs. Mobility refers to crawling, which happens between five and twelve months; walking, which starts between nine and nineteen months; and anytime your baby is in a baby walker. Make sure the gap between the bars of safety gates is the same as that recommended for cribs—no less than 2 inches (50 mm) or greater than 3 inches (85 mm)—so your baby's head or limbs don't get stuck.

# Playpens

Playpens seem to be something used more in the past when women had fewer household aids and had to use playpens to keep their babies away from danger while they worked.

Playpens can still have a use depending on your lifestyle and your baby's temperament (some babies won't stay in playpens very long). Playpens can be an effective barrier to dangerous areas, and I'm sure we all know someone who irons in the playpen while the baby has free run of the room. At other times a playpen provides a handy space for toddlers and young children to play in when they are playing with small toys that need to be kept away from the baby. However think about it before you buy—playpens are often bought and not used.

# Portable cribs

Portacribs are lightweight fold-up cribs designed for visiting or vacations and are an optional item for families who travel a lot. Take care when purchasing, as portacots are often badly designed and dangerous. Sadly, a number of babies have died following collapse of their cots. Cribs that incorporate a rotating lock mechanism that locks the top rails of the crib are the design that causes concern.

Look for the following safety features in both portacribs and playpens:

- Check the crib/playpen has not been recalled by the CPSC and is JPMA certified.

- If mesh design that the mesh is less than ¼ inch in size and has no tears, holes or loose threads. Also that the mesh is securely attached to the top rail and floorplate.

- If wooden that the slats are 2⅜ inches (60mms) apart or less. That the slats are not missing, cracked or splintered. The corner posts should be ⅟₁₆ inch (1½ mm) high or less.

- For portacribs, use only the original mattress purchased with the crib. It should be low and firm, not thick and soft.

- For both, check there are no missing, loose or exposed staples and that the collapse mechanism is baby-proof.

## Eating equipment

Between three and six months, your baby may start eating food from a spoon. Any unbreakable plate and spoon will do, but you might feel like choosing a special baby set from the wide selection available. Don't waste money on sets that include a host of things you don't need. One plate and one spoon is fine. Training system cups that offer a nipple, a straw, and a spout are a needless expense at this stage. Wait until your baby can use a straw or a spout, then buy whichever one she uses. Buying the three systems is unnecessary, especially when one is a nipple—if you're bottle feeding, you already have one, and if you're breastfeeding, you may never use it.

### FOR MORE INFORMATION
Chapter 18: Feeding Your Baby, page 425
Chapter 24: Feeding Your Baby, (tips for drinking from a cup, page 507)

chapter **e i g h t e e n**

# Feeding
# Your Baby

*We put cereal into his mouth and it kept going in,*
*but it also kept oozing out. My husband said to me,*
*"Why are we doing this?"*

Helen Townsend, *Baby Crazy*

## Starting new food

Fashions in feeding babies have ranged from starting solids at
nine to twelve months (eighty years ago), to six weeks (thirty
years ago), to four to six months at the present time. Flexibility to
allow for individual babies' needs and family lifestyles is often
ignored under the weight of scientific theory. For example: past
enthusiasm for early food from a spoon meant six-week-old
babies were swallowing things they didn't need. Present recommendations are at times followed to such extremes, breastfed
babies are sometimes kept unnecessarily hungry until the magic
age of six months is reached.

Don't get too bogged down by rules. Food is fun. Be flexible,
be relaxed, and above all be guided by your baby.

For most babies, human milk or formula is all they need for the
first four to six months. There are no advantages in giving food

425

from a spoon any earlier. Mothers often feel pressured into starting food early because they are told it will make their babies good eaters or because they have big babies. I have never seen any evidence that babies who start food early eat any better. The variations of the way babies eat are endless and rarely have anything to do with the age at which they start to eat food other than milk. Babies who are born big and are thriving do not need to eat food any earlier than other babies.

Lots of extra food from a spoon given early may have contributed to making some babies overweight in the past and caused problems for those with allergies or food intolerance.

In the few families where allergies and food intolerance are a problem, special care should be taken. Seek advice from a health professional who specializes in such things (a doctor or a dietitian). Even if your family doesn't have these problems, it is advisable to avoid foods most commonly associated with allergic responses until your baby is six months old (for foods such as egg yolk, wheat, milk, fish) and twelve months old (for foods such as peanut products and strawberries). Honey should also be avoided until babies are over twelve months because of the risk of botulism.

## When to start extra food

First, a note on the tongue thrust reflex. As a young baby's main way of obtaining food is by sucking, the tongue has an up-and-down movement that is different from the movement of the tongue when food from a spoon is eaten or fluid is drunk from a cup. Sometimes when a spoon or a cup is put into a baby's mouth, the baby's tongue automatically pushes forward, so food is pushed away. This is called the tongue thrust reflex, and much has been made of it in recent years in relation to giving babies new food, often confusing mothers who are told to "wait until it's gone" before starting food. From a practical sense, I have never found

tongue thrust information to be particularly useful. From my observations, if a baby wants to eat, she eats, and if she doesn't, she
doesn't, regardless of tongue thrust. Here are the guidelines I use.

## THINK ABOUT STARTING EXTRA FOOD ANY TIME
## BETWEEN THREE AND SIX MONTHS IF

- Your baby is breastfeeding and there hasn't been quite enough
  milk for some time. This shows by slow weight gains or no
  weight gains over an extended period, and there are times
  when, despite all efforts to increase the amount of milk, a baby
  still needs more food. If you want to keep breastfeeding, food
  from a spoon doesn't interfere with breastfeeding the way formula in a bottle does, so it is an alternative to bottle feeding.

- Your baby is bottle feeding and drinking excessive amounts.
  Extra food might be needed, but it's important to rule out overtiredness and incorrect preparation of the formula first. Your
  early childhood nurse can help you with this.

  **N.B.:** Some babies who are bottle feeding are never keen on
  their bottles and only ever drink relatively small amounts. Once
  offered food from a spoon, they show much more interest and
  quickly start enjoying a variety of different foods—this is fine.

- Your baby reaches six months of age and is still only having
  breastmilk or formula.

Food from a spoon is often tried for a whole range of reasons that
have nothing to do with nutrition. Here they are:

- To encourage "sleeping through." Once your baby is over three
  months old there is no harm in this, but don't be disappointed
  if nothing changes, and remember—sleep problems aren't

427

solved by forcing babies to eat. If she's not interested, forget about it for the time being.

- To help space frequent breastfeeds. This is fine, and if your baby enjoys the food, it can make life easier, but thriving breastfed babies often are not interested in any food other than breastmilk.

- To help prevent reflux vomiting. Starting food from a spoon rarely makes any difference to reflux vomiting or to crying babies who may have reflux heartburn. If your baby is vomiting a lot, you just end up with technicolor vomit instead of white.

- Curiosity. When babies start to show great interest in every mouthful of food going into everyone else's mouth around them, parents become agog with curiosity to see what they will do with food of their own and can't wait to try! If your baby is thriving on milk alone, don't rush it—wait until she is at least four months.

- Pressure from relatives often influences parents to start food from a spoon before their baby needs it. If this is not what you want to do, ignore uncalled-for advice.

## What do you need?

- A spoon without sharp edges. An unbreakable dish. You don't have to sterilize the dish and the spoon.

- Something to grind up the food. If your baby doesn't mind eating food mashed with a fork, a fork is all you need. Most babies like their food smooth to begin with—which means using something mechanical like a handheld electric mixer, a hand blender, or one of the small electric blenders specifically designed for grinding up baby food.

- Something to sit your baby in. When you start, you may find it easier to sit her on your lap. Once you're in the swing of things, a portable baby chair is useful until your baby can manage a highchair or a chair attached to a table (six to nine months).

- Plenty of mopping-up cloths.

## Which foods?

- Rice cereal;

- Cooked apples and pears;

- Mashed banana;

- Mashed avocado;

- Full-fat yogurt; ricotta cheese;

- Cooked veggies; chicken soup; veggie broth;

- **Rice cereal:** Rice cereal can be purchased at supermarkets or you can make your own. Rice cereal is the only cereal that does not contain wheat (which can cause problems for some babies) and is recommended until your baby is six months old.

- **Cooked apples and pears:** You may cook your own and puree them or buy commercially prepared fruit for babies available in jars. Once you have determined your baby likes home-cooked fruit, you can prepare and freeze it. Make sure your baby is going to eat the food first before going mad and filling up the freezer with ice-cube trays of cooked fruit and veggies.

  Cooked food in clean containers or jars of commercially pre-pared baby food last up to three days in the fridge as long as you always scoop out portions with a clean spoon.

Commercially prepared baby food is nutritionally sound and convenient but it is more expensive; it has no advantages for babies (advertising often implies it is superior), does not offer the range of tastes that home-prepared or fresh food does, and when you prepare your baby's food yourself, you know exactly what she's getting.

- **Mashed ripe banana:** Mashed or banana pureed with a little orange juice is excellent first food for babies. It does give some babies hard poo, so if this happens, you may have to stop the banana for a while. Banana also makes a strange poo sometimes, so don't panic if there are a few dark red stringy bits in your baby's poo after she eats banana—it's harmless.

- **Avocado:** Mashed or blended avocado is very nutritious and enjoyed by many babies. For some it is a little rich, which results in a bright green vomit. If this happens, wait a few weeks before trying again.

- **Yogurt:** Yogurt is an excellent first food for babies either on its own or combined with fruit or vegetables. Yogurt is far superior to custard, which is best avoided. Custard is sweet and addictive, so give it a miss and try yogurt instead. If your baby likes and tolerates yogurt, it's a wonderful, healthy convenience food. When served with fresh fruit, it makes a good meal on its own for older babies.

  The healthiest yogurt for babies is plain full-fat yogurt. If you can't persuade your baby to eat the plain yogurt, try one of the fruit-flavored yogurts without added sugar. Stay away from caramel and honey yogurts—they are sweet and addictive.

  Lactose-intolerant people who can't drink milk can tolerate yogurt because the lactose is partially broken down by the bacteria which cause the milk to thicken.

Commercial baby yogurt desserts are a diluted version of the real thing. They contain twenty-six percent yogurt, which is then sterilized so that the yogurt's culture is destroyed. What's left is mixed with fruit juice. Those are fine to use as an alternative now and then or to start with but are not as nutritious as full-fat yogurt.

Yogurt does make a small number of babies regurgitate, gives a few a red bottom, and some a rash around their lips, so wait until your baby is four months and start slowly. If any of these things happen stop, wait a month, and try again.

- **Fruit gels:** Fruit gels are simply pure fruit juice made into a jelly. Babies enjoy them from time to time, especially in hot weather when gels can be a useful way of getting extra fluid into babies who don't have bottles. You can make your own or use commercially prepared gels.

- **Vegetables:** I suggest potato, pumpkin, and carrot to begin with as they are all easy to cook and mash or make into a puree. You can try them separately or combine them. Babies often like potato and pumpkin together. Once you establish that your baby is going to be a veggie eater, try the full range of veggies blended up together (broccoli, spinach, sweet potato, zucchini, and so on). You do not have to give one little bit of a veggie weekly to test the result—it would take a year to try them all!

  If your family eats meat, when your baby is around five to six months and eating veggies well, try cooking a little ground beef or chicken and blending it up with the veggies. Grate some cheese and stir it in as well.

- **Chicken soup** is a regular item in the homes of many of the families I see, and traditionally in families of European descent this wonderful, nourishing dish is offered as baby's first food. This is fine.

# How do you begin?

Pick one of the items from the list. Rice cereal is usually suggested for the first choice, but feel free to try one of the others if you would rather. Cereal is convenient and easy to prepare until you work out how your baby takes to this new style of eating. It's a bit frustrating cooking up nutritious fruit and veggies for one little teaspoon, which initially may be spat back.

If you are using rice cereal, try one or two teaspoons mixed with ½ oz-1 oz (15–30 ml) of expressed breastmilk, warm water, or prepared formula. Express your own milk if it's easy; if it's difficult, select one of the other options.

Offer one or two teaspoons of food to your baby once a day until you have some idea of how she takes to it. Try any time of the day that suits you. For convenience, offer the food at the same time as the milk. If you offer the food in between the milk feedings you will find you are offering your baby food every two hours—this is time-consuming and unnecessary, but remember there are no strict rules. If you find it suits you and your baby to give the food from a spoon in between the breast or bottle, please do.

## MILK OR FOOD FIRST?

The endless discussion about the order in which babies should be offered food and milk when half the world's babies don't have enough to eat emphasizes the ridiculous extremes the simple act of giving babies something to eat has come to in our society. Mothers are led to believe their baby's entire future hangs in the balance over this one issue. Here's my view:

It's better to offer the milk first in the following situations:

- When younger babies of three or four months are given extra food because there is not quite enough breastmilk.

- Fussy bottle feeders who are slow to gain weight should be offered their bottle first.

- If you and your baby are happier for her to suck before eating, by all means do it that way.

For most babies it doesn't matter. Initially your baby will probably want to suck when she's hungry—that's what she's used to. Offering her a spoon first will probably frustrate and annoy her. You might like to offer one breast or half the bottle, try the food, then give her the other breast or the rest of the bottle.

Once spoon feeding is well under way, most babies who enjoy food usually like to eat first, then finish off their meal with the breast or bottle, often before having a nap. Sucking at the end of a meal is calming and pleasurable for you both. It is also a nice time for a cuddle.

## How to proceed

Sit your baby on your lap or in a portable chair. Take up a small amount of food on the tip of the spoon and place it in her mouth, well back over her tongue before emptying it, to encourage her to swallow. Expect some or all of the food to come back out of her mouth when you first start. Take it slowly, stay relaxed—food is fun, if a little messy.

If you have twins, you might find it easier in the beginning to offer the food to each baby separately to see how they take to it. Once it's well under way, sit them in portable chairs and use one dish and one spoon and feed them both at the same time unless there's two of you around to do the job. Babies quickly develop individual tastes, so don't be surprised to find one baby's eating style is different from the other's.

The same guidelines apply to premature babies as full-term babies, but if your baby was very premature, you will probably find she is not ready to start food from a spoon until she is around six to nine months.

It's all experimental until you find out what your baby thinks of this new way of eating.

If after a day or two it's going down with a minimum of fuss, increase an extra teaspoon of cereal every day or two up to a maximum of two tablespoons. If you think your baby is interested but doesn't like rice cereal, try mixing some fruit with the cereal or try one of the other suggested foods. When she is comfortably eating one to two tablespoons of food every day, try a second meal after two weeks. Two or three weeks later, offer a third.

Never try to force the food if your baby doesn't want it. If you have an interested eater, resist the temptation to try everything on the menu in three days. Try a new food every two or three days.

## A word about veggies

Veggies are wonderful. Veggie-eating babies make us all feel good, but I would estimate about half of all babies won't eat veggies, so don't let it get you down if you have a non-veggie eater. She will be fine. It's best to stop cooking and offering them after a few weeks if the veggie refusal looks like it's here to stay because you will get angry and your baby will get stressed. Just offer two meals a day or think of something else for the third. A second round of rice cereal and fruit is fine; babies don't look for endless variety.

## Some normal variations

It is difficult to be precise about food and babies. They all respond to food in their own way, and you must be guided by your baby. Wide variations exist across the eating spectrum that have little to do with the mother's feeding techniques. Here are the main ones I observe:

- **Loves food, eats anything:** Some babies just open up and down it goes! Be careful not to overdo it if you have one like this. Three to four tablespoons of food three times a day as well as the breast or bottle is ample. As babies like this eat anything, they are just as happy with a plate of veggies as anything else, so it's easy to give them a healthy diet that won't cause excessive weight gains.

- **Eats well, then suddenly refuses:** Don't panic. Stop completely and try again in a month. Remember food from the spoon is an optional extra at this stage. Continue milk only for the time being.

- **Complete refusal:** Not a problem. If, after you try a few different things over a week or two and you are getting nowhere, stop—try again in a month. Continue milk only for the time being.

- **Loves some things, refuses others:** Give her what she likes even when it is the same old boring things each day. Avoid the temptation to try sugary baby biscuits, flavored custards, and added sugar to vary the diet. They are not needed.

- **Keeps refusing all food from a spoon indefinitely:** About twenty percent of all babies are finger-food babies who constantly refuse food until *they* can feed themselves with their fingers. Parents find this frustrating, but it's their baby's decision, and respecting this is the only rational approach. If you have a finger-food baby, start to allow her two or three pieces of food to suck herself anytime between five and six months. After ten minutes, call it quits until around the next mealtime. Sometimes

**435**

finger food gets eaten and sometimes it gets thrown around the room, but healthy babies who eat like this thrive when left alone to get on with it without a lot of agonizing and soul searching from the parents about the five food groups and so on and so on. Offer the breast or bottle after the food. Here are some finger-food suggestions: steamed veggie sticks; grated carrot or apple (because of choking risks, do not give whole); small pieces of ripe pear, melon; pieces of home-made meat patties; pieces of home-made salmon or tuna pieces (after six months); pieces of bread or toast (seedless); crackers; pieces of cheese on toast.

- **No food at all for a long time:** A number of very healthy, thriving breastfed babies have mothers with such an abundant milk supply that they see no need to eat anything and end up exclusively breastfed for a very long time. They often refuse most food until they are nine to twelve months old. The issue of iron deficiency in babies who are exclusively breastfed beyond six months has been raised in the last few years. There is some evidence that ten to thirty percent of babies who are exclusively breastfed after six months may become iron deficient.

  Unfortunately, when babies are obviously thriving and look healthy, the only way to monitor this is to take blood tests or give all babies iron supplements if they are exclusively breastfed in the second six months. Because opinion is still divided over the age at which iron levels are depleted in breastmilk and the usefulness of such strategies, I suggest feeding on. Try foods with your baby in a relaxed way. If you are worried about the possibility of iron deficiency, talk it over with your nurse practitioner, or pediatrician. If anyone's advice puts you in panic mode, seek a second opinion.

## HERE IS A GUIDE TO FOLLOW ONCE YOUR BABY IS EATING WELL

*(Offer up to two or more tablespoons three times a day)*

| | |
|---|---|
| **Early morning** | Breastfeed or bottle feed |
| **Mid-morning** | Rice cereal with cooked fruit plus breast/bottle (breakfast) |
| **Early afternoon** | Blended veggies (add meat and chicken from five months) plus breast/bottle (lunch) |
| **Early evening** | Yogurt and fruit or mashed banana or try avocado/cottage cheese blended or some nutritious chicken soup plus breast/bottle (dinner) |
| **Late evening** | Breast or bottle (if needed) |

If your baby is not an avid eater, don't be tempted to give food in a bottle instead of off the spoon. Traditionally, parents from some cultures do give fruit, veggies, yogurt, and soup from bottles with big holes cut in the nipples.

While recognizing that generations of babies have grown into adults where this has been the practice, it is not recommended for the following reasons:

- The baby has no control over the amount of food she is "drinking." It just goes down and weight gains can become excessive.

- Food in a bottle is not teaching your baby the skills she needs to learn to eat in a socially acceptable way.

- Sucking food from nipples increases the chance of tooth decay, especially when this way of eating goes on into the second year, which it often does because it is very habit forming.

The guide on the previous page offers four breastfeedings a day. If you wish to breastfeed more, continue in the way that suits you and your baby. Juice or water in between meals is optional. Bottles and nipples do not need disinfecting after the first six months.

## Paid work and breastfeeding

Organizing their return to the workforce and arranging the best care possible for their babies is a concern for many women around this time. Combining breastfeeding and work is part of this, and many women are keen to continue breastfeeding but unfortunately often feel that breastfeeding has to stop once work starts.

Because of this, many women who intend returning to work during the first six months often feel discouraged from starting breastfeeding in the first place. Others think that even if they do start, it has to stop once work starts.

Many women are also under the impression that they have to either breastfeed or formula feed, and that once formula is started, they have to wean. This is not the case; breastfeeding and formula feeding can be combined. When you are unable to fully breastfeed, breastfeeding is great for you and your baby whenever you are together, which will still be a considerable amount of the time. Continuing part-time breast-feeding is also a comfort for many women who find that leaving their babies to go back to work is a very emotional time.

On the following page is a guide so that you can get organized before you start work. It can be used for expressed breastmilk or formula or a combination of both. If using formula, use a cow's milk-based formula labeled "suitable from birth."

**438**

## WEEK ONE

| Monday | Tuesday | Wednesday | Thursday | Friday |
|---|---|---|---|---|
| 6am | 6am | 6am | 6am | 6am |
| breastfeed | breastfeed | breastfeed | breastfeed | breastfeed |
| 10am | 10am | 10am | 10am | 10am |
| *bottle feed* | breastfeed | *bottle feed* | breastfeed | *bottle feed* |
| 2pm | 2pm | 2pm | 2pm | 2pm |
| breastfeed | breastfeed | breastfeed | breastfeed | breastfeed |
| 6pm | 6pm | 6pm | 6pm | 6pm |
| breastfeed | breastfeed | breastfeed | breastfeed | breastfeed |

## WEEK TWO

| Monday | Tuesday | Wednesday | Thursday | Friday |
|---|---|---|---|---|
| 6am | 6am | 6am | 6am | 6am |
| breastfeed | breastfeed | breastfeed | breastfeed | breastfeed |
| 10am | 10am | 10am | 10am | 10am |
| *bottle feed* | *bottle feed* | *bottle feed* | *bottle feed* | *bottle feed* |
| 2pm | 2pm | 2pm | 2pm | 2pm |
| breastfeed | breastfeed | breastfeed | breastfeed | breastfeed |
| 6pm | 6pm | 6pm | 6pm | 6pm |
| breastfeed | breastfeed | breastfeed | breastfeed | breastfeed |

## WEEK THREE

| Monday | Tuesday | Wednesday | Thursday | Friday |
|---|---|---|---|---|
| 6am | 6am | 6am | 6am | 6am |
| breastfeed | breastfeed | breastfeed | breastfeed | breastfeed |
| 10am | 10am | 10am | 10am | 10am |
| *bottle feed* | *bottle feed* | *bottle feed* | *bottle feed* | *bottle feed* |
| 2pm | 2pm | 2pm | 2pm | 2pm |
| *bottle feed* | breastfeed | *bottle feed* | *bottle feed* | *bottle feed* |
| 6pm | 6pm | 6pm | 6pm | 6pm |
| breastfeed | breastfeed | breastfeed | breastfeed | breastfeed |

## WEEK FOUR

| Monday | Tuesday | Wednesday | Thursday | Friday |
|---|---|---|---|---|
| 6am | 6am | 6am | 6am | 6am |
| breastfeed | breastfeed | breastfeed | breastfeed | breastfeed |
| 10am | 10am | 10am | 10am | 10am |
| *bottle feed* | *bottle feed* | *bottle feed* | *bottle feed* | *bottle feed* |
| 2pm | 2pm | 2pm | 2pm | 2pm |
| *bottle feed* | *bottle feed* | *bottle feed* | *bottle feed* | *bottle feed* |
| 6pm | 6pm | 6pm | 6pm | 6pm |
| breastfeed | breastfeed | breastfeed | breastfeed | breastfeed |

Here is some information to help you continue breastfeeding after you go back to your other job.

## Get breastfeeding off to a good start

Try to delay returning to work until your baby is at least three months old as this gives your baby and your body time to learn to work together to get the milk flowing. It also gives you time to sort out feeding difficulties and overcome any problems.

## Planning

Most things in life work a little better with some planning. Combining work and breastfeeding is no exception. In the early days, learning to express is of great benefit. You can get help with this from a midwife, a lactation consultant or a La Leche League International leader. Once you have the idea, practice as often as you can—it's like any skill; the more you do it, the easier it becomes.

Approaches to breastfeeding and work vary depending on the age of your baby and the hours of work involved, so working out a plan to suit your particular needs *well ahead of time* is very useful. Your nurse or La Leche League International leader can help with this.

A cup instead of a bottle has many advantages, especially for babies who are reluctant to take bottles. This is possible at any age after four months, but is easier with older babies who are also eating food from a spoon. Starting a cup well before you go back to work means your baby is used to it and makes life easier for your caregiver. Give small amounts frequently throughout the day from a small cup.

Planning is important, but stay flexible, as there is usually a period of trial and error during the first month.

## Here are the choices

Having your baby looked after at work and being able to feed her there is the ideal way to combine breastfeeding and work. Unfortunately, moves to make this option a reality are very slow, so work-based care is only available to a limited number of women in the United States.

Apart from being able to go to your baby for feedings there are three other options:

- Replacing breastfeedings with expressed milk from a bottle when you are not there.

- Replacing breastfeedings with formula from a bottle when you are not there.

- Replacing breastfeedings with food from a spoon and a cup—a possibility from five months onward. (See Starting New Food, page 425.)

### OPTION 1

Once your breastfeeding is going well (six to nine weeks), you can replace one of your breastfeedings with a bottle of expressed milk. You will need to express 4–5 oz (120 to 150 ml), depending on the size of your baby and her appetite. This amount increases quite quickly as your baby grows. By three months, she will need 5 oz–8 oz (150 to 210 ml) in each bottle. If your partner gives the replacement bottle, it leaves you free to express at the time of the missed feeding. Starting a regime of expressing and giving one bottle a day well ahead of returning to your job gives you a chance to learn how to express and helps your baby get used to a bottle. Once you are in a routine with one feeding, add another so that your baby has two bottles of expressed milk and about four breastfeedings every twenty-four hours. Continue this schedule after you return to work when the bottles of expressed milk are given by your babysitter.

Ideally, to maintain your supply, you should express once or twice at work, store the milk in a clean container in a fridge, and bring it home with you in a cold storage pack. If it is not possible for you to do this, you will need to express and store the milk during the time you are not at work. This can be done after a feeding, between feedings or any time your supply is abundant. If there is neither the time nor facilities to express and store milk while you are at work, you will still need to express once or twice a day for comfort for a week or two until your breasts adjust to missing feedings. Unfortunately in many workplaces the only room to do this is in the women's restroom.

Problems arise with this option either because some women can't express or because the amount they are able to express starts to dwindle after being back at work for a while. It's important to remember an inability to express does not mean you have a low supply; your baby will still get plenty when she goes to the breast. Nevertheless, not being able to express much leads you to option two.

## OPTION 2

If you decide to use formula instead of breastmilk, before you go back to work it's a good idea to start one bottle of formula a day, then to increase the bottles slowly until your baby is having the number of bottles a day that she will be having once you are back at work. If you are going back full-time, you need to start this about three or four weeks before you start work in order to give your breasts time to adjust. The guide on page 439 will help you to organize this and can be used for expressed breastmilk or formula or a combination of both.

If you are already back at work and the amount you are expressing is diminishing, start making up the difference by leaving bottles of formula with your caregiver as well as any expressed breastmilk you have.

In order to keep your milk flowing, give your baby extra feedings on weekends and in the evenings. Try not to give any more formula than is necessary when you are around to nurse as an increase in formula can result in a decrease in breastmilk. Ask your caregiver to give your baby her last bottle well before you pick her up so that she is ready to go straight to the breast as soon as you both get home. A bottle of water or juice will often keep your baby happy until you arrive.

## OPTION 3

Babies who start food from a spoon from four months and like it can have food instead of the breast twice a day while you are at work once they are eating well. Fluids such as expressed breastmilk or formula can be given from a cup as well as a little diluted juice for variety. The earliest, realistic age this is a possibility is from about five to six months, as food can only be introduced at the baby's pace, and it takes about six weeks for most babies to learn to drink a reasonable amount from a cup. If the time frame fits your return to work, it's a much gentler option than forcing your baby to take a bottle.

## FOR MORE INFORMATION

Chapter 8: Breastfeeding Your Baby After the First Two Weeks (*how to express and store breastmilk, page 125, low supply, page 135, baby won't take a bottle, page 170*)

Chapter 7: Bottle Feeding Your Baby For the First Two Weeks (*What's in formula? page 106, equipment, page 111, care of bottles and nipples, page 112*)

Chapter 16: For Parents (*tips for grandparents, page 384, conflicting advice, page 381*)

Chapter 14: Sleeping and Waking in the First Six Months *("sleeping through," page 315)*

Chapter 15: The Crying Baby *(reflux heartburn, page 344, and vomiting, page 344)*

Chapter 24: Feeding Your Baby, page 425

# chapter nineteen

# Common Worries and Questions

## *Bathing*

At some stage between three and six months, your baby will grow out of the baby tub and will need to be bathed in your tub. Moving into the big tub goes smoothly for most babies who enjoy the added space and freedom, but a few are not happy. If your baby is like this, take it slowly and gently—bathing her in the baby tub in the big tub or perhaps sharing the tub with her might help get her used to the idea.

Bathing babies in the big tub when they can't sit on their own is not great for adult backs, so if you have a back problem, it may be worth investing in a baby bath seat which provides support for your baby until she sits well on her own. *Never* leave your baby unattended while she is in a baby bath seat for any reason as babies have slipped out of them and drowned. If the phone rings, take her with you, or don't answer the phone. If you are still using baby bath lotion and it is a drain on your resources, stop using it as it is unnecessary. Avoid bubble bath solutions as they do cause problems for some babies' skin—mild soap and water is fine.

# Swimming

Parents often wonder when it is okay to take their baby swimming. Full-term healthy babies can start going for a swim any time after four months. A few guidelines follow:

- Make sure your baby is well protected from the sun (see page 242).

- Cold water frightens babies, so test the water yourself first; it should be comfortable.

- Sadly many of our cities' beaches and natural pools are often polluted, so avoid them following heavy rain or if you have any concerns at all about the cleanliness of the water.

- Limit the time to thirty minutes or less to avoid sun damage or overchilling.

- Inflatable tubes and water wings are not safety devices and do not replace adult supervision. With babies, all water activity should be on a one-to-one basis with a responsible adult. Never leave your baby with an older child.

- Swimming lessons should be conducted by qualified instructors who are certified in infant Heart Lung Resuscitation. Learning or updating your own skills is also very worthwhile.

- Be aware that while water play and swimming lessons give babies and toddlers confidence and enjoyment of water, they do not give them skills that prevent them from drowning even if they learn to float or dog paddle from a young age. Constant vigilance is vital.

# A little more about routines

I am returning to this because I know it is something that occupies lots of mothers' thoughts.

A reminder—if you are a routine person, don't despair if things are a trifle chaotic still. Once your baby is sleeping all night or most of the night without waking you and eating three meals a day, your days will become much more predictable. This happens between six and nine months for many mothers and babies.

You might find your days are in some sort of pattern now without you realizing it. Feeding and sleeping times often vary from day to day. That's to be expected, but if you feel like it, write down your schedule over a weekly period and you will probably find a predictable pattern is emerging. Strict routines are difficult to maintain. Trying to keep to one means structuring your life exactly around the baby's schedule, which limits your movements and usually means putting up with an intolerable amount of baby crying for no constructive purpose when she wakes early for a feeding or suddenly varies her sleep patterns. Illness, holidays, moving, or visitors can also play havoc with strict routines.

Here's a flexible guide *if you are looking for one.*

**5AM TO 8AM:** Baby wakes. Breastfeed or bottle. Stays up for about an hour. Bath may be here. Put to sleep—may sleep half an hour to two hours.

**9AM TO 12 NOON:** Breastfeed or bottle plus food from a spoon if appropriate. Bath may be here. Up for about an hour. Put to sleep or go out. Baby may sleep half an hour to two hours.

**1PM TO 4PM:** Breastfeed or bottle plus food from a spoon if appropriate. Baby may only sleep for a short period. Awake the

**447**

remainder of the time. This may be a challenging part of the day. Go for a walk.

**5PM TO 7PM:** Bath may be here. Breastfeed or bottle and/or other food if appropriate. Avoid letting your baby have a late catnap if you can as this interferes with bedtime.

**7PM TO 8PM:** Bedtime. Try and keep bedtime regular and consistent regardless of what happens the rest of the day. Total sleeping in the day varies from one to four hours. A number of babies only ever catnap. It is usually very difficult to make babies who catnap in the day sleep more or longer. (See page 320 for more on daytime sleeping.)

If some sort of pattern is important to you, follow a similar plan each day and don't keep radically changing the times you feed, bathe and put your baby to sleep, but stay flexible because she might radically change what she does from time to time. The main aim is to have a nice time with your baby, so don't do anything that doesn't suit your lifestyle or nature.

# The crying baby

The majority of crying, unsettled babies are much happier by three to four months. Unfortunately a number of otherwise healthy babies stay the same, which is distressing for the baby and demoralizing and exhausting for the parents. Most of the time a definite cause is never found. Living with the baby the way she is until she gets more used to the world is usually the only option. Continued support from a sympathetic health professional you can talk to and uncritical friendship from other parents helps through the difficult times.

If your baby doesn't sleep much during the day, go out as much as possible and try to be with people who care about you as much as you can so that you are not on your own.

A few babies stay distressed for the first year, but the overwhelming majority are much happier and quite different little people by the time they are six months old.

## Sudden crying episodes or a sudden change in behavior

Babies, like all of us, don't stay the same day in and day out. Sudden erratic changes are quite common. Bad days, sometimes weeks, continue to happen. Most of the time it is difficult to know exactly why the baby is behaving differently. Sometimes it might be because of one of the following:

- **An impending infection:** This may be a head cold and involve an ear infection, a sore throat, or a tummy bug that causes diarrhea and vomiting. Ear infections are not common under six months, but it's always worth having your baby's ears checked if she suddenly starts crying a lot and sleeping less. If the unhappiness is accompanied by a high fever and no other symptoms the urine should be tested. A cross baby may signal a dose of the measles, rubella, or chicken pox—not common in the first year but can happen.

- **Reflux heartburn:** This can be a cause of distress for babies after the first three months when previously it wasn't a problem. Reflux heartburn is always difficult to diagnose and, as in the first three months, probably diagnosed far more frequently than it actually occurs. Sometimes medication for reflux heartburn helps babies who suddenly become unsettled when other causes can't be found.

- **Change in diet:** Starting new food does upset some babies, even when it's only bland old rice cereal, so it might be worth stopping the food for a week if the change in behavior coincided with starting new food. Go back to milk only and see what happens.

- **Hunger:** Some babies suddenly become irritated or upset if they are hungry. Check your baby's weight. More food might be needed.

- **No obvious cause:** When there's no obvious cause you will probably find your baby settles again in a short time without you doing anything. Sometimes it's boredom (try to go out more), overtiredness (try staying in more), or some disruption in the home (visitors, moving or building an extension).

# Growing teeth

Many people, of course, will tell you your baby is teething when she is unsettled. Teething is an explanation that supplies a reason at times when it's difficult to know if anything is wrong and replaces colic once babies are over three months old. As babies grow twenty teeth during their first three years, there are always going to be times when the emergence of a tooth coincides with developmental changes, normal but strange baby habits, diaper rash, and illness.

The emergence of teeth during the baby years is surrounded by intense fascination, even obsession, which has led to a lot of myths about growing teeth. The term *teething* implies a medical condition, and teething is often used as a diagnosis by health professionals for baby behavior or to account for a whole range of minor illnesses that are common for all babies and toddlers in the

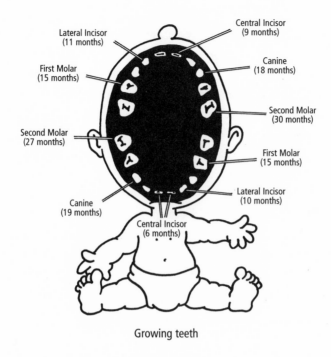

Lateral Incisor
(11 months)

Central Incisor
(9 months)

First Molar
(15 months)

Canine
(18 months)

Second Molar
(27 months)

Second Molar
(30 months)

Canine
(19 months)

First Molar
(15 months)

Central Incisor
(6 months)

Lateral Incisor
(10 months)

Growing teeth

first two years. I can understand the community at large doing this, but I think it's time health professionals and writers of baby information stopped perpetuating teething myths.

Let's look at the growing of teeth.

The first tooth appears between fourteen weeks and sixteen months of age. It announces its presence by simply appearing— sometimes a small lump comes first. No secret signs heralding the arrival of a tooth exist, so a health professional cannot peer at a toothless gum and announce that a tooth will or won't appear next week! After the first tooth arrives, others pop up at varying intervals. The central bottom teeth are usually the first to appear, and while most teeth do emerge in a set sequence, it is not at all unusual for some babies' teeth to appear out of sequence. For example, sometimes the top side teeth come before the top central teeth, which gives a gleeful Dracula appearance until the top teeth

**451**

appear. Occasionally the top central teeth arrive before the bottom central teeth.

The first twenty teeth arrive during the first two and a half years. They are lost and replaced by thirty-two permanent teeth between the ages of six and twenty years.

Growing and losing teeth is normal for all humans and happens on and off for twenty years or longer. Several hundred years ago, the emergence of teeth in babies was frequently given as a cause of death. At the turn of the twentieth century "dentition" appeared in dental textbooks as a cause of epilepsy. Science has made us realize how ridiculous these notions are, but to a lesser degree we are still being just as ridiculous. When seven- and eight-year-old children are growing teeth (some teeth at this age growing for the first time), scant attention is paid. Teething is never a suggested cause for illness or behavior changes in this age group because older children can communicate and have more predictable behavior, so it is easier to identify exactly what the problem is.

I understand that on an individual basis there are many times when an emerging tooth coincides with a bad day or night, a diaper rash, or an illness, but overall there are many more times when "teething" is blamed for a variety of conditions and the tooth never arrives.

After observing many babies for many years, I am convinced that the perception that growing teeth causes problems in babies is confused with normal development and illnesses caused by other things. While this may not be a popular approach, I think it is more useful for parents to understand the many more rational reasons relating to their baby's development, behavior, and health than simply pushing it all off as teething. Teething also gives rise to the overuse of medications and gels for gums that are sometimes used for months on end waiting for the appearance of the elusive tooth.

Growing teeth does not cause a fever, diarrhea, colds, coughs, ear infections, smelly urine, or diaper rash. Persisting with these myths may mean treatment is delayed or a serious illness is not diagnosed.

Funny baby habits such as pulling at ears and constantly putting fists in the mouth are developmental and part of a baby's growing intense curiosity with her own body. I observe or hear about babies doing these things all the time. Most of the time it is not in conjunction with growing a tooth; when it is, I suspect it is a coincidence.

Red cheeks appear a lot and are due to sun, wind, saliva, and cheeks constantly rubbing on clothes and sheets. Baby cheeks are sensitive, stick out a lot, and are easily affected by these things.

Dribbling is a constant feature of babyhood from three months to eighteen months or longer. Saliva first appears around three months in copious amounts, and until babies learn to swallow their saliva, the dribbling continues regardless of the growing of teeth.

Sleep problems are not caused by teeth emerging, and once your baby is over six months, if her sleep patterns are causing distress for the family, constantly blaming teeth does not solve the problem.

Does teething cause babies discomfort? Certainly not for three months before they are visible! Nor do they cause pain by moving around under the gum. An uncomfortable sensation just before the tooth emerges may worry some babies, and if you decide an emerging tooth is causing a problem for your baby, acetaminophen is the safest medication to use. If your baby is very distressed and behaving in an unusual way, never assume the problem is simply teething. Look further and if necessary seek a second opinion.

## Other teeth tidbits

A bluish swelling is often present on the gum when a tooth is emerging. This is normal and not painful for the baby.

Growing teeth is not a developmental milestone, and the stage at which they appear has nothing to do with a baby's future intelligence.

Babies do not need teeth for eating a variety of food, for example, bread, crusts, fruit, cheese, and so on.

## Care of teeth

Teeth cleaning can be started once a day once they arrive. Use a soft toothbrush without toothpaste. Cleaning an active baby's or toddler's teeth is easier said than done, and many parents take the line of least resistance and wait until their child is between two and three before getting into regular teeth cleaning. The main line of defense against tooth decay is the right diet.

Pacifiers dipped in sweet things and endless around-the-clock bottles cause black teeth. Apart from water, all other drinks in bottles are a potential problem when they are sucked for a large part of the night and day. This includes fruit juice. Think about limiting bottles to three every twenty-four hours sometime between six and nine months. Try giving fruit juice in a cup instead of a bottle. There are no nutritional reasons to continue bottles after the first year unless a baby has medical or developmental problems.

## Blood in vomit

Occasionally a breastfed baby damages the nipple after teeth arrive. The nipple bleeds, so she swallows a little blood, which may then appear when she regurgitates. This is usually only a temporary problem—I have included it because it can cause a moment of panic to suddenly see blood in a baby's vomit.

# Thumb-sucking

Thumb-sucking is a normal activity for babies—many do it while in the womb. Thumb-sucking has a few advantages over pacifiers. Skin is nicer to suck than silicone or rubber, the baby can make her own decisions about when to use her thumb, and thumb-sucking doesn't cause sleep problems because babies don't lose their thumbs in the night. Some parents worry about thumb-sucking because they don't like the look of older children sucking their thumbs, they see thumb-sucking as a sign of stress, thumb-sucking in older babies sometimes causes skin irritation on the thumb, and of course there's the worry about the orthodontic bill.

Thumb-sucking does not indicate stress and has no effect on a baby's progress if the thumb-sucking continues throughout early childhood. Nor does it affect teeth until the permanent teeth are through, at which time the ten percent of children who continue thumb-sucking push their teeth up and out and orthodontics may be needed. I can't help noticing how many children have ortho-dontic treatment anyway whether they were thumb-suckers or not, so it's not an issue I see as highly significant. If your baby is a thumb-sucker, there's not a lot you can do about it. Trying to get thumb-sucking babies to take pacifiers instead is generally stressful and unsuccessful.

Giving a pacifier from birth to avoid thumb-sucking because "you can throw the pacifier away" may introduce your baby to a habit you find as unattractive as thumb-sucking, which is just as hard to break, may interfere with breastfeeding, and causes sleep problems to boot. Lots of babies use neither.

If your baby develops a skin irritation on her thumb, try using a tiny dab of 0.5% gentian violet on the affected area three times a day for a couple of days. Don't knock over the bottle, it's messy.

Some babies are so enamored of their thumbs they suck them

while they eat. This is a harmless habit that may continue into the second year.

# More about poo

Poo is a fascinating topic for those involved with babies and promotes endless discussion at each age and stage.

**A reminder about breastfed babies:** Breastfed babies of this age who are having no other food or milk may go up to three weeks without doing a poo. It is normal for their farts to be smelly. When they go, it will be a very large, soft one—everywhere! You do not have to do anything to make your baby poo, but if you feel better seeing a poo a little more often, try a little diluted prune juice.

**Constipation:** Bottle-fed babies and breastfed babies who are eating other food will do firmer poo that may be a variety of colors. Breastfed babies often get a little constipated when they first start food from a spoon. It is normal for babies to grunt and groan and go red in the face when they do a poo. If your baby's poo gets hard and she gets very distressed beyond the normal grunting, here are a few suggestions:

- Stop banana for a while.

- Stop rice cereal for a while—cooked pureed pears. Some babies respond well to a piece of ripe orange (seeds removed).

- Increase fluids when possible (extra breastfeedings, water or fruit juice).

- Try diluted prune juice. If your baby doesn't drink from a bottle, put the prune juice in with her cereal or try prune juice and yogurt.

- A little added sugar in her cooked fruit or on her cereal helps.

- When your baby is trying to do a poo and it seems difficult, lie her on her back and bend her knees toward her stomach gently for two minutes. Repeat a few times if necessary.

You should not have to resort to medication and suppositories unless the constipation is extreme; the use of these things should be limited. Constant constipation that can't be helped by diet needs a trip to a pediatrician.

**Recycled food in the poo:** Once babies are eating a wide variety of food, quite a lot of food appears in the poo in its original state, so don't be amazed to see carrots, crusts or spinach. This is quite normal—no need to change the diet.

# Ammonia-smelling urine

Mothers are often amazed at how smelly their babies' urine becomes as their babies grow; this is especially noticeable the first diaper change after a long sleep. As long as your baby is otherwise well and the urine is pale and straw-colored (although a little darker and concentrated first thing in the morning), there is nothing to worry about. Naturally, if you are at all worried, see your pediatrician.

# Skin things

Baby rashes in the first three months tend to be a normal response to adjusting to wearing clothes and life outside the womb and generally need no treatment. After three months, rashes and skin things

457

are either caused by medical conditions or because of contact dermatitis caused by the baby's natural secretions coming in contact with her fine baby skin—for example, saliva, urine, sweat, or tears—and may need treatment. Let's look at the most common ones.

## Atopic dermatitis or eczema

Eczema or atopic dermatitis is a dry-skin condition that affects some babies in varying degrees. The exact cause is unknown but the condition is strongly affected by hereditary influences. Eczema is more likely to occur when there is a family history of allergic conditions such as asthma, hay fever, eczema, and reactions to food. However, about one in five toddlers who has eczema has no family history of allergies.

Eczema in babies is rarely caused by an allergy to one particular thing, so it is usually not possible to "cure" the eczema by removing a specific substance.

Most babies outgrow their eczema by the age of five.

Eczema can be mild, moderate, or severe. Treatment is aimed at keeping the skin supple, relieving inflammation and itching, treating infections if they occur, and avoiding things that make it worse.

### THE FOLLOWING ARE COMMON IRRITANTS FOR PEOPLE WITH ECZEMA

- Sand.

- Soap, detergent, bubble bath, perfumed and medicated products.

- Wool and acrylic materials found in clothes, carpets, furniture, and car seat covers.

- Chlorinated swimming pools.

- Dry air (air-conditioning and heating).

- Increased sweating.

Eczema appears as a dry rash that may become red and moist and itchy. Often the first place it is noticed is around the ankles; the other main areas are the neck, behind the ears, the upper chest and in the elbow and knee joints. The more severe the eczema, the more widespread and itchy it becomes.

Mild eczema often presents as a round, dry patch that is frequently confused with a ringworm infection. A ringworm infection has to come from somewhere, and if your baby has not been in contact with a person or animal who has ringworm, the round, dry patches are more likely to be mild eczema.

Using hypoallergenic moisturizers, the occasional use of a mild hydrocortisone cream, and avoiding common irritants usually keeps mild to moderate eczema under control.

It is advisable to consult a skin specialist in severe eczema cases as the treatment is more complicated. Stronger cortisone cream may be used, and sometimes the skin becomes infected and needs oral antibiotic treatment.

Research about the relationship between food and eczema is conflicting, and the success of dietary measures varies tremendously with individual babies. When these measures work, the eczema is improved but not cured. Exclusive breastfeeding for the first six months helps delay the onset and may reduce the severity.

Babies with eczema should avoid woollen and synthetic clothes, chlorinated swimming pools, and should be kept away from people with cold sores as they are particularly susceptible to the cold-sore virus. These babies are also more prone to the contact dermatitis lots of babies get from time to time that causes diaper rash, red cheeks, rashes around the mouth or eyes, cracking behind the ears, and red, moist areas under the chin and on the skin in between the joints.

## Red cheeks

Red cheeks are very common in babies and toddlers until dribbling stops and their cheeks stop constantly coming into contact with clothes and food. Baby cheeks are very soft and chubby and stick out, so they catch the wind and sun easily, becoming dry and chapped especially in winter. Red cheeks (or sometimes only one red cheek) are not related to ear infections, teething or diet, although once the cheeks are red and dry, acidic food such as oranges may irritate them further.

Red cheeks are often hard to clear up as the irritants can't be removed, but they don't seem to bother babies at all. Try to keep the skin around the area dry, apply moisturizing cream whenever you can (a tricky job—babies don't like it much), and last thing before bed apply a soothing barrier cream. A mild cortisone ointment helps if the redness is very severe. Ointment always works better than cream on moist areas.

## Rash around the mouth

Again, very common and caused by saliva, milk, and food being constantly on the baby's face. Using a pacifier contributes as the fluid gets trapped under the plastic shield which surrounds the nipple. Certain food may make the rash worse (orange juice, tomatoes, eggs, or yogurt). This is a frustrating rash as it's often difficult to clear completely until the baby stops dribbling.

Try to keep the area as dry as possible. Apply a soothing barrier cream at night. Experiment a little with food—don't get too uptight about food or you may find your baby's diet is very restricted and the rash is still there anyway.

If this rash gets really bad, check with your pediatrician or a skin specialist to make sure there is no underlying bacterial infection (from a snotty nose) that needs antibiotic treatment. If not, the only way to clear it is to apply a mild cortisone ointment (not cream) regularly. This takes some time to clear it, but it does eventually.

## Red under chin

Another maintenance problem until your baby holds her chin out from her neck and stops dribbling (around twelve months). Here's how to look after it:

Always dry well under your baby's chin. To do this, lie your baby down and firmly but gently pull her chin away from her neck. After you have dried the area, apply some zinc and starch powder (for example, Destin) with your fingers under the chin from ear to ear. The Destin absorbs moisture and separates the skin surfaces. The more often you can apply it, the better the results, so see if you can do it most diaper change times when you are at home. Your baby might not like it much at first, but she will get used to it quickly.

If the area becomes very inflamed, shiny, and weepy, see your family doctor. A combination of a mild cortisone and anti-fungal ointment will clear it. Afterward, it is better to continue to use the Destin powder. Diet makes no difference to this rash.

## Cracking behind ears

This may be related to eczema or simply to moisture behind the ears causing irritation to the skin. It tends to be an on again, off again little problem that can go on throughout the first year. It's another maintenance problem—here are a few tips:

Always dry well, but gently, behind your baby's ears every day and check to see what's happening.

Frequent applications of moisturizing cream help keep the

area supple, so apply a little every diaper change time while you are at home.

If the area behind the ears becomes very inflamed, cracked, and weepy, see your pediatrician. A combination of a mild cortisone and anti-fungal ointment will clear it. Continue with the moisturizing cream when it is clear. Diet makes no difference to cracking behind ears.

## Heat rash

Heat rash continues to return from time to time, often until the age of three. Heat rash in older babies looks like little reddish blue separate dots and appears mainly at the back of the neck, on the tummy and the top of the chest, and often arrives with hot weather. It mostly doesn't bother babies but is sometimes itchy, especially around the back of the neck. Heat rash is not related to diet.

## Mosquito bites

Mosquito bites look like flat red, tiny spot, almost like dots from a red felt-tip pen. Mosquito bites usually disappear without incident.

## Pigeon lice bites

Pigeon lice bites are often confused with chicken pox as they appear as small, raised pink spots that form a blister and a crust. If your baby gets a few lesions like this when she is otherwise well and has not been in contact with chicken pox, pigeons are likely to be the culprit.

## Impetigo

Impetigo happens when a lesion on the skin becomes infected, usually because the baby scratches it. The lesion slowly enlarges and spreads. It may be crusty, pus may be present, and other lesions may start to appear. See your pediatrician—impetigo needs antibiotics.

# Baby acne

Occasionally a baby develops inflamed pimples and blackheads on her face that look very similar to a mild form of teenage acne. It is not related to the hormone rash most babies get in the first three months, which is often misnamed "baby acne." It is an uncommon condition called infantile acne and tends to happen to babies who come from families where there is a strong history of acne in the teenage years, although this is not always the case. There is no wildly successful treatment; it doesn't bother the baby and dissappears sometime in the first two years, maybe to return in the adolescent years. Baby acne is not affected by diet.

# A yellow baby

If your baby is otherwise well but turning yellow before your eyes, it's almost certainly because of her consumption of foods containing beta carotene, such as pumpkin, carrots, spinach, tomatoes, peaches, apricots, and prunes. Quite a few babies eat a lot of pumpkin and carrot. Beta carotene is a yellow pigment that is converted by the body into vitamin A. The yellow skin is harmless; the beta carotene does not have this effect on the skin after age three. There is no need to reduce the offending food items as they are all very good for your baby; however, regular large amounts of carrot juice pose a slight risk of a buildup of vitamin A. This can pose a health risk, so avoid overdosing your baby on carrot juice.

# Small lump under nipple

It is quite common to be able to feel a lump under the nipple in one of your baby's breasts. This has nothing to do with the swollen breasts that babies under three months develop due to hormones (red, swollen breasts, page 212). Small lumps in older babies are normal breast tissue and nothing to worry about, but check with your doctor if you are unsure.

## FOR MORE INFORMATION

# chapter twenty

# Growth
# and
# Development

## *Growth*

Babies roughly gain 5 to 6 oz (140 to 170 grams) a week in the second six months and grow about ¾ inch (2.5 cm) in three months. Before you start to worry, here are a few statistics that so you can see the wide normal range.

### AT SIX MONTHS

|  | Small/Normal | Large/Normal |
|---|---|---|
| **Boys** | Weight 13 lb 2 oz (6.2kg) | 10kg (22lb) |
|  | Length 63cm (26 inches) | 73cm (29 inches) |
|  | Head circ. 41.5 cm (16 inches) | 46cm (18 inches) |
| **Girls** | Weight 5.8kg (13lb) | 9.2kg (20lb) |
|  | Length 61cm (24 inches) | 70cm (27 inches) |
|  | Head circ. 40cm (15 inches) | 45cm (17 inches) |

# Development

## Gross motor skills

Between three and six months, your baby starts a lot of new movements, some at four months, some at five months. By six months you will notice that:

- When she lies on her back, she raises her head to look at her feet.

- She lifts her legs to play with her feet.

- When she is on her tummy, she takes her weight well on her forearms.

- She has great head control. When you pull her from lying to sitting, she braces her shoulders and pulls herself toward you to sit.

- She might be able to sit on her own. Some babies can sit on their own by six months; for most sitting unsupported happens between six and nine months. It's fine to let babies sit, well supported so that they don't fall and hurt themselves, before they can manage to sit on their own—doing this doesn't damage their backs.

- She is probably rolling. By six months, a lot of babies roll from front to back and/or from back to front, but the age at which babies intentionally roll is extremely variable. Some do it once or twice and don't do it again for a long time; others still haven't rolled by nine months. Safety is an important consideration in relation to rolling. Never assume your baby can't roll because the very time you leave her unattended on a bed or change table could be the first time she does it—onto the floor!

- She likes to be held standing so that she can take her weight and bounce up and down. Most babies do this by six months;

however, some still have collapsible legs. If your baby doesn't weight bear, give her some practice when you can, as well as plenty of floor play and no walker.

## Vision and fine motor

- Babies of this age are delightful, vitally interested in everything and everyone around them. Eyes should now move together. If they look uneven or crooked, have them checked.

- By now your baby will be reaching out and grabbing everything in sight. She passes toys from one hand to another, usually via her mouth, for a chew and a suck. Exploring things with her mouth and tongue is her way of getting additional information about all the things she sees and touches. At times she will get quite frantic about this process of discovery. It is important that your baby is able to suck, bite, and mouth safe objects without too many inhibitions placed upon her.

- When an object is dropped to the floor, your baby will look for it purposefully rather than continuing to stare at the spot from where it disappeared.

## Hearing and speech

### HEARING
By six months, babies turn consistently to a voice or a noise as long as they are not too distracted. This might be a voice from across the room or a quiet noise from something like a rattle behind each ear.

### SPEECH
Speech is in the form of tuneful, sing-song vowel sounds. Some babies of this age start single or double syllables (ga-ga, da-da, ma-

ma), although most don't start these sounds until a little later. A number of babies go through a quiet stage between five and seven months where they don't make as many talking noises as they did when they were younger. Don't worry—it all starts up again! Laughing, chuckling, squealing, and screaming are all part of their speech now.

## Social and play

Your baby will now start to bang things together. When you offer her a rattle, she will reach for it immediately and shake it deliberately. She will laugh at things and people and especially enjoy games with a surprise element.

# Toys

This is the age for movement, kicking, reaching and grasping, and chewing. A mesh bag full of cellophane makes interesting noises and attracts attention.

Washable safe rattles and shakers are popular. An unbreakable mirror mounted about seven inches (18 cm) away from your baby's face on a wall where she can look at herself is good entertainment value.

Mobiles still attract attention. By six months,, your baby will be reaching and grabbing, so make sure they are well out of reach.

Activity centers manufactured by various companies are a great favorite, especially between six and nine months. Balls are always fun.

Specially designed playmats for babies to lie on give them things to grab and chew and make noises with while they are on the floor.

# Books

Babies need books, and you can start to introduce them from any age.

Chewable plastic books are one idea. As well, read to your baby using simple, rhythmical language from books with realistic pictures. Do it for a short time and don't worry if she doesn't seem to be listening. Establishing a storytime just before sleep can be part of your baby's life as soon as you like.

# Developmental summary: 6 months

## Gross motor

- on back—lifts head to look at feet;

- lifts leg and grabs foot;

- pulled to sit—braces shoulders, no back curve;

- can roll, front to back (very variable).

## Vision and fine movements

- moves head and eyes eagerly;

- a squint is abnormal;

- uses whole hand to grasp objects and passes them from one hand to another;

- watches falling toys.

## Hearing and speech

- turns immediately to parents' voices;

- turns to minimal sound;

- makes tuneful talking noises and may use single or double syllables;

- laughs, chuckles, squeals, and screams.

## Social and play

- puts everything into mouth;

- reaches out and grabs things;

- may be wary of strange faces and places.

# Growing and developing—when to worry

It is natural for you to watch your baby closely and to be concerned if she doesn't seem to be growing or is late to reach a milestone. Constant comparisons with other babies and listening to other parents' experiences may increase the worry that something is wrong. Here are some guidelines for action if you are not sure that your baby is growing and developing normally.

## Growth

Sometimes parents are concerned or are made to feel concerned because their baby's weight is less than would be expected for her age and height. Family and friends make comments or it might be noted by a health professional.

If you are concerned about your baby's weight, have her weight, length, and head circumference taken by someone reliable, then plotted on a percentile chart. None of these measurements mean as much taken on their own as they do taken together and plotted on a growth chart so that her overall pattern of growth can be looked at. Her weight should be around the same percentile as her height, but there are always a number of babies who weigh one or two percentiles below their height or one or two above. When they are bright, active, and feeding well, there is unlikely to be a problem.

Appearances can be quite deceptive and comments made by onlookers ("what a small baby!") are generally quite wrong, so if you're worried, nine times out of ten this simple procedure is all that's needed to put your mind at rest.

If low weight is a pattern and your baby's weight percentile is a long way below her height percentile, here are the most common reasons, which do vary with ages and stages of development:

## DIET

Persistent low gains in healthy babies in the first three months are often related to breastfeeding problems. Once these are overcome, the weight should increase. Care must be taken before abandoning breastfeeding as some babies continue to gain only small amounts on formula.

Incorrect mixing of formula is occasionally a cause of low weight gains in the early months.

If your baby's weight stays the same over several weeks or drops and she is over four months old, giving some food from a spoon as well as milk is a good idea.

Older babies who are given very restricted diets may not gain weight for long periods. An abundant supply of breastmilk still supplies most dietary needs beyond six months of age, but when the supply is noticeably diminished, it is very important to include other fats in the diet such as milk, cheese, and yogurt. Babies do not thrive well on small amounts of breastmilk and fruit and vegetables only. If for some reason dairy products are eliminated, a fortified soy formula is the best choice of extra milk as it has added fat.

It is quite common for babies to start refusing food sometime between nine and twelve months, which is a constant source of worry for lots of parents. It is also a time when the weight of many babies, especially breastfed babies, levels out. As this is normal for most babies, try not to worry. Babies cannot be forced to eat, so the best thing you can do is to make sure you offer your baby an adequate diet that includes a range of foods. Health problems in healthy "non-eating" older babies only happen when they are consistently offered the wrong food or put on crazy fad diets.

## ILLNESS

Continuing stationary or low weight gains may be caused by illness. During the first year, medical problems such as a urinary tract infection, pyloric stenosis (a narrowing of the passage between the stomach and the small intestine), a heart problem, or other rare illnesses may be diagnosed and treated. Acute illnesses such as viral diarrhea, upper respiratory tract infections, ear infections, or tonsillitis can all affect weight gains. Medical problems are nearly always accompanied by signs other than low weight such as strange-smelling poo, apathy, fever, delayed development, irritability, or constant unhappiness.

Most underweight babies and toddlers have nothing at all wrong with them and no one knows precisely why they are underweight. The difficulty always is deciding when the reasons for being underweight need investigating. The approach of health professionals to underweight babies and toddlers varies tremendously, so parents find they often receive conflicting advice. Techniques used to diagnose possible medical causes are invasive, often expensive, and should not be done as a matter of course on all underweight babies.

When your baby is bright and active, lives in a loving home, is offered an adequate diet, does normal poo, and continues gaining some weight every so often, there's unlikely to be anything wrong. Chasing diagnosis after diagnosis is a nerve-racking exercise that rarely changes anything.

If your baby has a sudden weight loss and shows obvious signs of illness, or if you are concerned about her milestones, see your practitioner, nurse, or doctor. Babies born small for dates will catch up, but some won't until their second year. Premature babies of very low birth weight tend to stay small for the first year or two but follow a steady growth pattern of their own.

Height problems, either too short or too long, are not common but do occur. Height anomalies tend to emerge over a period of time and are more likely to be noticed in the second year. When it appears height is outside the normal range, special attention is needed from specialists in the field. As with weight, the first thing to do is to work out whether a height problem exists. Your nurse practitioner or pediatrician can help with this.

## Development

Remember, milestones are a guide. Listening to other proud parents boasting about their baby's achievements can be hazardous to your peace of mind. Variations in skills and personality differences between babies just as diverse as they are between adults.

Unless there is a generalized delay in a few areas over several months, it doesn't matter if your baby seems slow to do some things compared to other babies. Gross motor skills such as walking, sitting, crawling, and rolling have the widest variations and are highly visible. Parents are very aware when their baby sits like a blob at twelve months while their friend's baby of the same age is ready to start little athletics.

Delay in gross and fine motor skills can be helped by physiotherapists and occupational therapists if you and your health care professional think it's appropriate. Communication skills are very important, so if you ever think your baby can't hear or see, seek help immediately. Here is a general guide about when to go for assessment. Start out with your nurse practitioner or pediatrician who can tell you where to go next if it's necessary.

### SEEK HELP IF

- your baby consistently doesn't respond to sounds;

- your baby doesn't seem to see things; white or cloudy eyes

- she isn't interested in what's going on around her;

- she can't hold her head up by three to four months;

- she squints a lot after three months; eyes not focusing

- persistent and excessive crying continuing after three to four months;

- there's no babbling by six months;

- she doesn't use or move **both** arms and/or legs;

- your baby is not sitting well by ten months;

- she doesn't want to weight bear by twelve months.

This is only a very general guide. Always get professional help if you are unsure. You know your baby better than anyone and have a good feel for what's happening. Too many opinions will drive you mad, but a couple of assessments by different people can give you a better idea of whether a problem exists or not, the degree of the problem, and the best course of action.

## FOR MORE INFORMATION

# chapter twenty-one

# Safety

The following chart emphasizes particular hazards associated with this developmental stage, but don't forget most safety hazards remain at any age and stage.

*Don't forget your baby's second round of immunization is due at 4 months.*

| Age | Developmental stage | Safety hazard | Precautions |
|---|---|---|---|
| **3–4 months** | • rolls over<br>• starts to mouth objects | • falls off heights<br>• inhalation of small, loose pieces of toys or other small objects<br>• scalds by baby grasping and spilling hot drinks while being nursed | • eyes off, hands on is the golden rule<br>• check all toys for small removable parts or household objects or equipment that can be sucked<br>• keep all hot liquids out of baby's reach<br>• think about the way you drink tea and coffee, especially when friends visit |

| Age | Developmental stage | Safety hazard | Precautions |
|---|---|---|---|
| **4–5 months** | •may feed self cookie, breadstick, or rusk | •suffocation by inhalation of food •choking, inhalation hazards as baby has increasing access to small, hard objects | •always supervise with food or bottle •constant supervision and monitoring of items left around the home |
| **5–6 months** | •increased mobility by crawling and rolling | •falls—from high chair, carriage, stroller, change table •burns—exposed fires, heating vents, grasping hot objects, sunburn | •safety harness and constant supervision in high chairs, carriages and so on •use fire guards, limit exposure to the sun, and cover up |
| **6–7 months** | •picks up small items •may sit alone •may pull to stand | •drowning—left alone in the tub •falls—from sitting or standing position | •never leave alone in the tub or in the company of older children •close supervision, especially if a baby walker is being used |

## FOR MORE INFORMATION
Chapter 12: Safety *(immunization, page 268)*

# chapter **twenty - two**

# For Parents

## Contraception

Here's a reminder: Change from the minipill to an IUD or the combined pill if you wean or dramatically decrease your breastfeeding.

## Night waking between four and six months

It is normal and common for babies to wake at night after three months. Some babies have never slept more than two to three hours at a time; others may have slept most of the night from eight weeks only to start waking frequently again around four to five months.

The amount of distress this causes parents usually depends on the number of times it happens, how quickly the baby goes back to sleep after a feeding, and whether both parents are working. Parents' expectations can cause added tension, especially when all their friends' babies are sleeping through. It is also hard to bear if the baby slept well at night for several months and then started waking again.

## What can you do?

Unfortunately, contrary to popular opinion, there is no safe, easy way to "make" (an unfortunate word used a lot in this context) your baby sleep all night.

Here is some information:

- Illness sometimes causes a return to night waking. Wait for a few days and see if something eventuates or ask your pediatrician to check her out, including her ears.

- **"Teething," "hunger"** and **"gas"** are explanations you will doubtless be given by most friends, relatives, colleagues, and health professionals.

  **Is it teeth?** Unfortunately, it's rarely that simple, but if a tooth appears and then she goes back to sleeping—hallelujah! I do not find the growing of teeth relates much to wakeful nighttime babies.

  **Is it hunger?** Starting solids is usually the next suggestion. Occasionally this does the trick, and if so—great! If your baby rejects the food completely, then forget about it; chances are it would not solve the night sleep problem anyway. Most of the time food seems to play a very insignificant role in keeping babies sleeping at night.

  **Is it gas?** When mothers are up a lot at night with babies, in their fog of weariness they often become very aware of their babies' farting and burping habits and tend to see this as the problem. However, babies who sleep all night burp and fart too—it's just that because everyone else is also asleep it passes by (or out) unnoticed. Troublesome gas is not likely to be a reason for nighttime waking unless your baby has a defined medical problem, which would give her gut pain, or is having a reaction to some new food.

- Is your baby too big now for wrapping and being in a bassinet? Sometimes moving the baby into a crib and stopping the wrapping helps. Sometimes it makes things worse; however, give it a try. Put her in the crib on her back with a sheet and blanket over her tucked in tightly around the crib mattress, leaving her arms free.

- If your baby has been managing without night feedings, then suddenly starts waking again, generally reintroducing a night feeding is the best thing to do. You can try replacing the night feedings with a pacifier or by rocking and patting; however, most of the time you will find you are up more and get less sleep than if you feed her. If you are only getting up once or twice at night and your baby is going straight back to sleep, I think it's better to carry on feeding and review the situation when she is over six months old.

- A lot of babies sleep from around seven at night until one or two in the morning, wake for a feeding then wake hourly until the daylight hours. If your baby is doing this, apart from the strategies already suggested, the only other possibilities are take her to bed, let her cry by following the teaching-to-sleep guidelines on page 543, or live with it and hope it gets better. Waking the baby at 10 to 11 pm and giving her a feeding is often suggested as a way of "making" her sleep through the night. By all means try it, but I find this strategy does not have a high success rate and often makes things worse.

- The pacifier. If you find you are getting up frequently to put the pacifier in, it's worth thinking seriously about getting rid of it. When the pacifier goes, there is the dilemma of what to do when the baby wakes. Unless you can quiet her quickly with a feeding or a pat, the only other alternative is to let her cry.

Leaving babies to cry at night to teach them to sleep is dealt with in detail in the next section, as six months is the earliest most babies and parents can handle this approach. However, if you are desperate and if your baby is well, please refer to page 543 for the best way to do teaching-to-sleep. If you have decided to take this approach, it is better to follow these guidelines than just lie in bed listening to your baby cry.

## TO SUMMARIZE

Generally babies wake at night as part of normal sleep patterns and do not know how to go back to sleep. Night waking is unlikely to be related to easily explainable things like teeth, hunger, and gas. Nor is it usually anything to do with what the parents have or haven't done.

If the night waking is not bothering you unduly, do nothing.

Once hunger and illness have been ruled out, the options are to feed the baby and live with it or let the baby cry. Replacing feedings with pacifiers, rocking, wrapping, patting, and so on usually doesn't work. Letting babies cry at any time is difficult and a controversial approach; however, there are times when parents feel there are no alternatives and wish to try.

If you want to do so before your baby is six months old, please follow the guidelines for teaching-to-sleep closely. If there has not been a change for the better in your baby's night sleep patterns within three nights, stop and wait until she is older. Stop before if you find it too distressing.

# Traveling with your baby

Traveling with a baby is different from traveling on your own. It is rewarding, exciting, can be better than staying at home, but it is hard work. Parents' tolerance, expectations, and anxiety levels when traveling with babies and toddlers differ greatly from one family to another. Lots of families travel vast distances regularly and thrive on it; other parents find long trips with babies too much to bear and decide to only take unavoidable trips until their babies are older. Don't feel like a wimp if you're in the latter category or feel pressured into taking unnecessary trips when you'd sooner stay home.

The first trip with your baby may seem quite daunting, but the more trips you take, the better you become at handling the tricky parts and enjoying yourself at the same time.

To ensure as smooth a trip as possible, planning is essential. Planning includes mental preparation so that you don't have too many unrealistic ideas of what's ahead. You will find you are not able to enjoy the same sort of things you did when you traveled before your baby arrived. Leisurely meals, shopping expeditions, fishing trips, extensive sightseeing, late nights, and long drives without stopping to get quickly from one place to another tend not to be compatible with babies.

Be mentally prepared for the unexpected so that you don't feel too let-down when things go wrong. Illness, crying attacks, and diarrhea are all possible baby events when you're on the road.

Many babies and toddlers find travel disrupting, which doesn't hurt them in any way, but you might find their eating, sleeping, and behavior patterns change temporarily.

You may wonder about using a sedative for your baby, especially if you are traveling overseas. Sedating babies under six months is not recommended and rarely needed anyway; most babies in this age group travel well and are fairly immobile. Some parents traveling with older babies and toddlers take a mild sedative in case of difficult times but find they usually don't use it.

Sedating older babies for a long car trip may be needed occasionally in an emergency, but sedatives should never be given as a matter of course for car trips and shouldn't be used on a daily basis for the duration of a long journey.

Try to avoid immunizing your baby just before traveling.

Whether traveling by car, train, or plane, the all-purpose baby bag is essential. In it you need:

- disposable or cloth diapers depending on the length of the trip;

- disposable wipes or damp washcloths in a plastic bag;

- cleaning lotion;

- diaper cream;

- cotton balls;

- extra pacifiers (if you are using pacifiers);

- several changes of clothing;

- soft gauze weave diapers

- safety pins, scissors, masking tape, flashlight, Band-Aids;

- tissues;

- plastic bag for dirty clothes, nappies;

- baby acetaminophen, sunblock;

- oral rehydration powder;

- a blanket that can be used as a changing sheet or to put on the floor so that baby can lie on something familiar and clean.

## Plane trips

Short trips within the United States don't cause too many difficulties; however, strollers are generally not allowed on board
domestic airlines, posing difficulties when there are stopovers if
you are hanging around an airport with an active baby for any
length of time. Some airlines have strollers available to borrow
while you wait; it's always worth asking. Domestic flights also do
not have a supply of disposable diapers on hand, so make sure
you have some with you.

Long overseas flights with babies are becoming more and more
common for families. The first overseas flight is often viewed with
trepidation by parents but usually their worst fears are never
realised and it all goes quite smoothly.

Here are a few tips:

- Book well in advance. Mid-week flights are more likely to have
spare seats.

- Most airlines will allow travelers to hold babies under 24 months
old on their laps, rather than purchasing an additional seat. You
may have to provide documentation to prove your toddler's age.
Notify the airline when you make your booking if you intend to
travel with a baby on your lap.

- Many airlines offer a 50 percent discount for babies under 24
months for travelers who want their baby to have her own space
so they can use a child safety seat.

- Travelers who opt to hold their baby may use an empty seat if
one is available and they've brought their safety seat along.

For international flights:

- A bassinet may be requested in advance on international flights but it is not confirmed. "Requested" is not a firm booking. The age/weight for babies using bassinets is different for every airline so make sure you check.

- Check about baby food availability as it varies with individual airlines. Best to take your own.

- Ask if the airline has change tables in the economy bathrooms

- Ask if you have to remove your baby from the bassinet when the seatbelt sign comes on during the flight (some companies insist on this—others don't).

- Are you able to take a lightweight umbrella stroller on board? If not, are they available to borrow during stopovers?

- If you are formula feeding, you can:
  Take some icy cold bottles of prepared formula in an insulated pack to be warmed up as needed.
  Take cleaned, disinfected bottles, formula powder, and your own water (in a thermos or bottled still water—not mineral water) and make up feedings as you go.

- Make sure you have plenty of diapers and supplies of formula. Most airlines carry these items, but they may not be suitable for your baby and supplies do run out.

- Ask if your baby bag will be charged as excess baggage.

- Giving your baby something to suck as the plane takes off and lands helps equalize the pressure in her ears and stops her becoming alarmed. Breast, bottle, pacifier, or your finger (for young babies) all fill the bill.

- When you reach your destination you might find your baby

comes down with a minor illness (cough, cold, or diarrhea) which unfortunately often seems to happen when babies leave their usual environment.

- Reorganizing sleep patterns might be tricky for a short time. Get your baby back into her normal sleeping patterns as soon as you can by keeping her up when she would normally be up during the day rather than letting her sleep for long periods. Using a sedative for older babies and toddlers for a night or two can be useful to help them back into regular sleep patterns. Talk to your family doctor or pediatrician before you leave.

## Car trips

Some babies travel well in their restraint or car seat for long stretches. Others only manage two-hourly stints without becoming irritable. Unfortunately a small number of babies go into full roar after departure and continue until the car stops and they are taken out. It's very hard to know why some babies do this—one of my children carried on in this fashion for a year or so, which meant our car travel was quite limited until she changed.

Have your baby dry, comfortably dressed, well fed, and, if possible, ready for a sleep before leaving. Make sure she is protected from the sun.

Long car trips are tiring for everyone. Plan to stop every two hours for a break. What do you do if your baby has a sudden screaming attack and you can't pull over?

- Sing a song, play a tape, or turn up the radio.

- If someone is available, rub your baby's head, stroke her arm, and soothe her as much as possible.

**486**

- Give a young baby your finger to suck. Try to distract an older baby with a toy, finger food, or a drink.

- Obviously, stop as soon as you can.

It's always worth asking well-traveled friends for tips. Extensive traveling with your baby is best avoided until early difficulties with feeding, crying, sleeping, and so on are sorted out, although if it's unavoidable, it won't hurt your baby—it just makes things a bit harder for you.

## FOR MORE INFORMATION

# part three

# 6 TO 9
# MONTHS

# Equipment

## *Clothes*

You are probably noticing now that your baby moves all over her crib at night, rarely staying under the covers, which, if it's winter, is a bit of a worry. As soon as this starts to happen, it's a good idea to buy one or two sleepers (sleeping bags with legs). A sleeper is worn over pajamas. It zips up the front and keeps your baby warm without restricting her movements.

## *A highchair*

The major piece of equipment to consider in this age group is a highchair. Types and prices vary tremendously, with new styles constantly available.

Here are some guidelines about what to look for:

### Safety

Check stability. Highchairs with a narrow base may be less sturdy—this particularly applies to older, secondhand highchairs.

Highchairs come with a waist and crotch harness, but it is advisable to purchase a shoulder harness to use as well, so there should be points on the highchair for you to anchor it.

A portable chair that hooks onto a table is a useful accessory for holidays and dining out or to use attached to the family table at home. Portable chairs don't fit all tables, so check when you buy. Babies can't manage portable chairs until they can sit well without support for a reasonable period of time. A harness should always be used and constant supervision is essential while the baby is in the chair because she has access to everything within her reach on the table, so the risk of scalds and inhaling small objects is increased.

The highchair should be made of non-toxic material. The simpler the design, the easier to clean and the less likelihood of small fingers becoming caught. Highchairs that convert to lowchairs should do so smoothly without the risk of pinching fingers or jamming midway.

## Practicalities

- The highchair should be light and easy to move.

- Think about the space available—you might need a fold-up model to stack away when not in use.

- The style of highchair that converts to an armchair, swing, potty, and table won't be particularly useful unless it converts quickly and you use all its features.

## A few tips when using a highchair

- Remember, it's quite normal for many babies to be just beginning to sit on their own around nine months. Until they can sit well independently for any length of time, they need support while in a highchair and should only be left sitting supported for a limited time, as they do get tired and upset when they start to slide forward or to one side.

- Always make sure your baby is secure and never leave her alone with food.

- Take her out when she is obviously restless or upset.

# chapter twenty-four

# Feeding
# Your Baby

*Alas! What various tastes in food,*
*Divide the human brotherhood.*

Hilaire Belloc, "On Food," *Cautionary Verses*

## More about food—the second six months

Between six and nine months, babies can be introduced to a wide range of food. Here is a plan for you to use as a guide if you need one. Remember, it is only a guide and must be adapted to your baby and your lifestyle. The times given are approximate:

Here is some information to help you with the diet plan:

- Babies who like eating will be following this plan by nine months. Don't rush things unnecessarily—on the other hand, there's no need to delay introducing a wide variety of food if your baby is enjoying it.

- If allergy is a consideration for you, follow recommendations from your pediatrician. If you are thinking of restricting your baby's

| 6am | Breastfeed or bottle (6 oz to 8 oz) | | | | | |
|---|---|---|---|---|---|---|

| 8am | Breakfast suggestions | | | | | |
|---|---|---|---|---|---|---|
| farina | and/or | stewed | or | full-fat | or | egg yolk |
| oatmeal | | fruit | | yogurt | | (whole egg |
| baby cereal | | | | | | after nine |
| (add made-up | | | | | | months) |
| formula or | | | | | | |
| full-fat milk) | *as well offer bread or toast* | | | | | |
| | *drink: water or juice in a cup or bottle* | | | | | |

| 10–11am | morning snack (optional) |
|---|---|
| choice of finger food | |
| bread | |
| cheese | |
| crackers | *drink: water or juice in a cup or bottle* |

| 12:30pm | Lunch suggestions | | | | |
|---|---|---|---|---|---|
| any veggies | add | ground beef | add | grated cheese |
| | | or chicken | | (stirred in) or |
| | | or fish | | tomato puree |
| | | | | or grated hard- |
| (ground up in an electric blender) | | | | boiled egg yolk |
| | *drink: breastfeed or bottle (6 oz to 8 oz)* | | | |

| 2–4pm | afternoon snack (optional) |
|---|---|
| Same as 10–11am | |

| 5–6pm | Evening meal suggestions |
|---|---|

*(Some time between nine and twelve months, cheese on toast, sandwiches, fishsticks, spaghetti, or baked beans may also be offered.)*

| avocado | or | mashed | or | soup | or | jars of | or | egg |
|---|---|---|---|---|---|---|---|---|
| & cottage | | banana & | | | | commercial | | (boiled or |
| cheese | | yogurt | | | | baby food | | scrambled) |
| mashed | | or tofu | | | | or fresh | | or family |
| | | & fruit | | | | yogurt | | food ground |
| | | | | | | & fruit | | up (e.g.: |
| | | | | | | | | pasta, rice, |
| | | | | | | | | casseroles, |
| | | | | | | | | spaghetti |
| | | | | | | | | meat sauce) |

*drink: breastfeed or bottle (6 oz to 8 oz)*

**495**

diet in any major way, please seek advice from a knowledgeable health professional so that your baby's diet is not nutritionally unsound.

- Offer the food before milk from now on if you have been doing the reverse.

- As well as changing from four-hourly feedings to three meals a day, this plan suggests cutting down the breast or bottle feedings to three every twenty-four hours. This will suit lots of mothers and babies but obviously not all.

## Breastfeeding

If you wish to breastfeed more often, continue in the way that suits you and your baby. Or if you decide to only breastfeed three times a day, the feedings do not necessarily have to be given according to the plan—again do what suits you both best.

## Bottle feeding

Three bottles of milk a day are all your baby needs once she is eating well. One or two drinks of juice a day are sufficient—try water at other times when your baby is thirsty. Leave your baby on the formula she is already having—changing to follow-up formula is unnecessary.

## Night feeding

Night feeding, whether breast or bottle, is related to sleep, not food, once babies are over six months.

If you wish to change your baby's nighttime feeding patterns please refer to Sleeping and Waking Six Months and Beyond on page 539. If you are happy with what's happening, carry on.

- If your baby is a 5 am waker, it is easier to give her the breast or bottle at that time than launch into breakfast at the crack of dawn.

**496**

Often, after a milk feeding, babies go back to sleep for a while. When your baby has breakfast later after an early feeding, there's no need to repeat the bottle or the breast—a little juice or water from a bottle or a cup with her breakfast is all that's needed.

- If your baby is a 7 to 8 am waker, give her breakfast as soon as she wakes up followed by breastfeeding, her bottle, or milk from a cup.

- Some breastfed babies whose mothers have an abundant milk supply do not want breakfast after their morning breastfeeding. The breastmilk supplies all they need, so don't worry if your baby does this—she will probably start eating breakfast sometime around twelve months.

- Think of your baby now as having family food rather than a special diet. Take a critical look at the family diet; if you have a healthy diet, your baby's diet will be healthy too.

## Food to avoid

Avoid junk food and unnecessary sugar (sometimes a little sugar on the morning cereal helps with constipation). On the other hand, things like basil, garlic, and tomato puree that you use in your food are fine.

Honey is a form of sugar and therefore can be a problem if given too often. It has been known to cause botulism (poisoning by toxins produced by a harmful bacteria) in babies under twelve months, so if you occasionally use honey on bread, wait until your baby is over a year old.

Other food to avoid includes whole apple, whole carrot, raw celery, corn chips, and popcorn because of the risk of choking. It is now recommended that these foods not be given until children are over four years.

Strawberries are known to cause an extreme reaction in some

babies; wait until she is a year old. Peanut products are also responsible for quite severe reactions in some babies, so wait until the second year before starting peanut butter.

## A word about fats

Fat is an essential part of babies' and toddlers' diets. They need fat as a concentrated source of energy and for brain development, so don't limit the fats in your baby's diet. Forty to fifty percent of a baby's energy intake should come from fat, decreasing to about thirty percent at age five to twenty-five percent after puberty. Always use full-fat dairy products and include a range of dairy products in the food you offer your baby or toddler. If for some reason you are eliminating dairy foods from your baby's diet and you are not breastfeeding, use one of the soy infant formulas as they have added fat.

## Cholesterol

Cholesterol is a fat used by the body to make some hormones and nerve and brain cells. Breastmilk has a lot of cholesterol, and it is believed, although not proven, that as breastfed babies do not need to make their own cholesterol, their bodies set up an important feedback mechanism that helps prevent overproduction later in life. We do not need to eat cholesterol as the body makes its own, and as we are all aware, an oversupply in adult life, usually caused by a diet high in saturated fats, can lead to problems. However, limiting food such as eggs, meat, and dairy products in babies' or toddlers' diets may be harmful as they contain valuable nutrients for proper growth and development, and limiting these foods in early childhood does not prevent high cholesterol in adult life. All soy infant formula has added fat. It *is* advisable to reduce the intake of saturated fat content by limiting things like butter, cream, margarine, fried food, and fatty meats at any age.

# Food safety

Food safety precautions are very important as soon as your baby starts eating family food. Small, hard items such as peanuts, and seeds are dangerous for babies. This means taking care with seeds in fruit and seeds bread. Offer plain bread and keep all nuts out of your baby's reach. Once your baby starts eating food herself, make sure she is always supervised and not allowed to crawl or walk with food.

## GAGGING AND CHOKING

Most parents worry about the way their baby gags at times and the possibility of her choking, and often confuse gagging with choking. It's a normal worry, but unfortunately it can lead to a baby's diet being too restricted and the delaying of finger foods at the ideal time to start them (between six and nine months).

## WHAT'S THE DIFFERENCE?

**(I) GAGGING:** Babies are born with a strong gag reflex that is part of their bodies' natural defense against food entering the respiratory tract instead of the esophagus. The gag reflex persists throughout life—for example, if you are forced to eat something you don't like, you will automatically gag. Babies have to learn to inhibit their involuntary gag reflex when they start eating finger foods or food of a lumpier consistency than they are used to. They also have to learn how much food to put in at a time when they feed themselves—biting off more than they can chew is common. The other common thing babies learn to do to confuse the issue is to gag voluntarily when they don't wish to eat something. The gagging-on-purpose habit can last well into the toddler years, making parents believe their toddler is physically unable to eat anything other than a liquid diet (and forgetting about the times a chocolate cookie or a packet of chips goes

**499**

down without a problem).

When a baby gags, the food sits at the back of her throat and either ends up going down where it's supposed to go or comes up again. As long as you are around to make sure she's all right and the food doesn't get stuck, gagging is harmless and part of the way she learns to feed herself and eat lumpier food. Most babies need the main part of their meal ground up until they are twelve months old as the gag reflex remains strong and, to some extent, involuntary until then, so lumpy food from a spoon tends to make mealtimes stressful because the lumps cause a lot of gagging. Mothers are constantly told to offer lumpy food from a spoon from six months on with dire warnings of babies never learning to chew if they don't. I find this a cause of great stress for many families. Oddly enough, when babies feed themselves finger foods, they control their gag reflex much more efficiently, so a good compromise is to give your baby the main part of her meal ground up, then offer her some finger food she can eat herself. Obviously if your baby manages chunky food from a spoon without gagging a lot, go for it!

**(II) CHOKING:** Choking occurs when the airway is obstructed, preventing air from reaching the lungs. When it is a small, soft item (a crumb or a soft lump), the baby will usually cough, which removes the object from the airway. Serious obstruction happens when the item is a small, hard object like an orange seed, a peanut, a sweet, or a piece of apple that gets stuck in the airway and partially or completely blocks it.

What follows is a basic guide for the first aid steps to take for choking, but it is not intended to be your sole source of information. As it is very difficult to learn basic CPR skills from a book, it is highly advisable for all parents to take a course in CPR (cardiopulmonary resuscitation). CPR classes are available at local YMCAs, hospitals, community centers or local chapters of the

American Red Cross or American Heart Association. It is becoming more common now for groups of parents to arrange for Red Cross personnel to conduct classes in private homes. If you are interested, call your local chapter (in the White Pages).

Once you have taken a course, it is also advisable to update your skills regularly.

Make sure you have an emergency number for paramedics by the phone. Check the inside of your phone book to find the best number for your area. In most areas the number is 911 (or another number). In other areas, the fire department handles paramedic services making it faster to call there directly.

## BASIC STEPS

Allow your baby to cough. If coughing does not dislodge the blockage, here is what to do:

- Sit on a chair with your baby face down on your lap and her head pointing away from you. Slide one arm under her body and support her face and neck with one hand. Use the heel of your other hand to gently but firmly thump her five times in the middle of her back, between the shoulder blades.

- Then turn her over on your arm, supporting the back of her head with one hand

- Find her sternum (the bone that ends just under the center point of the chest between the nipples) and press on it five times. Stop if the baby starts to cough and let her try to cough up the obstruction.

- Continue blows and thrusts until the airway is cleared.

- If breathing still has not occurred, start resuscitation. Ask someone to call 911 (or your emergency number) immediately. If you

**501**

are on your own give your baby rescue breathing for one minute before you stop to call for help.

These guidelines are from www.babycenter.com, where you will find an excellent Illustrated Guide for infant First Aid for Choking and CPR.

It must be emphasised that choking is not a hazard normally associated with introducing a wide range of food to babies in their second six months as long as you take a few sensible precautions. Don't let fear of choking keep you from allowing your baby to try different food and new ways of eating.

## Teeth and food

Teeth emerge anytime between three and a half and sixteen months. The arrival of teeth has nothing to do with when and what your baby eats. Many twelve-month-old babies with no teeth eat a wide variety of chunky food as they learn to use their gums very efficiently.

## Breakfast suggestions

You may give your baby adult cereal after six months or continue with baby cereals if you prefer or use both for variety. Whole, full-fat cow's milk is fine to use on the cereal. Cooked fruit may be added to the cereal or yogurt and fruit can be offered at times instead of cereal.

Egg yolk may be commenced anytime after six months. Soft boil an egg and try the yolk off a spoon or dip a piece of bread or toast into the egg and let your baby suck or chew it. A hard-boiled egg yolk can be grated and mixed into her veggies at lunch or dinner. When she is accustomed to lumps, try scrambling the yolk with a little milk. The whole egg may be given anytime between nine and twelve months. Minor reactions to egg white are things like mild swelling of the lips and/or a sudden appearance of a red rash around the mouth. If this happens, leave eggs for a month and try again. Extreme reactions to egg white are rare.

Try your baby on pieces of toast or bread after breakfast.

## Morning and afternoon snacks

When you are changing from four-hourly feedings to three meals a day, you might find a snack and a small drink a handy substitute while your baby is getting used to her new routine. It can also provide distraction from the breast if you are limiting your breastfeedings to three a day. Morning and afternoon snacks are optional, and if your baby sleeps or is quite happy without a snack at this time, forget it.

## Lunch suggestions

The main meal (that is, the veggie one) may be given in the middle of the day or in the evening. There is no truth in the rumor that heavy food shouldn't be given in the evening. If your baby is a non-veggie eater, substitute veggies with some of the breakfast or dinner ideas.

## Dinner suggestions

I think everyone has trouble at times working out what to give for the third meal. Babies don't need endless variety, and cooking lots of separate little dishes that may not get eaten is time-consuming and stressful. Remember, babies who eat anything will eat easily prepared family foods and babies who are fussy eaters usually won't eat the specially prepared fancy baby dishes made to tempt them, so keep it simple. Your baby may start eating some of your food that is suitable for grinding up such as casseroles, stews, pasta, rice dishes, or spaghetti. Obviously avoid hot things such as chile, pepper, and so on.

By nine months, lots of babies are able to eat sandwiches or cheese on toast. Sandwiches can be made with a variety of fillings such as banana, cream cheese, tomato, salmon or tuna, and cheese. Water or juice may be given with dinner and the breastfeeding or bottle saved for bedtime if that's what you and your baby prefer.

## Juice

Try not to overdo the juice. Juice tends to be given to babies and toddlers for a whole range of reasons like relieving their boredom, getting them to sleep, and to stop them from crying, all of which relate to behavior, not nutrition. Sucking juice from bottles is extremely habit forming. Endless bottles of juice cause diarrhea, and black teeth, interfere with babies' appetites, and prevent them from developing good eating habits, which are a normal part of healthy weaning.

Use unsweetened pure juice or make your own. If your baby is having juice from a cup, she will not drink nearly as much as from a bottle, so give it full strength. If she is using a bottle halve the juice with water. Two bottles of juice a day are plenty—4 oz (120 ml) in each bottle. Try water at other times; if she is really thirsty, she will drink it. If you are having a few hard poo problems, prune juice may be given for a drink at morning or afternoon snack times.

## Whole cow's milk

Unfortunately the issue of milk seems to have gotten completely out of hand, to the point where it is viewed by many as akin to some sort of nasty poison, drops of which should never pass babies' lips. Manufacturers of infant formulas have a lot to gain from the move to encourage the prolonged use of formula. At the time of writing, the general recommendation is to use formula for twelve months, but toddler formulas are appearing on supermarket shelves. How long will it be before the recommendation will be up to the age of two? The emphasis on the use of formula means many parents today assume manufactured milk is an essential part of infant feeding for at least the whole of the first year and maybe beyond.

Many babies bypass formula by breastfeeding, and, in the second six months, combine breastfeedings with milk from a cup. Most bottle-fed babies who eat well and drink only two to three bottles of milk should be able to drink whole milk from their bottles from nine months without any detrimental effects. I have not found any health professional able to tell me the physiological difference between a baby of nine months and a baby of twelve months in regard to the strict formula until twelve months rule so one wonders why it exists apart from increasing profits for formula companies.

## WHY THE RECOMMENDATIONS? WHAT ARE THE PROBLEMS WITH WHOLE COW'S MILK?

- When babies under six months are not breastfed or have a combination of breastmilk and formula, formula is the best and safest option to put in their bottles. Whole cow's milk lacks ingredients that are essential for a young baby's proper growth and development when it is supplying their total food requirements. Whole cow's milk is also not suitable for babies over six months as the *major* part of their diet. A large amount of whole milk in conjunction with little or no food is obviously nutritionally unsound for babies and toddlers. This does not mean babies cannot have whole milk as part of their diets, in a cup or on cereal, once they are over six months.

- Allergy/intolerance is a problem for a small number of babies. Some babies can tolerate cow's milk-based formula, but when introduced to whole cow's milk in any volume, they vomit, get cramps, and perhaps a shiny red bottom. Babies with a true milk allergy will not be able to drink cow's milk-based formula either—naturally it would not be a good idea to give these babies whole cow's milk.

- Research has shown that whole cow's milk plays a part in contributing to iron deficiency in a small number of vulnerable babies and toddlers when it is started early and used excessively. Iron deficiency is cause for concern but is more strongly associated with poverty, fad diets, and ignorance. Whole cow's milk has a relatively low iron concentration and has been found to cause minuscule bleeding into the gut (detectable only by a special test), which increases the chance of iron deficiency in these babies. This information has been used widely to justify the prolonged unnecessary use of infant formula, particularly follow-up-formula, for all babies rather than the small number who may need it. Formula certainly contains mammoth amounts of added iron, only four to ten percent of which is absorbed by the baby. Babies who eat well will get good iron from natural sources such as red meat, chicken and fish, legumes, and grains. Citrus fruits, cauliflower, broccoli, and melons provide vitamin C to help efficient iron absorption.

So, it's fine to include full-fat whole cow's milk in your baby's diet (on her cereal or in her food) after six months. If she is bottle fed, continue to use formula in her bottles until sometime between nine and twelve months (depending on how much she eats) when you can change to full-fat whole cow's milk. If she is breastfed and starting to use a cup or straw, whole cow's milk is fine to use in the cup from six months of age—you do not have to go out and buy formula.

Whole cow's milk is preferable to soy milk as it contains more naturally occurring ingredients (fat, calcium, iron) than soy milk. Soy milk has no advantages, and in fact may cause problems for some babies.

## Babies who will only eat commercial food

This is another cause of anxiety for some mothers. Try not to worry. Remember you can't force babies to eat things they don't want to eat. Commercial food is nutritious and there's an incredible array around now to choose from. Stop cooking your own food if your baby is not eating it and the situation is becoming tense. Give her what she likes, but as soon as she can sit for a while in a highchair, follow the jar of food with some finger foods for her to eat herself. Offer some fresh easy food (fruit, bread, cheese) regularly.

**506**

## Teaching your baby to use a cup

Drinking from a cup is a skill that has to be learned—it is not a developmental milestone that suddenly happens at a certain age. Teaching babies to drink from cups takes time and patience, but there are lots of advantages for you and your baby should you decide to teach her to use a cup during her first year.

Teaching your baby to use a cup has lots of advantages

- Once she's drinking well from a cup, the bottles can go, so there's one less hassle for you to worry about.

- Bottles of milk do interfere with the eating of food, and in the second year when lots of babies become fussy eaters bottles of milk and juice become a quick fix for feeding difficulties at a time when eating should be encouraged, not drinking.

- The risk of tooth decay is increased the longer the bottles are used.

- Going directly from breast to cup is the only option for breastfed babies who don't like bottles.

Here are some tips if you would like to teach your baby to drink from a cup.

**NOTE:** The definition of a cup is any container that does not have a nipple on it.

As all babies are different, you need to experiment to find out what suits your baby best—a small cup, a spout, or a straw.

A small cup is often the most successful to start with. Start with two teaspoons of fluid only. If you fill up the cup, your baby will be drenched and you will quickly lose patience. The main aim in the beginning is to gently teach your baby what to do, not to try and get her to drink the same amount she has from the breast or a bottle. Offer her a small amount in a cup at morning or afternoon snack time or after one of her meals. Use breastmilk, milk, water, or juice.

The more she has the opportunity to practice, the better she will become at drinking. The amount she drinks steadily increases; it takes about six to eight weeks for a baby to learn to drink 2 to 3 oz in one. Naturally, you have to hold the cup!

You might like to try a cup with a spout as they are less messy; however, I find spouts don't suit a lot of babies because they suck them like a nipple and end up coughing and spluttering a lot.

**508**

Straws can be very successful once the baby gets the idea. Start by offering one of the fruit juice packs that comes with a straw. Show your baby what to do, then put the straw to her lips and squeeze the pack so that a little juice squirts out to encourage her to suck on the straw. Practice whenever you can. One day she will go sip and get such a surprise she will probably open her mouth and let the fluid drop out. Once she's got the idea of sipping, keeping her mouth shut and swallowing, buy one of the cups available with a built-in straw. These have the great advantage of not spilling everywhere.

Breastfed babies going from breast to cup never consume the quantities of fluid that bottle-fed babies consume, so if you have a breast-to-cup baby, don't panic about this. There is rarely any need to force a healthy, breastfed baby to take a bottle after six months of age. This includes babies who only have three to four breast-feedings every twenty-four hours. Babies following this plan thrive on their meals, steadily increasing amounts from a cup, spout, or straw and their breastfeedings.

## Vegetarian diets for babies

Many families now choose not to eat meat. A vegetarian diet that includes milk, eggs, and other dairy products is fine for babies too.

Vegetarian diets that do not include any animal fats (vegan diets) pose problems for babies and young children, as these diets tend to be bulky and offer a very limited range of food that small people with fussy appetites are likely to have difficulty with. A con-tinuing shortage of protein, vitamin B12, iron, calcium, and fat as well as an overall shortage of calories can put a baby or toddler's growth at risk. Some of the problems can be overcome by breast-feeding and/or using a soy infant formula, mixing liberal amounts of smooth peanut butter (not until over one year) and tahini (sesame seed paste) into dishes before serving, and giving a vita-

**509**

min B12 supplement. The use of a soy infant formula (as opposed to soy drinks) should be continued for the second year, and when replaced by a soy drink, a brand should be chosen that has added fat, calcium, B12, and iron.

## Premature babies

Premature babies can follow the same dietary guidelines, although babies born earlier than thirty-four weeks will take longer to get to the stage of sitting and eating finger foods. Babies born very early may not be ready for the diet sheet on page 495 until about nine to twelve months, but all premature babies should be offered a variety of foods including finger foods by twelve months. It is fine to teach premature babies to drink from a cup anytime in their second six months as well as cutting down the number of bottles they have as suggested in the diet chart. The information for breastfed premature babies at this stage is the same as for full-term babies.

### FOR MORE INFORMATION

Chapter 25: Common Worries and Questions *(flexible sleeping and eating guide for six months and beyond, page 513)*

# Common Worries and Questions

## *Funny habits*

Babies have lots of funny little habits that are either related to reflexes that they have no control over or the normal changes happening to their bodies as they grow. Other funny habits are part of babies' inbuilt urges to explore their own bodies and the world around them. Whenever they are tired or bored, they become more obsessive and frantic about the particular strange habit they are into. Mothers often notice that the behavior often stops when their babies are out and about being entertained and distracted.

Here are some examples of a few interesting actions and activities common to all healthy babies—none of them are anything to worry about unless there is a whole range of odd behavior accompanied by signs of illness.

- Pulling and rubbing ears is a common action from six months and is not a sign of an ear infection or teething. Once your baby discovers her ear, it becomes a fascinating pastime to play with it because it makes an interesting sound and it's fun to grab hold of. If your baby is into pulling and rubbing her ears, you may notice she does it more when she is bored or overtired.

- Head-banging is another habit some babies indulge in, especially just before sleep. Try not to get disturbed by head-banging or to get worried by people who tell you it indicates baby anxiety. Pad up the crib if necessary and avoid long hours of boredom on the home front by getting your baby out and about as much as possible. Like all the other actions, it stops eventually.

- Sometimes you might notice your baby coughs almost deliberately even though she has no sign of a cold—another funny little habit that shows your baby has reached an age where she imitates and does things on purpose. Often, once a parent realizes what's happening, he or she coughs back, which encourages their baby to do it again, so it becomes a game.

- Babies find their tongues fascinating parts of their equipment, and many babies go through stages where they keep sticking out their tongues. Adults often find this amusing and do the same thing back, so the tongue-sticking-out game is as popular a pastime as the coughing game!

- Some babies make a peculiar grunting noise deep in their throat. Making a similar noise is quite irritating to adult throats, but babies manage to do this continually without any ill effect. Grunting noises in healthy babies is not a sign of constipation, bowel or tummy problems—just another strange habit that passes.

- Another habit is sucking the top or bottom lip, which looks most peculiar but is harmless.

- Babies often find constantly opening and shutting their hands is an interesting occupation, which can develop into a habit for a while. Another common hand habit is to sit moving hands and wrists as if driving a motor bike.

- Ear-piercing screeches are fun and often repeated over and over again. If the screeching and squealing gets a bit much, tell your baby firmly and consistently, no every time she does it. Eventually she will stop. If you keep laughing and encouraging her to do it, the screechy habit will last longer.

- Rubbing eyes is another common habit. As long as your baby is otherwise well and her eyes are not excessively watery, red, or have a discharge, rubbing eyes is not significant.

Babies repeat all sorts of actions. These are just a few normal habits, disappearing as they grow to be replaced by others. Don't try too hard to interpret them by projecting deep and meaningful adult thoughts onto harmless baby habits.

## Routines—one last time

Here's a flexible guide for six months and beyond if you are looking for one.

**5 AM TO 6 AM:** Breastfeed or bottle.

**7 AM TO 8.30 AM:** If your baby sleeps this late, offer her breakfast as soon as she wakes (choose something from the diet sheet on page 497) before her breastfeeding—give her a breastfeeding right after her food.

**9 AM TO 11 AM:** Bed—after some morning snack (if she wants it—see diet sheet). Baby may sleep from forty minutes to two hours.

**12 NOON TO 1.30 PM:** Make sure she's up by 1:30 at the latest—it's okay to wake her. Give her lunch—choose something from the diet sheet and give her a breastfeeding, bottle, or cup after her food.

**2 PM TO 3 PM:** Bed, but make sure she's up by 4 pm, and keep her up until bed at 7 or 7:30 pm. Baby may sleep forty minutes to two hours.

**4 PM:** Afternoon snack (if she wants it). You'll probably need to devote this time to amusing her or going for a walk.

**6 PM:** Dinner—choose something from the diet sheet.

**6.30 PM:** Bath followed by breastfeeding or bottle.

**7 TO 7.30 PM:** Bed—if you are having trouble helping your baby to go to sleep, read Chapter 28, page 543, and follow the teaching-to-sleep guidelines, which will teach her to go to sleep without the breast or bottle.

Total sleeping in the day varies from one to three hours. Changing from one to two daytime sleeps happens anytime between nine months and fifteen months and depends a lot on what time the baby wakes in the morning. Babies who catnap (only sleep for thirty-to-forty-minute stretches) do better having several small sleeps throughout the day. Trying to make babies who catnap sleep for longer periods is usually not possible. For more on sleep, see page 539.

# *Spoiling and discipline*

Between six and twelve months, babies gain skills that make them mobile and keen to explore, and this is the time you will find you have to start to set limits, to discipline. Discipline means to guide, to teach, to lead by love and example. Discipline does not mean withholding love, smacking, shouting, or imposing rigid rules. Babies of this age need a few reasonable limits so that they can begin to understand how their world operates, to develop healthy eating habits and to keep them safe.

At this stage, limit-setting is centered around activities associated with normal development. It is not centred on behavior as babies don't act in a premeditated fashion and still have no control over their behavior. So, again, spoiling in the sense of turning a baby into a nasty person no one likes is a meaningless expression. Not setting a few limits may lead to injuries, or, as the baby becomes a toddler, completely unacceptable, exhausting antics that do not contribute to the parent's well-being or a loving home atmosphere.

Here are a few tips on limit-setting:

- When saying no, limit it to a few important things. Always say no, in a firm voice that is different from your normal conversational tone.

- Childproof your house and put away as many forbidden objects as you can.

- Try diversion when you want your baby to stop what she's doing or about to do.

- Go out and about as much as possible. Babies quickly become bored at home when they are not eating or sleeping. The need for limit-setting is less when they are stimulated by new sights, sounds, and people.

- If your older baby's antics are driving you mad, timeout is acceptable for short periods—her crib is the best place for this.

- Work on a united front approach with your partner. Babies don't respond well to chaos and conflict on the home front.

- Repetition and patience are essential, especially between the age of nine months and three years, as it takes this long for children to *start* to develop the ability to make sensible and safe judgments about their behavior and the possible consequences of their actions. Learn all you can about baby and child development so that you know if your expectations and discipline are reasonable.

All babies and parents are different, so the limit-setting and discipline practiced will be different for each family. Babies thrive equally well and grow into well-balanced young people whether the discipline is very structured or more easygoing as long as their environment is safe, stable, and loving.

# Diaper rash

Diaper rashes in older babies usually need a combination of a mild hydrocortisone ointment and an anti-fungal cream to clear them up, so it's always best to seek advice from your nurse practitioner or family doctor before buying out the pharmacy. A sudden bright red shiny bottom can be the result of a dietary change. Whole cow's milk, soy milk, or yogurt can all have this effect, and stopping or cutting down the offending food clears the rash up. Antibiotics and a bout of viral diarrhea can also cause sore red bottoms. Red weeping bottoms caused by food, medication or viral diarrhea need a good barrier cream thickly applied to help them heal. Here are the two I find the best:

- Ask your pharmacist to mix one percent Ichthyol and ten percent zinc in yellow soft paraffin.

- Desitin ointment is made by Pfizer, and I find it a marvelous barrier cream for babies with sensitive skin who are prone to diaper rash. It both heals and prevents diaper rash, so it's worth getting some in if your baby has a sensitive bottom.

# Common illnesses 6–12 months

## Diarrhea and vomiting

Diarrhea means that there are a lot of loose, watery bowel movements different from your baby's normal poo. Sudden diarrhea is usually caused by a viral infection of the gut. It may or may not be accompanied by vomiting. Some gut infections cause vomiting without diarrhea. It is often confusing sorting out viral diarrhea and vomiting from loose poo caused by food or medication or other illnesses, so if you are ever in doubt, seek help from your pediatrician.

Medication is not a part of treatment for most infectious diarrhea. Antibiotics are only used occasionally for a specific, diagnosed bacterial infection. Medications such as adults take to stop diarrhea are dangerous for babies and should not be used. **Simultaneous diarrhea and vomiting is potentially serious and needs medical assessment.** Diarrhea or vomiting on its own usually only needs simple dietary measures.

- The correct treatment for either diarrhea or vomiting is to give small amounts of clear fluids only for twenty-four hours. If you

**517**

are breastfeeding, continue breastfeeding—if you have an abundant supply, try short, frequent feedings.

- If you are bottle feeding or using a cup, the amount of fluid should not exceed ½ teaspoon per pound of the baby's body weight every hour.

## SUITABLE FLUIDS

- A commercial preparation such as Pedialyte. Make as directed.

- White grape juice.

- Rice water: Boil ¾ cup of white rice in 5 cups of water until the water is milky—not too thick! Strain the rice and add four level teaspoons of sugar to every litre of rice water.

- Boiled water: Add four level teaspoons of sugar to one litre of boiled water.

## A FEW IMPORTANT POINTS

- A commercial preparation such as Pedialyte is not a medication. It is a fluid replacement to be given instead of formula for twenty-four hours. Parents are often given confusing messages about using a commercial fluid replacement and they give it as well as formula in the mistaken belief it is a medication that will cure the diarrhea.

- Babies under four months should be given a commercial preparation in preference to white grape juice, rice water and sugar, or boiled water and sugar.

- Older babies with simple diarrhea or vomiting do not need commercial preparations. Any of the other suggested fluids are fine.

**518**

- Follow the guidelines for the addition of sugar closely. A small amount of glucose or sucrose helps the baby absorb fluid more efficiently and makes the fluid more palatable, but too much causes more diarrhea. Do not give flat lemonade at any age— the sugar content is too high.

After twenty-four hours of small, frequent breastfeedings or clear fluids, reintroduce your normal breastfeeding regime or half-strength formula.

Older babies who are eating food should resume a balanced diet as soon as possible, but continue to give small amounts often for a few days. Make sure some fat is introduced during the second twenty-four-hour period (e.g., breastmilk, formula, or milk), as constant clear fluids and fruit and veggies alone aggravate acute diarrhea.

Recommence full-strength formula by day three. Sometimes babies develop a temporary lactose intolerance following gastroenteritis, which means their watery diarrhea comes back once full-strength formula or milk is reintroduced. When this happens a special lactose-free formula is required for two to three weeks until the bowel recovers.

Breastfed babies tolerate breastmilk well following gastroenteritis and do not need lactose-free formula.

Most babies respond well to these simple measures, but unfortunately there are times when the correct advice is not given or parents and health professionals underestimate the severity of the illness.

**Always seek help or a second opinion if:**

- You are worried.

- You are given a diagnosis of teething (growing teeth does not cause diarrhea).

- Your baby is under three months of age.

- Your baby suffers from another illness such as diabetes, heart disease, urinary tract infection, or is on any medication.

- Your baby is simultaneously vomiting and having diarrhea, especially if she is not keeping down breastmilk or clear fluids.

- Your baby is lethargic, drowsy, has a dry mouth, and is passing less urine than normal.

What about the well, happy baby with mild diarrhea, no burning bottom, no vomiting, no weight loss, and no fever?

When this happens, it is difficult to decide whether or not to start the diarrhea regime as the baby gets very unhappy and very hungry. Wait one or two days and see what develops. Continuing loose poo in an otherwise well baby can go on for some time after an episode of viral diarrhea. It's inconvenient and messy but harmless and eventually stops.

Note: Endless bottles of juice exacerbate loose poo. If your baby is drinking juice, once or twice a day is plenty. Try water at other times if she is thirsty.

## Ear infections

Ear problems in older babies are very common.

The problems usually occur in the middle ear because the eustachian tube that connects the middle ear to the throat is short and straight in this age group. This allows easy entry of mucus, milk, and germs into the chamber of the middle ear. Older babies and toddlers also catch a lot of colds until they build up some resistance to bugs. The extra mucus colds created by blocks the eustachian tube, which stops the middle ear from draining properly.

A problem with ears is caused by either:

- An acute infection from infected mucus. This is painful, so the baby's behavior may change dramatically. She may have screaming attacks, whine more than usual, or develop a sudden sleep problem. It's always worth having your baby's ears checked when these things happen. Antibiotics and pain relievers are needed;

OR

- A collection of uninfected mucus in the middle ear, called glue ear. Glue ear is generally not painful, but transient earaches occur, especially at night, so a change in night sleep patterns may occur even when a baby is happy during the day. Treatment for glue ear ranges from none to medication to insertion of tubes depending on the frequency of infections, the discomfort, and the amount of hearing loss.

## Urinary tract infection

A urinary tract infection (UTI) is caused by a growth of germs— usually in the bladder but sometimes in the kidneys. It is common in babies, toddlers, and children. Approximately thirty percent of urinary tract infections in babies occur because of an underlying structural problem in the urinary system. It is routine for all babies to have X-rays and an ultrasound when a UTI is diagnosed to treat such conditions to prevent chronic renal problems later in life.

### SYMPTOMS

Symptoms in babies and toddlers under three can be vague and confusing, which is why urine is routinely tested when the cause of a fever is not clear. Irritability, vomiting, and failure to thrive can also be symptoms of a urinary tract infection.

Symptoms may include odd-smelling urine or urine that looks

cloudy or thick, and occasionally the baby may show signs of distress when peeing.

## TREATMENT

A urine specimen is collected and tested and antibiotics commenced if an infection is present. Collecting urine samples from babies can be a challenge. An attempt is made to catch a clean sample of urine in a suitable specimen jar (plastic urine bags are no longer used as contamination causes unreliable results when the urine is tested). If this proves too difficult, or if the baby is very ill, the urine may have to be collected in hospital by inserting a fine tube or needle into the bladder via the abdomen.

With the antibiotics, infections will clear in five to seven days, but the baby may continue a smaller dose of the medication until the results of the investigations are known.

Treatment for underlying kidney and bladder problems ranges from protective antibiotics for a period of time to surgery, depending on what the problem is.

# Coughs

Coughing is a reflex we are all born with. Babies cough to clear their throats, which helps clear their air passages. Coughing accompanies many illnesses. When your baby has a cold, the reason for coughing is obvious. When coughing is associated with wheezing, a high fever, breathlessness, or sleepless nights, see your pediatrican. It is dangerous to give cough suppressants to a baby or a young child. Worrying coughs should always be investigated.

# Croup

Croup is a form of laryngitis that follows a viral infection in the upper respiratory tract and affects the voice box and trachea. It is more common in babies and toddlers than in older children and adults because they have small soft windpipes that collapse easily when inflamed. The baby's cough sounds like a baby seal barking and is accompanied by a crowing noise as she breathes in. Her voice may be hoarse and she may have trouble breathing.

Croup is more severe at night when the air is cooler, and the worst period usually lasts about two nights. Some babies have what is known as spasmodic croup—frequent attacks of a small duration. These tend to occur at night, lasting for a few hours, and occasionally recur the following night.

## TREATMENT

The previous treatment of using steam to alleviate symptoms is no longer recommended as the risks of burns and scalds far outweigh any benefits, which have been shown to be negligible. Calm your baby as much as you can by sitting her on your lap while the bout lasts.

### Go to the hospital immediately if:

- You are worried about your baby's breathing or drawing her chest right in.

- She becomes pale and sweaty or blue.

Croup is usually mild, but it can get worse quickly. If you are worried, seek medical help.

## MEDICATIONS

Since croup is caused by a virus, antibiotics are not an appropriate treatment. The only medications used for croup are steroids and adrenaline, which are administered in a hospital.

# Wheezing and asthma in babies under twelve months

Accurate diagnosis of asthma in this age group is difficult. Episodes of prolonged coughing are common among babies and toddlers under two. The endless cough is usually associated with upper respiratory tract infections and is unlikely to be associated with asthma when there is no wheeze or history of allergic conditions such as eczema, hay fever, and reactions to food. Some babies under twelve months have troublesome episodes of wheezing but are otherwise thriving and happy. Most of them lose the wheeze after the first year. Consult your pediatrician if you are worried about your baby's coughing or wheezing.

## Pneumonia

Pneumonia is a viral or bacterial infection of the lungs that causes swelling and blockage in sections of the lung. It is also often referred to as a chest infection. Pneumonia occurs at all ages but is most common in babies and toddlers.

### SYMPTOMS

Pneumonia may follow a mild infection of the nose and throat. It can be tricky to initially diagnose in babies as the symptoms vary greatly and can be very subtle. For example, neck stiffness, lack of energy, fever, and loss of appetite (a baby's sudden refusal to feed or disinterest in breast or bottle usually means something is wrong). Other symptoms include rapid breathing, grunting while breathing, and a bluish tinge around the mouth. A chest X-ray is usually needed to confirm the diagnosis.

### TREATMENT

Antibiotics are used when bacteria is the cause of the infection. Serious pneumonia needs hospitalization for intravenous therapy

**524**

to administer fluids and antibiotics (if appropriate). Acetaminophen is used for pain and fever. Recovery usually takes seven to ten days.

## Fevers

Babies and toddlers are much more prone to running fevers than older children and adults are.

Fever is the body's natural defense against infection, so fever may accompany an illness such as a cold, a urinary tract infection, gastroenteritis, or an infectious disease like chicken pox.

A baby's fever can also be caused by other things not related to an infection—for example, overdressing, being kept too long in a hot car, a hot day, sunburn, following immunization or crying for a long time.

Sometimes babies run fevers for two to three days and nobody knows why.

Growing teeth does not cause a fever. Constant mild fevers that come and go over a period of time should always be investigated.

A fever is not always the best indicator of an illness. Some serious illnesses only cause a mild fever.

### HOW DO YOU KNOW YOUR BABY HAS A FEVER?

If your baby's temperature is above 99° F (37.2° C) she has a mild (low-grade) fever. Babies' temperatures may be taken by placing a (regular glass thermometer), under her arm or by using an ear thermometer.

Most parents quickly become skilled at estimating fever by touch. Hot or warm heads do not necessarily indicate a fever and baby hands and feet usually remain cool whether a baby has a fever or not. The best method is to place the back of your hand on your baby's tummy. You will soon learn the difference between a warm, hot, or burning feeling.

**525**

## WHAT IF HER TEMPERATURE IS BELOW NORMAL?

Usually this is because the thermometer is not registering properly—not because there is something wrong with your baby. If her body and head are warm and if she is a good color with good skin tone and a loud cry, there is unlikely to be a problem. However, if she is pale and floppy and feels cool to touch, seek help immediately.

## HERE ARE THE THINGS TO DO IF YOUR BABY IS HOT

- Give the recommended dose of baby acetaminophen or ibuprofen if your baby is over 101° F (38.4°C) and/or if she is miserable. If your baby is too distressed to swallow and it is important for her to have the medication, suppositories are available.

- While waiting for it to work, undress your baby down to her body suit and diaper. Keep her under a light sheet in a cool room.

- If you feel uneasy and the cause of the fever is not obvious, see your pediatrician. Any baby with a fever during the first three months after birth should be seen by a pediatrician.

## Fever fits (convulsions)

A fever fit is a convulsion caused by a high temperature. The most common age for this to happen is between eighteen and twenty-four months, but overall it happens to about four percent of all babies and children between six months and five years.

## WHY DOES IT HAPPEN?

Babies and young children have immature brains that are particularly sensitive to outside stress. Some just can't handle a high body temperature, so their brains respond by giving off an abnormal electrical discharge that results in a fit. Having a fit means the baby loses consciousness and twitches all over. It can happen out of the blue when it is not obvious that the baby has a fever; however, there is usually a history of an illness such as a bad cold, an ear infection, tonsillitis, or sometimes gastroenteritis. Urinary tract infections are less common but can cause very high fevers, which is why a urine test is done when the cause of the fever is not clear.

## WHAT DO YOU DO?

It's very scary, but don't panic! The fit usually lasts less than five minutes, but that can seem like forever when you're the parent. Stay with your baby. Place her on her side or tummy with her head on the side. Loosen any clothes around her neck and gently support her head with your hands. Don't put anything in her mouth or force open her gums. Urgent medical help should be sought if it lasts longer than five minutes.

When your baby comes around, take her to your pediatrician or your nearest children's hospital, as it is important to confirm that it is only a fever fit. This may mean some tests being done depending on the age of the baby and how long the fit lasted.

Febrile convulsions can recur. After the first convulsion, there is a thirty percent chance of recurrence (fifty percent if the baby is under a year); after the second convulsion, a fifty percent chance. Once a toddler has had a fever fit it is important to try to keep any fevers under control with acetaminophen (remember suppositories are available) and appropriate clothing, but there still might be times when a fever sneaks up on you. Frightening though they are, febrile convulsions are usually brief and harmless, and when you know one may occur, you can be prepared.

# Infectious diseases

These are not common in a baby's first year but do happen. Identifying a rash as a particular disease (e.g. measles, roseola, rubella, viral rash, or an allergy rash) is often an educated guess in the first year as strange rashes at this time are not always easy to diagnose accurately.

The time between the infection (before the symptoms appear) and the illness (when the symptoms appear) is called the incubation period.

### CHICKEN POX

Chicken pox is preceded by a mild fever and a fussy baby. The rash starts as small, raised pink spots that turn into blisters, then form crusts. The incubation period is fourteen to twenty-one days so there can be a three-week gap between one family member and another becoming infected. Parents often worry about the likelihood of their very young baby catching chicken pox from older babies and toddlers. New babies can catch chicken pox, but their natural immunity protects them to a large extent, so it is unusual to see chicken pox in the first six months after birth.

Treatment aims to relieve the itch and fever. Give acetaminophen and warm to hot baths. Add some oatmeal to the bath water if the itch is severe. Benadryl helps. Calamine lotion applied directly to the spots helps.

A vaccine is available for chicken pox. You may have your baby vaccinated at twelve months. See your pediatrician.

### MEASLES

Measles immunization is started at twelve months, but a small number of babies do catch measles before they are immunized. If this happens, your baby still needs her immunization at twelve months.

The incubation period is seven to fourteen days. Measles first appear as a cold. The baby is miserable with a runny nose, watery eyes, a cough, and a fever. Two days later, spots appear on the neck, behind the ears, and on her face.

Within hours the whole body is covered. The rash often joins together and becomes one red mass or a series of blotches. Give acetaminophen to bring the fever down and encourage extra fluids.

## RUBELLA (GERMAN MEASLES)

Rubella immunization is included with the measles and mumps immunization at twelve months. Rubella has an incubation period of fourteen to twenty-one days. It is often difficult to diagnose in babies and is frequently confused with measles, roseola, an allergy, or a viral rash. The baby may have mild cold symptoms. The rash rapidly spreads over her arms and body. It appears as small, pink separate dots unlike the measles rash, which is red and blotchy.

The most reliable sign confirming rubella is swollen glands at the back of the neck and behind the ears.

Care should be taken to avoid contact with women who are in the early stages of pregnancy as the rubella virus is dangerous to the developing baby. The introduction of the rubella vaccine as part of the measles/mumps/rubella immunization, as well as the rubella immunization of adolescents, has done a lot to eliminate the risk, but if there is any doubt about the possibility of a problem, your pediatrician or obstetrician should be consulted.

## ROSEOLA

Roseola is an acute viral disease that is most commonly seen in babies between six and twelve months. The incubation period is about ten days.

Roseola starts with a sudden very high fever that remains for four to five days. Just after the height of the fever, a pale pink blotchy rash appears on the chest and spreads to the arms and legs.

It is rarely on the face. The rash fades quickly, usually within twenty-four to thirty hours. Treatment involves bringing the high fever down with acetaminophen.

### WHOOPING COUGH (PERTUSSIS)

Whooping cough is still around—partly because the immunization only gives eighty to ninety percent protection, but mostly because there is a rise in the number of parents who are choosing not to immunize their babies.

If your baby has been immunized and does get whooping cough, the illness is much milder and easier to manage. Whooping cough starts as a short, dry cough with a fever developing a short time later. After a few days, the whoop develops and vomiting occurs. Small babies tend not to whoop but have difficulty breathing and get blue attacks. They are at great risk and need hospital care so that they can have around-the-clock attention. Even a mild case lasts six weeks.

### FOR MORE INFORMATION

Chapter 10: Early Worries and Questions *(diaper rash, page 191)*
Chapter 12: Safety *(immunization, page 268)*
Chapter 15: The Crying Baby *(lactose intolerance page 349)*
Chapter 19: Common Worries and Questions *(recycled food in the poo, page 457)*
Chapter 24: Feeding Your Baby *(diet chart, page 495)*

chapter **twenty-six**

# Growth and Development

## *Growth*

During the third three months of their lives, lots of babies gain around 2 to 3 ounces (60 to 90 grams) a week and between six months and twelve months will grow 3 to 4 inches (8 to 10 cm).

### AT NINE MONTHS

|  | Small/Normal | Large/Normal |
|---|---|---|
| **Boys** | weight 17 lb (7.5 kg) | 11.6kg (24lb) |
|  | height 67cm (26 inches) | 78cm (29 inches) |
|  | head circ. 43cm (16 inches) | 48cm (18 inches) |
| **Girls** | weight 7.0kg (15lb) | 10.8kg (22lb) |
|  | height 65cm (25 inches) | 75cm (28 inches) |
|  | head circ. 42.5cm (15½ inches) | 47cm (17½ inches) |

## *Development*

### Gross motor development
- By nine months, your baby will be sitting alone. If she has only just learned to do it, she may only manage ten minutes at a time.

**531**

- While she sits, she will lean forward to pick up toys and examine them. If she leans sideways, she might fall.

- She may be crawling very efficiently, starting to crawl, or still just sitting.

- She may be starting to pull herself up onto furniture. This gives her a new view of the world; suddenly she can see what the top of a coffee table looks like. After standing and holding for a short time, she may fall backward—bump!

- When you hold her, she will weight bear and take alternate stepping movements.

## Vision and fine movements

- She is visually very eager with a fine eye for detail.

- She will start to pick up dust, crumbs, and small objects with three fingers and may at times have difficulty releasing what's in her fingers. Her forefinger constantly leads the way, exploring like a little antenna—poke, poke, poke.

- When she drops things, she looks for them. By now she is probably playing the dropping game so that you can pick things up for her.

It's important to provide a safe environment so that your baby can explore fully without too many inhibitions.

## Hearing and speech

- Your baby is very attentive to voices (especially yours), music, and everyday sounds.

- She will turn to a tiny sound behind each ear if she is not too distracted.

- She makes talking noises constantly and deliberately, which may be friendly or surprised or noises that show she is upset or annoyed.

- Most babies are now stringing together consonants followed by vowels like da-da, ma-ma, adaba, agaga, and so on.

- She will start to imitate noises such as a cough.

- She understands no, no (but doesn't necessarily obey) and bye-bye.

## Social and play

- Fussiness with strangers and distress when separated from their mothers is common for many babies now in varying degrees.

- Your baby can hold finger food well at this age and eat it without too many mishaps.

- Everything still goes into the mouth for a thorough checking.

- If asked, she will offer you a toy (if she's in the mood) but mostly can't let go of it into your hand.

- She loves playing peek-a-boo and bashing two blocks together. If she has been taught, she can clap hands, although not necessarily on request.

- When you partially hide something and she is interested and watches you do it, she will often find it.

# Developmental summary: 9 months

## Gross motor skills

- sits alone for 10–15 minutes;
- leans forward to pick up toys;
- attempts to crawl;
- pulls to stand.

## Vision and fine movements

- vision attentive;
- stretches out to grab things;
- pokes with forefinger;
- inferior pincer grasp;
- looks in correct direction for falling toys.

## Hearing and speech

- attentive to voice and everyday sounds;
- vocalizes (ma, da, ba);
- shouts;
- babbles;
- turns to minimal sound.

## Social and play

- holds and chews;

- distinguishes strangers from familiars;

- imitates;

- plays "boo":

- claps hands (if taught), bangs two blocks together.

# Serious developmental delay due to unknown causes

Chapter 13: Growth and Development (page 287) gives a general guide to developmental delays in babies that need investigating. A tiny number of babies appear to develop normally until around nine months, when it starts to become apparent that possibly things are not quite right. Unfortunately it may be a long time before a definite cause or prognosis is established. Needless to say, it is an ordeal for parents who face months, even years, of repeated assessments before knowing what the problem is and what the future holds. Parents, understandably, sometimes ignore their secret worries, but if you ever have any concerns, it is better to seek advice as soon as possible so that you can get all the help and support available. Health professionals can be over-reassuring, so if deep down you feel things are not right with your baby, find someone who is an expert at assessing baby/child development. Children's hospitals have child development units where detailed assessments can be made.

**FOR MORE INFORMATION**

Chapter 32: Becoming a Toddler *(separation anxiety and stranger awareness, page 585)*

# chapter **twenty-seven**

# Safety

The following chart emphasizes particular hazards associated with this developmental stage, but don't forget most safety hazards remain at any age and stage.

*Don't forget your baby's third round of immunization is due at 6 months.*

| Age | Developmental stage | Safety hazard | Precautions |
|---|---|---|---|
| **7–8 months** | • increasing dexterity at picking up small objects | • greater manual skills increase the risk of swallowing or inhaling foreign objects<br>• cuts from sharp or breakable objects left within reach | • remove small, sharp, and breakable objects from reach<br>• be careful of lotions, creams, and equipment on the change table—keep safety pins out of reach |
| **8–12 months** | • may drink from a cup<br>• may walk | • poisoning—does not discriminate between food, drinks, and other substances | • store all poisons, cleaning agents, medications, and insecticides in a locked cabinet; don't forget alcohol! |

| Age | Developmental stage | Safety hazard | Precautions |
|---|---|---|---|
| **8–12 months (cont)** | •increasingly mobile | •scalds—pulls tablecloth and dangling electrical cords, spilling hot liquids •insect stings, bites, scratches •strangulation— head caught between railings of fence, deck, or banisters •suffocation— plastic bags over airways •electrocution— playing with electrical power appliances and power sources *falls—from stairs, porches, beds, highchairs, and so on | •take care when medicating your baby •constant supervision •supervision near animals •wear covering on feet out of doors where there is a risk of a bee sting •destroy or tie a knot in unused plastic bags. Don't leave them anywhere near the baby, day or night. This includes shopping bags. •use socket covers on power sources •supervision •constant vigilance •stair gates |

## FOR MORE INFORMATION
Chapter 12: Safety *(immunization page, 268)*

# chapter twenty-eight

# Sleeping and Waking Six Months and Beyond

*To sleep—perchance to dream, ay, there's the rub.*

William Shakespeare, *Hamlet*

## Night waking—your options

First, a refresher about "sleeping through." Sleeping through is a confusing expression as it implies sleeping soundly, without stirring, all night. In fact, humans of all ages have brief waking periods during the night following a light sleep and dreaming phase before going into a deep sleep. Babies who disturb their parents at night become fully awake at this time and are unable to put themselves back to sleep, so eventually they start to cry.

At this stage, they are given a breastfeeding, pacifier, bottle, are rocked and patted, or are put into bed with their parents. I call these external aids. There is nothing wrong with using external aids

**539**

to help babies get back to sleep as long as parents are happy to keep doing them. They do not spoil a baby, but most babies aged six months and beyond do not voluntarily give them up.

As babies get older, some of them rely on certain conditions being in place before they can fall asleep (for example, the external aids). Adults also get used to certain conditions like using the same bed and pillow. If we go on vacation and change our conditions of sleep (the bed and the pillow), we invariably have trouble sleeping but usually get used to new conditions of sleep after a few nights—if they remain consistent—and sleep well again.

Overall, about forty percent of babies between six and twelve months are waking at night. The night waking varies between waking once for a quick feeding, and going right back to sleep to waking every two or three hours.

Many babies start to sleep for longer periods at night without disturbing their parents by the time they are three months old only to start crying again at night between six and twelve months. Some research suggests this is because babies of this age have intense dreaming phases from which they wake easily.

Babies who are still sharing their parents' bedrooms seem to wake and want attention more often after six months than babies who are in their own room.

All parents and babies are different, and parents have their own individual expectations and tolerance of nighttime waking. Some are quite prepared for months, even years, of broken sleep while others hope their babies will sleep all night without disturbing them by the time they are six months old. This expectation is not unreasonable, but unfortunately a lot of information circulating about babies and sleep suggests there is nothing that can be safely done to change an older baby's night waking. Consequently, many sleep-deprived parents live with night waking, believing that there is no other safe option.

## Night waking under six months

I believe that not a lot can be done about night waking (once any feeding problems are sorted out) until babies are over six months of age for a few different reasons:

- Young breastfed babies need to wake and feed frequently in order to keep breastfeeding working the way it's supposed to.

- Leaving young babies to cry at night instead of feeding them can mean weeks of crying, which is distressing and unkind for everyone and rarely changes what the baby is doing.

- It often takes six months for parents to get to know their baby, work out which babycare options they wish to follow, learn the difference between food, health, and behavior and gain confidence in caring for their baby.

## By six months or beyond things are different

- Babies are old enough to learn new conditions of sleep.

- Parents who wish to change what's happening during the night are more confident about deciding what to do.

- It is also much easier at this stage to separate a sleep problem from hunger or a medical problem. Hunger is never a cause of ongoing nighttime waking after six months—unfortunately it's not that simple. Nor is teething.

   The tendency to view ongoing sleep problems as teething is misleading and unhelpful. Babies get twenty teeth sometime between three and a half months and three years whether they sleep all night or not. Waiting for all the teeth to come through before teaching your baby to sleep means facing disturbed nights for another three years.

**541**

## Common causes of night waking apart from sleep patterns and conditions of sleep

• Illnesses (coughs, colds, and ear infections are the most common).

• A change of environment (different room, different bed, different house).

• A change of routine (holidays, travel, visitors, separation/divorce, childcare).

Some babies will experience one or more of the above and return to sleeping all night after the drama is over, but for many the ear infection gets better, the visitors leave, but the night waking remains.

## What's a parent to do?

Part of deciding to do something about your baby's sleep pattern is to work out whether it is a problem or not. Parents often feel pressured by those around them, so try and learn to ignore uncalled for, unwanted advice.

Lots of advice about night sleeping only emphasises one option, which tends to make parents feel bad if they do something different. For example, "letting the baby cry is wrong," "control crying is harmful and dangerous," or "sleeping with your baby is wrong."

There are a few options—the trick is to find what works for you and some parents go around in circles a few times before working out what they are prepared to do.

**If you are happy with what's happening, there's no need to do anything.**

Most parents ask themselves whether the night waking dilemma could have been prevented. The answer is probably not, and there is very little value in soul-searching, agonizing, and going back over what you did or didn't do over the last six months. Caring for babies is not always easy, and everyone does what they have to do, especially during those exciting, strange, and anxious early months.

## The three options

Options are limited, and despite a multitude of variations on the sleep theme, when you peel back all the layers there are only three. Changing or living with your baby's nighttime sleep patterns always involves one of the following:

1. Teaching your baby to sleep (involves stopping all the external helping-to-sleep aids and leaving her to cry).

2. Living with it (continue feeding, rocking, patting, and bed sharing).

3. Using a sedative (a very limited option and only appropriate under certain circumstances).

## Option 1: Teaching-to-sleep

Teaching-to-sleep means changing the conditions of sleep so that the baby learns how to go back to sleep on her own after she wakes following a light sleep phase.

The other name for teaching-to-sleep is, of course, "control crying." I know I can't fool you by calling it something different. Other names are "control comforting" and "crying down." The different names reflect creative attempts aimed at making parents feel better about leaving their babies to cry.

Regardless of what it is called, every structured sleep program is a variation of leaving the baby to her own devices at night and providing only minimal attention during the withdrawal period. Techniques vary according to the health professional giving the advice and the parents' feelings on the matter. Because all parents are different, and there are endless variations in how babies and toddlers respond, none of the programs (including mine) provides the definitive solution to all sleep problems despite extravagant promises. However, they do have the potential to safely improve the baby's frequent night waking and to help everyone in the family get more sleep.

Some programs are simple; others are more complex. Some favor (as I do) a direct jump-in-at-the-deep-end approach; others prefer a softer, more gradual withdrawal of the parents' attention. In my experience, the latter approach often doesn't achieve a great deal apart from more exhaustion for the parents and mixed messages for the baby, who ends up not having a clear idea of what her parents want her to do.

One of the problems faced by parents who would like to change things is the fear that control crying is harmful. With overuse, the meaning of the term has become blurred to the extent that it now has a negative, if not sinister, aura around it. So before launching into my version, let's put it into some perspective.

Control crying means that the baby is left to cry until she puts herself back to sleep instead of being breastfed, rewrapped, given a pacifier, or a bottle, rocked, patted, rolled over, or taken to her parents' bed. A parent visits the baby at varying intervals, briefly comforts her, then leaves.

Success rates for babies under six months are highly variable and I do not recommend control crying programs for young babies. Not because such regimes are necessarily harmful, but because there are too many times when the baby cries endlessly and the parents get more distressed trying to put the regime in place than they were before they started.

Consistent, reliable research involving large numbers of older babies and toddlers supporting unqualified success is hard to find. However, anecdotal reporting from hands-on practitioners supports

**544**

a high degree of success in changing older babies' and toddlers' sleep patterns quickly with no negative effects. In fact, the reverse seems to happen. Parents and children become much happier and family life is vastly improved.

On the negative side, not all parents can see it through, it doesn't always work, and sometimes the pleasing results are not permanent. Regardless of these potential negatives, just having the option presented in a positive manner and trying it often contributes to parents working out what they want to do in relation to their baby's sleep patterns.

Conversely, it is also hard to find any concrete evidence that shows using the various forms of control crying causes permanent emotional and psychological damage to healthy babies in loving homes. And in one form or another, it has been done regularly throughout the world at least since the sixties and almost certainly for decades prior to that.

The critics of control crying are usually people who do not have the day-to-day experience of the range of normal families that hands-on practitioners have. They do not have to come up with suitable, practical ways of helping all parents, rather than just some.

Conflicting views are to be expected and discussion encouraged so that parents can come to their own informed decisions. Unfortunately, many critics present their opposition to control crying in ways designed to make responsible parents, particularly mothers, feel guilty and alarmed.

Suggestions that control crying leads to suboptimal brain growth, diminished relationship skills and serious personality glitches are examples of such criticism. However, there is no long-term properly conducted scientific research that provides evidence for these opinions.

Some present the view that parents are forced by experts to do control crying by and are thus turned away from trusting in their own instincts. Parents learn as they go, and I have always found that they are highly unlikely to be pushed into a strategy like control crying unless they decide that this is what they really want to do.

The decision to let babies cry to teach them to sleep ultimately rests with the parents, who hopefully receive balanced information about the issue. When making the decision, they must bear in mind that:

- Apart from the baby's habits naturally changing over time, it is the only safe way of bringing the frequent night waking of a healthy baby to an end when all other avenues have been exhausted.

- Good results are not always permanent.

- It doesn't always work.

- There are some situations when it is not safe.

## WHEN IS IT NOT SAFE?

- Deliberately letting babies cry in a home where there are serious emotional and social problems.

- Letting babies cry at night for weeks on end puts their emotional and psychological development at risk.

- Letting babies cry at night when they are unwell or emotionally upset by family events is not advised.

Sometimes ongoing sleep problems are about more than just sleep. There are times when baby sleep problems are an indication of more deep-seated family problems that need to be addressed before dealing with the sleep problems on a practical level. It is impossible when writing a book to cover every reader's individual experience, so if you are aware of such a possibility in your household, I recommend that you seek professional advice and help.

A quick rule of thumb is that if you feel that you are continually distressed about your baby's nighttime waking and you can't put a teach-to-sleep plan into action or come to a suitable compromise, then further help is advisable. Further help involves counseling to resolve other issues that may be affecting your ability to deal satisfactorily with the sleep hassles.

## A PLAN FOR TEACHING YOUR BABY TO SLEEP

Teaching your baby to sleep is not a form of discipline or some sort of endurance test for parents. It is safe to do after your baby is six months old (in my opinion the ideal time is between six and twelve months) and does not cause emotional and psychological problems in a loving, stable environment where all your baby's needs are being met. Teaching-to-sleep is also necessary when mothers wish to wean older breastfed babies who are still nursing at night.

Letting babies cry is never easy, so it's best to teach your baby to sleep in the most efficient way possible so that it's all over quickly and everyone can start enjoying a good night's sleep. This means planning. The more haphazard you are, the more exhausting and drawn out the whole thing becomes, with little chance of anything changing.

## BEFORE YOU BEGIN

- Your baby must be in a room on her own. This may mean temporarily moving family members around.

- If your baby shares your room and there is no other bedroom I suggest you and your partner sleep in another room for a week. Once your baby is sleeping all night, move back to your bedroom. Unfortunately, shared accommodation sometimes means a return to disturbed nights. But if you're getting desperate for sleep, it's certainly worth a try. If you are about to move to a bigger apartment or house, wait until you move before teaching your baby to sleep.

- If you have an older child in another room and the baby shares your room, bring the older child into your room for five nights (move the bed in or put a mattress on the floor). Make sure you tell your older child this is a temporary arrangement as well as explaining what it's all about. Put the baby into the room on her own. Once she's sleeping all night, move your older child back with the baby. I find this works very well. Often older children sleep better when their baby brothers or sisters are in the room with them. As well, babies do not wake and call for room service when they share the room with their siblings the way they do when they share the room with their parents.

- As the aim is to teach your baby to sleep on her own, all external aids must stop. Remember, swapping one for another will not stop the night waking—all must be stopped.

   **Here is a list of all the external aids I can think of:** Breastfeeding; bottles of milk, water, or juice; pacifiers; rocking and patting; walking the floor; driving around the block in the car; playing games or watching late-night television; flipping your baby over from front to back or changing her position. Videos taken of babies who sleep through the night show that these babies wake, sit up, talk to themselves, and roll all over the crib, often ending up in some very strange postures and positions, yet they do not call for attention. Getting up every few hours at night to change your baby's position quickly becomes an external aid. Babies can learn to sleep where they land without any harmful effects.

- You and your partner must cooperate, so talk over your plan of action well in advance. Teaching your baby to sleep is easier when partners agree on the course of action and both take part. However, this is not always possible. In the situation where one is prepared to follow the plan and the other isn't, the non-participator must either bury their head under the pillow, or if this is too difficult, sleep somewhere else for three to five nights. Listening to a baby cry is not easy, but it's doubly difficult when one partner undermines the other's actions.

- Let your neighbors know so that they don't give you a hard time. Impress upon them that you are up with your baby—she is not being left to cry on her own—and that you would appreciate their patience for a few nights.

- Pick a time that suits you, bearing in mind things like work commitments, visitors, holidays, and moving. It's important to make sure your baby continues to sleep in the same bed, in the same room, for at least a month afterward.

- Your baby must be in good health (ignore teething).

- You and your partner must be well and not under too much other stress when you decide to teach your baby to sleep. Babies respond well as long as their parents stay calm and confident— if you become visibly upset and worried, your baby will get distress signals from you and take much longer to go to sleep.

### THE FIRST EVENING

Here are three key words for you to remember while you are teaching your baby to sleep. Write them in capital letters and put them on the fridge: Stay **calm, confident, and consistent**.

It's a good idea to start from bedtime so that your baby learns how to go to sleep without breast, pacifier and so on. Put her

**549**

to bed at about 7.30 pm without any of the external aids. Make sure she has been up since 4 pm at the latest—a late catnap after 4 pm makes it very difficult for her to go to sleep before 9 pm or 10 pm.

Since she is used to having help to sleep, she will cry as you leave the room. This is the hard part—do not linger; leave. Wait three minutes, then go back in and give brief comfort. Brief comfort means telling her you love her and a gentle stroke on the cheek. Brief comfort does not include picking her up, replacing the pacifier, a breastfeed, a bottle, rolling her over, or a rock and a pat. If you keep doing these things, she will not learn to sleep on her own. Remember, it is not your job to get her to go back to sleep anymore—it is hers.

After a brief time with your baby, leave the room. Do not linger.

Continue to go to your baby, but make the intervals longer—wait five, ten, fifteen, then every twenty minutes until she falls asleep. It may take one or two hours before she sleeps. Remain calm and confident; she *will* sleep.

Before going to bed, mentally prepare yourself for a stint of night duty. When your baby wakes next, leave your bed and stay up until she sleeps. It is much more stressful scrambling in and out of bed than staying up. Make a cup of tea; perhaps turn on the TV or some calming music. Think of greener pastures. Repeat the evening procedure.

There is likely to be a fair bit of crying the first night—maybe up to two or more hours. Each night there is less, and by the third night there will only be a little bit of crying and lots of sleeping. Your baby should be sleeping well within five nights with a small cry of about ten minutes before she falls asleep at 7:30 pm. This pre-sleep cry may go on for a few weeks. It's best to ignore it. Whatever you do, don't start any of the external aids again.

**550**

## TIPS

- It is often hard to accept that the pacifier must go, but if you continue to use it, the night waking will start up again—the pacifier is a problem, not a solution. I find that once parents make the commitment to follow the teaching-to-sleep guidelines, throwing the pacifier away does not cause any added disruption; in fact, it often turns into a non-event. Put your baby to bed without the pacifier on the first evening you start teaching-to-sleep and never reintroduce it. The daytime sleeps may not be great for about a week because the pacifier has gone, but once your baby sleeps all night without the pacifier, the daytime sleeps will improve. For more on daytime sleeping after six months, see page 557.

- There is no need to change her diaper—if she slept all night, you would not get up at 2 am to change her.

- Vomiting is certainly distressing, but remain calm, clean your baby up with a minimum of fuss, and continue from where you left off. Whatever you do, don't start going back to the old sleeping aids because of vomiting. Unlike healthy adults, healthy babies and toddlers vomit very easily, and providing they are otherwise well, it is not a sign of anything drastic. I find babies who throw up when left to cry as part of teaching-to-sleep stop quickly as long as their parents stay calm and consistent so that the baby gets a clear message.

- Once babies are able to pull themselves up, they often stand at the side of the crib and cry until they are ready to fall asleep. If your baby is at this stage, there is no point in lying her down, as she will stand up again before you can blink. Just gently stroke her cheek and leave. It does not hurt her to stand at the side of the crib until she is ready to lie down and go to sleep.

- There is no advantage in picking your baby up each time you go into her room—it simply makes it harder for both of you.

## WHAT ABOUT TWINS?

It's a little harder with twins, but the procedure is exactly the same. When both babies are waking, leave them in the same room, plan things carefully around work schedules and so on, and be mentally prepared for a stint of night duty. You will probably get less sleep than parents with one baby while you are following the guidelines, but the end results are excellent—both babies will learn to sleep within the same time frame as one. It's much easier when both parents participate, so try and arrange a time when this is possible, or if you are a sole parent, perhaps your mother or a friend can help you.

If only one baby is waking, it's better to put her in a room on her own, then move both babies in together again as soon as she's sleeping.

## AND PREMATURE BABIES?

You can start anytime six months after birth, but if your baby was sick as a newborn and/or premature, please wait until you feel confident and sure that teaching-to-sleep is what you want to do. When the beginning is difficult, it's often harder and takes longer for parents to come to terms with leaving their babies to cry. Thinking it all through carefully and waiting until you are ready rather than stopping and starting is much less stressful for you all.

## TEACHING YOUR BABY TO SLEEP MAY NOT BE AN OPTION IF

- You think it is wrong to leave babies to cry.

- Your living arrangements involve a shortage of bedrooms, paper-thin walls, or sharing a house with others who may object.

552

- You and your partner cannot come to an agreement over what you should do.

Some parents would like to change things but cannot bear the thought of leaving their baby to cry. This is not a sign of weakness and quite understandable. However, unless the baby obligingly changes herself, you will have to come to terms with the night waking and find other ways to manage it (for example, sharing the bed).

## Commonly asked questions

### WHAT IF IT TAKES LONGER THAN THREE NIGHTS?

Sometimes it takes up to seven nights. As long as you are following the guidelines, keep going. It should not take longer than five to seven nights. If it does, perhaps you are not ready for this option yet—you may be combining teaching-to-sleep with rocking, patting, a pacifier, and so on.

Or perhaps your baby is not ready. Some babies need to be a little older (nine to ten months).

**Here are some other reasons why it might not be going according to plan:**

- Lack of support from your partner.

- A lack of confidence due to disapproval from extended family members; fear of doing the wrong thing after reading of the dangers of control crying; or fears that the baby won't love you any more and that the attachment is threatened.

- Inadequate planning or it's the wrong time (sick baby, moving, visitors.

- Doing it for the wrong reason—"it's time I taught her to sleep now that she's six months old."

- A basic child-rearing philosophy that is at odds with this strategy.

- Unknown (it doesn't always work).

If the teaching-to-sleep is not going to plan, it is best to forget about it for the time being. Consider the above points. Are you able to do something about any of them that may be causing you problems? Try leaving it for a month and start again if you haven't come to a suitable compromise in the meantime.

### WILL MY BABY BE UPSET AND CLINGY DURING THE DAY?

Most aren't, but a few are. The ones who do become clingy are fine after about a week. Stay calm and consistent throughout—avoid guilty behavior that might upset your baby.

### MY BABY SEEMS TO BE MORE UPSET WHEN I GO IN AND OUT OF THE ROOM

Going in and out of the room is optional. If you prefer not to or want to make the times in between visits longer, that is up to you.

### WILL THE RESULTS LAST FOREVER?

Unfortunately, maybe not. Illness, holidays, a change in routine, and so on can change babies' sleep patterns, and you might find she starts crying again during the night. If this does happen, and you know that you don't want to go back to regularly getting up at night and/or sharing beds, start teaching her to sleep again as quickly as possible.

## MY BABY STILL WAKES BETWEEN 4 AM AND 5 AM. LEAVING HER TO CRY MEANS SHE CRIES AND CRIES UNTIL IT'S TIME TO GET UP AND WE'RE ALL WRECKS

Unfortunately, a number of babies only manage to sleep from around 7 pm until 4 am after teaching-to-sleep (which is a vast improvement from waking every two hours) and there usually isn't an answer to this. Leaving them to cry in the early hours of the morning for weeks on end is not recommended. I suggest giving them a quick feeding, after which most will go back to sleep.

## SHOULD I PUT HER TO BED LATER SO THAT SHE'LL SLEEP LONGER IN THE MORNING?

As a general rule, no. She will almost certainly still wake at the crack of dawn. Babies sleep very well in the early part of the evening. Putting them to bed late means they get less sleep and you miss your quiet time in the evening.

## SHOULD I TRY TEACHING-TO-SLEEP IF MY BABY SLEEPS THROUGH SOME NIGHTS AND WAKES OTHERS?

This is a tricky situation. Teaching-to-sleep is really a strategy for the two-hourly night waker who has never learned to sleep for longer periods without calling for help. If your baby sleeps through more nights than she wakes and goes to sleep quickly after minimal attention, carry on with what you're doing. If the night waking starts to cause you serious sleep deprivation, you might like to think about starting teaching-to-sleep. It is difficult when babies are not consistent because the very night you get yourself ready for action she will probably sleep all night. By the time the next bad night comes around, you may find you have lost the plot. It's a dilemma I have no answer for.

## Option 2: Living with what's happening

For some parents the potential drama involved in control crying is far worse than getting up once or twice a night for their babies. Some parents are fans of co-sleeping in the family bed, and if that is what appeals to you, fine. It can be a very positive experience.

Even if it is not what you originally planned, you may find it preferable to the alternatives (teaching-to-sleep or getting up several times a night). I talk to many parents who come to terms with night waking and bed sharing when it becomes apparent it is the only option for them. From your baby's point of view, it doesn't matter; she will be fine whatever you decide.

The most important thing is to be as consistent as possible. If you combine bed sharing with leaving to cry and a drop of sedative when you are really desperate, the nights are always going to be fraught. Try to go with the flow and find the best way for all members of the family to get optimum sleep.

## Option 3: Sedatives

Sedatives do not solve baby sleep problems but must be included as an option so that parents are fully informed. Some health professionals suggest sedatives as the only option. When parents are exhausted, a sedative does seem like an easy, peaceful solution. But giving a sedative does not teach a baby how to sleep. It's similar to adults taking diet pills to lose weight rather than changing their eating and exercise habits.

Parents are often advised to slowly decrease the dose over a period of time until the baby can sleep without the sedative. I have never seen this work—once the sedative is stopped, the night waking returns.

Sedatives also have the following difficulties associated with them:

- They have the reverse effect on some babies, so rather than calming, the sedative stimulates them.

- A safe dose often only promotes sleep for about four hours, so there is the dilemma of deciding whether to repeat the dose again during the night or go back to using external aids. A dose that makes babies sleep all night may be unsafe, and apart from anything else, will keep them in a zonked-out state during the day—not the best way to promote optimum growth and development.

Sometimes exhausted parents who cannot face either teaching-to-sleep or continuing to get up for their baby try sedatives. They invariably find that sedatives either don't work, or if they do, a stage is reached where they are constantly increasing the amount in order to get their babies to sleep. It soon becomes apparent that sedatives are not the answer and it's time to reconsider other options.

# Daytime sleeping—six months and beyond

The range of daytime sleeping for babies and toddlers varies from almost nil to three hours a day, and the ranges of variations in daytime sleep patterns and habits are similar to those in babies under six months except that many babies now sleep more predictably.

When babies are not sleeping much day or night, it is possible to help them sleep longer at night by stopping external aids and teaching them to sleep (see page 543). It's always best to *do teaching-to-sleep during the evening and night* and forget about the day because helping them to sleep better during the night is achievable. Babies always eventually go to sleep at night—during the day they don't, and may cry for two hours, after which time a distressed mother picks up a distressed baby and nothing is achieved. This can

**557**

go on day after day for an unlimited time. Often when the nights are better, the daytime sleeps improve, but even if they don't, it's much easier to manage because at least everyone is sleeping at night.

Unfortunately I have found no sure way to encourage consistent daytime sleeping in babies who don't sleep much or who have twenty- to-forty minute catnaps during the day. It doesn't hurt a baby not to have much sleep, but there is much more of the day to fill in, so the baby has more time to get bored, irritable, and overtired, which in turn makes life more difficult for the mother who never gets much of a break.

If this is happening to you, I think it's more stressful trying to keep making the baby sleep more or longer day after day. It's probably better to accept what's happening, try for three catnaps (make sure the last one starts no later than 3:30 pm), go out as much as you can, put your baby to bed by 7 pm, and if you haven't yet done so, follow the teaching-to-sleep guidelines so that you are all sleeping at night.

Babies who sleep more and longer will have one or two hours in the morning and/or one or two in the afternoon. Daytime sleep times depend a lot on what time the baby wakes and goes to bed. Sometime between nine and eighteen months, lots of babies stay up all morning and have one sleep of one, two, or three hours after lunch.

# Early morning waking

Early morning waking is part of the baby package. Not all babies wake at the crack of dawn, but lots do, and most of the time there's not much you can do about it. Leaving babies to cry from 5 am onward doesn't teach them to sleep longer, and when they have been asleep since 7 or 7:30 pm, it's not really a fair or reasonable thing to do.

If you have an early morning waker, whatever you do, don't start putting her to bed later. Babies tend to wake at the same time in the morning regardless of when they go to bed, so keeping her up means she gets less sleep and you don't get your time off in the evenings.

## Here are the usual strategies to deal with early morning waking

- Get up and start your day. It's unfair when it's always the same person, so some sort of roster system should be worked out so that both parents get a chance to sleep in at times. If you're a single parent, there's not much you can do unless you've got a friend who will step in sometimes.

OR

- Bring your baby into bed and give her a breastfeeding or a bottle and see if you can all get some more sleep together.

OR

- Give your baby a breastfeeding or a bottle or a drink from a cup and put her back to her bed for another sleep.

OR

- Some parents try to slowly extend the time by going in five minutes later each week.

**FOR MORE INFORMATION**
Chapter 14: Sleeping and Waking in the First Six Months (*stages of sleep, page 312, "sleeping through," page 323, "spoiling," page 325*)

## FURTHER READING

The following book is centered on the teaching to sleep theme (leaving your baby/toddler to cry) but varies slightly in the approach:

*Solve Your Child's Sleep Problems*, Richard Ferber, Fireside, revised edition, USA.

(Dr Richard Ferber is an American pediatrician whose specialty area is sleep—what a hero. This book is based on his work at the Children's Hospital in Boston.)

These books provide comfort and ideas on the bed-sharing theme for those who wish to explore this option or are looking for confirmation of their choice. The information is largely based on the authors' personal experiences.

*Three In A Bed,* Deborah Jackson, Bloomsbury, U.S.A., 1999.

*The Family Bed,* Tine Thevenin, Avery Publishing Group, USA, 1987.

part **four**

# 9 TO 12 MONTHS

# chapter twenty-nine

# Feeding
# Your Baby

## *Breastfeeding*

### Late mastitis

Mastitis (see page 152) mostly happens in the first three months, but it can happen anytime while you are breastfeeding. Signs and symptoms are the same as previously described as is the treatment. A sudden change in night feeding, a baby who suddenly loses interest in the breast, return to work, ill health, or trauma to the breast (perhaps from a sports injury) are all possible reasons. Sometimes the 'flu-like symptoms appear first, making the diagnosis uncertain until the breast symptoms appear. If it doesn't subside in six to twelve hours, you will need antibiotics.

### Weaning older babies

Weaning can happen from soon after birth up to three or four years of age. It might be your decision or your baby's, or it might be mutual. All the benefits of breastfeeding are there for as long as you and your baby wish to continue, so if you are happy with what's happening, carry on.

The following information is for women who wish to stop breastfeeding at night and/or wean between six and twelve months. If your baby is breastfeeding a lot day and night and you wish to do less feedings or weanings here are some guidelines to follow.

## ADDRESS THE NIGHT WAKING FIRST

Babies who are still breastfeeding frequently during the second six months usually breastfeed a lot at night, and a number of women find they become increasingly frustrated and depressed because of the constant night waking.

If this is happening to you, waiting for your baby to decide to nurse less or wean might mean waiting until she is a lot older. It's fine for you to make the decision to wean and/or stop night feeding rather than leaving it up to your baby.

Stopping breastfeeding at night involves teaching your baby to go back to sleep without the breast. Swapping the breast for a pacifier, a bottle, a rock and a pat, and so on is not the answer—it simply teaches your baby to rely on something else and will probably take even longer to get her back to sleep. Trying to make older breastfed babies take bottles who don't want to is a catastrophe and does not teach them to sleep at night.

Teaching your baby to sleep without the breast involves letting her cry, which is never easy, but by reading Chapter 28 and following the guidelines carefully, you can help her sleep all night without the breast within three to five nights. It takes three to five nights for your breasts to adjust to not being used at night so don't forget to hand express for comfort once or twice a night, for three to five nights. If they are really uncomfortable, cold cabbage leaves (see page 177) and a firm bra help.

## DAYTIME—DIET AND FLUIDS

Once your baby sleeps all night without needing the breast to go back to sleep, only breastfeed her three times during the day with meals. Be firm and consistent and don't give her the breast at sleep time. Changing your daily activities helps until she forgets about the breast.

If your baby takes a bottle, you can then replace each daytime breastfeeding with a bottle of formula or milk over the next month or two at a pace that suits you. If your baby will not take a bottle, forget about bottles; give her three meals a day and gradually replace each breastfeeding with milk from a cup. Once your baby is not drinking all night and only having a few breast-feedings during the day, you will find she will drink more and more from the cup.

Some mothers worry about their babies' fluid intake when they use a cup instead of a bottle because it seems they drink so much less than babies who drink from bottles. Try not to let this bother you—babies who drink from bottles drink more than they need a lot of the time. When the weather is hot extra fluids can be given as fruit gels, fruit ice blocks or by putting extra fluid in the food. Letting your baby sit in the tub and suck the washcloth is another way of giving extra fluid in hot weather.

Once you decide to breastfeed less or wean, be consistent so that your baby gets a clear message. If you do one thing one day and something else the next, she won't know what's going on. Never reintroduce a breastfeeding once it's gone.

# Babies who wean themselves

A number of babies take themselves off the breast sometime between six and twelve months. This can be upsetting whether you planned to breastfeed indefinitely or planned to wean around a year. Unfortunately it's usually something you have to accept unless the breast refusal is temporary because your baby is unwell, in which case she might go back to the breast when she is better. When it's permanent, talk about it to someone sympathetic and have a good cry—the sad feelings will pass.

Again, there is no need to start bottles if your baby is happy to drink from a cup. Give her small amounts of milk, juice, or water frequently throughout the day. The amount she drinks will gradually increase.

## Biting the breast

Mostly, the arrival of teeth makes no difference to breastfeeding, but a few babies do start to bite, which is very painful indeed. Deliberate biting in older babies (whether it's a breast or a shoulder) is part of their development and one way they find out about the world and what their bodies can do. It has nothing to do with teething, nor is it intentionally done to hurt; however, they have to learn that biting another person hurts, is not a game, and is unacceptable behavior. Here are a few tips to help with biting:

- Playing with the nipple rather than sucking it for food or comfort is a diversion for older babies and a time when biting may occur, so try not to let yourself get distracted while nursing and allow the feeding to go past the time your baby is really interested. Older babies are able to drain the breast in two or three minutes and may not be interested in extra sucking time when other things are attracting their attention.

- Try not to overreact to a bite (easier said than done, especially when the first nip takes you by surprise) as a major response from you may mean your baby refuses all breastfeedings. The minute she bites, a quiet but firm no is required. Take her off the breast immediately and don't breastfeed again for several hours.

Resist offering her your breast every time she starts to whine—try diversionary tactics such as a snack, a drink from a cup, or going out.

- Like everything to do with babies, try to stay consistent. If you laugh sometimes, go ouch sometimes, and keep letting her play with your breast, the biting is likely to go on indefinitely.

## Breastfeeding into the second year and beyond

Rather than wean, some women decide to continue breastfeeding for as long as their babies want to. The night waking is not an issue for them and they feel the rewards of this option outweigh any disadvantages. As well, the thought of teaching their babies to sleep by leaving them to cry is an unacceptable option. Unfortunately I find mothers who choose to do this often get a hard time from all and can be made to feel they are doing the wrong thing. If this is your choice, continue to enjoy your baby, your breastfeeding, and sharing your bed for as long as you feel like doing it. Learn to shrug off negative comments—some view your approach as optimum. It is fine to nurse a new baby and a toddler if you are happy to do that.

# When should a baby feed herself with a spoon?

Sometimes there is no choice about this because a number of babies won't eat unless they can feed themselves. If your baby is an independent eater and you don't mind the mess, by all means let her use a spoon and her fingers to feed herself mushy food as well as the less messy finger foods.

If your baby is happy to let you be in charge of the spoon, there is no urgency about teaching her to do it herself until she is older and has better coordination. Most toddlers can use a spoon reasonably neatly around eighteen to twenty months.

# Bottle feeding

When you are breastfeeding, it is fine to use full-fat cow's milk in your baby's food, on her cereal, and to drink from a cup from six months of age. There is no need to go to the expense of using formula when you are following this plan. If you are breastfeeding and for some reason don't want your baby to have cow's milk, it's better to use a soy-based infant formula on cereal, in a cup, and so on until she is a year old rather than soy drinks.

When babies are bottle fed or if you wean between six and nine months, infant formula is recommended. Follow-up formula has no advantages for healthy babies who are eating a wide variety of food.

Anytime from nine months you can change your baby to full-fat cow's milk. An unlimited amount of milk is not part of a well-balanced diet so three bottles of 7 to 8 ounces every twenty-four hours is plenty. Encourage your baby to eat food. There's no need to boil the milk; when you decide to change, swap one bottle of formula for one bottle of milk each week so that in three weeks your baby will be having milk in all her bottles.

### FOR MORE INFORMATION
Chapter 25: Common Worries and Questions *(options for night waking, page 513)*

# Growth and Development

## *Growth*

Lots of babies are three times their birthweight by twelve months. From nine to twelve months onwards, weight gains are often slow and irregular, but length continues to increase steadily. The weight of breastfed babies in particular can level out quite dramatically. As long as they are otherwise fit and healthy, this is rarely a sign of anything being wrong.

### AT TWELVE MONTHS

|  | Small/Normal | Large/Normal |
|---|---|---|
| **Boys** | weight 18 lb (8.2 kg) | 26 lb (12 kg) |
|  | height 28 inches (72 cm) | 32 inches (80 cm) |
|  | head circ. 17 inches (45 cm) | 20 inches (50 cm) |
| **Girls** | weight 16 lb (7.8 kg) | 25lb (11.2 kg) |
|  | height 27 inches (70 cm) | 31 inches (79 cm) |
|  | head circ. 16½ inches (43.5 cm) | 19½ inches (49 cm) |

# Development

## Gross motor

- By twelve months, your baby will be sitting well, on her own, for long periods.

- She will probably be cruising (some babies still just sit).

- Lots of babies are "cruising" (walking around the furniture) by twelve months.

- Many are walking on their own.

- If you have stairs, your baby may be able to crawl up the stairs but not down.

## Vision and fine motor

- She now uses her index finger and thumb to pick up anything she finds (crumbs, fluff off the carpet, paper clips, and so on).

- She can drop objects or release them deliberately (if she wants to). She can give you a toy willingly (if she's in the mood).

- Both hands are used to play, eat, and manipulate objects.

- Pointing at everything starts at about a year. It is often not noticed much because obvious skills like walking and crawling attract much more attention.

- Pointing is a way of communicating found only in humans, and babies start to point around twelve months, some as early as nine months, but intentional pointing is never any earlier.

  Pointing is a clear communication signal and the way a person singles out an object as being important enough to consider and contemplate. By pointing, the person draws someone else's attention to the object to get them to consider and contemplate the object as well. Pointing is always done with someone, not alone. I find pointing a fascinating part of the development of baby communication skills that happens long before babies have the verbal skills to draw their parents' attention to objects in the astonishing world around them.

- Your baby can recognize you from a distance of twenty feet (6 meters) or more.

## Hearing and speech

- She knows and turns to her name immediately and will also turn to a quiet noise behind each ear.

- Vocalizes constantly as if having a conversation using lots of vowels and consonants; a few babies may have one or two words.

- Your baby shows by her behavior and response that she understands conversation and simple instructions like "Come to Mummy," "Don't touch" and so on.

## Social and play

- Loves to empty cabinets and tip things out of containers.

- Likes having a cuddle, although if you have a "busy" baby, cuddles may be few and far between at times.

- Offers a kiss to people she knows and trusts.

- Waves "bye, bye," plays pat-a-cake and "boo."

- From twelve months on, things tend to go into the mouth less often.

- Lots of babies start being able to put shapes into the correct hole, particularly if encouraged and given help.

- Your baby will now examine things much more closely before waving them about and dropping them. She will also start to use things like a hairbrush or a small broom appropriately.

- It's now quite obvious what mood she's in—sad, happy, cross and so on.

# Bottom shuffling—a normal variation

Bottom-shuffling babies are normal late walkers. Babies who bottom shuffle move about in a sitting position by extending their legs and then moving their bodies forward by pushing with their hands behind them.

Bottom shuffling often runs in families, and babies who move around like this are late to pull themselves up onto furniture, as it's much harder to pull up onto furniture from a sitting position than a crawling position. This means they are also later to walk (usually around eighteen months), but this is no cause for concern.

# Non-crawlers—a normal variation

A number of babies bypass crawling. There is no evidence that this causes problems, and opinions as to whether some sort of intervention makes any long-term difference vary. Like many areas in babycare, the decision whether or not to give your baby therapy is ultimately yours. Ask a few different people for their opinion before becoming committed to time-consuming exercises and activities for your baby that will make you feel guilty when you don't do them.

**573**

# *Developmental summary: 12 months*

## Gross motor

- sits well, indefinitely;

- crawls;

- cruises, walks.

## Vision and fine motor

- pincer grasp;

- watches toys fall to the ground;

- points with index finger;

- recognizes familiar people from twenty feet (6 m).

## Hearing and speech

- knows own name;

- vocalizes—vowels and consonants;

- understands the meaning of many concepts and words as well as simple instructions.

## Social and play

- may drink from a cup;

- holds a spoon;

- helps with dressing if in the mood;

**574**

- tips things out of containers;

- likes having a cuddle;

- demonstrates affection;

- plays "pat-a-cake";

- waves "bye-bye."

## FOR MORE INFORMATION

Chapter 32: Becoming a Toddler *(toys and activities, page 590)*

# chapter thirty-one

# Safety

## *Vacation safety*

It's essential to be aware of the added hazards to your child's safety when the family leaves home for a while.

Vacations with babies are different from vacations on your own. Parents often feel there's no such thing as a vacation with babies and toddlers; it's simply a change of scenery with fewer conveniences and more work. Despite this, everyone still does it. Parents enjoy the change of scenery and the opportunity to spend time with their babies without having to worry about the demands of life in the suburbs and the routine of the working week for a while.

The hard work of vacations does center around keeping little ones safe. Constant vigilance is essential.

Going to live in an unfamiliar environment is the first hazard. Whether you are staying in a motel or camping, check the surrounding areas to make sure they are safe for playing. Ask about potential drowning hazards such as pools, spas, ponds, septic tanks, or post holes. Find out the whereabouts of any barbecues or incinerators. Make a note of driveways and which way cars come and go (especially in campsites) so that your baby or toddler plays in a safe spot.

A rented house is unlikely to have any of the safety features around that you have in your home, so pack some of the equipment you use at home to make the surroundings safer.

Appliances such as the stove, the toaster, or the washing machine may not be as safe or in as safe a place as they are at home. Also, check baby furniture such as the crib if it is supplied with the house. Watch out for flimsy curtains near the stove or for venetian blind cords that may hang over the crib. Old-style holiday cottages often have strange containers of liquid in outside toilets or laundries that need putting out of reach.

Access to windows may be easier, which increases the risk of a toddler falling out. Look in the bedroom your baby is going to occupy and remove any mirrors or fans that might be broken or played with.

## Camping holidays

These need to be planned very carefully. Camping usually means a confined cooking, sleeping, and living area. The combination of this and active young babies can lead to tensions, especially in wet weather, which makes accidents more likely to happen.

Keep cooking, sleeping, and lighting equipment simple and safe. If you are in a tent, it is much safer to have equipment without a flame. When sleeping bags are dry-cleaned, you should allow at least a week before they are used. After dry-cleaning they need to be aired for four to five days. Children have died in unaired sleeping bags due to breathing fumes from the dry-cleaning chemicals.

If you are staying with friends or grandparents who normally do not have babies or children around, there are likely to be many hazards within easy reach of curious minds and fingers, not to mention potential damage to prized possessions in your host's home.

Check where medicines are kept and poisons are stored. I remember leaving my son to sleep on his grandparents' bed only to find when we went to get him up that he had emptied out every drawer in the bedroom and liberally applied every bit of makeup he could find to himself and the cream-colored wool carpet. Luckily there were no medications in their bedroom.

Water plays a big part in summer fun. Unfortunately drownings keep happening. Remember small children fall into water with so little sound it cannot be heard above normal conversation. There is no such thing as a "drown-proof" child, even those who have been to swimming lessons.

## HERE ARE SOME GENERAL GUIDELINES TO FOLLOW FOR WATER SAFETY

- Never leave your baby alone in water such as the tub or a wading pool while answering the phone or door. Take her with you when you go if there is no other adult around to supervise her in the tub or pool.

- Don't leave younger children in the care of older children at bath time or when they are playing at the beach, near a creek, or near a river.

- Flotation toys and swimming aids are not lifesaving devices and do not replace adult supervision.

- Alcohol increases water hazards. During the vacation season there is likely to be more risk of being in situations where there is both water and alcohol. If you are taking your baby to a pool party, decide beforehand which parent is going to drink and which parent is going to drive *and* take care of the baby in a hazardous environment.

- Remember to drain wading pools after use and remove the access ladder from above-ground pools when swimming is over for the day.

The following chart emphasizes particular hazards associated with this developmental stage, but don't forget most safety hazards remain at any age and stage.

*Don't forget your baby's immunization, which is due at twelve months.*

| Age | Developmental stage | Safety hazard | Precautions |
|---|---|---|---|
| **12–18 months** | •watching<br>•learning<br>•imitating<br>•absorbing<br>•exploring<br>•finding out<br>•mastering gross motor and fine motor skills | •scalds—pulls protruding handles on the stove<br>•burns—clothing catches on fire (open fires and barbecues)<br>•drowning—in tub, buckets of water, fish pond, wading pool, swimming pool<br>•poisoning—medication, confuses tablets with sweets. Drinks fluids from bottles (especially soft drink bottles)<br>•cuts—from knives and sharp utensils | •turn handles away from edge of stove or bench. Get a stove guard.<br>•non-flammable clothing such as wool or treated fabrics. Fitted nightwear.<br>•always supervise near water. Do not leave older child in charge. Cover fish ponds; empty tub, buckets, wading pools when not in use. Safe storage of diaper buckets. |

| Age | Developmental stage | Safety hazard | Precautions |
|-----|---------------------|---------------|-------------|
| **12–18 months** **(cont)** | •very mobile | •suffocation— airtight spaces such as old fridges, wardrobes | •keep poisons in locked cabinets. Don't take medication in view of small children. Store poison in correct containers (not unlabeled bottles). •keep tools and knives out of reach. •remove doors from old fridges and lock wardrobes—put key somewhere out of reach. |

## FOR MORE INFORMATION

Chapter 12: Safety *(immunization, page 268)*

Chapter 22: For Parents *(travelling with your baby, page 482)*

# chapter **thirty-two**

# Becoming a Toddler

*You used to lean
on that cot rail
and wait
with the vigour of a flame
to leap into my arms
two feet tall and two years old.*

Kate Llewellyn, "The Flame," *The Mountain*

The toddler age is from about twelve months, when toddling starts, to three years. It is a time of tremendous development when babies discover they are able to use their minds and bodies to do things and make things happen.

Learning to do things and make things happen can be quite frustrating for the toddler as well as for her parents. Children of this age have a strong desire to be independent but still need a great deal of help and security. As they learn to do things more efficiently and to understand the world around them more they experience less frustration, and lots of the exasperating things they do fade away. So it's important to realize that the things your baby or toddler does to assert herself and her attempts at independence are by no means indicative of her future temperament or character.

Toddlers do many things that adults find exasperating and some toddlers do them more than others.

Temper tantrums, not eating, not sleeping, biting, hitting other toddlers, not wanting to poo in the potty, and whining are some of them, to name a few. All of this sounds very negative—a lot of the time, of course, toddlers are rewarding and delightful, and parents find they are well compensated for the exasperating times by the enormous amount of pleasure they get watching and helping their baby through this stage.

Some babies don't get into the full swing of toddlerhood until they are fifteen months old; others start to change from the easy, cuddly baby stage as early as nine months. When your nine-month-old suddenly refuses to eat lunch or launches into a mini-temper tantrum by flinging herself backward when something upsets her, it marks the beginning of a new era for you both.

Here are some of the things you might find your baby starts to do from nine months onward. They are all normal, and the suggestions to help are aimed at managing your life together and not making things worse rather than providing solutions, since in time they disappear.

# Difficulty dressing, undressing, and changing diapers

And very frustrating this is! Suddenly you find your baby does not lie peacefully while you attend to her daily care and it all becomes a monumental struggle. Changing a pooey diaper is a major catastrophe, which is particularly trying if your baby poos four or five times a day, not to mention if you are on vacation somewhere in the woods with no decent changing facilities. Your baby's resistance to dressing and diaper changing may last well into the second year.

What can you do? Not a lot, unfortunately. Distract your baby as much as possible with toys and music, and obviously have everything ready to do the job as fast as you can. Holding and distracting a determined baby is much easier with two than one, so always get help if help is around.

# Not eating

Finicky appetites in healthy babies and toddlers between nine months and three years are quite normal and often start to happen between nine months and twelve months. Some babies of this age have never eaten happily from a spoon, so not eating is not new. Others who used to eat with gusto suddenly start refusing all their lovingly prepared nutritious meals, particularly veggies.

What can you do? Remember your job is to offer your baby food, not force her to eat it. This means a change in your behavior and it may take a little while to come to terms with. Leaving the job to your baby will probably give you a feeling of neglecting her, but babies understand from a very early age that the decision to eat is theirs and they will exercise this choice in a very human way. When healthy babies are in a loving environment and are being offered the right food, they do not suffer.

There are several reasons why toddlers lose interest in food and why their bodies still function efficiently even when they appear to eat very little:

- After the first year, their growth rate slows down, they do not need as much food, and they are not as hungry.

**583**

- Most have accumulated stores of fat and other nutrients, which keep them going.

- Their bodies use what they do eat very efficiently.

- Food becomes relatively unimportant for many toddlers compared to other things in their lives.

As so many older babies and toddlers have little interest in food yet remain active and healthy, it is reasonable to assume this is a normal state of affairs for the human body at this time.

## Here are a few tips

- A lot of babies will not eat unless they can feed themselves with their fingers. There's no doubt it's not nearly as rewarding to have finger food thrown around the room as to have a nice plate of pureed veggies disappear neatly into an open mouth, but if this is your baby's choice, save yourself a lot of angst and accept it.

- Resist the temptation to keep replacing meals with extra bottles of milk and juice. This only fills your baby up and makes her less inclined to eat. Three bottles of milk a day is more than enough for babies between nine and twelve months. If you are breast-feeding, do what suits you and your baby. Three breastfeedings a day are plenty for babies in this age group; if you want to breastfeed more frequently, that's fine, but if your baby is having a lot of breastfeedings, she may not eat much.

- Give breast or bottle after the food and avoid any drinks an hour before the meal if you can.

- Nourishing snacks throughout the day are quite acceptable. Make sure they are nutritious, not chips, sweets, and cookies.

**584**

But if your baby snacks a lot, don't expect her to eat three formal meals a day as well.

- If your baby is or has become a fussy eater, try not to let it turn into a major issue. Avoid cooking and preparing a million nourishing meals that do not get eaten. Your efforts will be unappreciated, you will become angry and upset—and probably overweight when you keep polishing off what your baby doesn't eat. Keep the food simple, stay calm and pretend you don't care whether she eats or not. As finicky food behavior frequently lasts at least until three years of age, constant confrontation and stress about eating can unnecessarily turn these years into a nightmare.

# Separation anxiety and stranger awareness

Part of a growing baby's mental development is all about learning how to tell the difference between things, places, and people and how to compare and judge them. Separation anxiety and stranger awareness refers to the time in a baby's life when she realizes the difference between her mother and a few other close acquaintances and the rest of the world. When this happens, lots of babies start to make a fuss when unfamiliar people look after them or even just pay them attention. Glasses and beards put some babies off; others shriek whenever a particular person comes near them (which is unfortunate when it's a grandparent). They also become distressed if they are taken to unfamiliar surroundings even when their mother is with them.

Stranger awareness and separation anxiety happens between

**585**

three to four months and nine to twelve months. It is most common and intense around nine months. Not all babies show signs of being upset while they are learning to tell the difference between faces and places, and it's difficult to come up with reasons why some do and some don't. Lots of exposure to new faces and places from a young age doesn't necessarily make any difference. In the same family where the environment is similar for all the children, one baby may be incredibly clingy and another may be social.

Becoming clingy, antisocial with unknown people, and distressed in strange places is normal for many healthy babies at this time, and is to a large extent outside your control. If your baby is like this, it does not mean she is spoiled or insecure. On the other hand, if she mostly doesn't give a hoot who she is with or where she is, it doesn't mean she is not attached or hasn't bonded. The normal range of separation anxiety varies tremendously. Some babies pass through it quickly. Others are unsure about being away from their mothers or meeting strangers until the age of two or even older.

Separation anxiety often puts women in a turmoil when they are trying to work out aspects of their lives—especially in relation to work, occasional care (for much needed time off), and solving nighttime sleep problems, particularly when older babies are still being breastfed frequently through the night.

Remember, if your baby is clingy and gets distressed at being somewhere strange, it is normal. In a good, loving environment it will not harm her to start learning to separate for short periods such as:

- Occasions when you want/need some time off to go to the dentist, shopping, classes, or part-time work.

- When it is essential for your sanity (moving your baby to her own room and teaching her to sleep) or leaving her somewhere safe while you attend to household chores or to your own personal requirements (showering, dressing, or going to the toilet).

## Some guidelines to help with separation anxiety

• Make whatever arrangements you need to and stick to them, including having a shower and going to the toilet alone. It doesn't matter if your baby performs for thirty minutes as long as she is left in a safe spot.

### TIPS FOR OCCASIONAL CHILDCARE

• A sensible babysitter and quality childcare is crucial. The caregiver needs to be someone who is very patient, understands the baby's distress is normal and temporary, and is willing to mind her without giving you a blow-by-blow description of the drama when you return.

• Babies will usually settle with a caregiver in occasional care after about seven weeks. If they are not happy within seven or eight weeks, chances are they are going to continue to be unhappy indefinitely. If the hours in care per week are short and you desperately need a break, it's difficult to see that it will cause any long-term harm as long as your caregiver is willing to continue. Full-time daycare is another matter (see next page).

• Spending time with her at daycare or at the babysitter's home until she becomes familiar with the place and the people helps.

• Try not to leave your baby with the babysitter in a flurry. Make sure she has her security items (pacifier, blanket, cuddly, or special toy).

- When you are leaving her, leave decisively. Don't stop and start and hang about. Remember, lots of babies and toddlers cry initially, are fine for the period you are not there, then cry again as soon as they see their mother.

- Resist the temptation to sneak off to avoid the fuss that occurs when she knows you are going. Overall this will only make her more anxious. Painful as it may seem, it is better for her to learn to trust you and know that when you go, you will always come back.

### CHILDCARE FOR FULLTIME PAID WORK PURPOSES (DAYCARE, HOME-BASED CARE)

A small number of babies never settle. If this happens, you do have to look at things again. You may decide an unhappy baby outweighs the benefits of work. If possible, other options have to be looked at that may include arranging one-to-one care at home with a nanny (obviously not an option for many families), a relative, your partner, or giving up the work temporarily.

## Feet and shoes

Many babies start walking between nine and twelve months, and their feet often go in all directions when they first start to walk. This is quite normal and rarely needs any special treatment or equipment. Feet turning in, feet turning out, bow legs, and flat feet are all common variations of normal posture that worry parents. Another interesting one is the baby who bends her outer ankle so that the edge of one foot rolls over.

All these things are seen frequently in many babies from the time they start to walk (nine to nineteen months) until the time their legs straighten and their feet point ahead (between two and five years). Plasters, night splints, inserts, and special shoes are generally not needed but if in doubt, ask a specialist such as a pediatric physiotherapist or a pediatric orthopedic surgeon.

## Shoes

Babies need shoes for warmth and protection, not for development. They learn to walk and run more efficiently in bare feet, so leave your baby barefoot whenever it's warm enough and she is not in danger of hurting her feet.

Wait seven to eight weeks after she starts walking before buying shoes. Until then, let her stay barefoot or use socks. Slipping and sliding can be a hazard—bootees with a non-slip sole are available for older babies.

The first shoes need not be expensive. Bear in mind that they don't last long.

- The fit should be the same size and shape as the foot with sufficient room for the toes.

- Rounded toes are preferable, but sandals with a firm heel are fine for the summer.

- Shoes should be flexible, not too heavy, and should have a firm heel. Ankle support is not required. The only advantage to expensive leather ankle boots it that they are more difficult for your baby to keep removing.

- Sneakers, preferably with a firm heel and ventilation holes, are fine.

# Toys and activities

This is a watching, learning, imitating, absorbing, exploring, and finding-out stage, as well as being a time when your baby is mastering her gross motor and fine motor skills.

## A few suggestions for toys and activities

• Continue books—babies love books.

• Short periods of watching television such as *Barney* and *Sesame Street* are fun for her, but resist the temptation to use the TV as a babysitter.

• Toys that give her practice with her hands are things like nesting cups; peg boards with pegs and string; pull-along-string toys (for practicing her pincer grasp); blocks (for building up, knocking down, and banging together); a collection of things in a container that can be taken out, examined, and put back. Babies love keys—organize a safe set for her; they also love old telephones.

• Bath toys; once she sits alone in the tub, dipping and pouring bath toys will interest and delight her.

• Toys that help her to practice gross motor skills are things like a weighted trolley she can push around when she is at the cruising stage. Balls are always popular. A big cardboard box she can crawl in and out of is lots of fun—make sure there are no sharp edges or staples.

   She will enjoy an obstacle course made of cushions, blankets, and boxes.

• Music is important; babies are musical and enjoy any music from birth. Your baby will quickly pick up simple nursery rhymes and repetitive tunes.

- Household items. Babies often prefer things in cabinets to things in their toy boxes, such as a flashlight; cardboard egg containers; old magazines and junk mail; pots and pans with lids; measuring cups and spoons; Band-Aids; wooden spoons; cardboard tubes (toilet rolls, foil and plastic wrap rolls); playing cards; funnels, strainers and a colander; a pastry brush.

  Don't forget to check everything for safety.

# Playgroups

As you reach the end of the first year with your baby you might find yourself wondering whether it's a good idea to look for and join a playgroup. A playgroup is simply a small group of parents and toddlers who meet regularly. The toddlers play under their parents' supervision. The parents usually take it in turns to hold the playgroup in their homes, but playgroups can also take place in the park, at the beach or in a community settings (a church hall for example). Playgroups are often an extension of mothers' groups formed in the early months after birth. Individual playgroups structure the group to suit the people involved. Some have arrangements where parents can take it in turn to leave their toddlers and so have some free time.

Playgroups allow toddlers to be able to see each other on a regular basis and start forming friendships. It is also a good way for toddlers to get to know other adults well.

Playgroups are not for everyone. They don't suit some toddlers' temperaments and they drive some parents crazy. It is important that you enjoy it as well as your toddler. If your toddler lives in a home where there is plenty of social contact with family friends and extended family, joining a playgroup is certainly not essential for her social development. The age at which toddlers start to enjoy extended time with other toddlers varies a lot. Some are not ready for extended group play until they are nearer to three years of age and until then, are happier in a one-on-one setting.

Finding a playgroup depends a lot on where you live. Some areas are highly organized and have facilitators who advertise in local newspapers, community newsletters and the phone book. In other areas you'll have to check with childcare centers, libraries, universities, pre-schools, churches or any parenting community organizations. If you are on the web, visit www.google.com. Go to advance search, keyboard in "playgroups" and up will pop playgroup choices from all over the country. Obviously, groups vary according to the people involved so you may have to try a few before you find one you feel happy with.

## FOR MORE INFORMATION

Chapter 19: Common Worries and Queries *(care of teeth, page 454, recycled food in the poo, page 457)*

Chapter 25: Common Worries and Questions *(spoiling and discipline, page 515)*

## FURTHER READING

*The Mighty Toddler*, Robin Barker, M. Evans and Company, Inc., New York, 2002.

*The Emotional Life of the Toddler*, Alicia F. Lieberman, Simon & Schuster, 1995.

# What's It All About?

(THE LAST WORD)

The end of your baby's first year is only the beginning of a never-ending story. My grandmother died at ninety-nine—her "baby," my father, was seventy when she died. There were no baby books around in the small country town they lived in when he was born to tell her what to do, how she should "feel" or what deeper meaning it all had. From my conversations with her it was part of life and you just got on and did it the best way you could. My parents got on and did it the best way they could, for which I am extremely grateful, as among other things it helped me to do the same for my babies, and so the story flows on . . .

When our children are babies it is very hard to see the whole picture, as the change to our lives is so immense and, often, the physical and emotional demands so overwhelming that we wonder what *is* it all about? My babies are now two delightful young adults and my pride and joy in them is a feeling so intense it must be equal to that a writer or a painter feels after completing a great work. The years between their first year and now were the usual mix of emotions and hard work that all parents go through, but, looking back, it was worth every minute.

And I guess that's what it's all about.

# Resources

America has many resources available for families, although there never seems to be quite enough. Some are constant, others wax and wane according to funding available and how much voluntary support is around to keep them going. In the U.S. resources for parents vary tremendously between urban and rural areas, from state to state right down to individual communities.

Resources come and go as do phone numbers, websites and name changes so it is not practical to have detailed resource lists in books as it is impossible to keep such lists up to date and relevant. The aim of the following is to let you know the main services that are available. The internet is an invaluable source of information but I am aware that it is still not available to many so I have included phone numbers and/or addresses as often as possible.

Use the following resources to find out what is in your area:

## Your family doctor/pediatrician

## The maternity hospital

## Your nearest children's or local hospital

## Your local county

## Your local library

## A church or synagogue

## The phone book

Here are some specific resources to give you an idea of what's around. Bear in mind there are many more than those listed here

# Breastfeeding Education, Information, Advice, and Support

## LA LECHE LEAGUE INTERNATIONAL (LLLI).

1400 N. Meacham Road
Schaumburg, IL 60173-4048
Telephone: (847) 519-7730 or (800) 525-3243
Website: http://www.lalecheleague.org

## LACTATION CONSULTANTS

Lactation consultants can be located via LLLI or http://www.breast-feeding.com has lists for every state.

# Child Safety

## U.S. CONSUMER PRODUCT SAFETY COMMISSION (CPSC)

CPSC is an independent federal regulatory agency created to protect the public against unreasonable risk of injuries and deaths associated with consumer products. The CPSC covers a wide range of baby and child consumer products.
Telephone: 301-504-0990.
Toll-free consumer hotline: 1-800-638-2772, 1-800-638-8270 (TTY)
Web site: http://www.cpsc.gov

## U.S. CONSUMER GATEWAY (CONSUMER.GOV)

Consumer.gov is a resource for consumer information from the federal government and has a category for children with information ranging from childcare to immunization to product recalls.

Telephone Federal Information Center: 1-800-688-9889
Web site: http://www.consumer.gov/children.htm

## NATIONAL HIGHWAY TRAFFIC ADMINISTRATION (NHTSA)

NHTSA, under the U.S. Department of Transportation was established to carry out safety and consumer programs in all areas relating to traffic and motor vehicle safety. NHTSA has a wide range of valuable information about baby/child motor vehicle passengers that includes a list of child safety seat recalls.
Telephone nationwide toll-free number: 888-DASH-2DOT 888-327-4236. TTY number is 800-424-9153.
Web Site: http://www.nhtsa.dot.gov

## NATIONAL SAFE KIDS CAMPAIGN

SAFE KIDS is dedicated to the prevention of unintentional childhood injury and has 300 state and local SAFE KIDS coalitions in all 50 states. SAFE KIDS provides information on all aspects of baby and child safety including a product recall list.
Telephone: 202-662-0600
Web site: http://www.safekids.org

## JUVENILE PRODUCTS MANUFACTURERS ASSOCIATION, INC (JPMA)

JPMA is a national trade organisation of over 400 companies that manufacture and/or import infant products such as cribs, car seats, strollers, bedding and a wide range of accessories and decorative items. JPMA developed an extensive Certification Program to help parents select baby/child products that are built with safety in mind. Parents can look for the seal on product packaging.
Telephone: 856-638-0420
Web site: http://pwww.jpma.org

## CONSUMER REPORTS

Consumer Reports Magazine and Consumer Reports Online is an independent, nonprofit testing and information organization that tests products, informs the public and protects consumers. The organization has a comprehensive Babies and Kids category that includes detailed ratings and reports for hundreds of products.

Address: 101 Truman Avenue, Yonkers, NY 10703.

Telephone number and email address is only given to subscribers.

Web site: http://www.consumerreports.org

Safety Belt Safe Ride Help Line (provides guidelines for proper infant/child car-seat installation as well as information on booster-seat and airbag safety).

Telephone: 1-800-745-7233

Website: http://www.carseat.org

# Immunization

### NATIONAL IMMUNIZATION PROGRAM HOTLINE: 1-800-232-2422

### NATIONAL IMMUNIZATION WEBSITE:

http://www.cdc.gov/nip

### NATIONAL VACCINE INJURY COMPENSATION PROGRAM:

**TELEPHONE:** 1-800-338-2382

Website: http://www.hrsa.gov/bhpr/vicp

Low-cost/free vaccinations: Telephone: 1-800 232-2522

## Multiple Birth

### NATIONAL ORGANIZATION OF MOTHERS OF TWINS CLUBS (NOMOTC)

PO Box 231188
Albuquerque, NM 87192-1188
Telephone: 800/243-2276 or 505/275-0955
Website: http://www.nomotc.org

## Postpartum Depression

### DEPRESSION AFTER DELIVERY

A postpartum delivery clearinghouse that has information on causes, symptoms, treatments as well as resources for women suffering from depression after the births of their babies.
Telephone: 1-800-944-4773 (4PPD)
Website: http://depressionafterdelivery.com (the website has links to other resources for postpartum depression).

## Sole Parents

Parents without partners:
Telephone: 1-800-637-7974
Website: http://www.parentswithoutpartners.org

## Sudden Infant Death (Crib Death)

### BACK TO SLEEP CAMPAIGN

Information on the National Institute of Child Health & Human Development's SIDS education program.

### NATIONAL SUDDEN INFANT DEATH RESOURCE CENTER

Devoted to promoting SIDS awareness and information sharing.

Websites include links to related organizations worldwide.
Telephone: 703-821-8955
Website: http://www.sidscenter.org
Sudden Infant Death Syndrome Alliance
Circulates information on SIDS and provides support for families.
Telephone: 1-800-221-SIDS
Website: http://www.sidsalliance.org

## Support for Parents Who Think They Might Hurt Their Babies

### PARENTS ANONYMOUS

Dedicated to breaking the cycle of child abuse. Don't be afraid to call.
Telephone: 90 9621-6184
Website: http://www.parentsanonymous.org

## Support for Babies with Gastroesophageal Reflux

### THE PEDIATRIC/ADOLESCENT GASTROINTESTINAL REFLUX ASSOCIATION (PAGER)

A non-profit organization offering support and information from other parents whose babies have reflux.
Telephone: (301) 601-9541 or (760) 747-5001
Website: http://www.reflux.org

# Acknowledgments

I am indebted to my family and the many friends and health professionals who have been involved in *Baby Love* and helped bring it to life.

Roger Barker has been my partner, lover, and friend for many years. Unbeknown to me when we started this arrangement, he had another hidden talent—that of being a great father to our children. I have never worked out whether it was instinct or if he reads father books on the sly, but I give thanks daily that my partner in life is not only a great lover and friend but a truly great father. As well, Roger has given me unlimited emotional and financial support for this never-ending project and even (most of the time) shown avid interest in its progress. Thank you, Rog.

Thanks to good friends Narelle and Peter Black, who let me take over a portion of their house to write the final draft and who continue to show genuine interest in all my projects, be they mad or sane, successful or not.

Several nursing colleagues let me use their ideas. Thank you to Jann Zintgraff for her delightful observation, " . . . the uncircumcised penis needs the same care as the elbow" and for her thoughts on sibling rivalry; to Sally Keegan for her ideas on "looking after yourself," to Patrizio Fiorillo for help with the relaxation exercise, to Liz Flamsteed for her expertise on the immediate postpartum area; and to Jan Annson for her help with the ever-important breastfeeding positioning. Thanks too to Murray Cox for his insights into fatherhood which made me think again about what it means to be a father.

I am grateful to an enthusiastic band of readers for their encouragement and forthright comments. Thanks to Carolyn Parfitt, Tina Matthews, Sally Zwartz, Janine Goldberg, Jenny Miller, Leah and Doug Shelton, Michelle Maxwell, Ruth Sainsbury, Jann Zintgraff, Maureen Fisher, Dasha Gilden, Mary Lynch, Laureen Laylor-Smith, Peter Hartmann, Hilary and Ian Jacobson, Mark Ferson, Lorraine Young, and Anthony Samuels.

Special thanks to three people who are the sort of friends who give our lives that extra dimension—Helen Wilmore, Margaret Sheens, and Jann Zintgraff.

During the course of *Baby Love*'s history I have developed a deep appreciation of the skills of editors and publishers. Oddly enough hands-on contact with the *Baby Love* manuscript seems destined to produce babies. The following women had no children when I first knew them. I am happy to report that they now have five babies and toddlers among them despite exposure to a manuscript full of sleepless nights, crying babies, sore nipples, and endless poo. Well done team! Thank you to Julia Stiles and Cath Proctor for their excellent editorial guidance and unflagging encouragement and support for my labors and to Jane Curry, publisher, for believing in the author and the book and making sure neither sink.

A special mention to Carolyn Parfitt for a thorough and vigorous job of copy editing, to Susie Baxter-Smith for the great illustrations magically produced in between caring for two toddlers, to Elspeth Menzies, editor, who helped me look at the material yet again with a fresh eye for this edition, and to Margaret O'Sullivan, friend and agent.

Finally, to all the mothers, fathers, and babies who have allowed me for a short time to share your lives—this book was born out of conversations with you, and your experiences provide a great deal of the material throughout the book—thank you.

## BOYS: BIRTH TO 36 MONTHS PHYSICAL GROWTH PERCENTILES

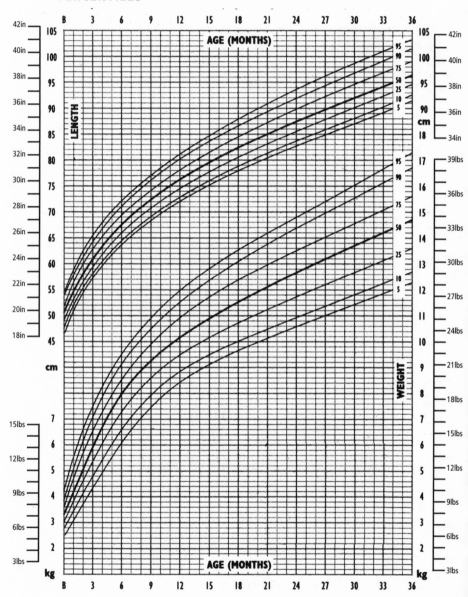

## GIRLS: BIRTH TO 36 MONTHS PHYSICAL GROWTH PERCENTILES

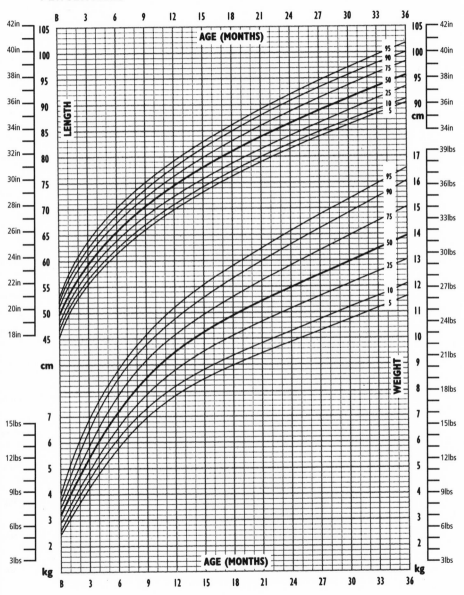

# Index

## OTHER EARLY CHILDHOOD MUST-HAVES AVAILABLE FROM M. EVANS

Robin Barker
### The Mighty Toddler

Robin Barker takes parents beyond the first twelve months into the toddler years of one, two, and three. **The Mighty Toddler** is the most comprehensive guide available to parents covering the five key areas of the toddler world:

- **Growth and Development**
Including the key milestones for each age group.
- **The Question of Behavior**
Perhaps the most vital section for parents with a complete ABC of typical toddler behavior and the best ways to respond.
- **The Basics**
A guide to day-to-day toddler care: including sleep, food, play, and safety.
- **Why Is He Always Sick?**
Explains toddler health, medical conditions, and illnesses.
- **For Parents**
Advice on keeping your life on track, childcare, and even when to have another baby.

Robin Barker's expert advice, wisdom, humor and sheer commonsense will keep you sane and smiling throughout the wonderful years with your mighty toddler.